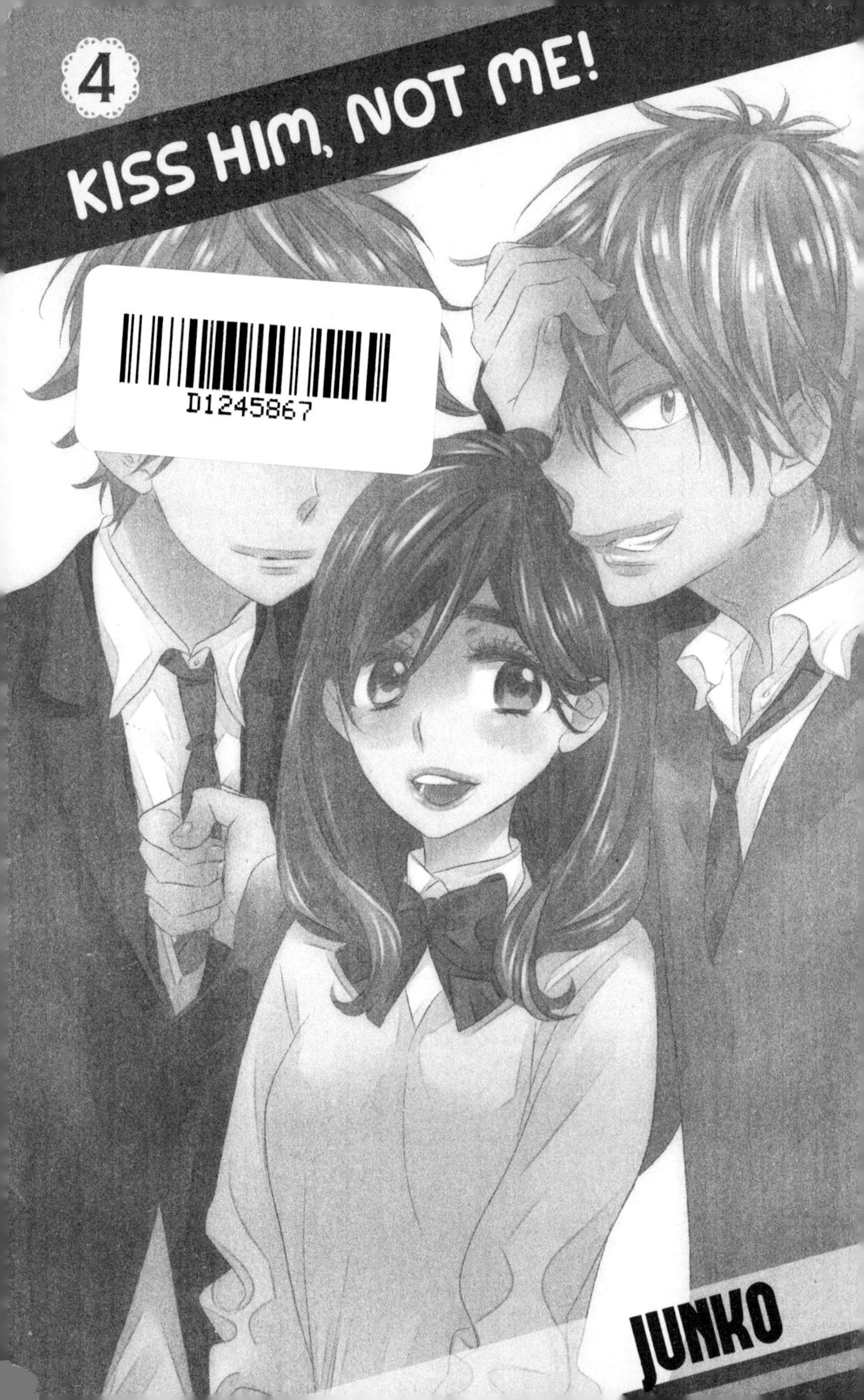
4
KISS HIM, NOT ME!
JUNKO

CONTENTS

STORY

KAE SERINUMA, A **FUJOSHI** WHO LOVES WATCHING BOYS INTERACT WITH EACH OTHER ON A MORE *INTIMATE* LEVEL, CHALLENGES HERSELF TO **MAKE CHOC-OLATES** SO SHE CAN SUBMIT AN ENTRY TO THE VALENTINE'S DAY PROJECT HELD BY HER FAVORITE ANIME, "MIRAGE SAGA." HOWEVER, SHE EATS TOO MANY OF HER RUINED CHOCOLATES, AND RETURNS TO THE WAY SHE LOOKED BEFORE...

KAE THEN STARTS A DIET, BUT SHE HURTS HER LOWER BACK AND STARTS TO GET DISCOURAGED, BUT THANKS TO EVERYONE'S COOPERATION, SHE'S ABLE TO GET HER STUNNING BEAUTY BACK. ☆ SEEING HER POSITIVE ATTITUDE AND HER GENTLE, BRIGHT PERSONALITY, **IGARASHI** FALLS FOR HER ALL OVER AGAIN AND HE **AGGRESSIVELY** GOES ON THE OFFENSE!! BUT WHAT WILL **NANASHIMA** DO WHEN HE SEES THAT CHANGE?!!

I ♥ BL

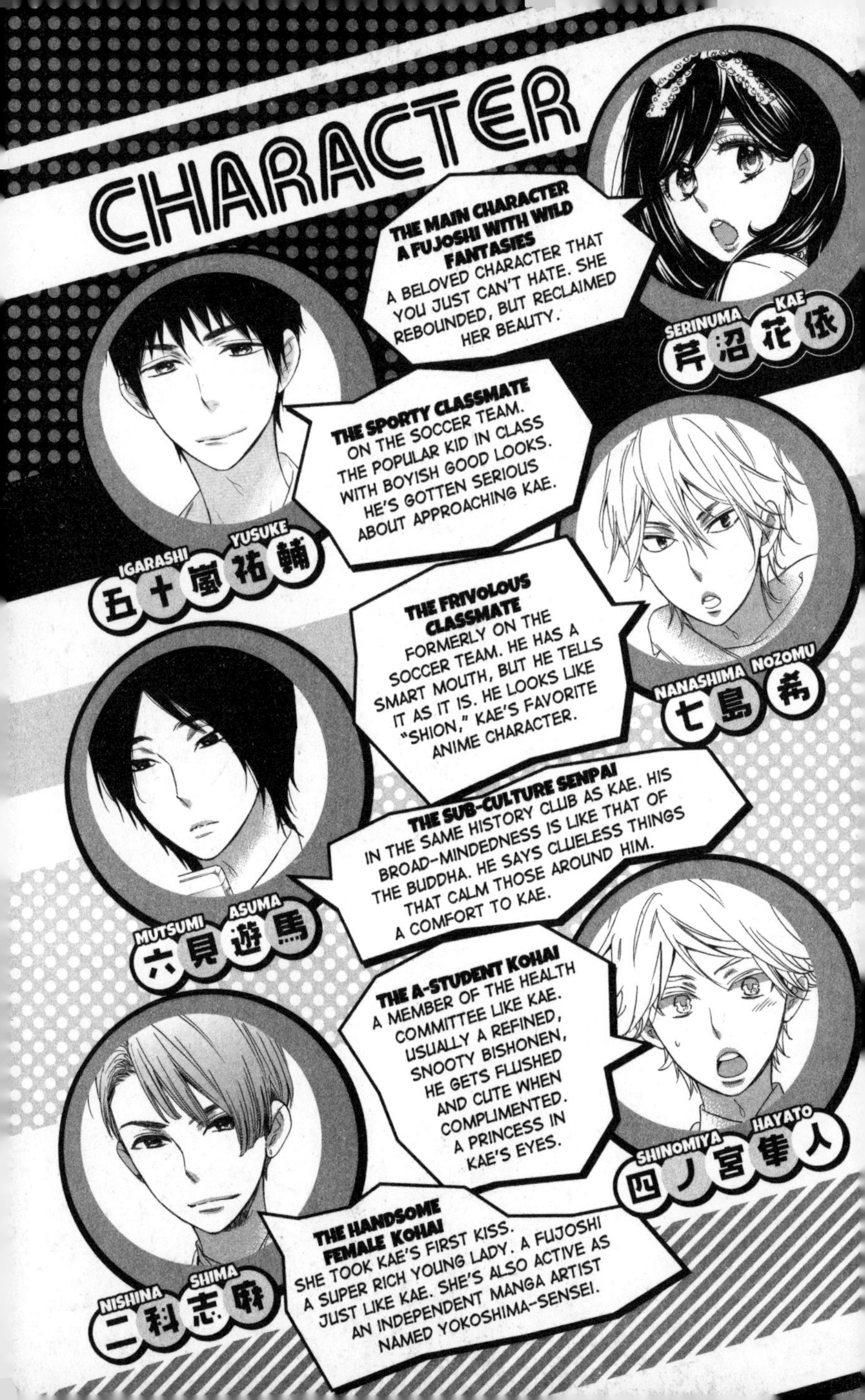
CHARACTER
THE MAIN CHARACTER A FUJOSHI WITH WILD FANTASIES
A BELOVED CHARACTER THAT YOU JUST CAN'T HATE. SHE REBOUNDED, BUT RECLAIMED HER BEAUTY.
SERINUMA KAE 芹沼花依
THE SPORTY CLASSMATE
ON THE SOCCER TEAM. THE POPULAR KID IN CLASS WITH BOYISH GOOD LOOKS. HE'S GOTTEN SERIOUS ABOUT APPROACHING KAE.
IGARASHI YUSUKE 五十嵐祐輔
THE FRIVOLOUS CLASSMATE
FORMERLY ON THE SOCCER TEAM. HE HAS A SMART MOUTH, BUT HE TELLS IT AS IT IS. HE LOOKS LIKE "SHION," KAE'S FAVORITE ANIME CHARACTER.
NANASHIMA NOZOMU 七島希
THE SUB-CULTURE SENPAI
IN THE SAME HISTORY CLUB AS KAE. HIS BROAD-MINDEDNESS IS LIKE THAT OF THE BUDDHA. HE SAYS CLUELESS THINGS THAT CALM THOSE AROUND HIM. A COMFORT TO KAE.
MUTSUMI ASUMA 六見遊馬
THE A-STUDENT KOHAI
A MEMBER OF THE HEALTH COMMITTEE LIKE KAE. USUALLY A REFINED, SNOOTY BISHONEN, HE GETS FLUSHED AND CUTE WHEN COMPLIMENTED. A PRINCESS IN KAE'S EYES.
SHINOMIYA HAYATO 四ノ宮隼人
THE HANDSOME FEMALE KOHAI
SHE TOOK KAE'S FIRST KISS. A SUPER RICH YOUNG LADY. A FUJOSHI JUST LIKE KAE. SHE'S ALSO ACTIVE AS AN INDEPENDENT MANGA ARTIST NAMED YOKOSHIMA-SENSEI.
NISHINA SHIMA 二科志麻

KiSS HiM, NOT ME!

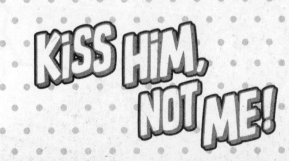

#13 BETWEEN YOU AND ME

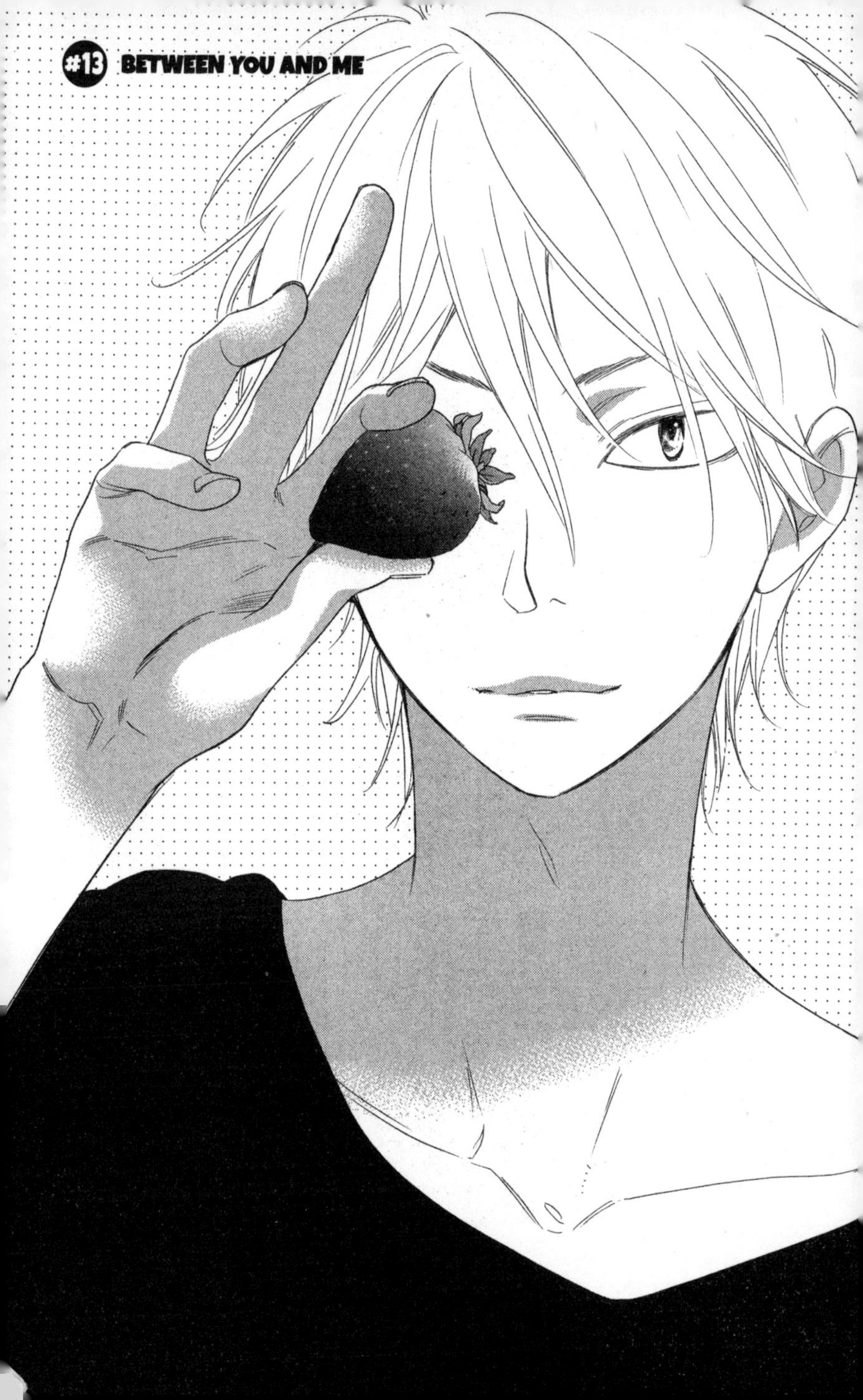

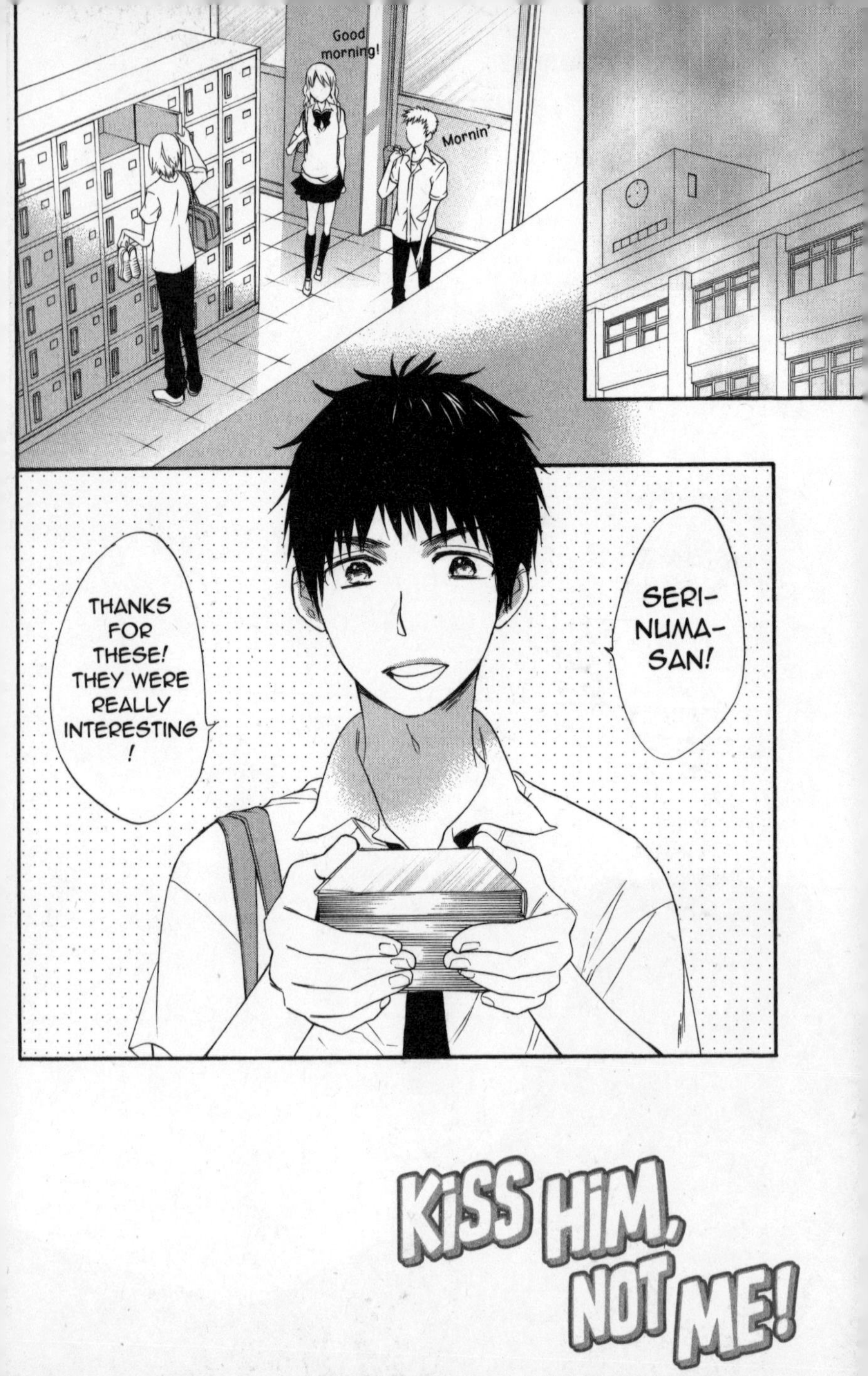
Good morning!
Mornin'
SERI-NUMA-SAN!
THANKS FOR THESE! THEY WERE REALLY INTERESTING!

KiSS HiM, NOT ME!

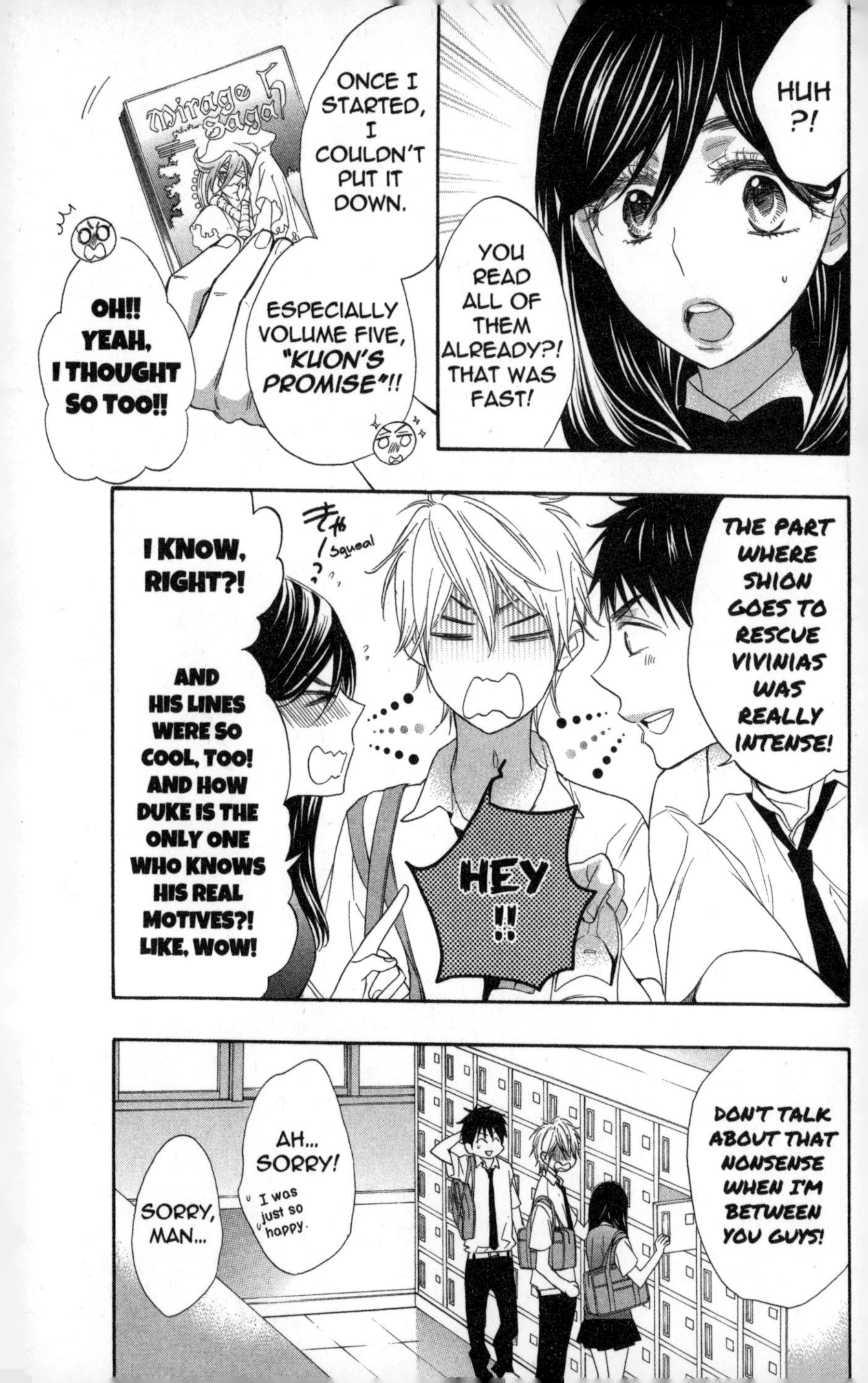
HUH ?!
YOU READ ALL OF THEM ALREADY?! THAT WAS FAST!
ONCE I STARTED, I COULDN'T PUT IT DOWN.
Mirage Saga 5
ESPECIALLY VOLUME FIVE, "KUON'S PROMISE"!!
OH!! YEAH, I THOUGHT SO TOO!!
THE PART WHERE SHION GOES TO RESCUE VIVINIAS WAS REALLY INTENSE!
HEY !!
squeal
I KNOW, RIGHT?!
AND HIS LINES WERE SO COOL, TOO! AND HOW DUKE IS THE ONLY ONE WHO KNOWS HIS REAL MOTIVES?! LIKE, WOW!
DON'T TALK ABOUT THAT NONSENSE WHEN I'M BETWEEN YOU GUYS!
AH... SORRY!
I was just so happy.
SORRY, MAN...

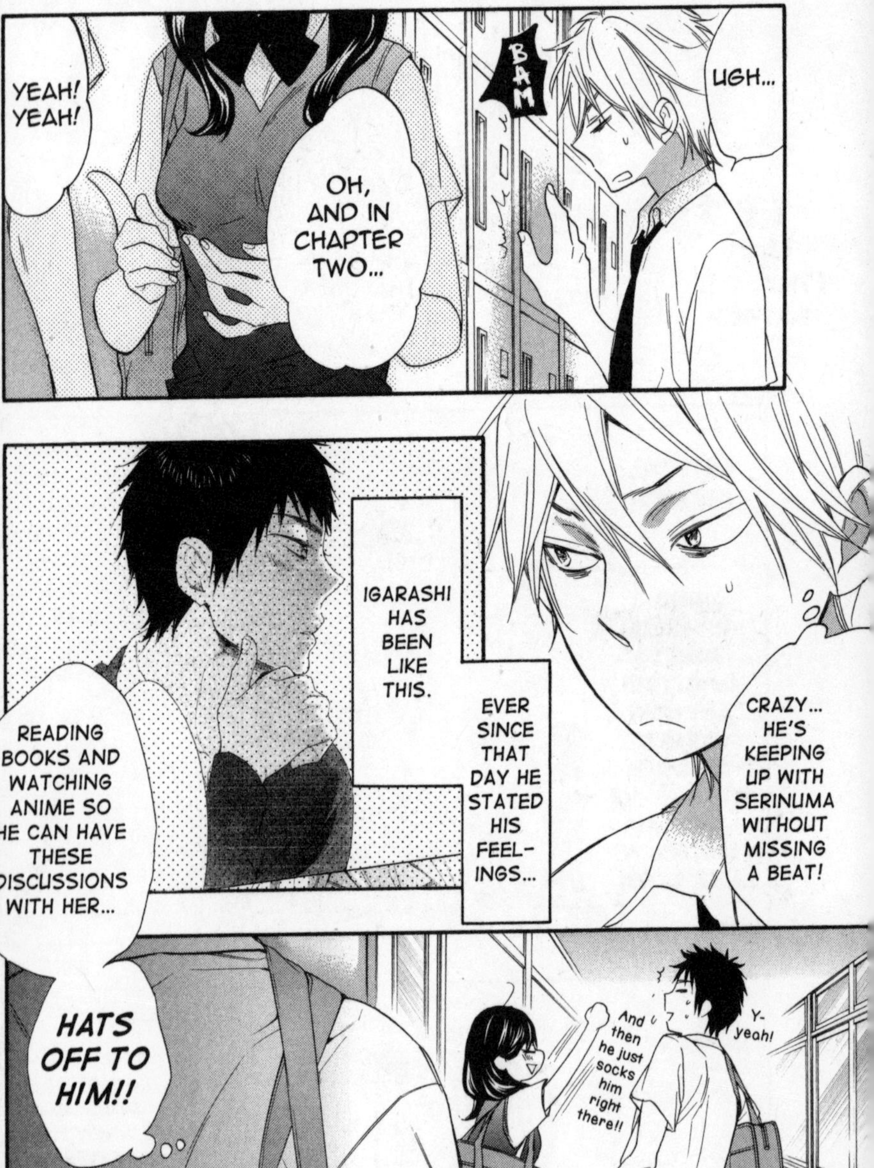
BAM
UGH...
OH, AND IN CHAPTER TWO...
YEAH! YEAH!
CRAZY... HE'S KEEPING UP WITH SERINUMA WITHOUT MISSING A BEAT!
IGARASHI HAS BEEN LIKE THIS.
EVER SINCE THAT DAY HE STATED HIS FEEL-INGS...
READING BOOKS AND WATCHING ANIME SO HE CAN HAVE THESE DISCUSSIONS WITH HER...
HATS OFF TO HIM!!
Y-yeah!
And then he just socks him right there!!

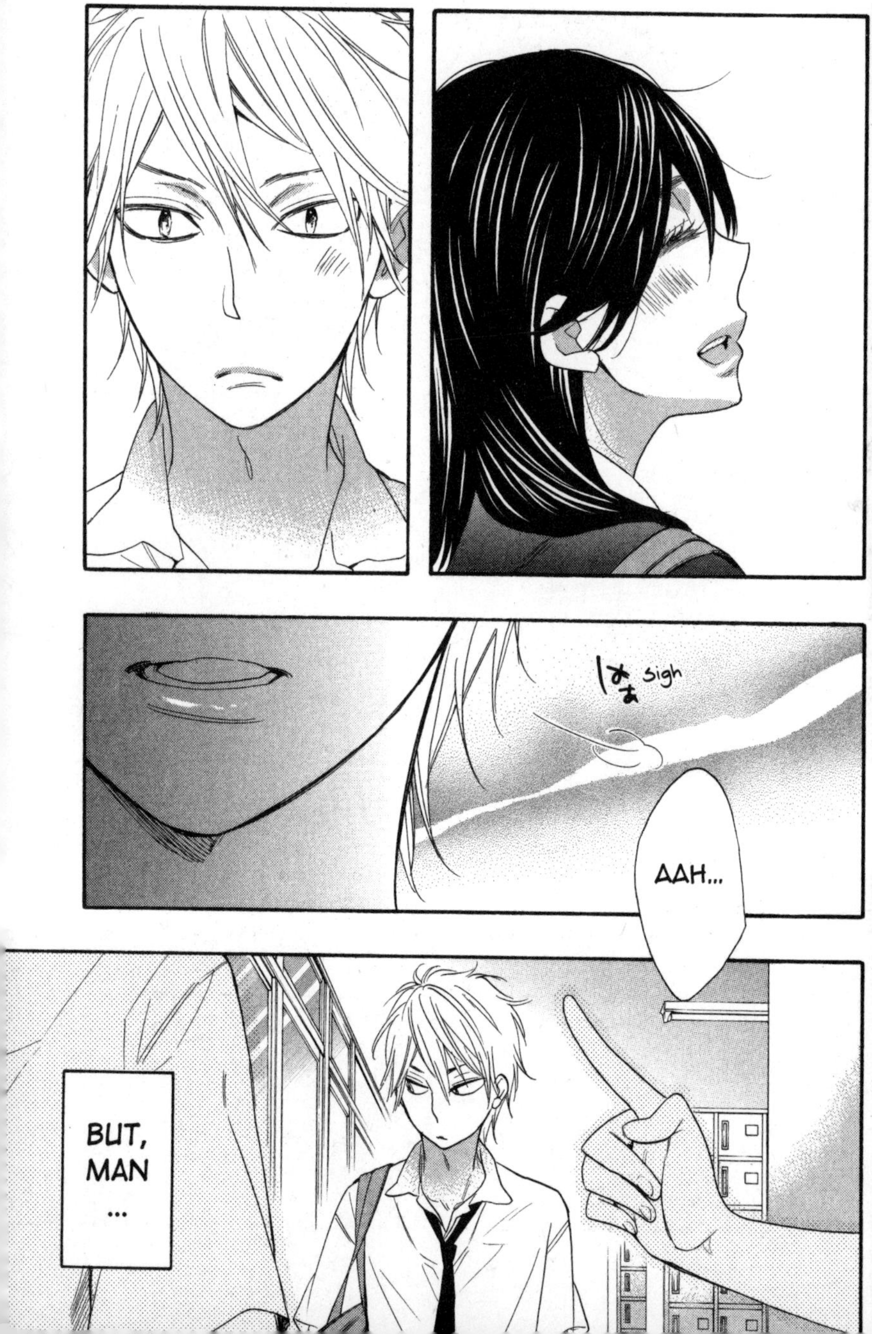
はぁ sigh
AAH...
BUT, MAN ...

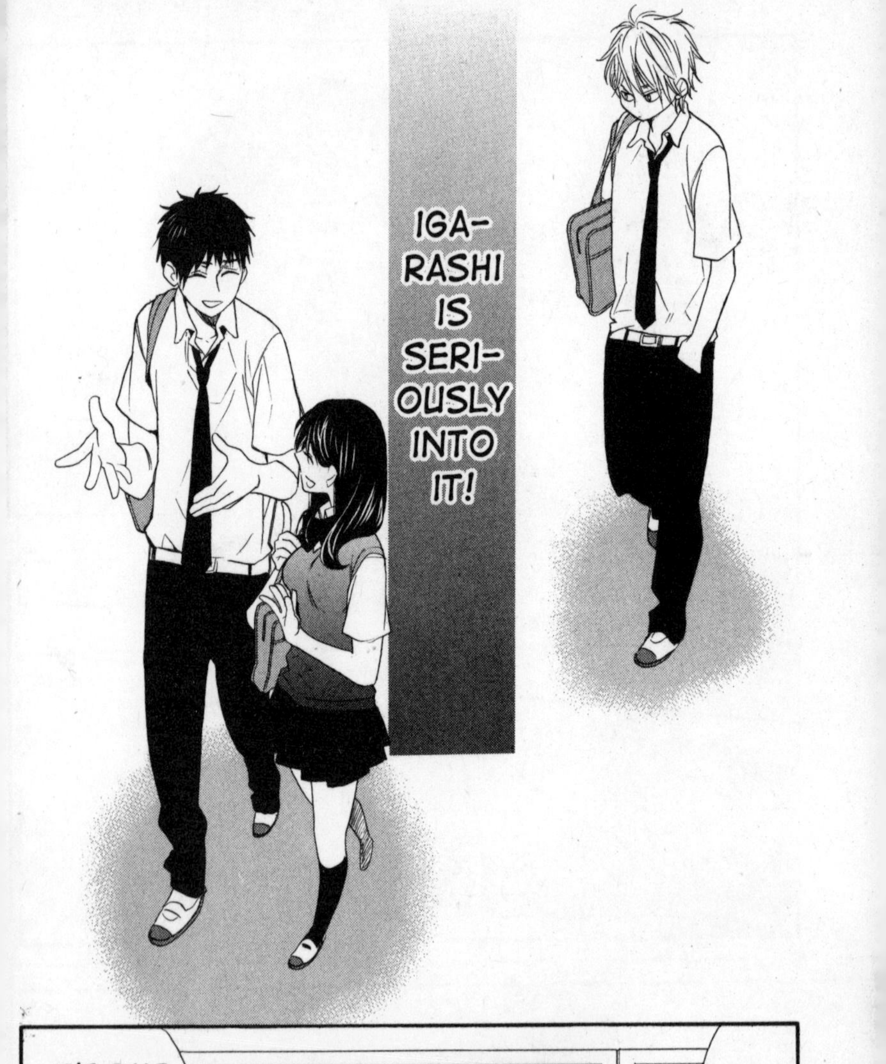
IGA-RASHI IS SERI-OUSLY INTO IT!

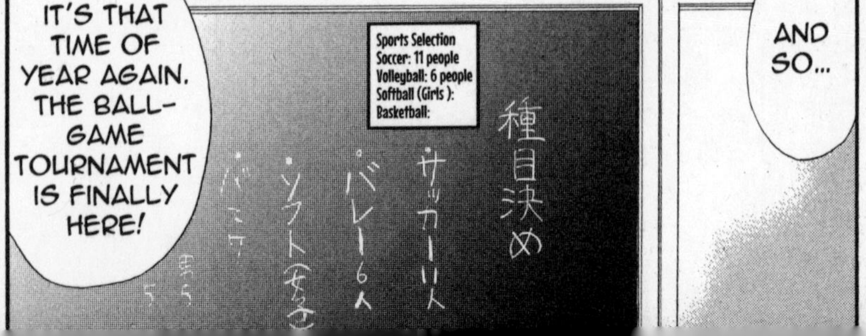
AND SO...
IT'S THAT TIME OF YEAR AGAIN. THE BALL-GAME TOURNAMENT IS FINALLY HERE!
Sports Selection
Soccer: 11 people
Volleyball: 6 people
Softball (Girls):
Basketball:
種目決め
・サッカー11人
・バレー6人
・ソフト(女子)

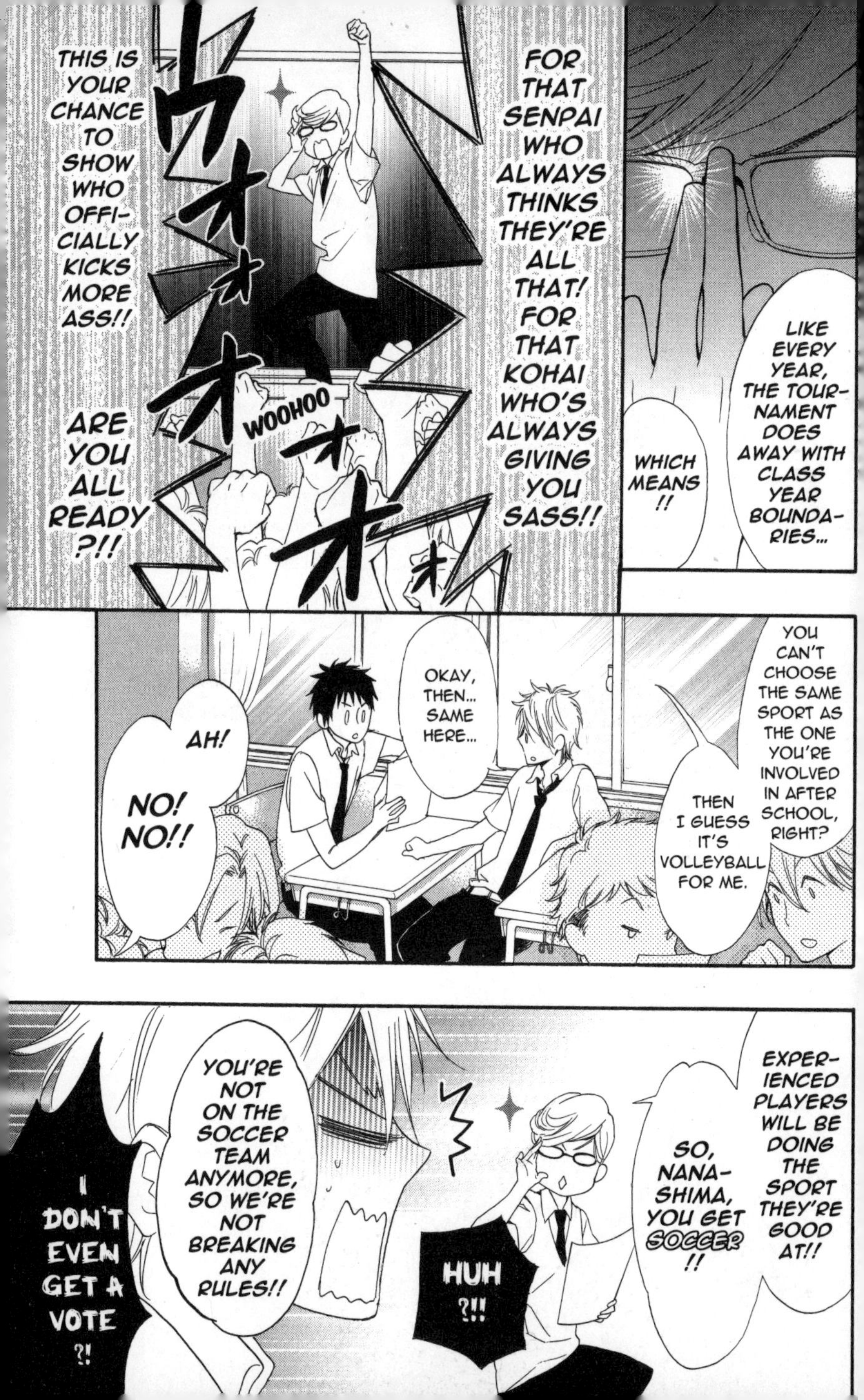
LIKE EVERY YEAR, THE TOURNAMENT DOES AWAY WITH CLASS YEAR BOUNDARIES...
WHICH MEANS!!
FOR THAT SENPAI WHO ALWAYS THINKS THEY'RE ALL THAT! FOR THAT KOHAI WHO'S ALWAYS GIVING YOU SASS!!
THIS IS YOUR CHANCE TO SHOW WHO OFFICIALLY KICKS MORE ASS!!
ARE YOU ALL READY?!!
WOOHOO
YOU CAN'T CHOOSE THE SAME SPORT AS THE ONE YOU'RE INVOLVED IN AFTER SCHOOL, RIGHT?
THEN I GUESS IT'S VOLLEYBALL FOR ME.
OKAY, THEN... SAME HERE...
AH!
NO! NO!!
EXPERIENCED PLAYERS WILL BE DOING THE SPORT THEY'RE GOOD AT!!
SO, NANASHIMA, YOU GET SOCCER!!
HUH?!!
YOU'RE NOT ON THE SOCCER TEAM ANYMORE, SO WE'RE NOT BREAKING ANY RULES!!
I DON'T EVEN GET A VOTE?!

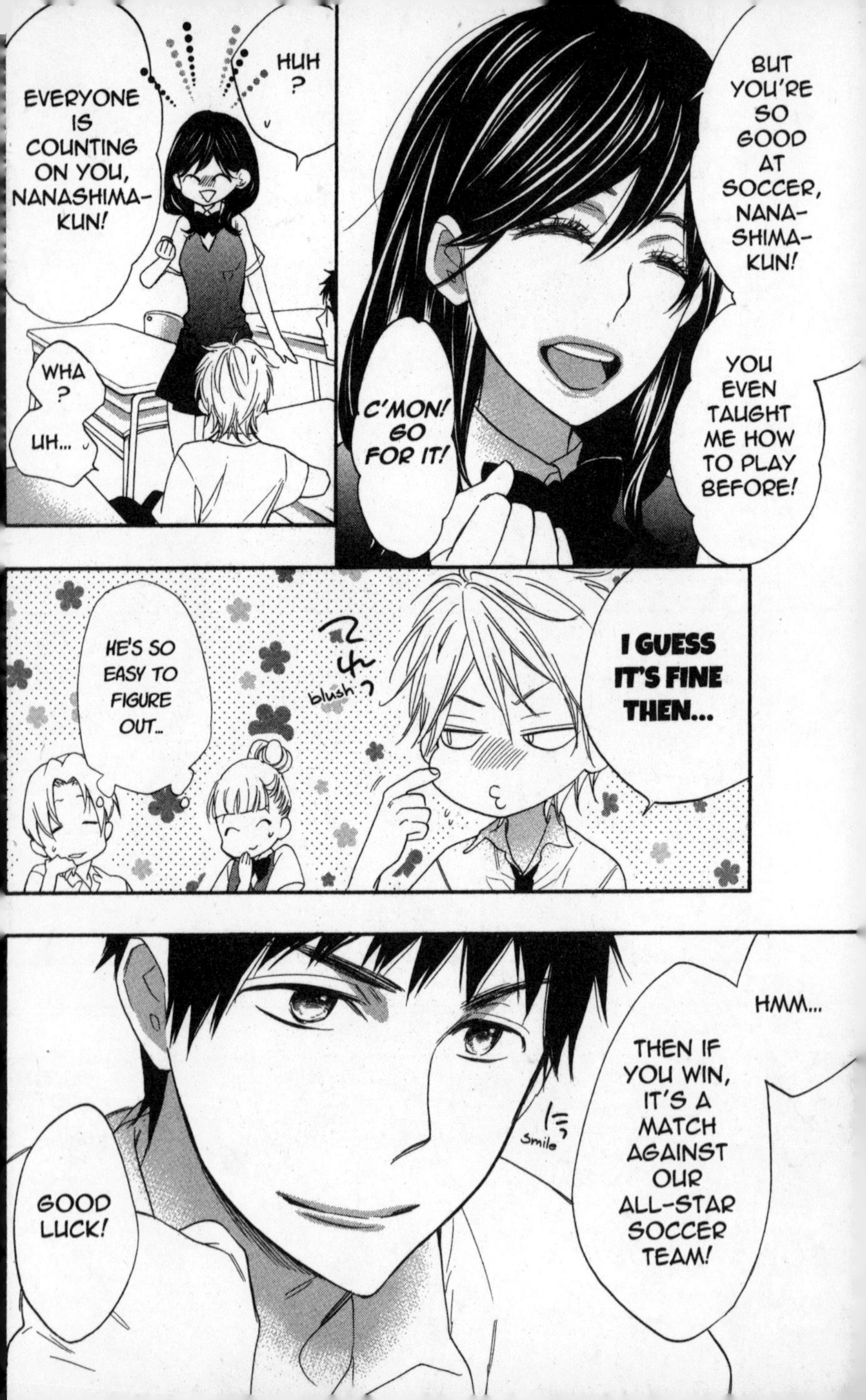
BUT YOU'RE SO GOOD AT SOCCER, NANASHIMA-KUN!
YOU EVEN TAUGHT ME HOW TO PLAY BEFORE!
C'MON! GO FOR IT!
HUH?
EVERYONE IS COUNTING ON YOU, NANASHIMA-KUN!
WHA? UH...
I GUESS IT'S FINE THEN...
blush
HE'S SO EASY TO FIGURE OUT...
HMM...
THEN IF YOU WIN, IT'S A MATCH AGAINST OUR ALL-STAR SOCCER TEAM!
Smile
GOOD LUCK!

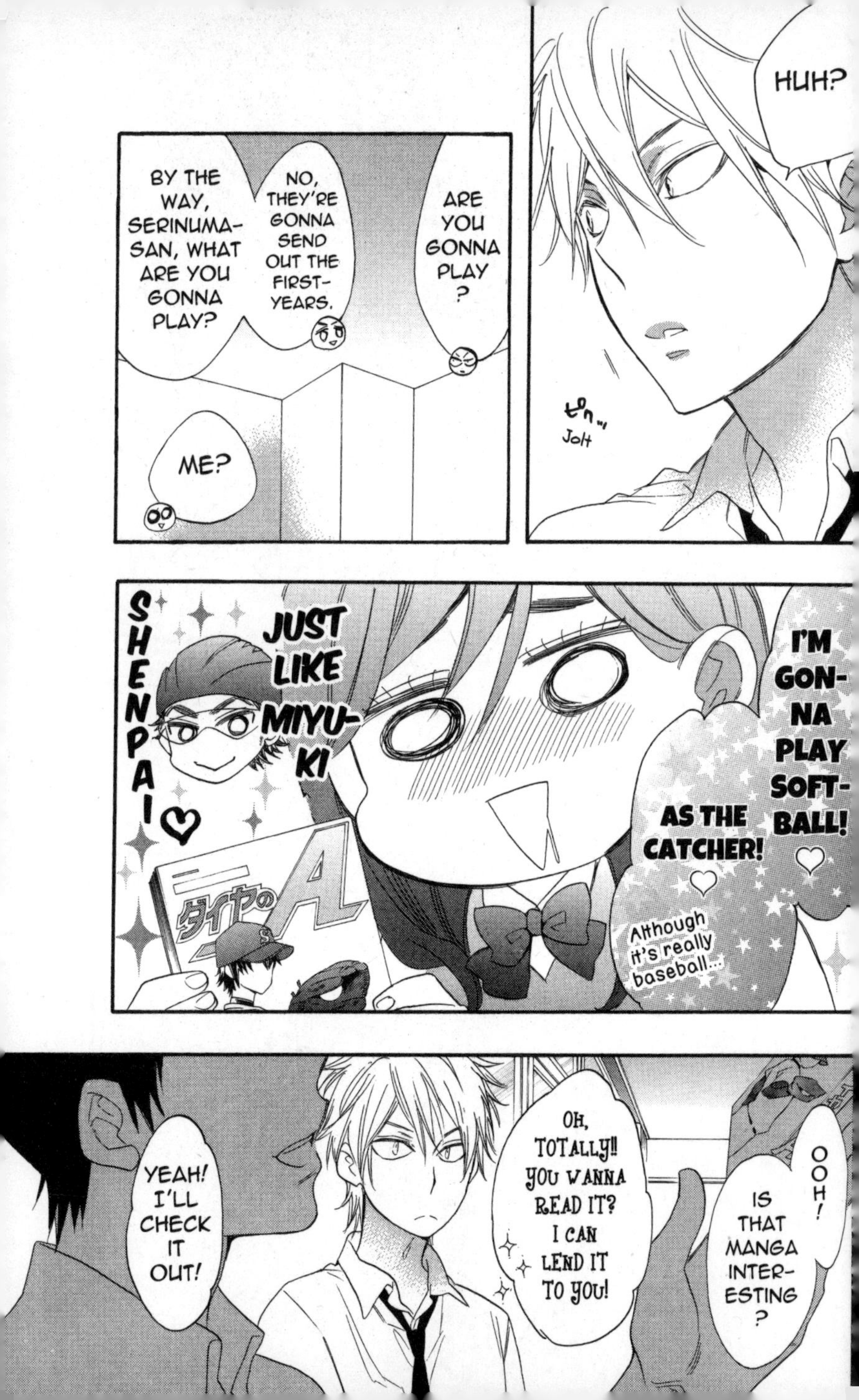
HUH?
Jolt
ARE YOU GONNA PLAY?
NO, THEY'RE GONNA SEND OUT THE FIRST-YEARS.
BY THE WAY, SERINUMA-SAN, WHAT ARE YOU GONNA PLAY?
ME?
I'M GONNA PLAY SOFTBALL!
AS THE CATCHER!
Although it's really baseball...
ダイヤのA
JUST LIKE MIYUKI
SHENPAI
OOH!
IS THAT MANGA INTERESTING?
OH, TOTALLY!! YOU WANNA READ IT? I CAN LEND IT TO YOU!
YEAH! I'LL CHECK IT OUT!

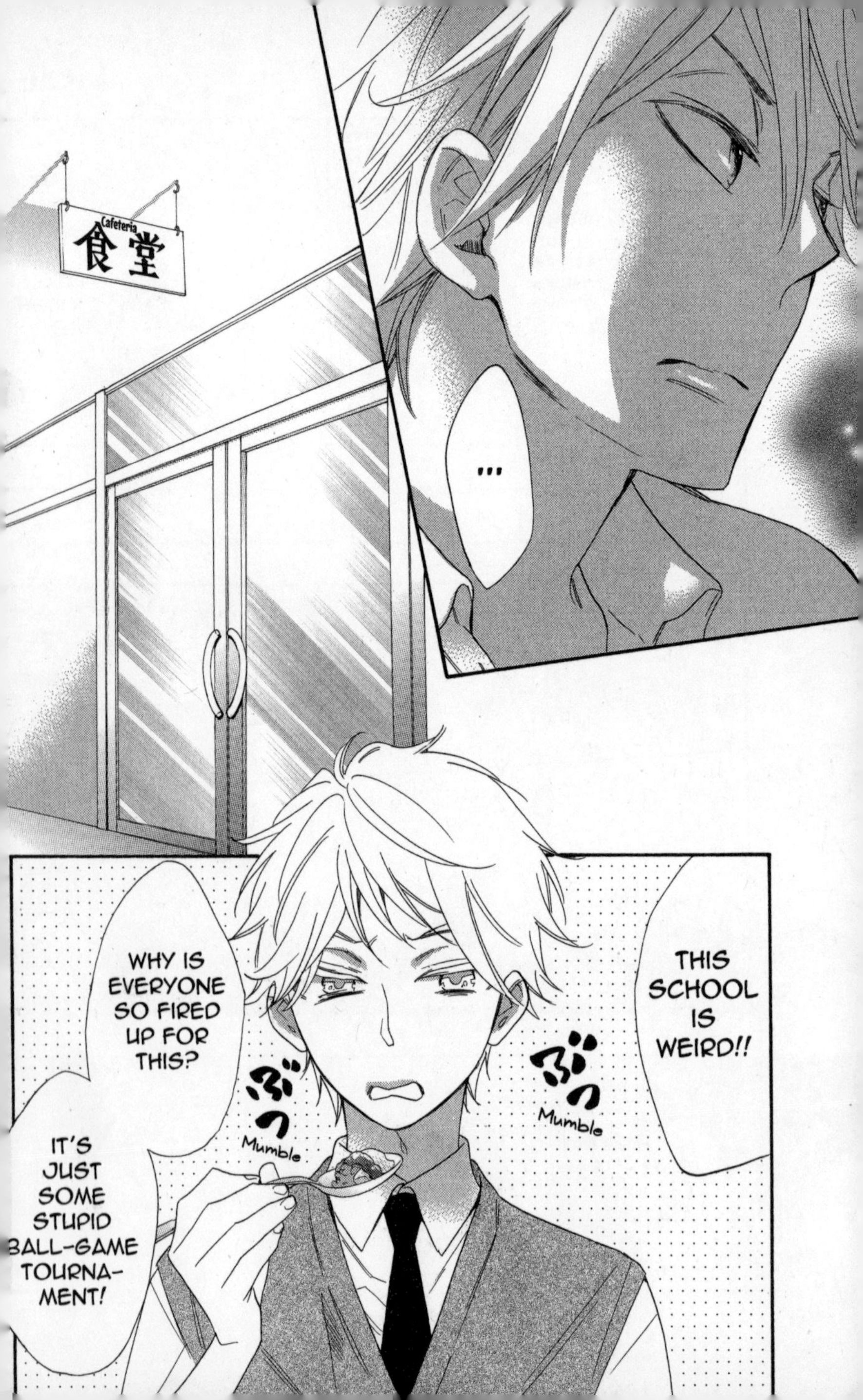
...
Cafeteria
食堂
THIS SCHOOL IS WEIRD!!
ぶつ
Mumble
WHY IS EVERYONE SO FIRED UP FOR THIS?
ぶつ
Mumble
IT'S JUST SOME STUPID BALL-GAME TOURNA-MENT!

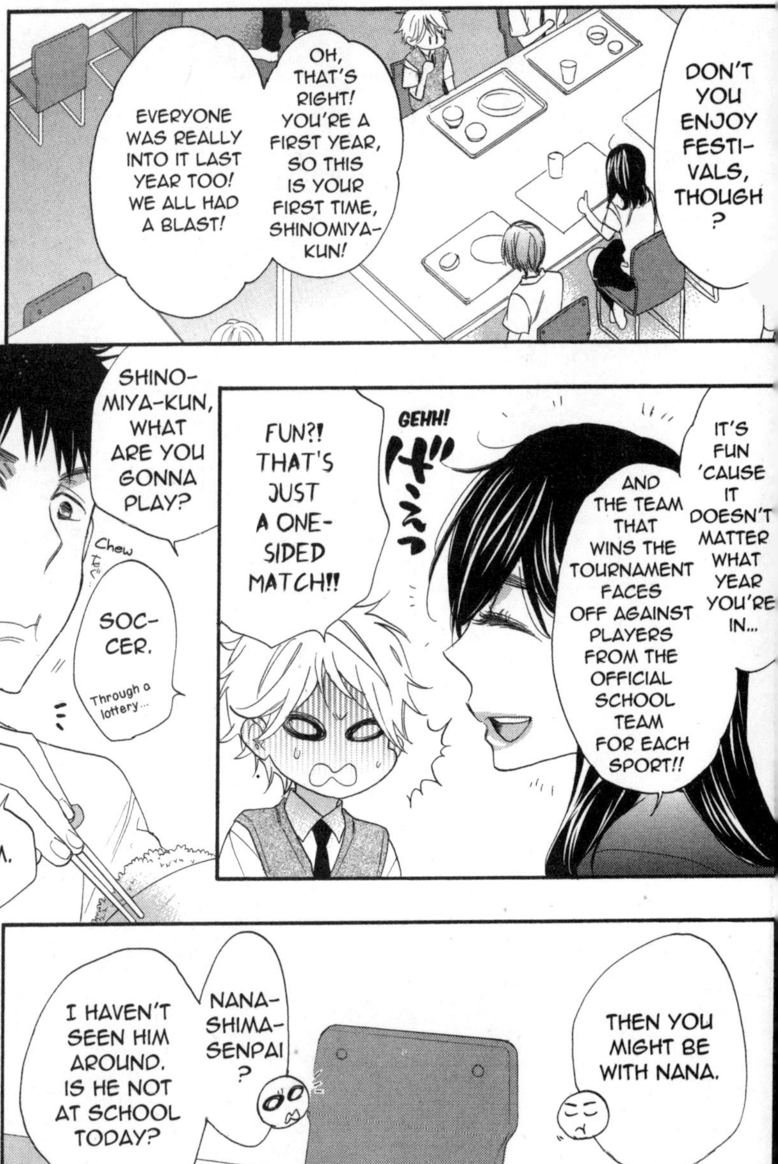
DON'T YOU ENJOY FESTIVALS, THOUGH?
OH, THAT'S RIGHT! YOU'RE A FIRST YEAR, SO THIS IS YOUR FIRST TIME, SHINOMIYA-KUN!
EVERYONE WAS REALLY INTO IT LAST YEAR TOO! WE ALL HAD A BLAST!
IT'S FUN 'CAUSE IT DOESN'T MATTER WHAT YEAR YOU'RE IN...
AND THE TEAM THAT WINS THE TOURNAMENT FACES OFF AGAINST PLAYERS FROM THE OFFICIAL SCHOOL TEAM FOR EACH SPORT!!
GEHH!
FUN?! THAT'S JUST A ONE-SIDED MATCH!!
SHINOMIYA-KUN, WHAT ARE YOU GONNA PLAY?
Chew
SOCCER.
Through a lottery...
MM.
THEN YOU MIGHT BE WITH NANA.
NANASHIMA-SENPAI?
I HAVEN'T SEEN HIM AROUND. IS HE NOT AT SCHOOL TODAY?

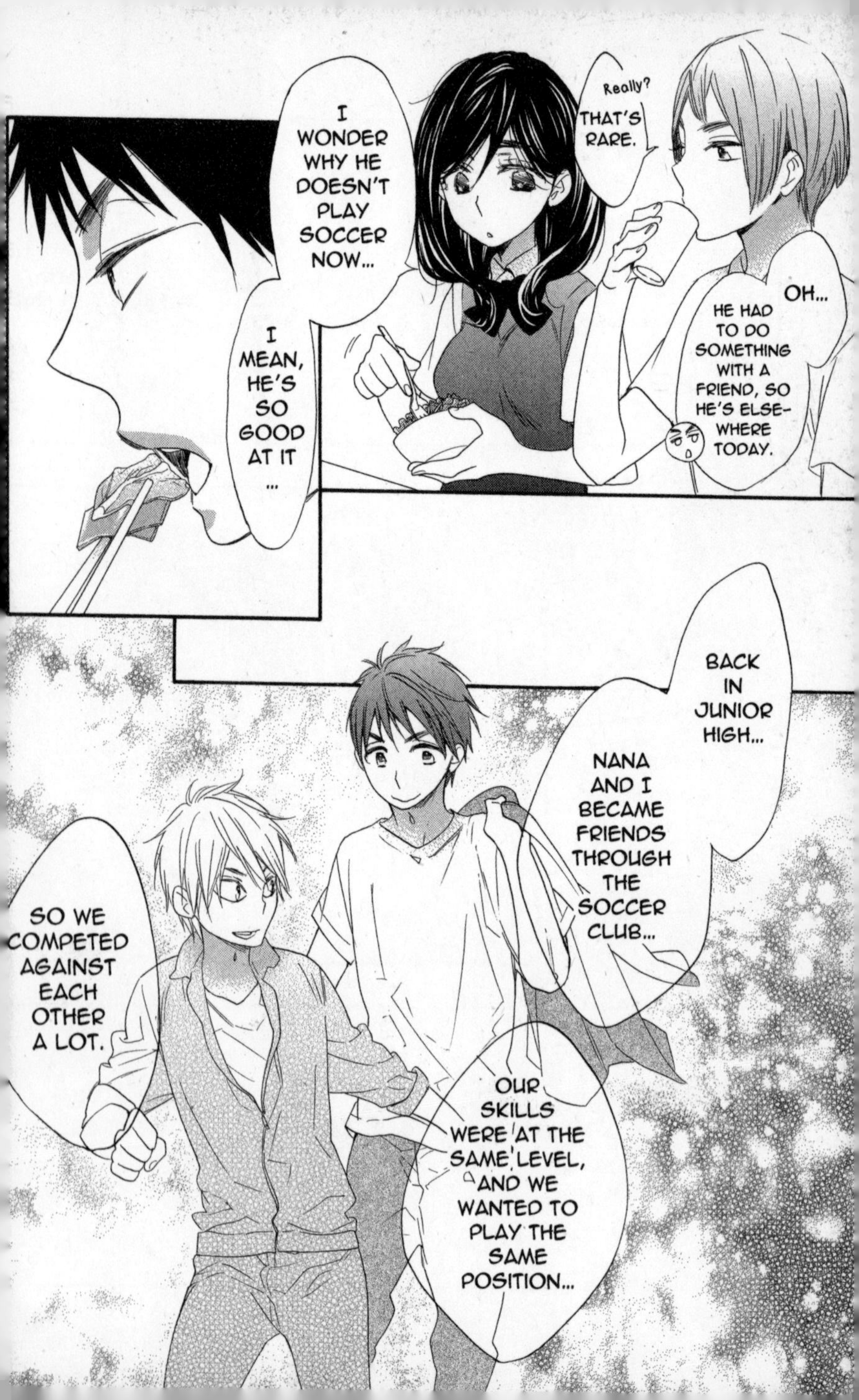
Really?
THAT'S RARE.
OH... HE HAD TO DO SOMETHING WITH A FRIEND, SO HE'S ELSE-WHERE TODAY.
I WONDER WHY HE DOESN'T PLAY SOCCER NOW...
I MEAN, HE'S SO GOOD AT IT ...
BACK IN JUNIOR HIGH...
NANA AND I BECAME FRIENDS THROUGH THE SOCCER CLUB...
OUR SKILLS WERE AT THE SAME LEVEL, AND WE WANTED TO PLAY THE SAME POSITION...
SO WE COMPETED AGAINST EACH OTHER A LOT.

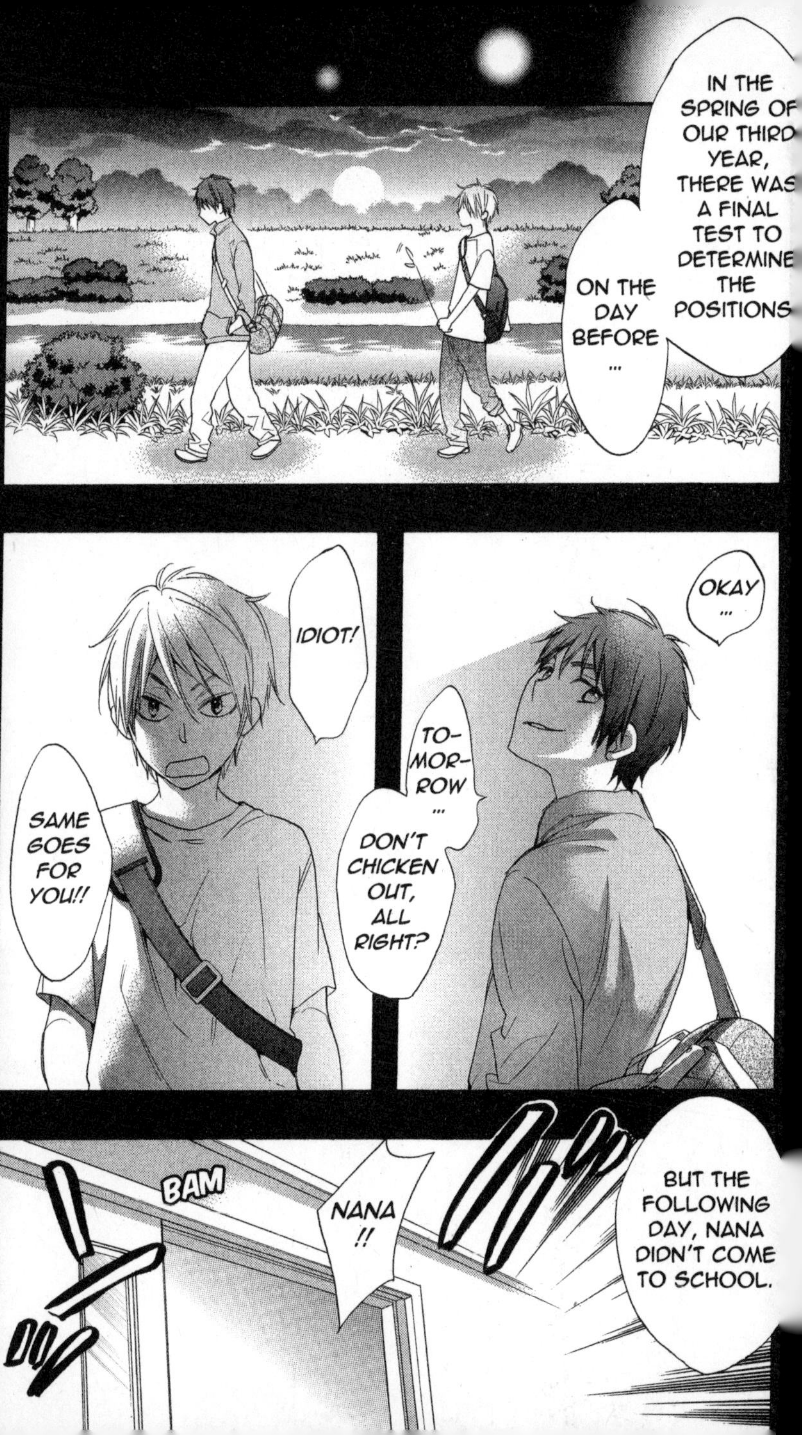
IN THE SPRING OF OUR THIRD YEAR, THERE WAS A FINAL TEST TO DETERMINE THE POSITIONS
ON THE DAY BEFORE ...
OKAY ...
TO-MOR-ROW ...
DON'T CHICKEN OUT, ALL RIGHT?
IDIOT!
SAME GOES FOR YOU!!
BUT THE FOLLOWING DAY, NANA DIDN'T COME TO SCHOOL.
NANA !!
BAM

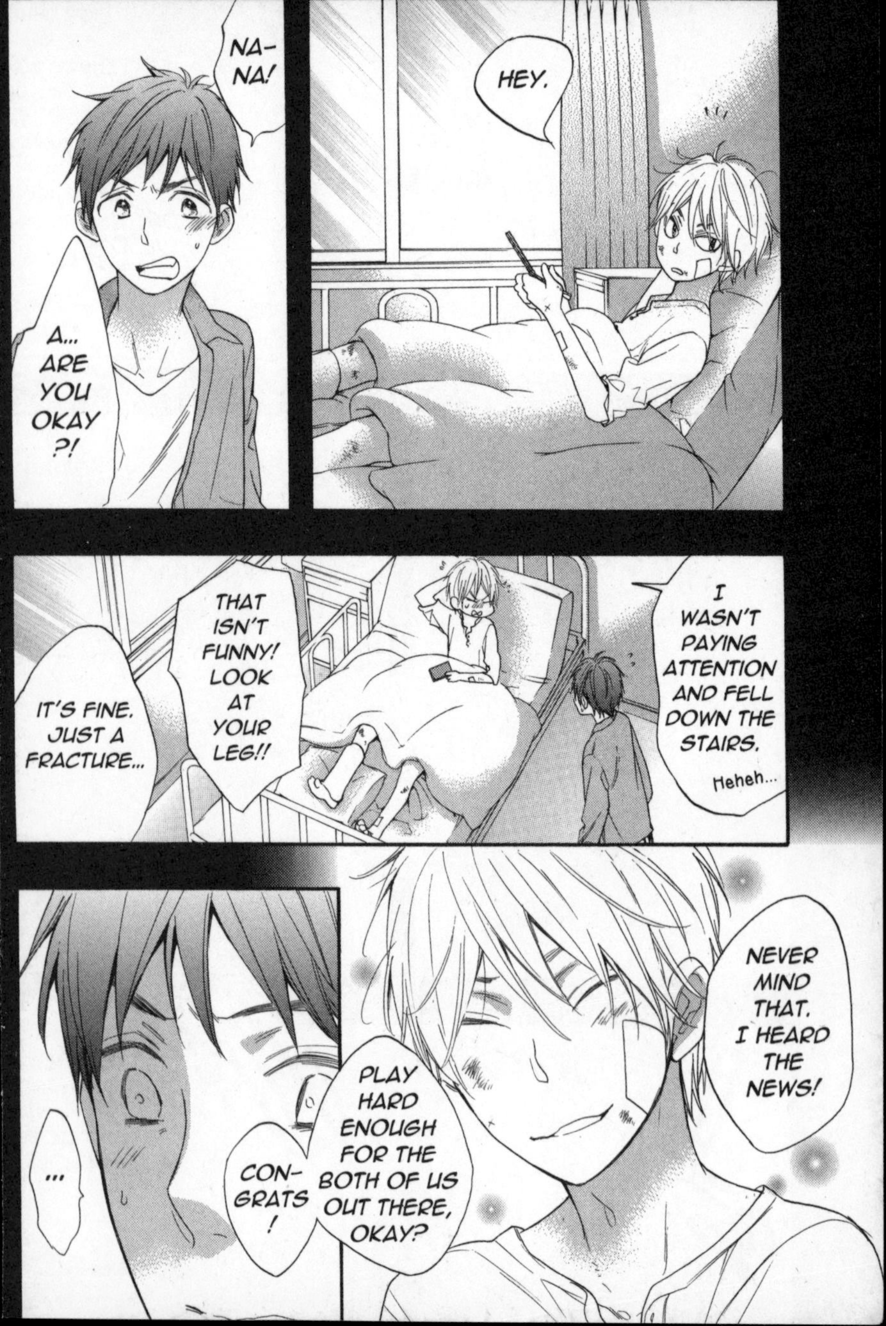
HEY.
NA-NA!
A... ARE YOU OKAY ?!
I WASN'T PAYING ATTENTION AND FELL DOWN THE STAIRS.
Heheh...
THAT ISN'T FUNNY! LOOK AT YOUR LEG!!
IT'S FINE. JUST A FRACTURE...
NEVER MIND THAT. I HEARD THE NEWS!
PLAY HARD ENOUGH FOR THE BOTH OF US OUT THERE, OKAY?
CON-GRATS!
...

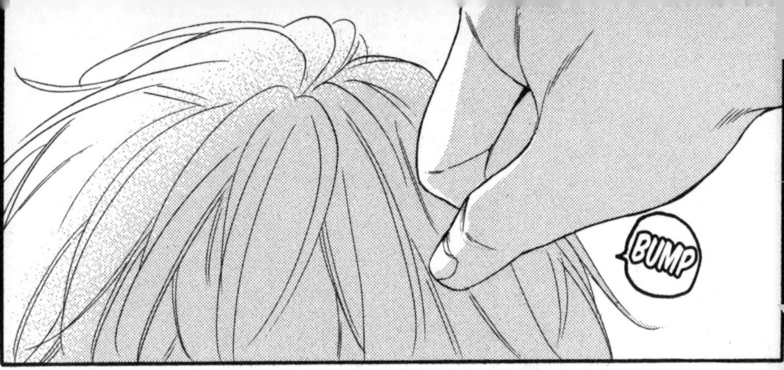
BUMP

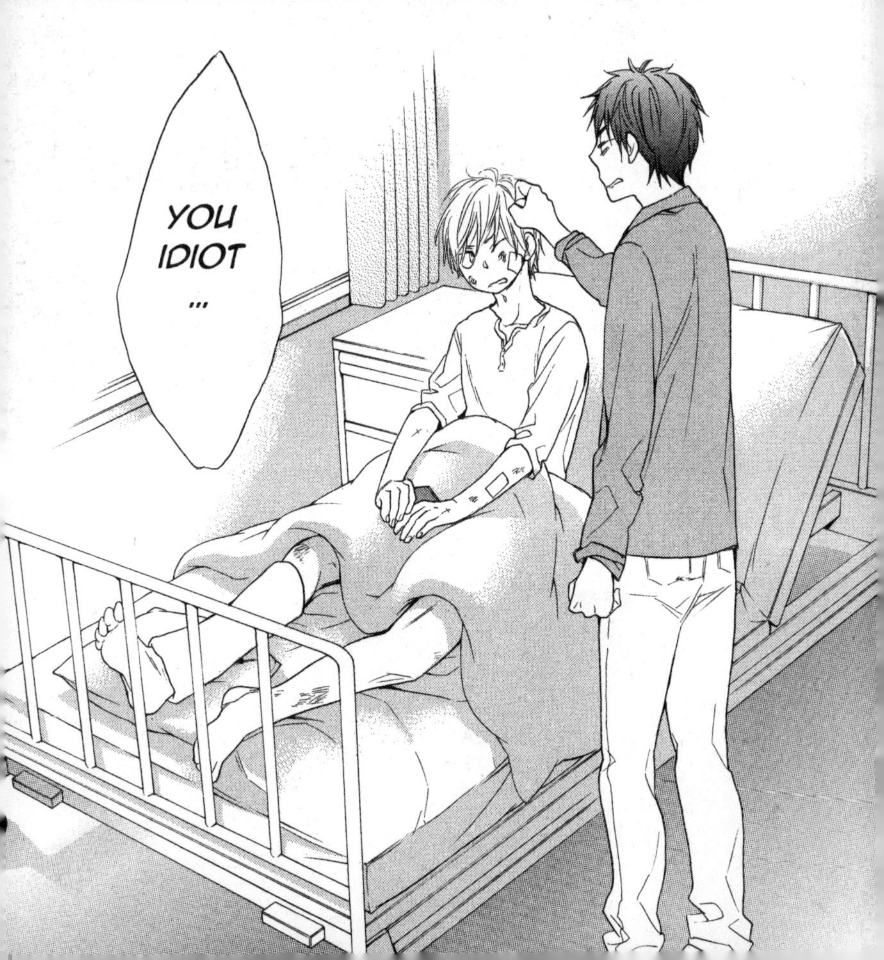
YOU IDIOT ...

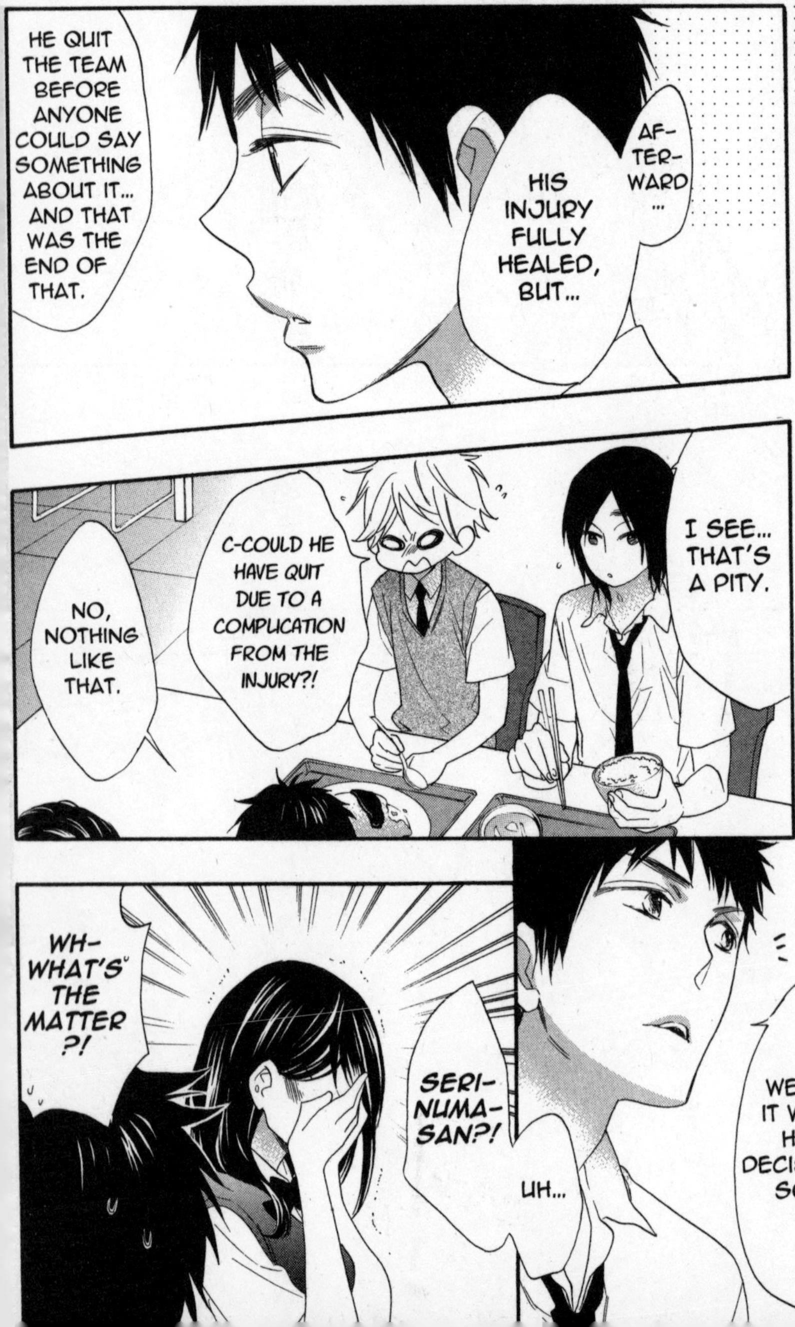
AFTERWARD...
HIS INJURY FULLY HEALED, BUT...
HE QUIT THE TEAM BEFORE ANYONE COULD SAY SOMETHING ABOUT IT... AND THAT WAS THE END OF THAT.
I SEE... THAT'S A PITY.
C-COULD HE HAVE QUIT DUE TO A COMPLICATION FROM THE INJURY?!
NO, NOTHING LIKE THAT.
WELL, IT WAS HIS DECISION, SO...
UH...
WH-WHAT'S THE MATTER?!
SERINUMA-SAN?!

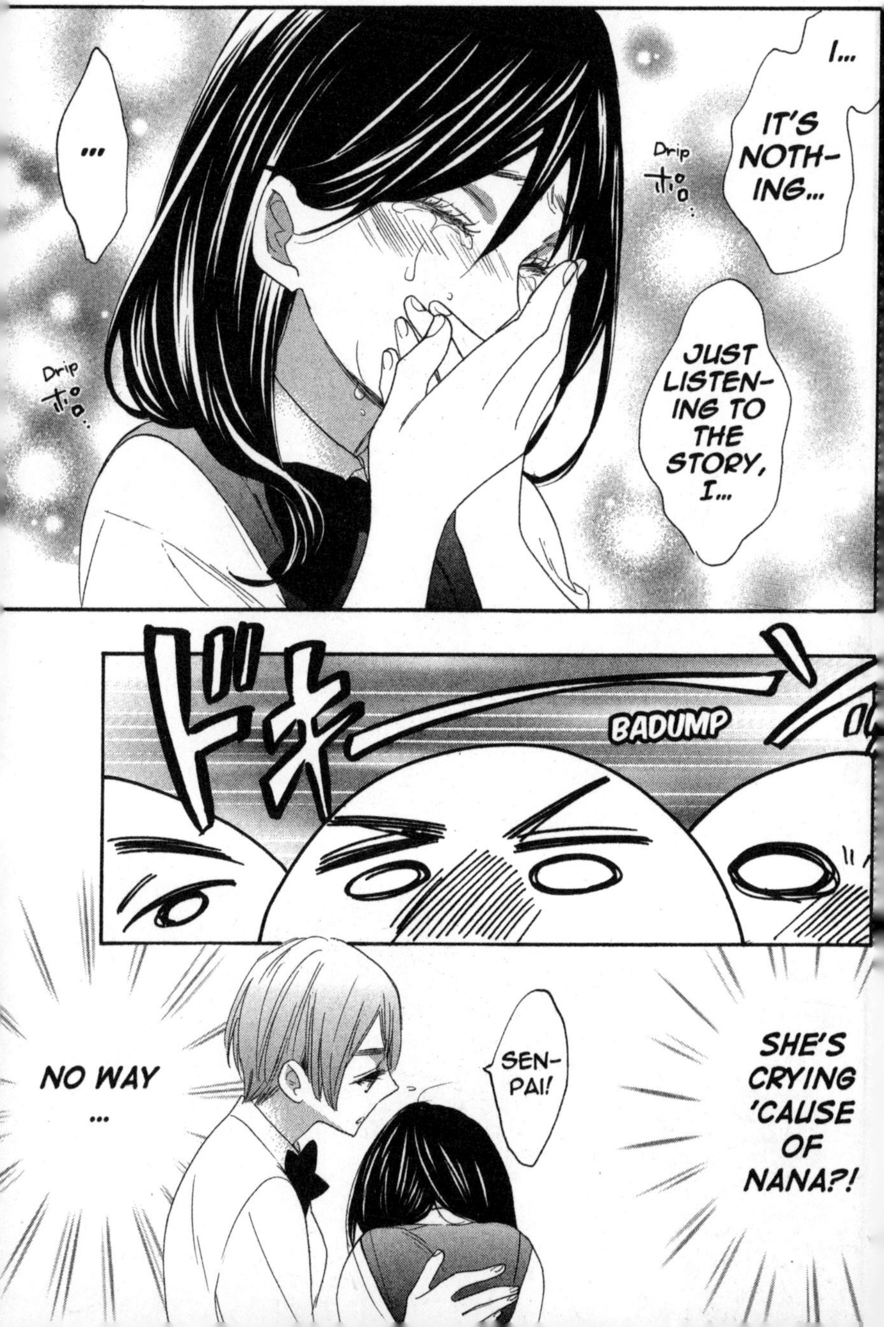

I...
IT'S NOTHING...
Drip
JUST LISTENING TO THE STORY, I...
...
Drip
ドキーン
BADUMP
SHE'S CRYING 'CAUSE OF NANA?!
SEN-PAI!
NO WAY ...

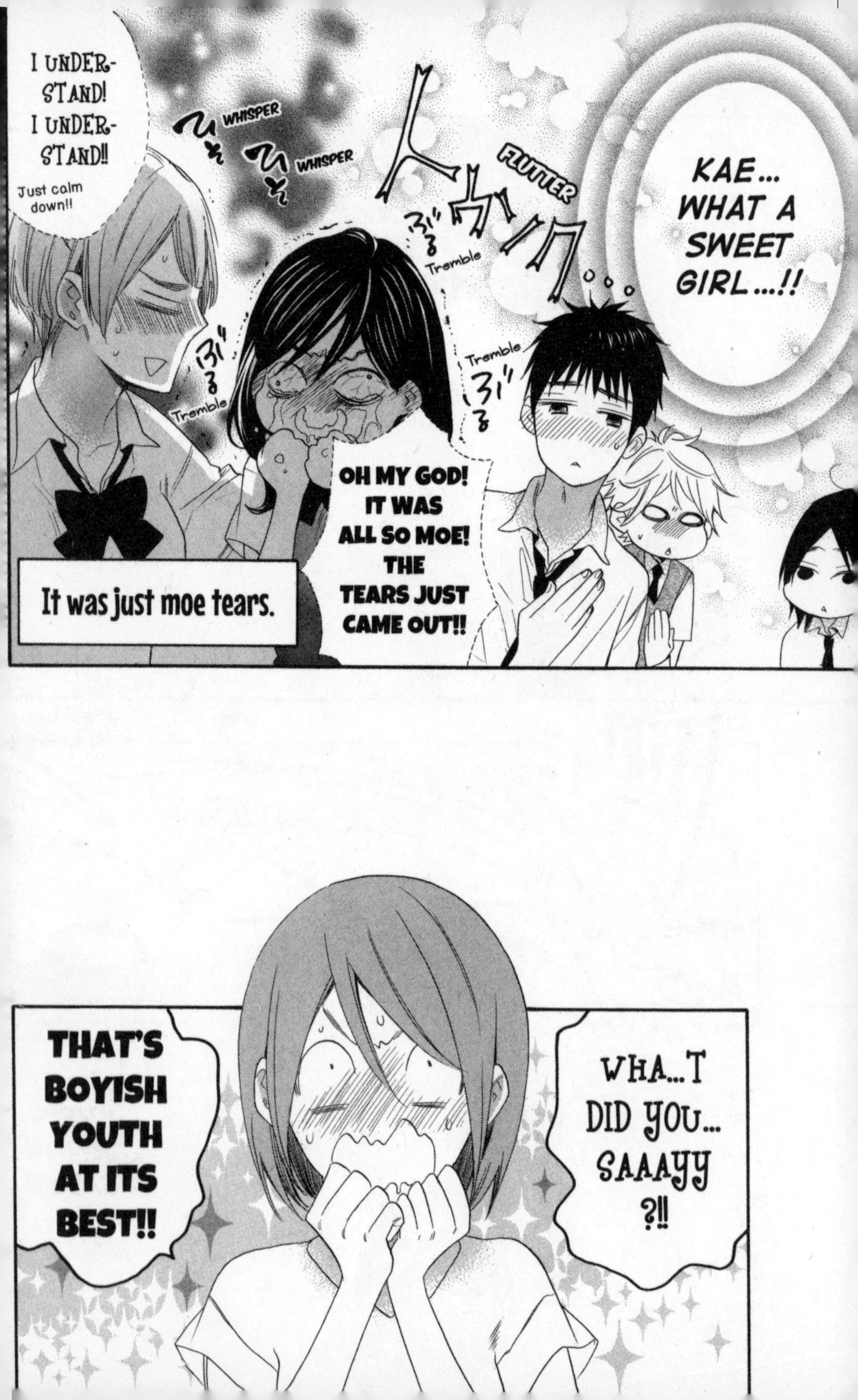

KAE... WHAT A SWEET GIRL...!!
FLUTTER
Tremble
Tremble
WHISPER
WHISPER
OH MY GOD! IT WAS ALL SO MOE! THE TEARS JUST CAME OUT!!
Tremble
I UNDER-STAND! I UNDER-STAND!!
Just calm down!!
It was just moe tears.
WHA...T DID YOU... SAAAYY ?!!
THAT'S BOYISH YOUTH AT ITS BEST!!

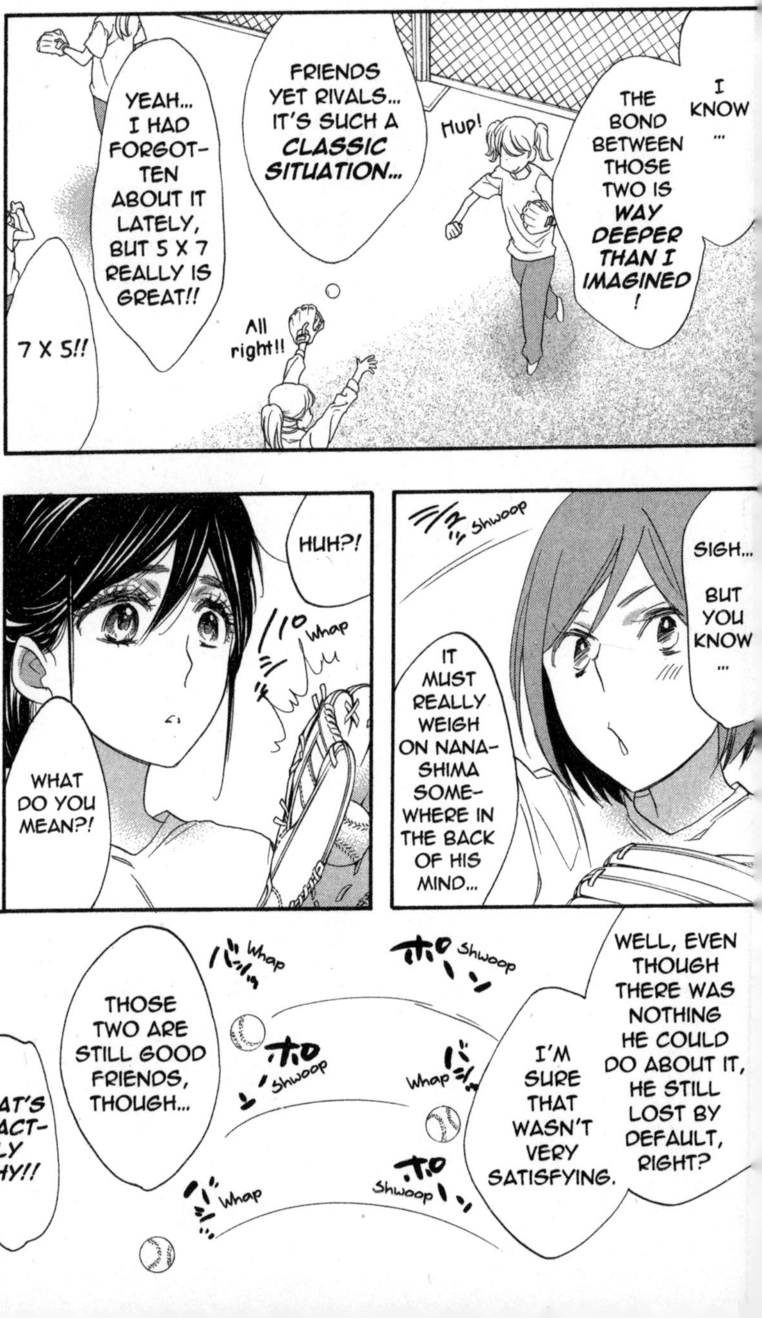
I KNOW...
THE BOND BETWEEN THOSE TWO IS WAY DEEPER THAN I IMAGINED!
Hup!
FRIENDS YET RIVALS... IT'S SUCH A CLASSIC SITUATION...
YEAH... I HAD FORGOTTEN ABOUT IT LATELY, BUT 5 X 7 REALLY IS GREAT!!
All right!!
7 X 5!!
Shwoop
SIGH...
BUT YOU KNOW...
IT MUST REALLY WEIGH ON NANASHIMA SOMEWHERE IN THE BACK OF HIS MIND...
HUH?!
Whap
WHAT DO YOU MEAN?!
WELL, EVEN THOUGH THERE WAS NOTHING HE COULD DO ABOUT IT, HE STILL LOST BY DEFAULT, RIGHT?
I'M SURE THAT WASN'T VERY SATISFYING.
Shwoop
Whap
Shwoop
Whap
Shwoop
Whap
THOSE TWO ARE STILL GOOD FRIENDS, THOUGH...
THAT'S EXACTLY WHY!!

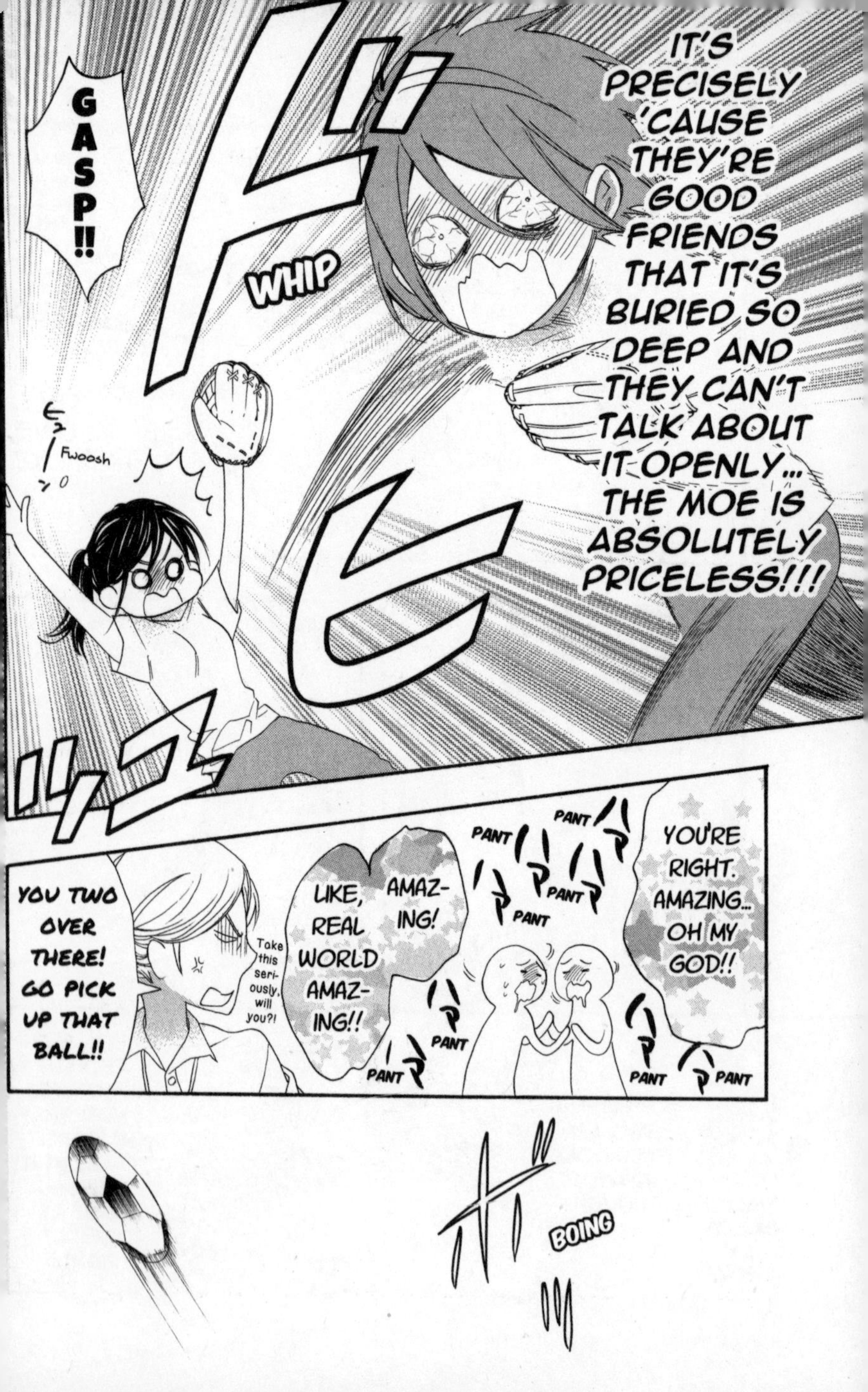
IT'S PRECISELY 'CAUSE THEY'RE GOOD FRIENDS THAT IT'S BURIED SO DEEP AND THEY CAN'T TALK ABOUT IT OPENLY... THE MOE IS ABSOLUTELY PRICELESS!!!
WHIP
GASP!!
Fwoosh
YOU'RE RIGHT. AMAZING... OH MY GOD!!
PANT PANT PANT PANT PANT PANT PANT PANT
AMAZ-ING!
LIKE, REAL WORLD AMAZ-ING!!
Take this seri-ously, will you?!
YOU TWO OVER THERE! GO PICK UP THAT BALL!!
BOING

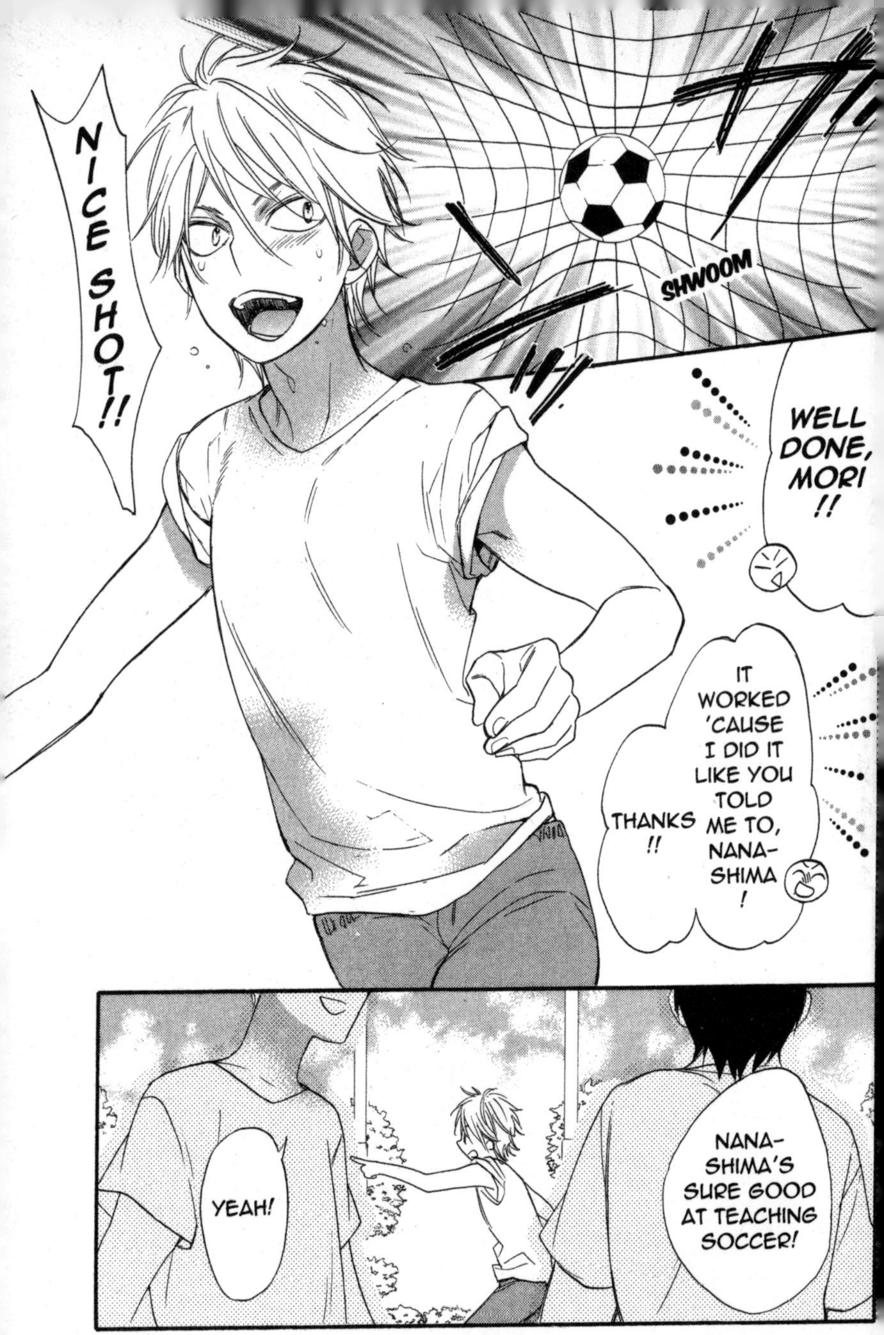
SHWOOM
NICE SHOT!!
WELL DONE, MORI!!
IT WORKED 'CAUSE I DID IT LIKE YOU TOLD ME TO, NANA-SHIMA!
THANKS!!
NANA-SHIMA'S SURE GOOD AT TEACHING SOCCER!
YEAH!

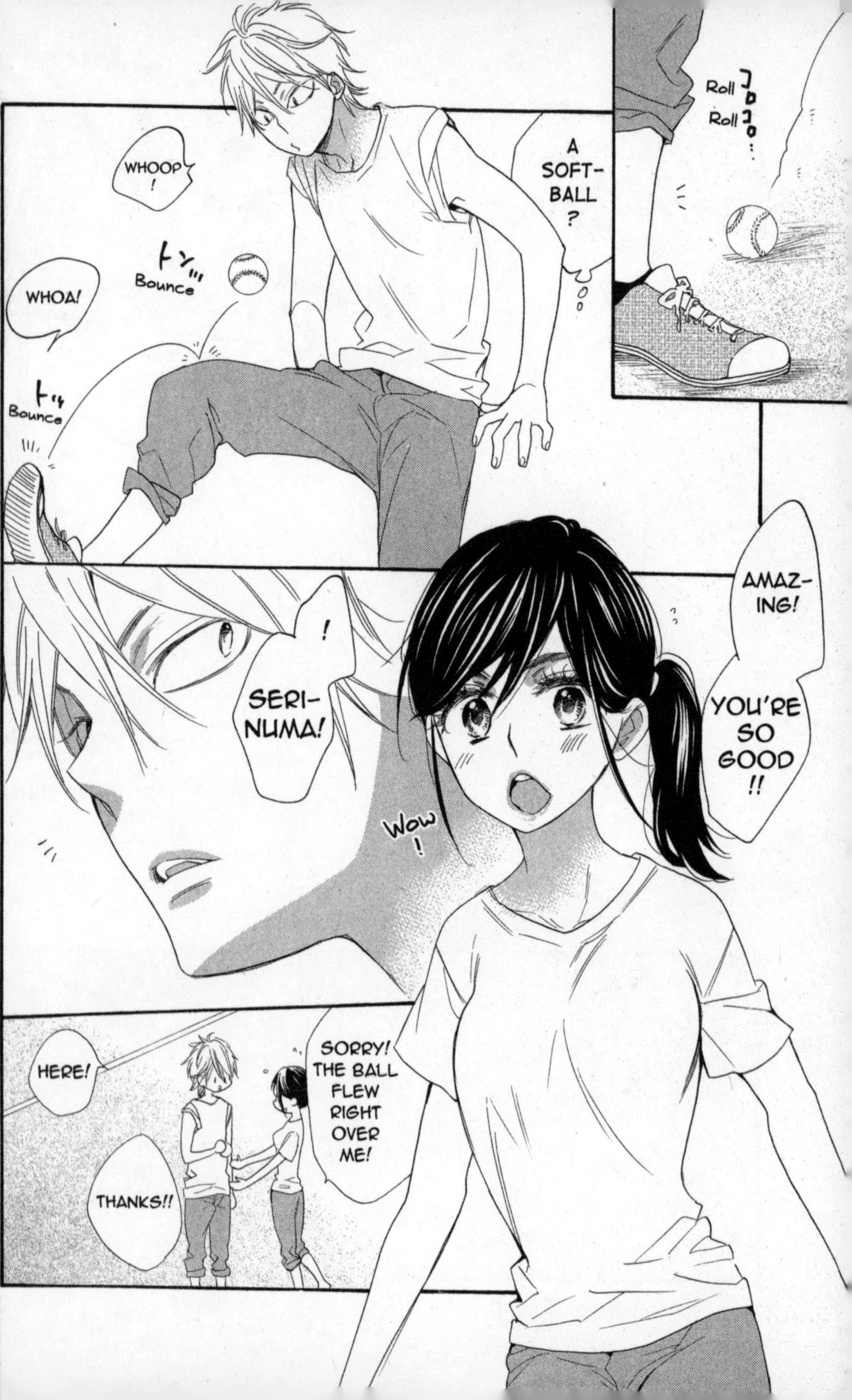
Roll
Roll
A SOFT-BALL?
WHOOP!
Bounce
WHOA!
Bounce
AMAZING!
YOU'RE SO GOOD!!
Wow!
!
SERI-NUMA!
SORRY! THE BALL FLEW RIGHT OVER ME!
HERE!
THANKS!!

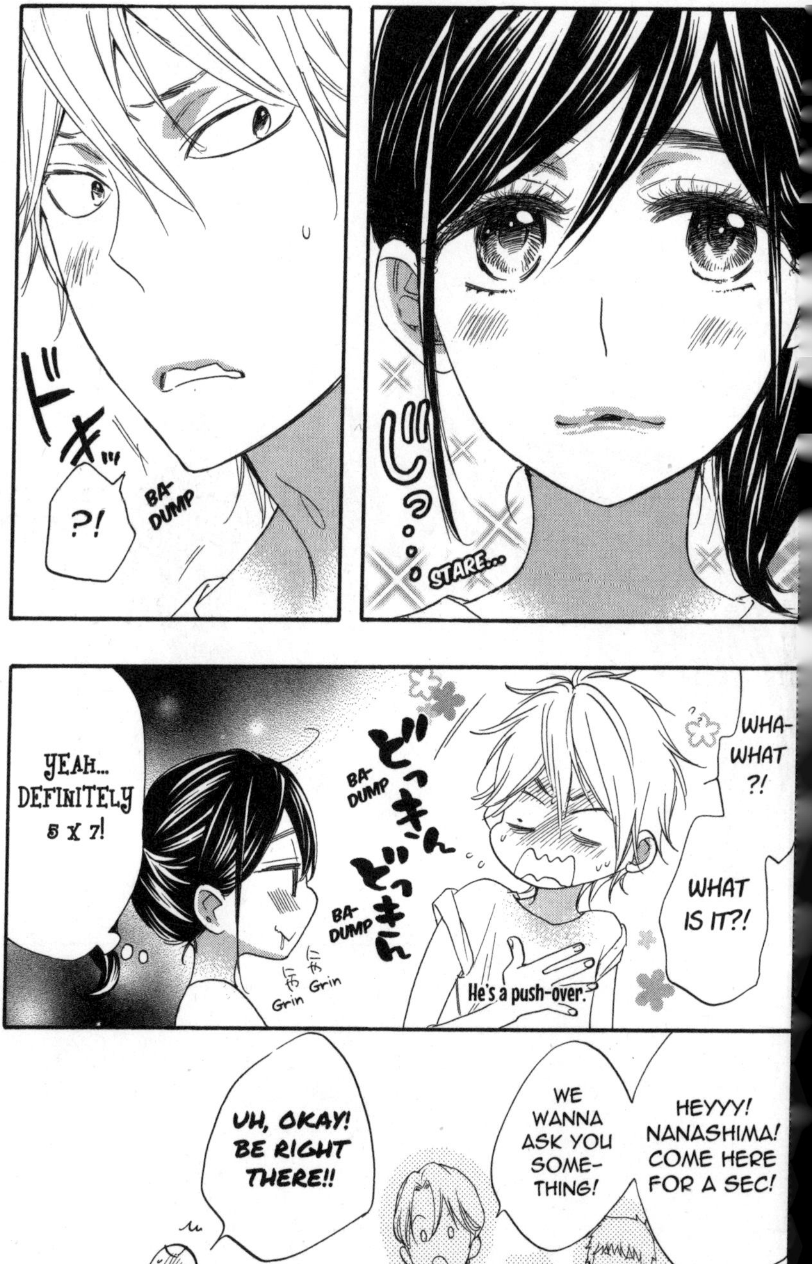

じーっ…
STARE...
ドキッ
BA-DUMP
?!
WHA-WHAT?!
WHAT IS IT?!
どっきん
BA-DUMP
どっきん
BA-DUMP
He's a push-over.
Grin Grin
YEAH... DEFINITELY 5 X 7!
HEYYY! NANASHIMA! COME HERE FOR A SEC!
WE WANNA ASK YOU SOMETHING!
UH, OKAY! BE RIGHT THERE!!

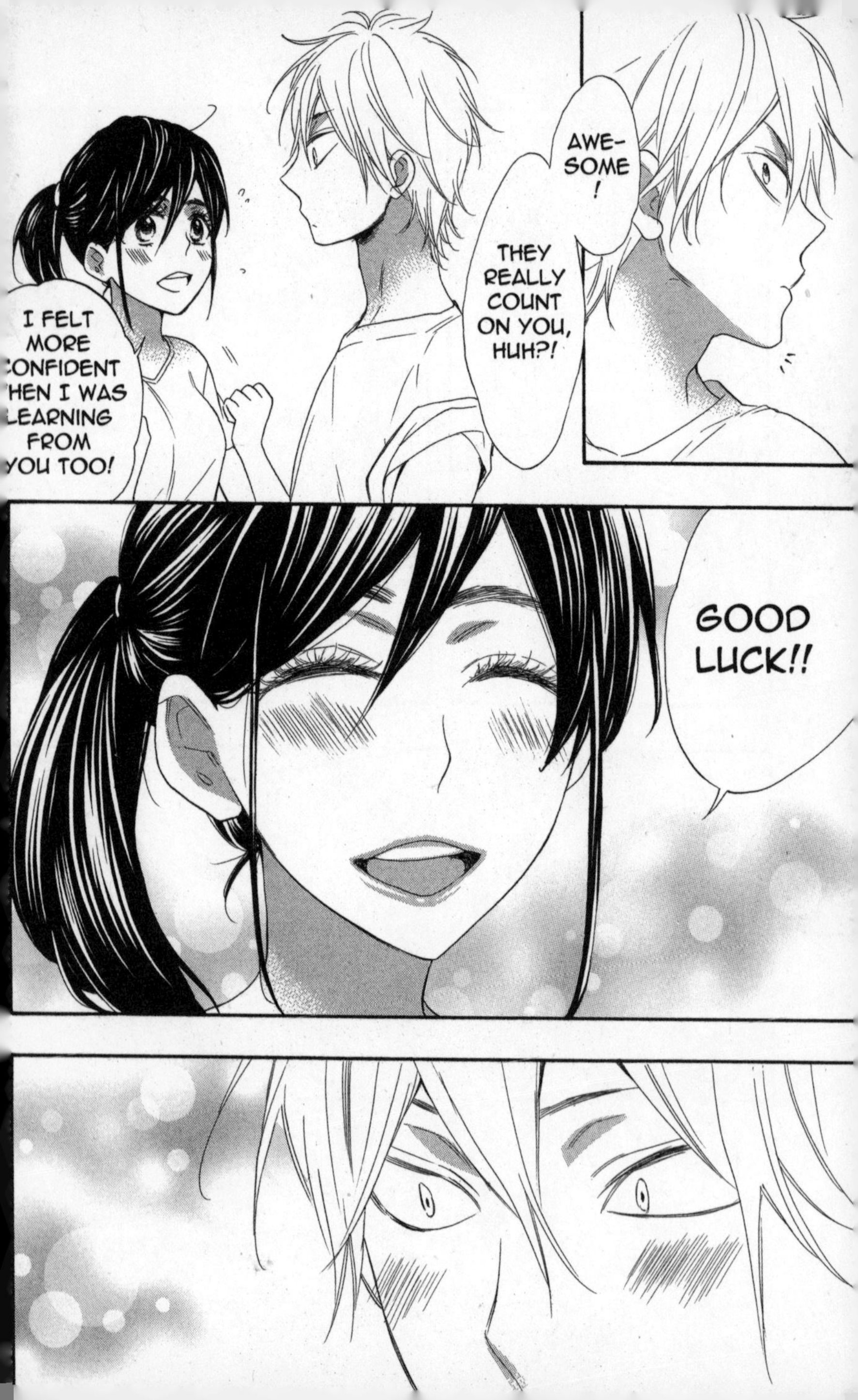
AWE-SOME!
THEY REALLY COUNT ON YOU, HUH?!
I FELT MORE CONFIDENT WHEN I WAS LEARNING FROM YOU TOO!
GOOD LUCK!!

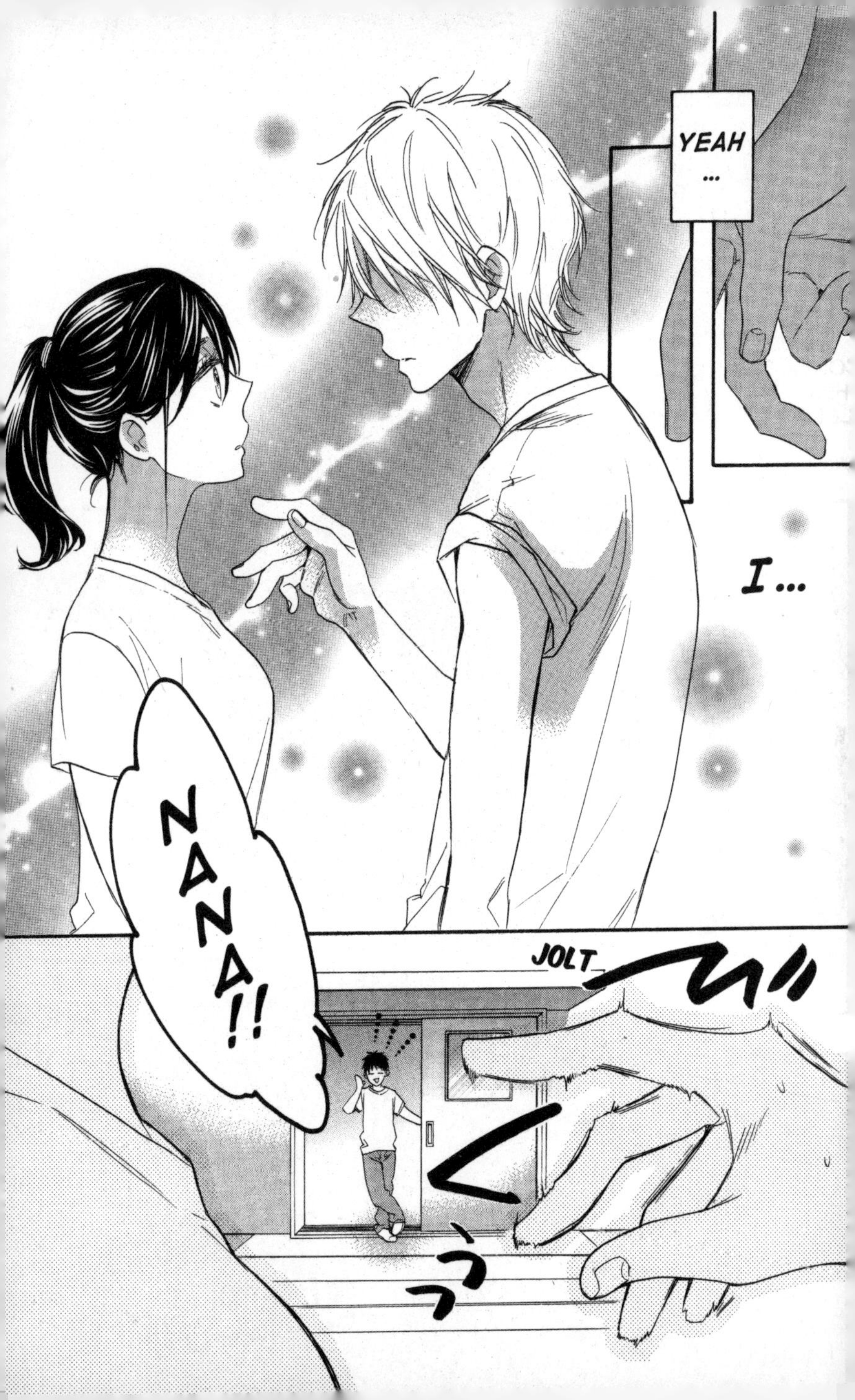
YEAH ...
I...
NANA!!
JOLT

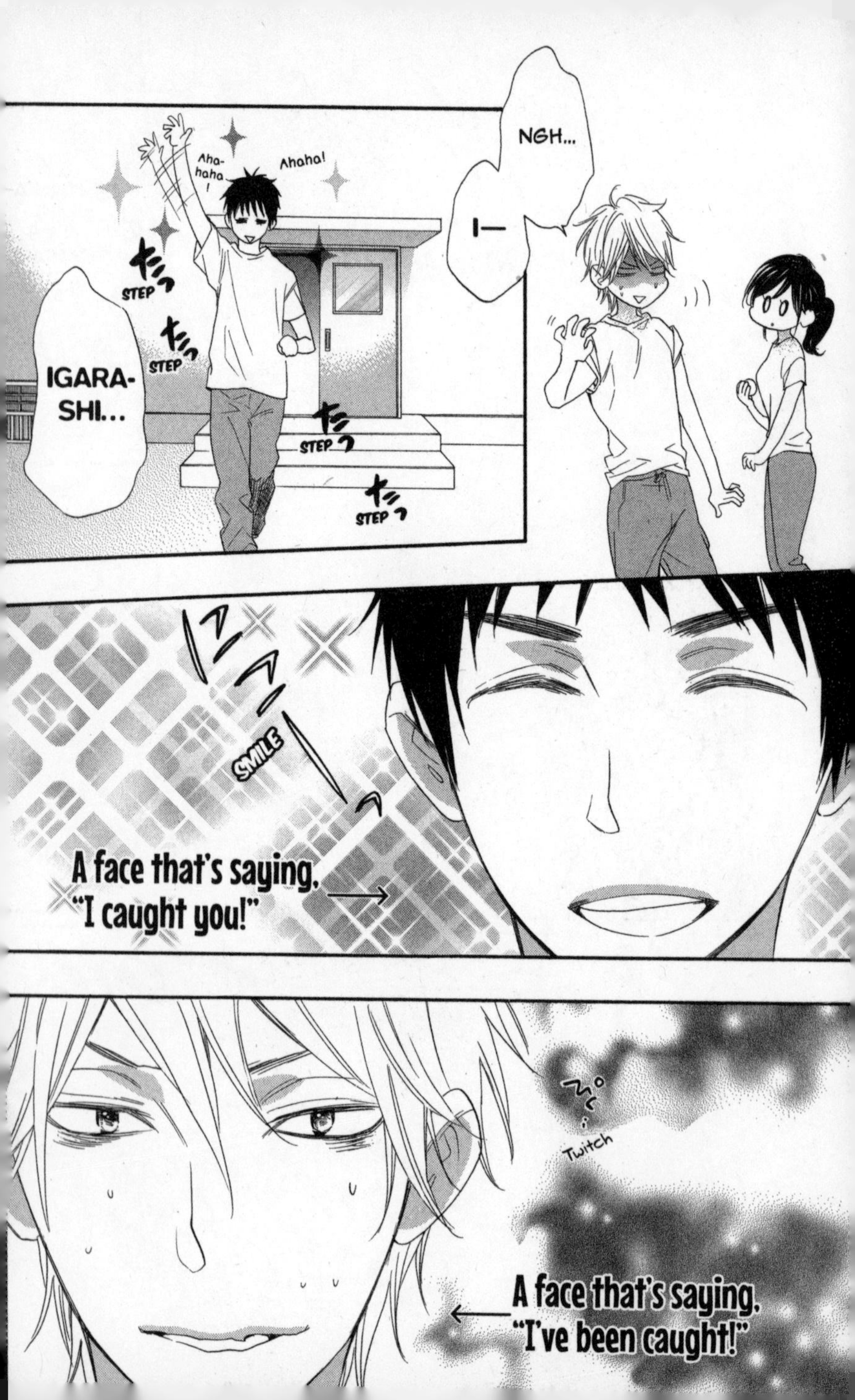
NGH...
I—
Ahaha!
Aha-haha!
STEP
STEP
STEP
STEP
IGARA-SHI...
SMILE
A face that's saying, "I caught you!"
Twitch
A face that's saying, "I've been caught!"

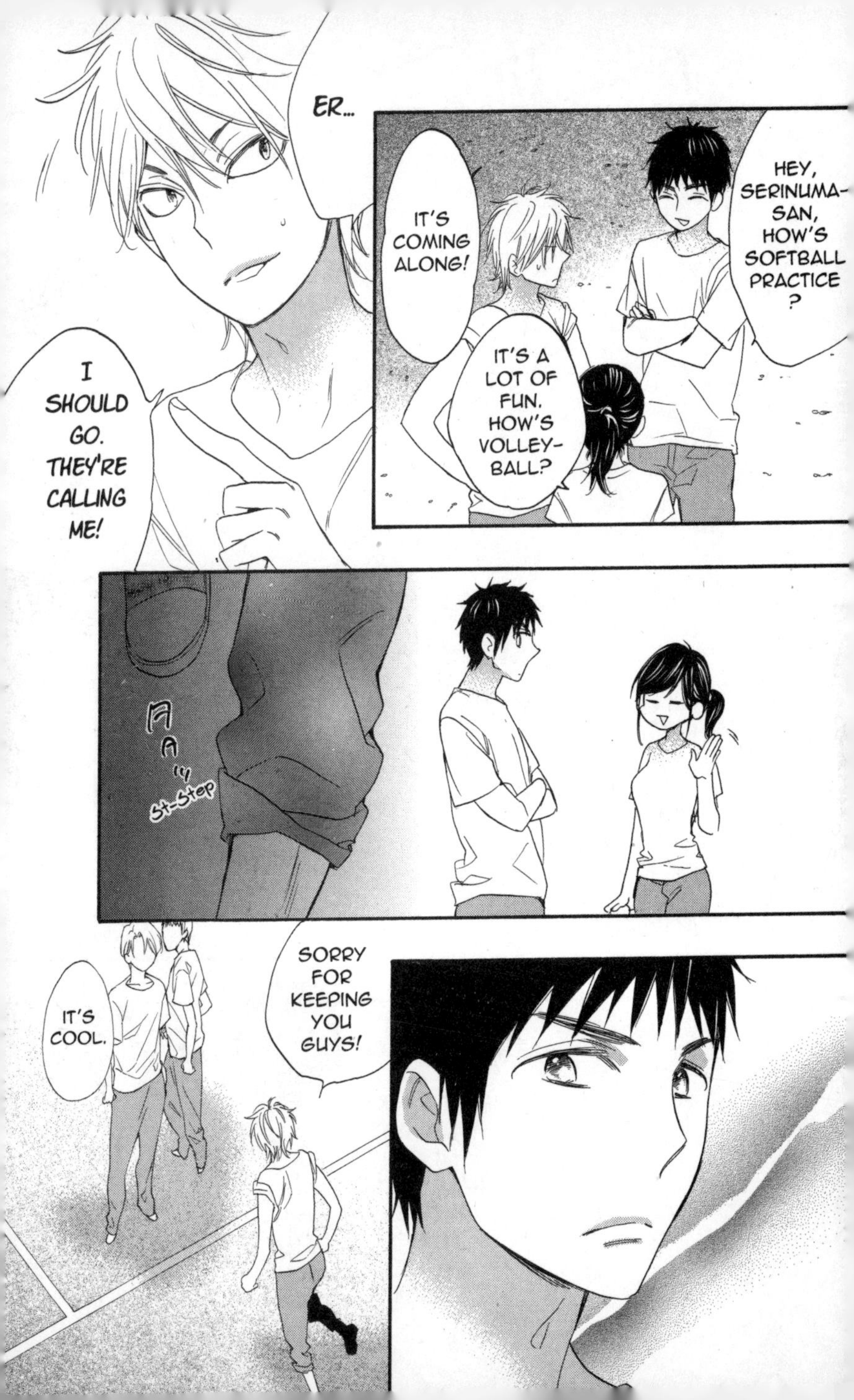
HEY, SERINUMA-SAN, HOW'S SOFTBALL PRACTICE?
IT'S A LOT OF FUN. HOW'S VOLLEYBALL?
IT'S COMING ALONG!
ER...
I SHOULD GO. THEY'RE CALLING ME!
St-Step
SORRY FOR KEEPING YOU GUYS!
IT'S COOL.

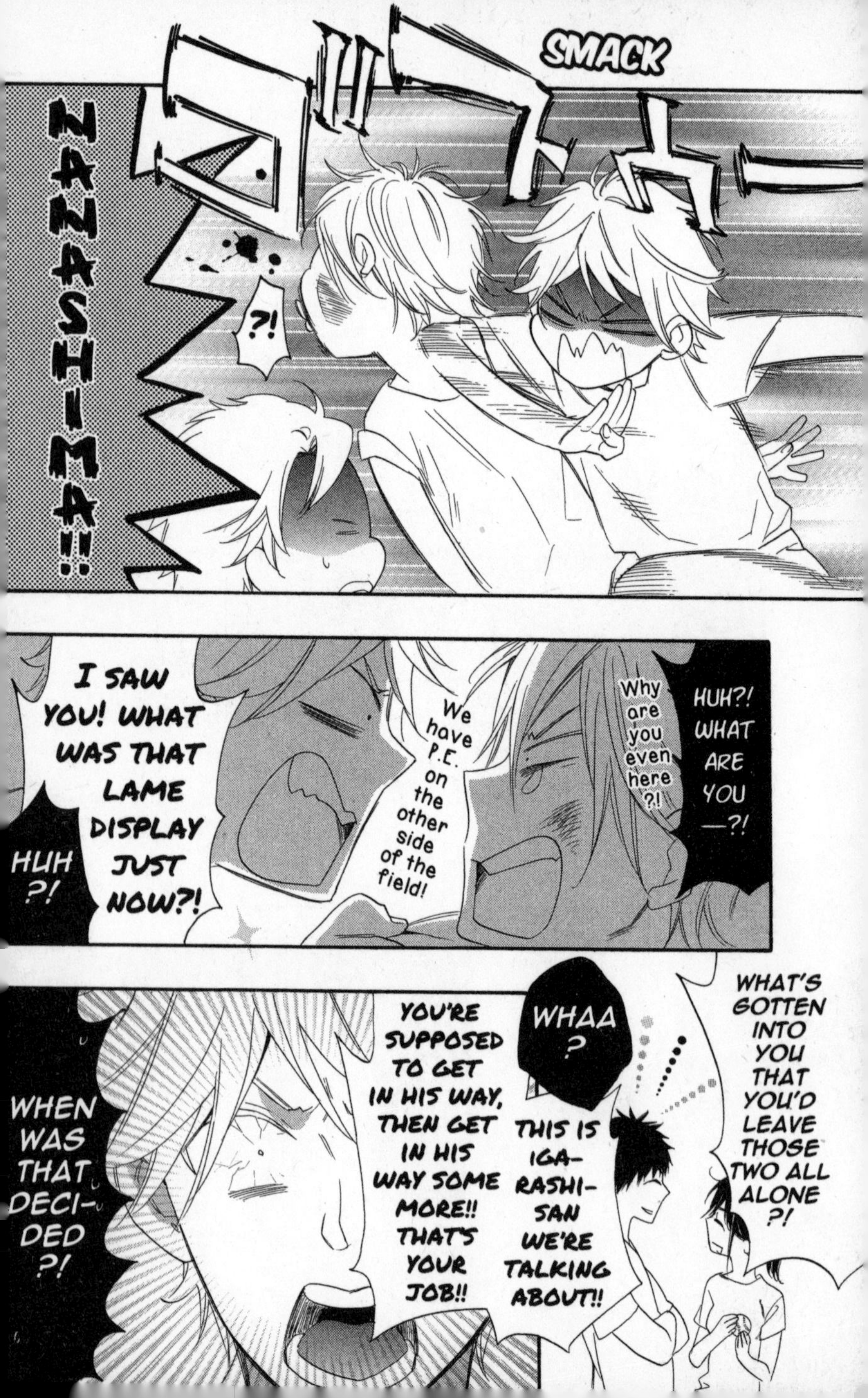
SMACK
?!
NANASHIMA!!
HUH?! WHAT ARE YOU—?!
Why are you even here?!
We have P.E. on the other side of the field!
I SAW YOU! WHAT WAS THAT LAME DISPLAY JUST NOW?!
HUH?!
WHAT'S GOTTEN INTO YOU THAT YOU'D LEAVE THOSE TWO ALL ALONE?!
WHAA?
THIS IS IGARASHI-SAN WE'RE TALKING ABOUT!!
YOU'RE SUPPOSED TO GET IN HIS WAY, THEN GET IN HIS WAY SOME MORE!! THAT'S YOUR JOB!!
WHEN WAS THAT DECIDED?!

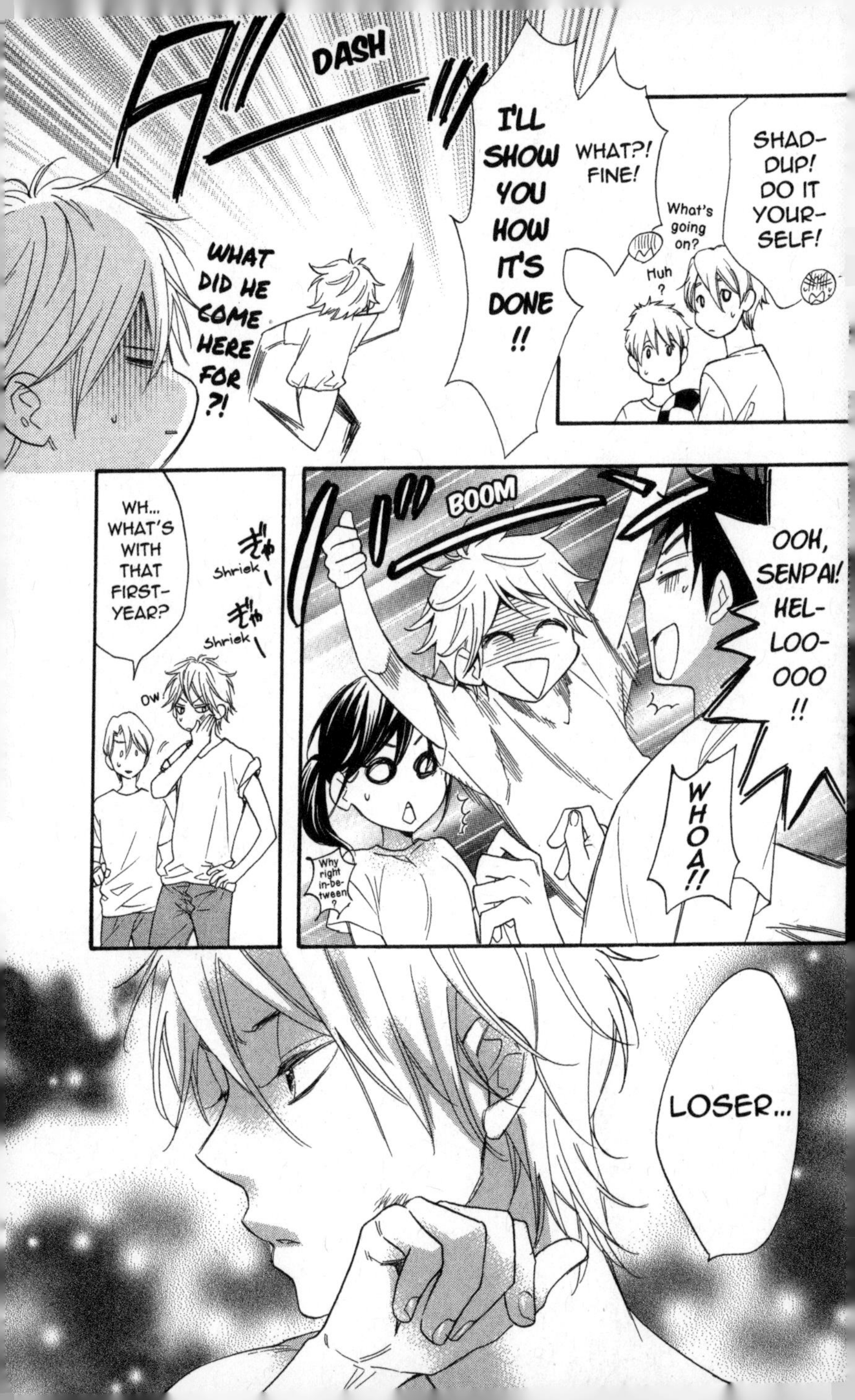
SHAD-DUP! DO IT YOURSELF!
WHAT?! FINE!
What's going on?
Huh?
DASH
I'LL SHOW YOU HOW IT'S DONE!!
WHAT DID HE COME HERE FOR?!
BOOM
OOH, SENPAI! HEL-LOO-OOO!!
WHOA!!
Why right in-be-tween?
Shriek
Shriek
WH... WHAT'S WITH THAT FIRST-YEAR?
OW
LOSER...

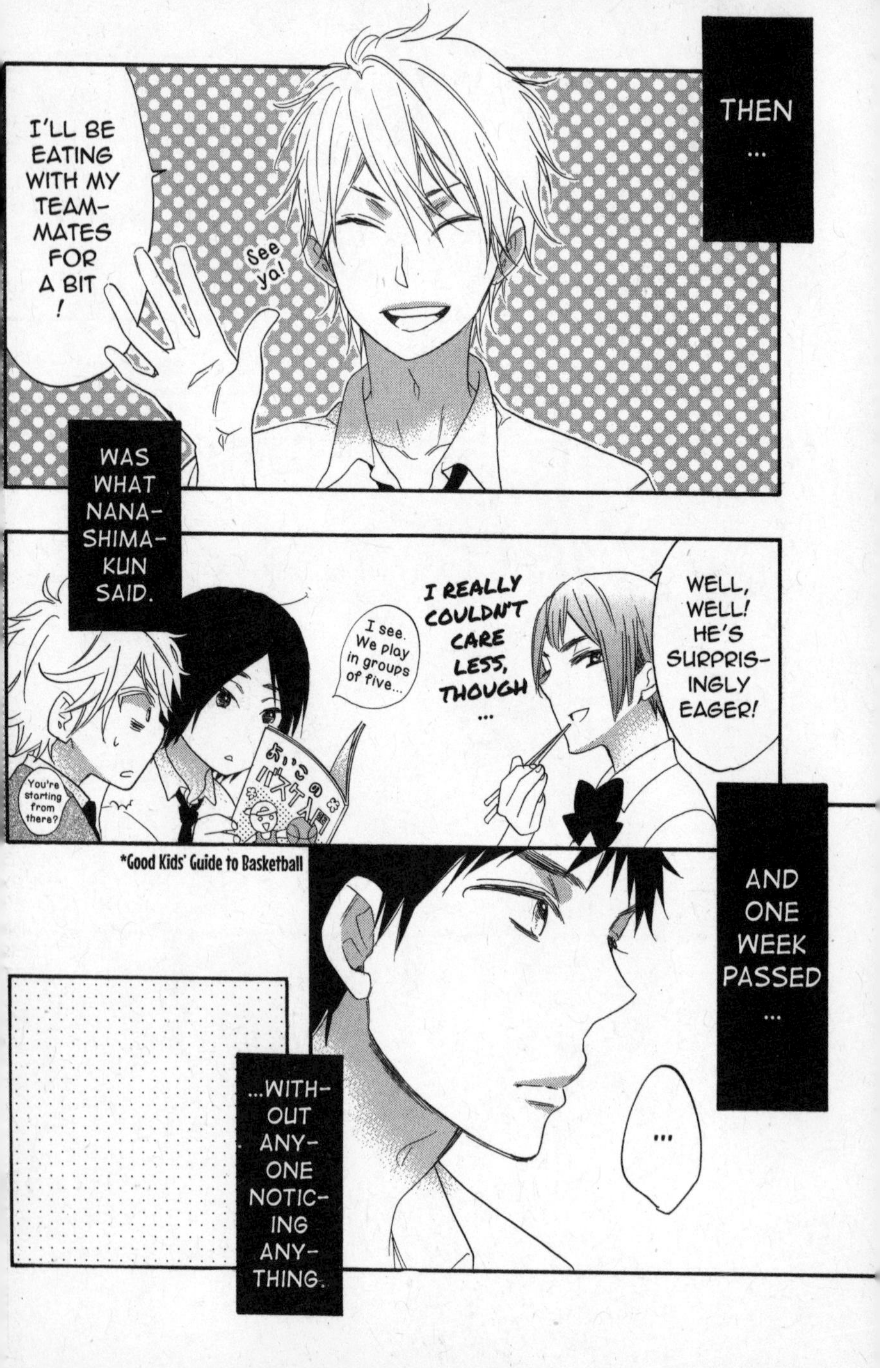
THEN ...
I'LL BE EATING WITH MY TEAM-MATES FOR A BIT!
See ya!
WAS WHAT NANA-SHIMA-KUN SAID.
WELL, WELL! HE'S SURPRIS-INGLY EAGER!
I REALLY COULDN'T CARE LESS, THOUGH ...
I see. We play in groups of five...
You're starting from there?
AND ONE WEEK PASSED ...
...
...WITH-OUT ANY-ONE NOTIC-ING ANY-THING.

*Good Kids' Guide to Basketball

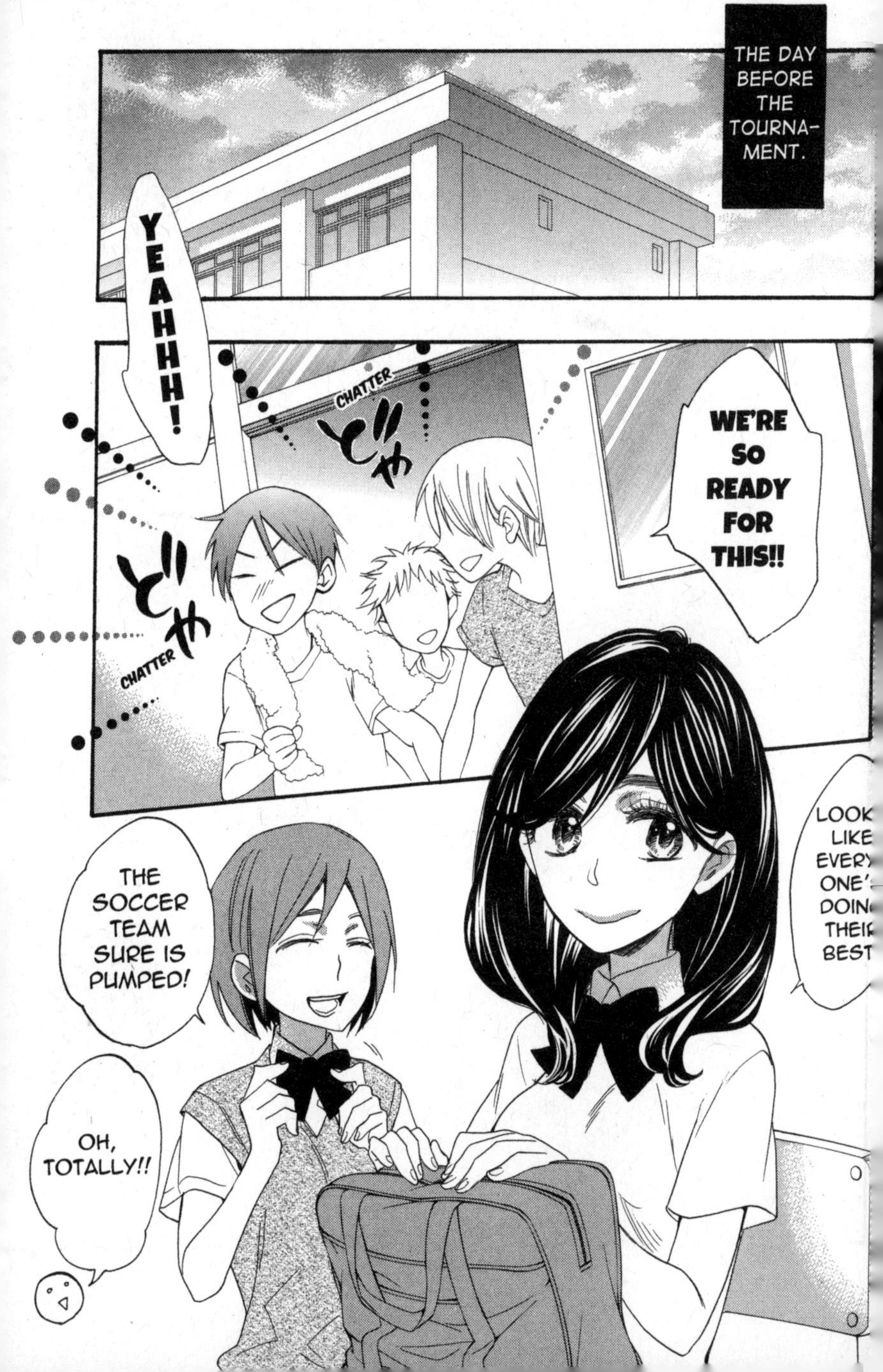
THE DAY BEFORE THE TOURNAMENT.
YEAHHHH!
WE'RE SO READY FOR THIS!!
CHATTER
CHATTER
LOOK LIKE EVERY ONE' DOIN THEIR BEST
THE SOCCER TEAM SURE IS PUMPED!
OH, TOTALLY!!

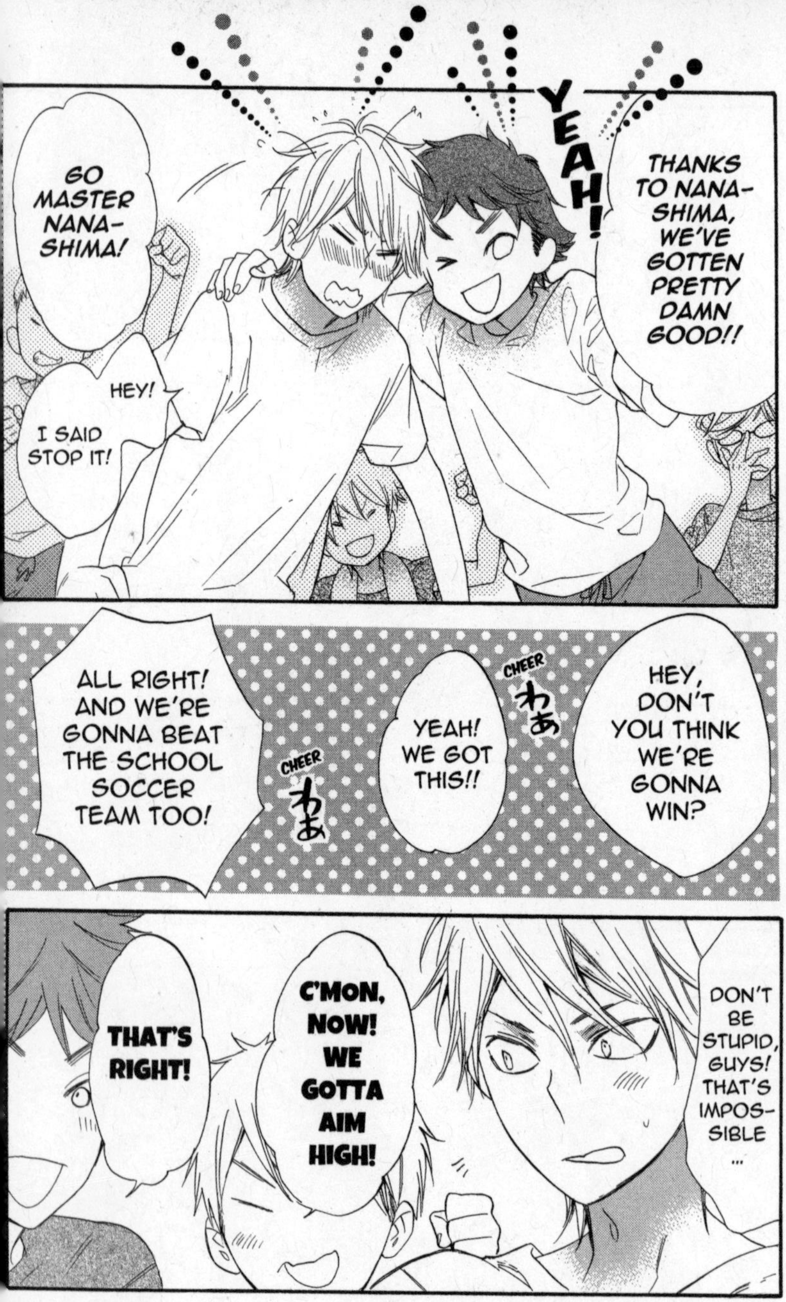
YEAH!
THANKS TO NANA-SHIMA, WE'VE GOTTEN PRETTY DAMN GOOD!!
GO MASTER NANA-SHIMA!
HEY!
I SAID STOP IT!
HEY, DON'T YOU THINK WE'RE GONNA WIN?
CHEER
わあ
YEAH! WE GOT THIS!!
CHEER
わあ
ALL RIGHT! AND WE'RE GONNA BEAT THE SCHOOL SOCCER TEAM TOO!
DON'T BE STUPID, GUYS! THAT'S IMPOSSIBLE...
C'MON, NOW! WE GOTTA AIM HIGH!
THAT'S RIGHT!

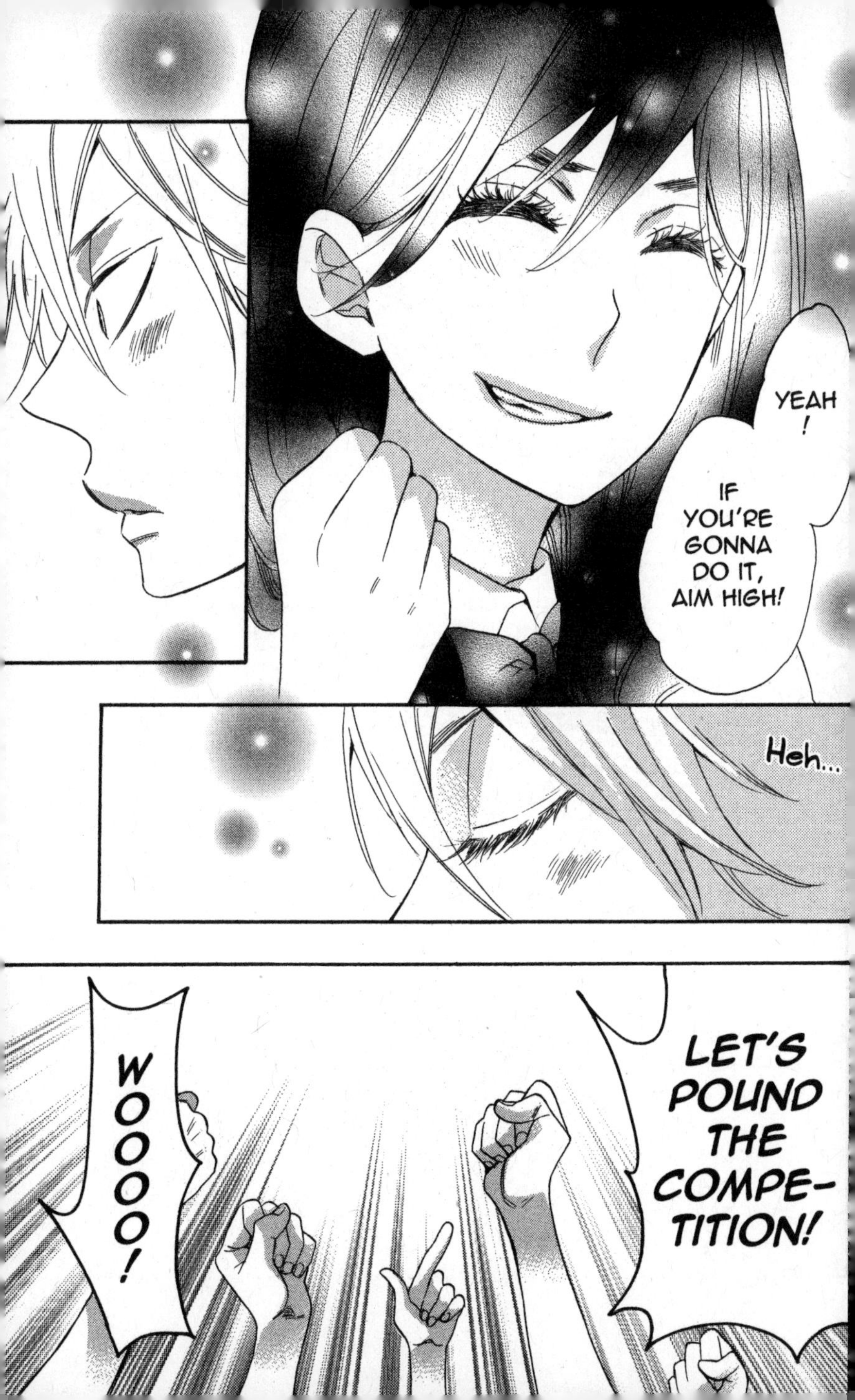
YEAH!
IF YOU'RE GONNA DO IT, AIM HIGH!
Heh...
LET'S POUND THE COMPE-TITION!
WOOOOO!

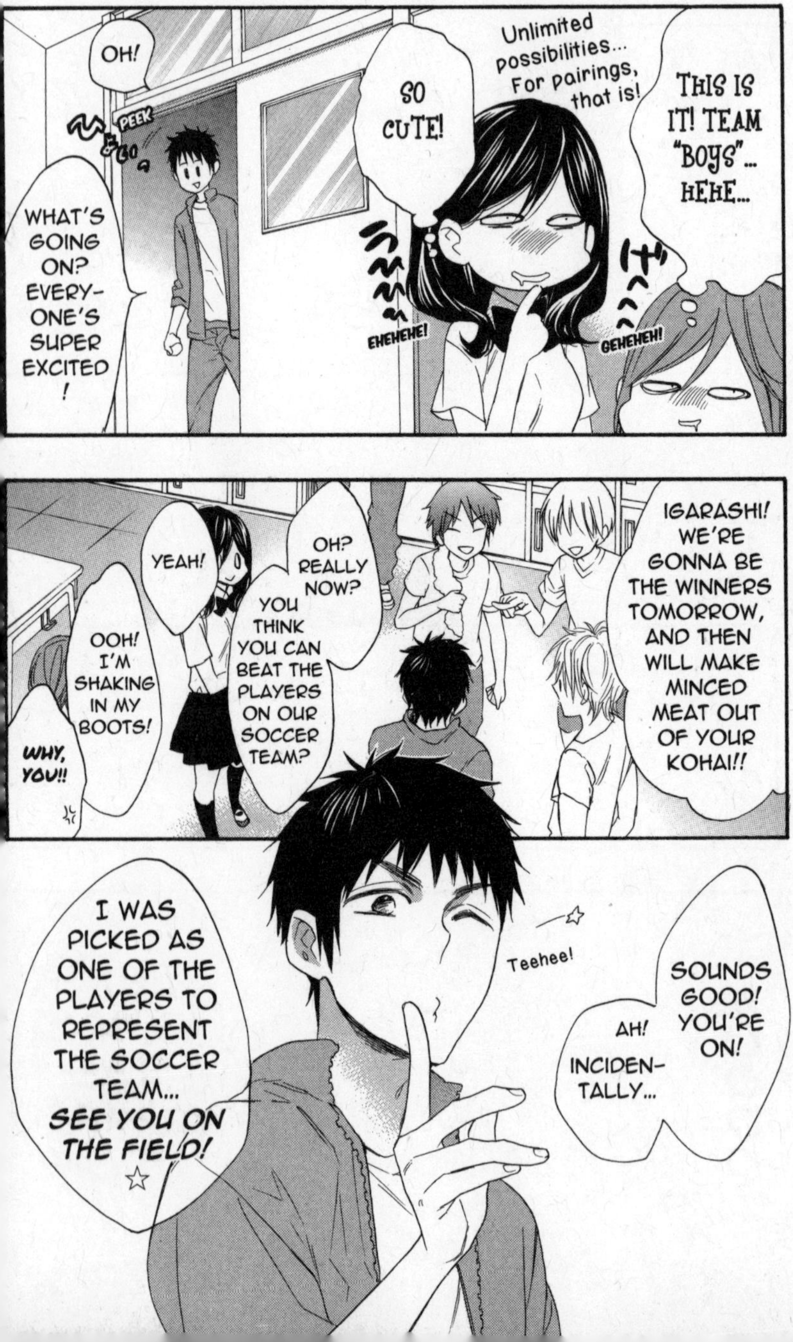
THIS IS IT! TEAM "BOYS"... HEHE...
Unlimited possibilities... For pairings, that is!
GEHEHEH!
SO CUTE!
EHEHEHE!
OH!
PEEK
WHAT'S GOING ON? EVERYONE'S SUPER EXCITED!
IGARASHI! WE'RE GONNA BE THE WINNERS TOMORROW, AND THEN WILL MAKE MINCED MEAT OUT OF YOUR KOHAI!!
OH? REALLY NOW?
YOU THINK YOU CAN BEAT THE PLAYERS ON OUR SOCCER TEAM?
YEAH!
OOH! I'M SHAKING IN MY BOOTS!
WHY, YOU!!
SOUNDS GOOD! YOU'RE ON!
AH! INCIDENTALLY...
Teehee!
I WAS PICKED AS ONE OF THE PLAYERS TO REPRESENT THE SOCCER TEAM... SEE YOU ON THE FIELD! ☆

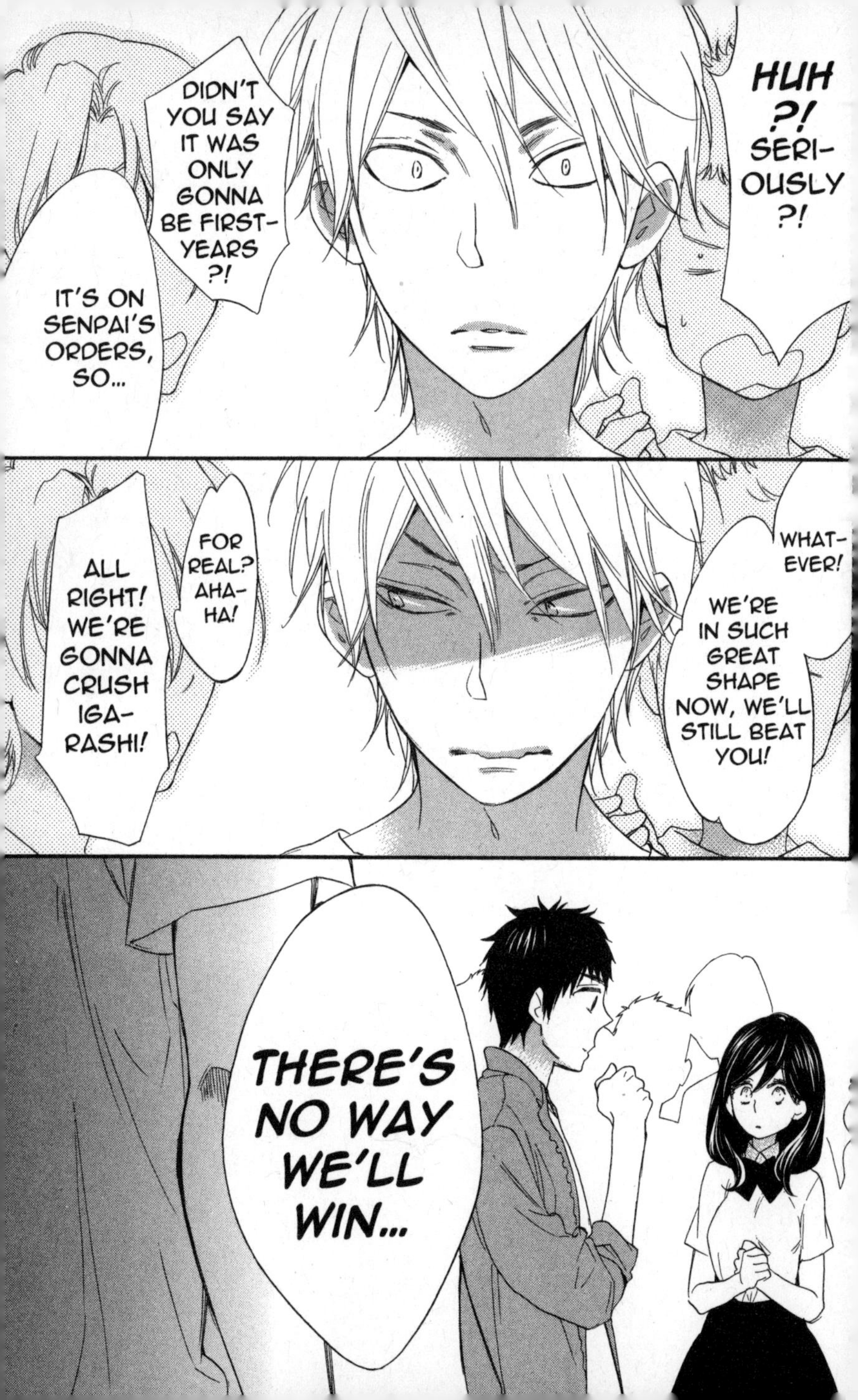
HUH?! SERIOUSLY?!
DIDN'T YOU SAY IT WAS ONLY GONNA BE FIRST-YEARS?!
IT'S ON SENPAI'S ORDERS, SO...
WHATEVER!
WE'RE IN SUCH GREAT SHAPE NOW, WE'LL STILL BEAT YOU!
FOR REAL? AHAHA!
ALL RIGHT! WE'RE GONNA CRUSH IGARASHI!
THERE'S NO WAY WE'LL WIN...

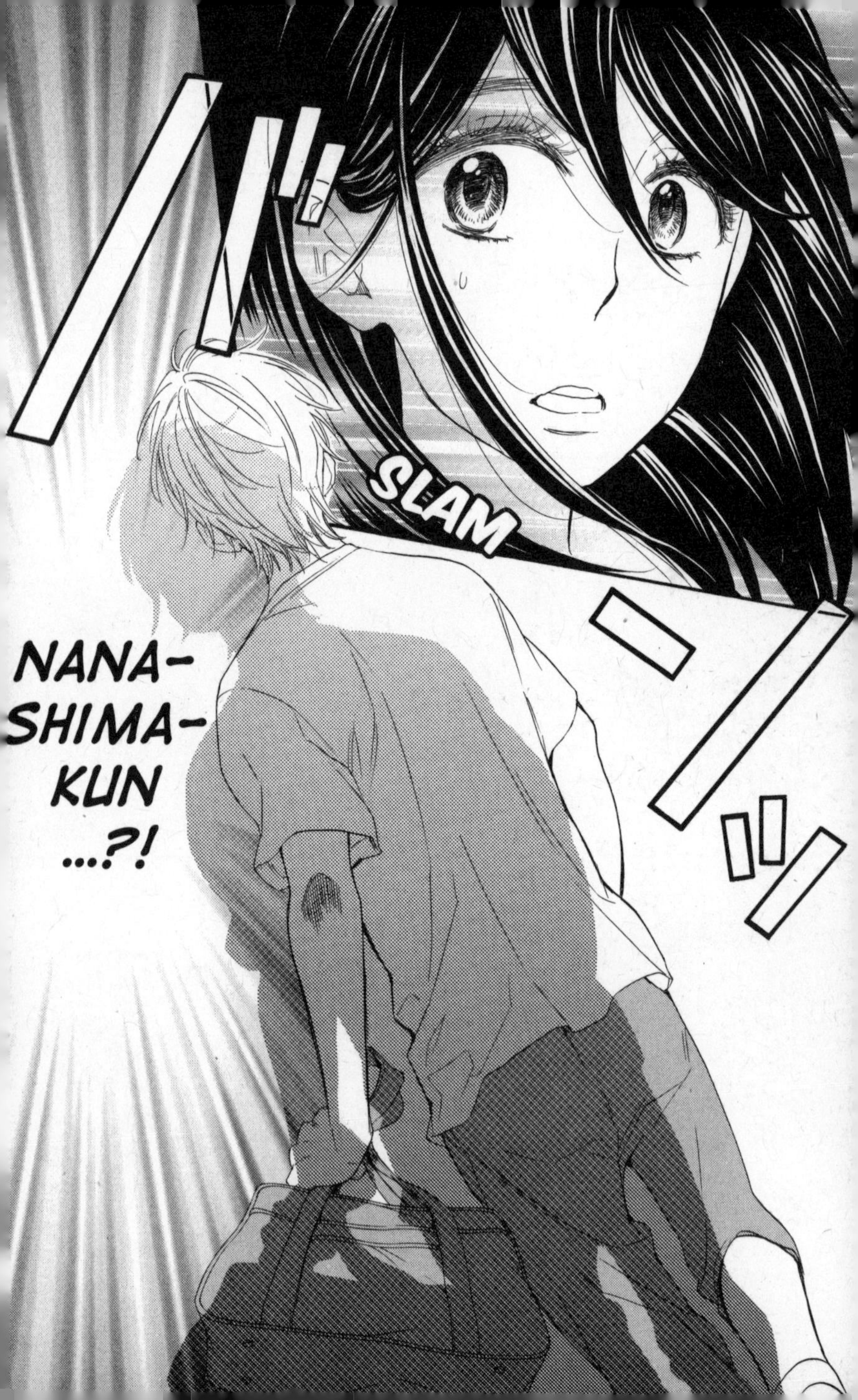
SLAM
NANA-SHIMA-KUN ...?!

#14 IGARASHI, I...

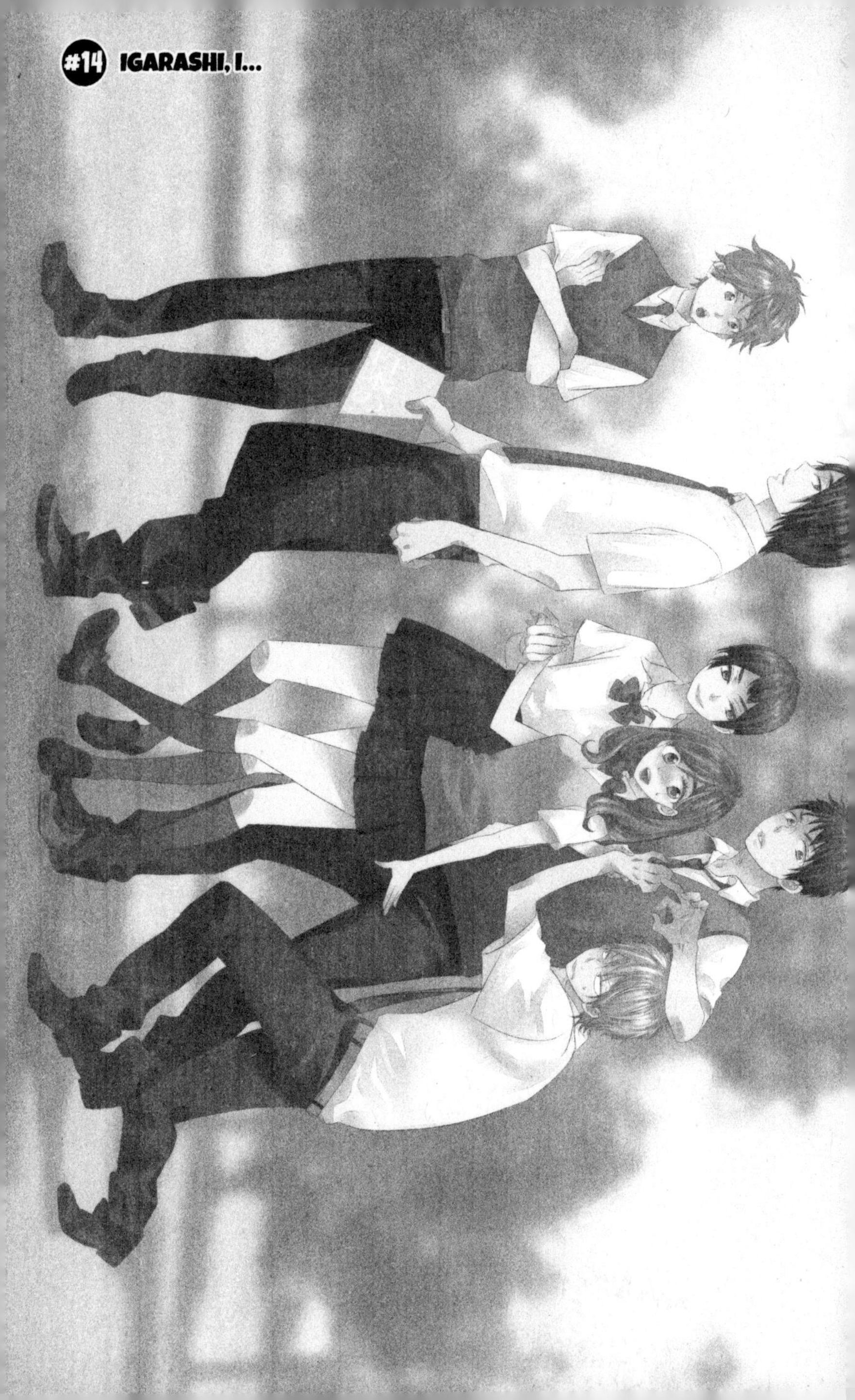

KiSS HiM, NOT ME!

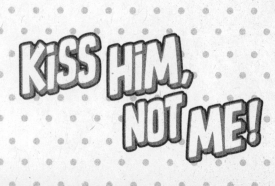

I THINK WE STARTED FROM AROUND THE SAME POINT...

To To

FWEE FWEEEEE

AWWW!
WE LOST!
YEAHHH!

KiSS HiM, NOT ME!

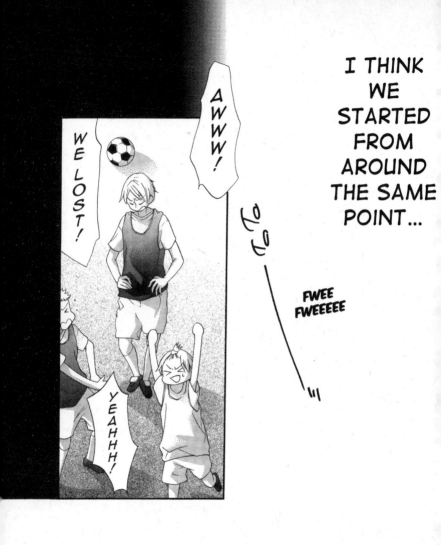

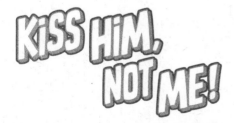

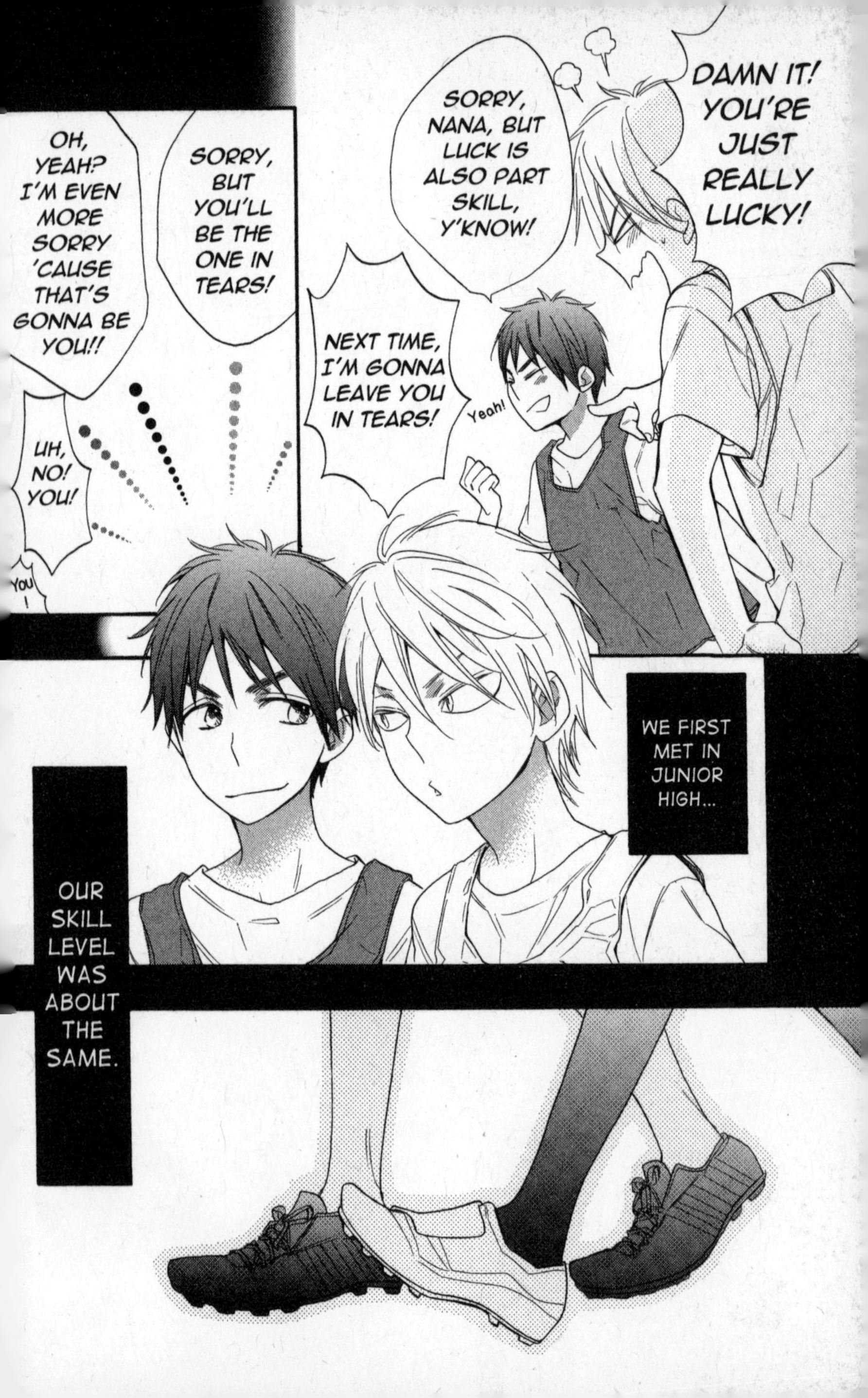
DAMN IT! YOU'RE JUST REALLY LUCKY!
SORRY, NANA, BUT LUCK IS ALSO PART SKILL, Y'KNOW!
NEXT TIME, I'M GONNA LEAVE YOU IN TEARS!
Yeah!
SORRY, BUT YOU'LL BE THE ONE IN TEARS!
OH, YEAH? I'M EVEN MORE SORRY 'CAUSE THAT'S GONNA BE YOU!!
UH, NO! YOU!
YOU!
WE FIRST MET IN JUNIOR HIGH...
OUR SKILL LEVEL WAS ABOUT THE SAME.

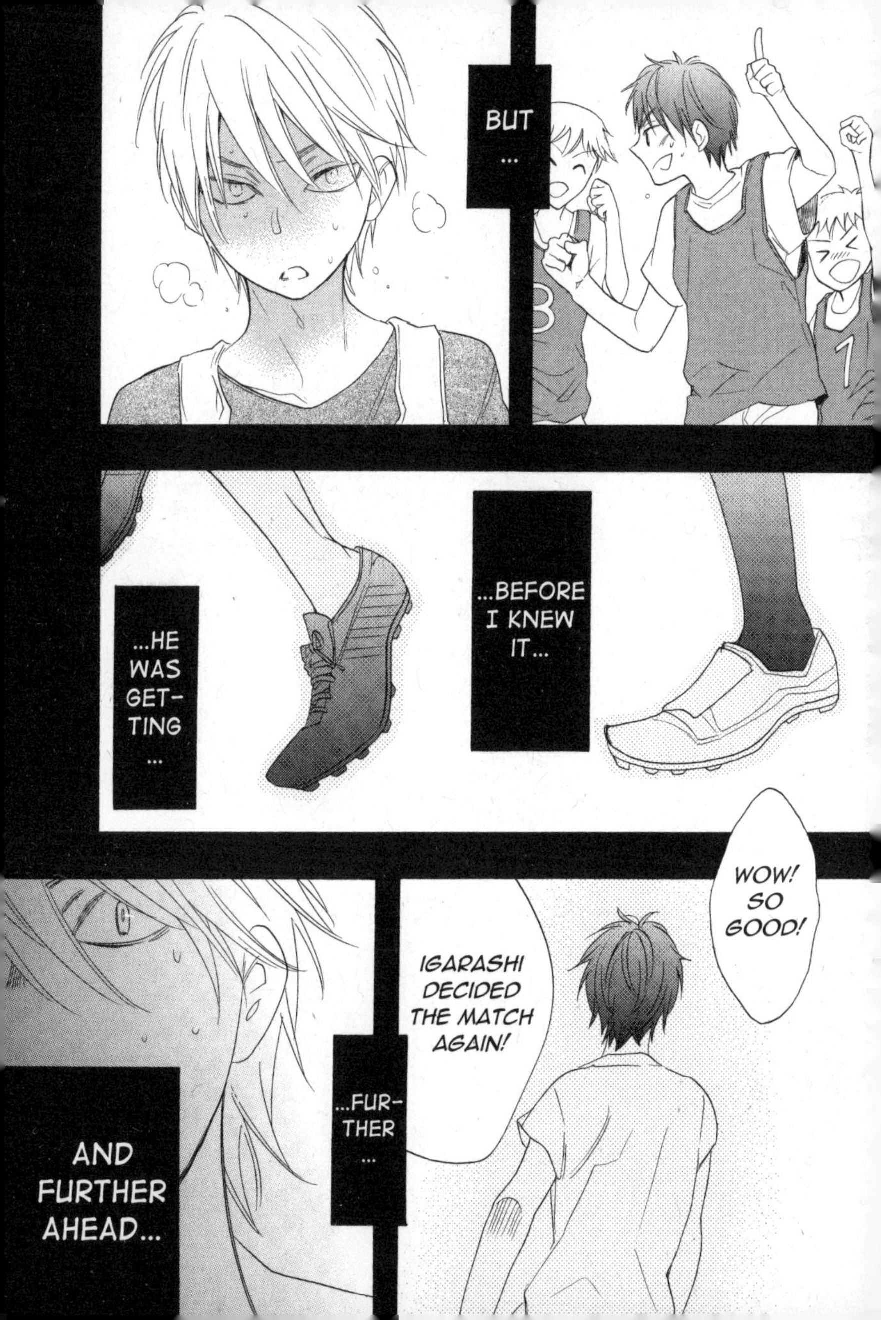
BUT ...
...BEFORE I KNEW IT...
...HE WAS GET-TING ...
WOW! SO GOOD!
IGARASHI DECIDED THE MATCH AGAIN!
...FUR-THER ...
AND FURTHER AHEAD...

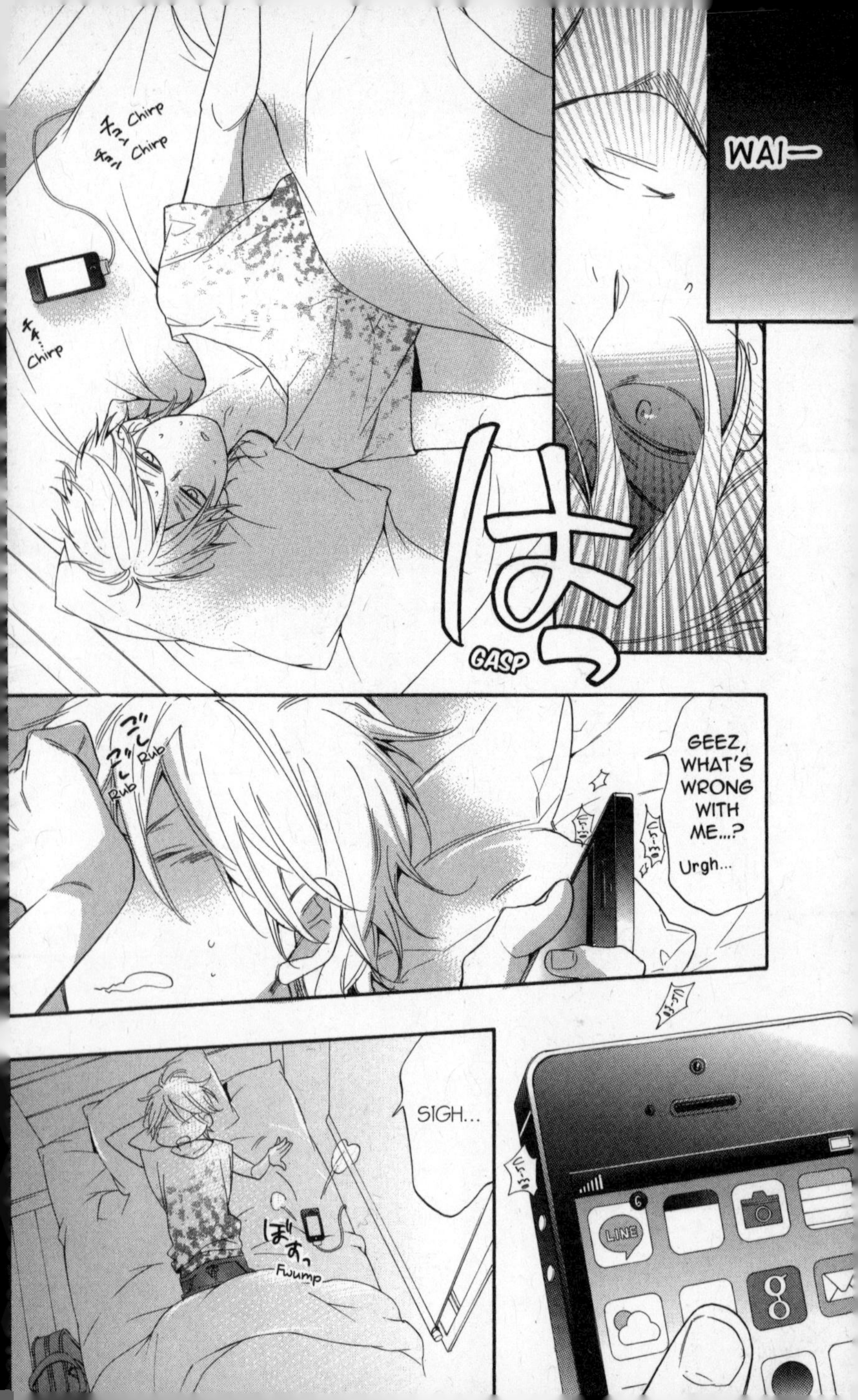

WAI—
はっ
GASP
チュン Chirp
チュン Chirp
チチ… Chirp
GEEZ, WHAT'S WRONG WITH ME...?
Urgh...
ごし Rub
ごし Rub
SIGH...
ぼすっ
Fwump
LINE

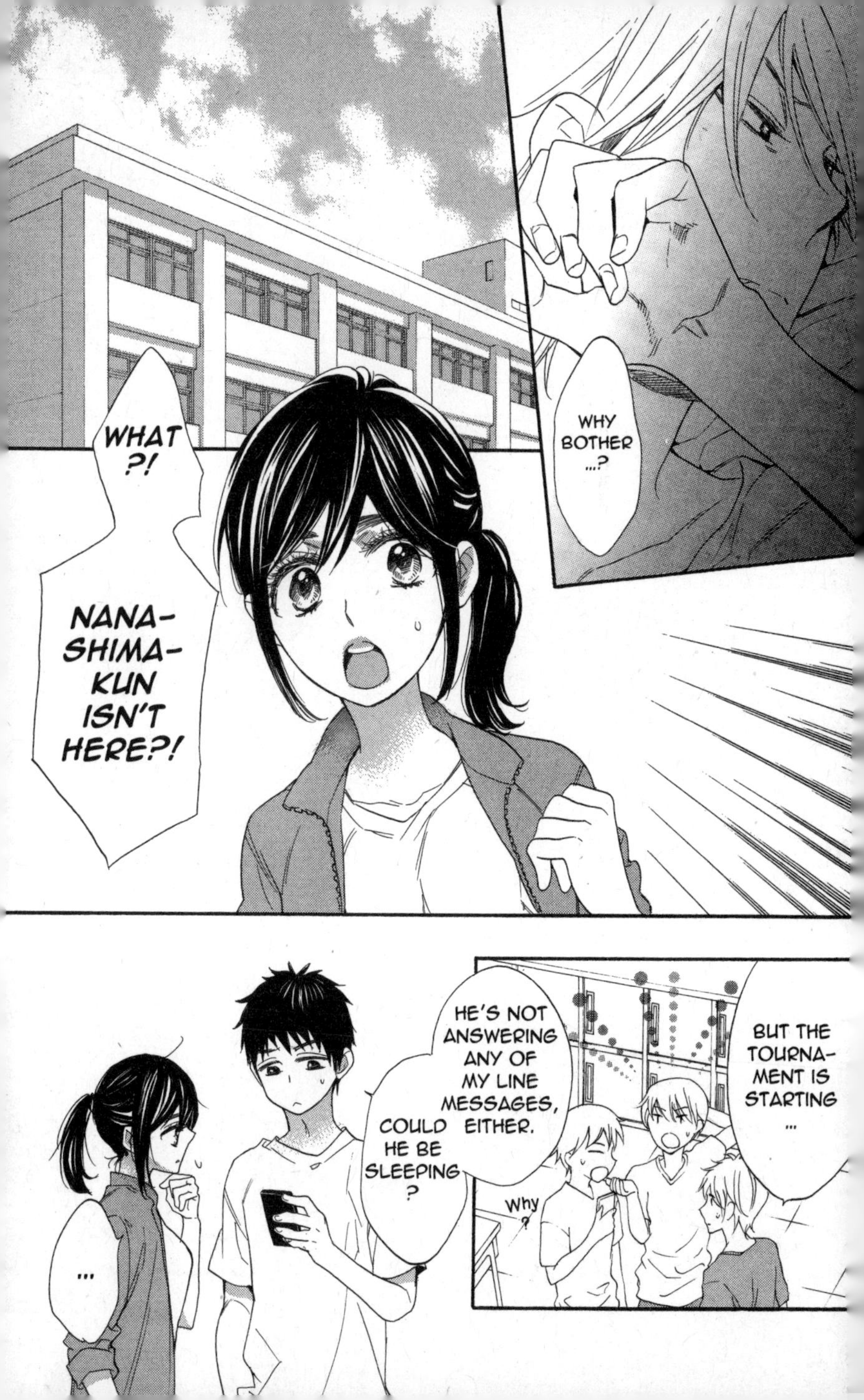
WHY BOTHER ...?
WHAT?!
NANA-SHIMA-KUN ISN'T HERE?!
BUT THE TOURNA-MENT IS STARTING ...
Why?
HE'S NOT ANSWERING ANY OF MY LINE MESSAGES, EITHER.
COULD HE BE SLEEPING?
...

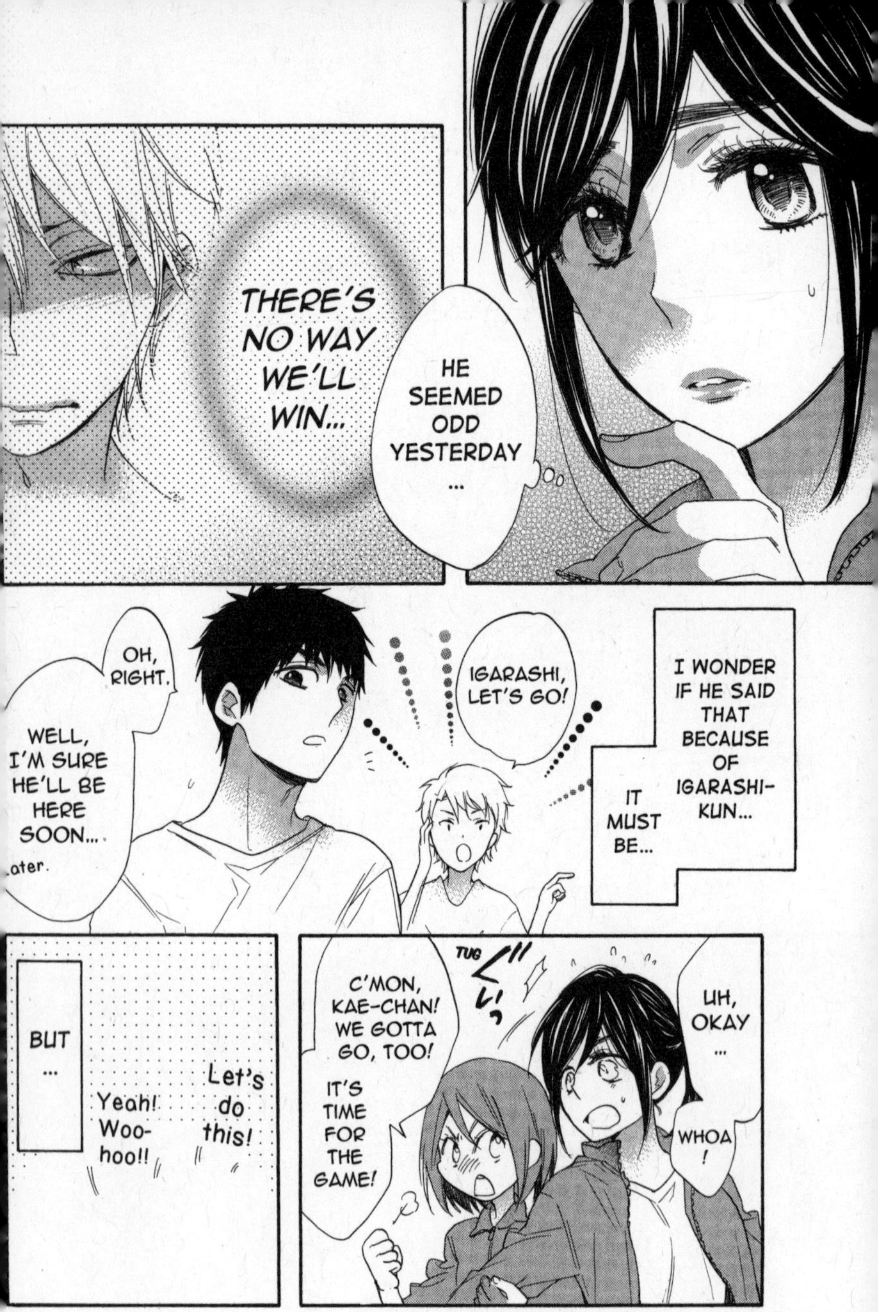
HE SEEMED ODD YESTERDAY ...
THERE'S NO WAY WE'LL WIN...
I WONDER IF HE SAID THAT BECAUSE OF IGARASHI-KUN...
IT MUST BE...
IGARASHI, LET'S GO!
OH, RIGHT.
WELL, I'M SURE HE'LL BE HERE SOON...
Later.
UH, OKAY ...
WHOA!
TUG
C'MON, KAE-CHAN! WE GOTTA GO, TOO!
IT'S TIME FOR THE GAME!
BUT ...
Let's do this!
Yeah! Woo-hoo!!

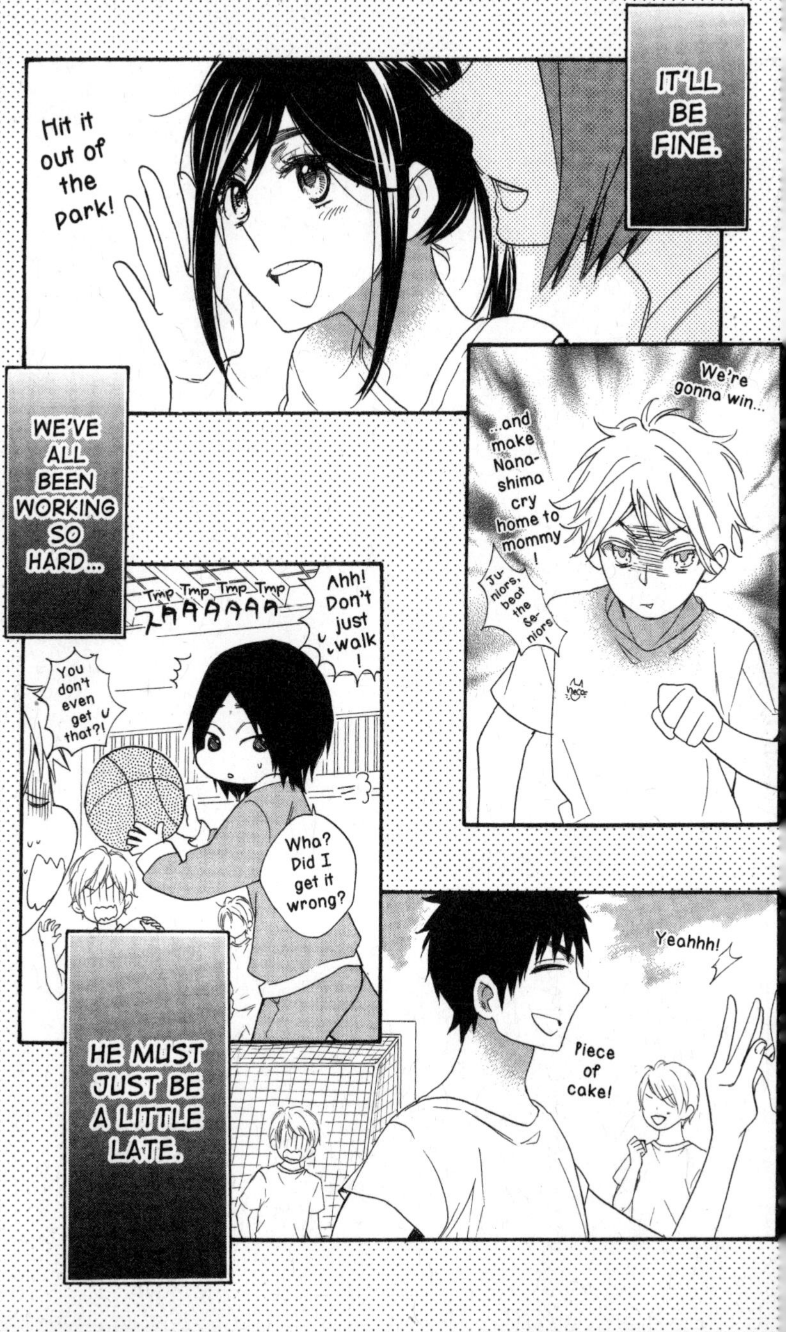
IT'LL BE FINE.
Hit it out of the park!
WE'VE ALL BEEN WORKING SO HARD...
We're gonna win...
...and make Nanashima cry home to mommy!
Juniors, beat the Seniors!
Tmp Tmp Tmp Tmp
Ahh! Don't just walk!
You don't even get that?!
Wha? Did I get it wrong?
Yeahhh!
Piece of cake!
HE MUST JUST BE A LITTLE LATE.

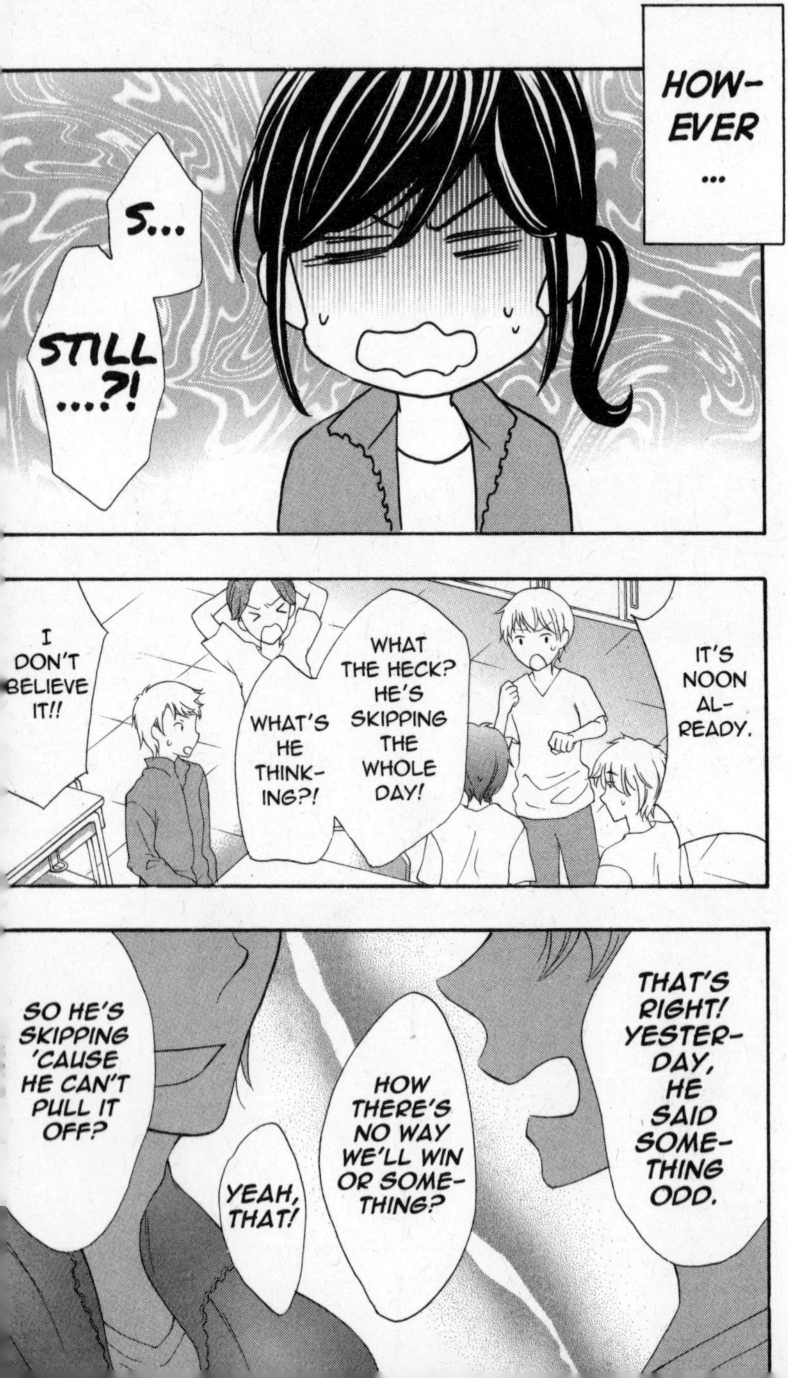
HOW-EVER...
S... STILL...?!
IT'S NOON ALREADY.
WHAT THE HECK? HE'S SKIPPING THE WHOLE DAY!
WHAT'S HE THINKING?!
I DON'T BELIEVE IT!!
THAT'S RIGHT! YESTERDAY, HE SAID SOMETHING ODD.
HOW THERE'S NO WAY WE'LL WIN OR SOMETHING?
YEAH, THAT!
SO HE'S SKIPPING 'CAUSE HE CAN'T PULL IT OFF?

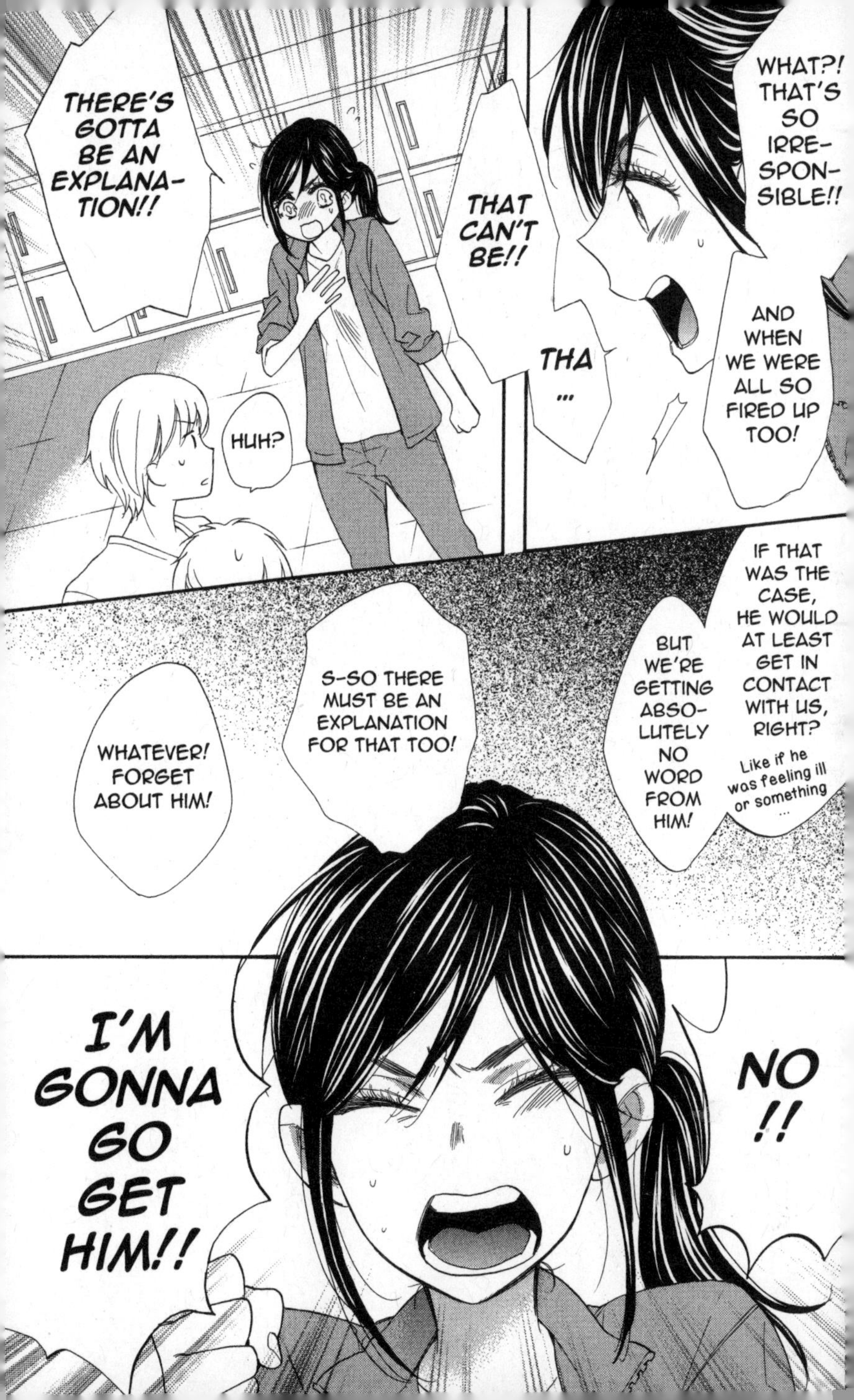
WHAT?! THAT'S SO IRRE-SPON-SIBLE!!
AND WHEN WE WERE ALL SO FIRED UP TOO!
THA ...
THAT CAN'T BE!!
THERE'S GOTTA BE AN EXPLANA-TION!!
HUH?
IF THAT WAS THE CASE, HE WOULD AT LEAST GET IN CONTACT WITH US, RIGHT?
Like if he was feeling ill or something ...
BUT WE'RE GETTING ABSO-LUTELY NO WORD FROM HIM!
S-SO THERE MUST BE AN EXPLANATION FOR THAT TOO!
WHATEVER! FORGET ABOUT HIM!
NO !!
I'M GONNA GO GET HIM!!

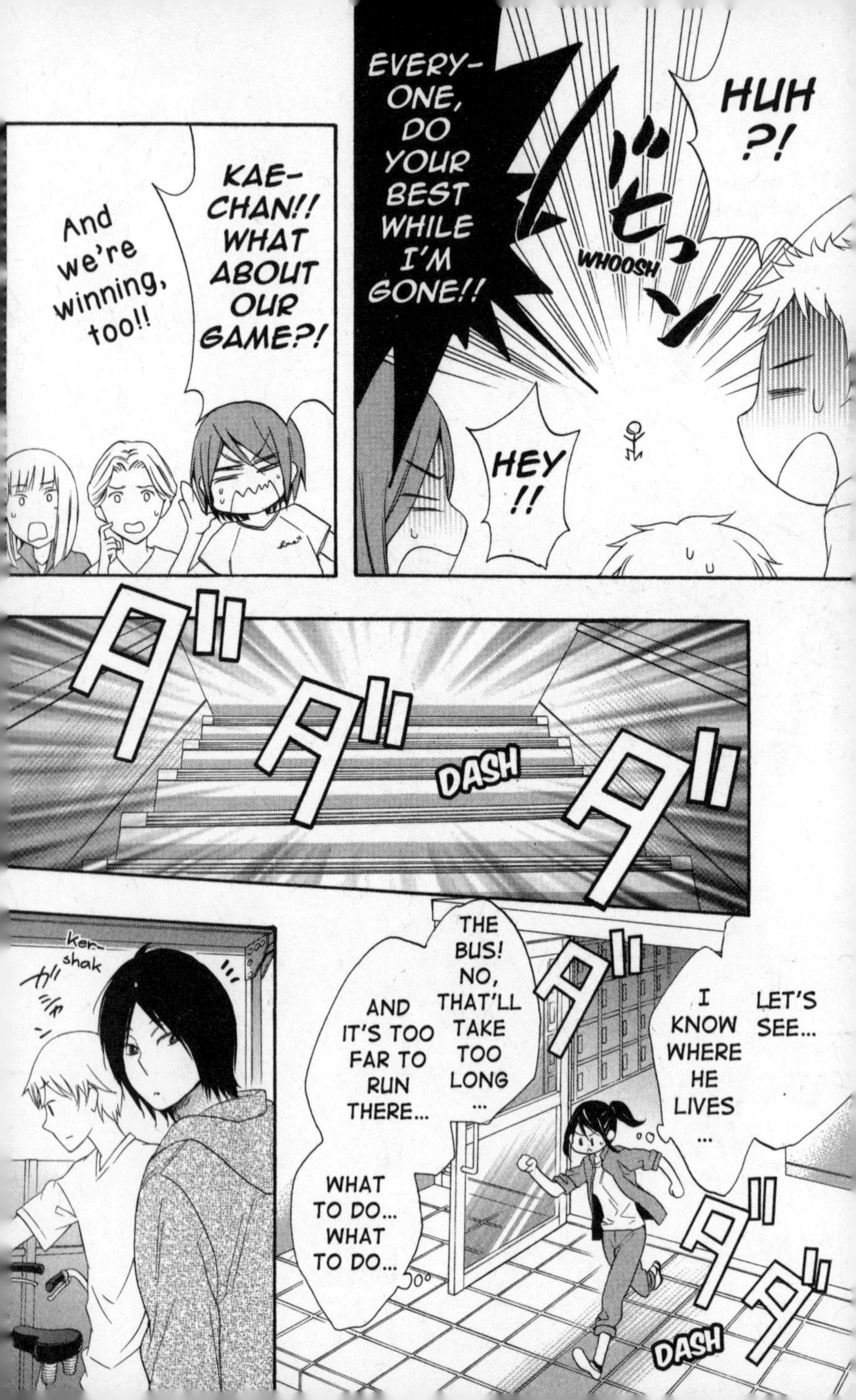
HUH ?!
EVERY-ONE, DO YOUR BEST WHILE I'M GONE!!
WHOOSH
HEY !!
KAE-CHAN!! WHAT ABOUT OUR GAME?!
And we're winning, too!!
DASH
LET'S SEE...
I KNOW WHERE HE LIVES ...
THE BUS! NO, THAT'LL TAKE TOO LONG ...
AND IT'S TOO FAR TO RUN THERE...
WHAT TO DO... WHAT TO DO...
DASH
ker-shak

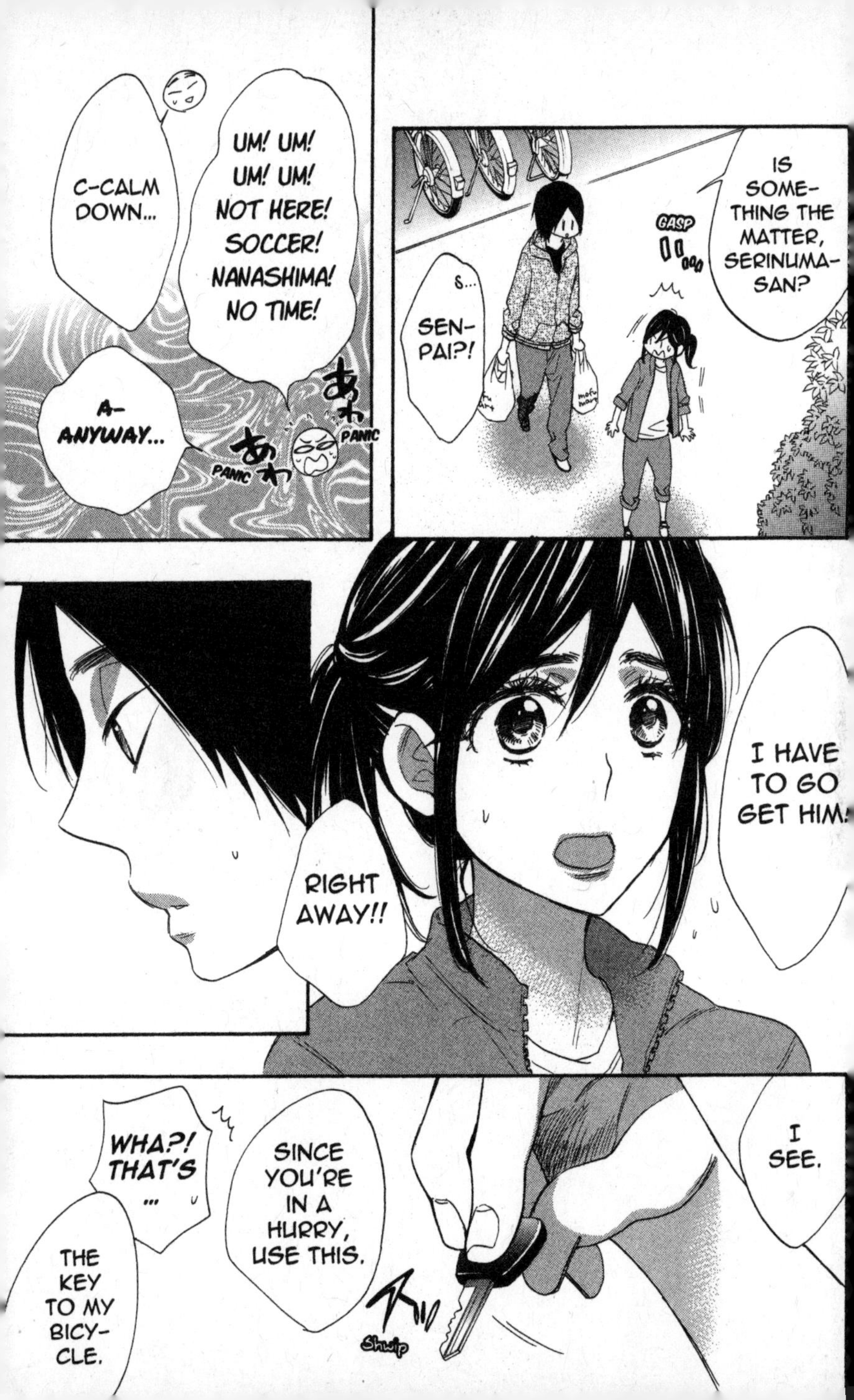

IS SOMETHING THE MATTER, SERINUMA-SAN?
GASP
S... SEN-PAI?!
UM! UM! UM! UM! NOT HERE! SOCCER! NANASHIMA! NO TIME!
C-CALM DOWN...
あわ PANIC
あわ PANIC
A- ANYWAY...
I HAVE TO GO GET HIM!
RIGHT AWAY!!
I SEE.
SINCE YOU'RE IN A HURRY, USE THIS.
Shwip
WHA?! THAT'S ...
THE KEY TO MY BICYCLE.

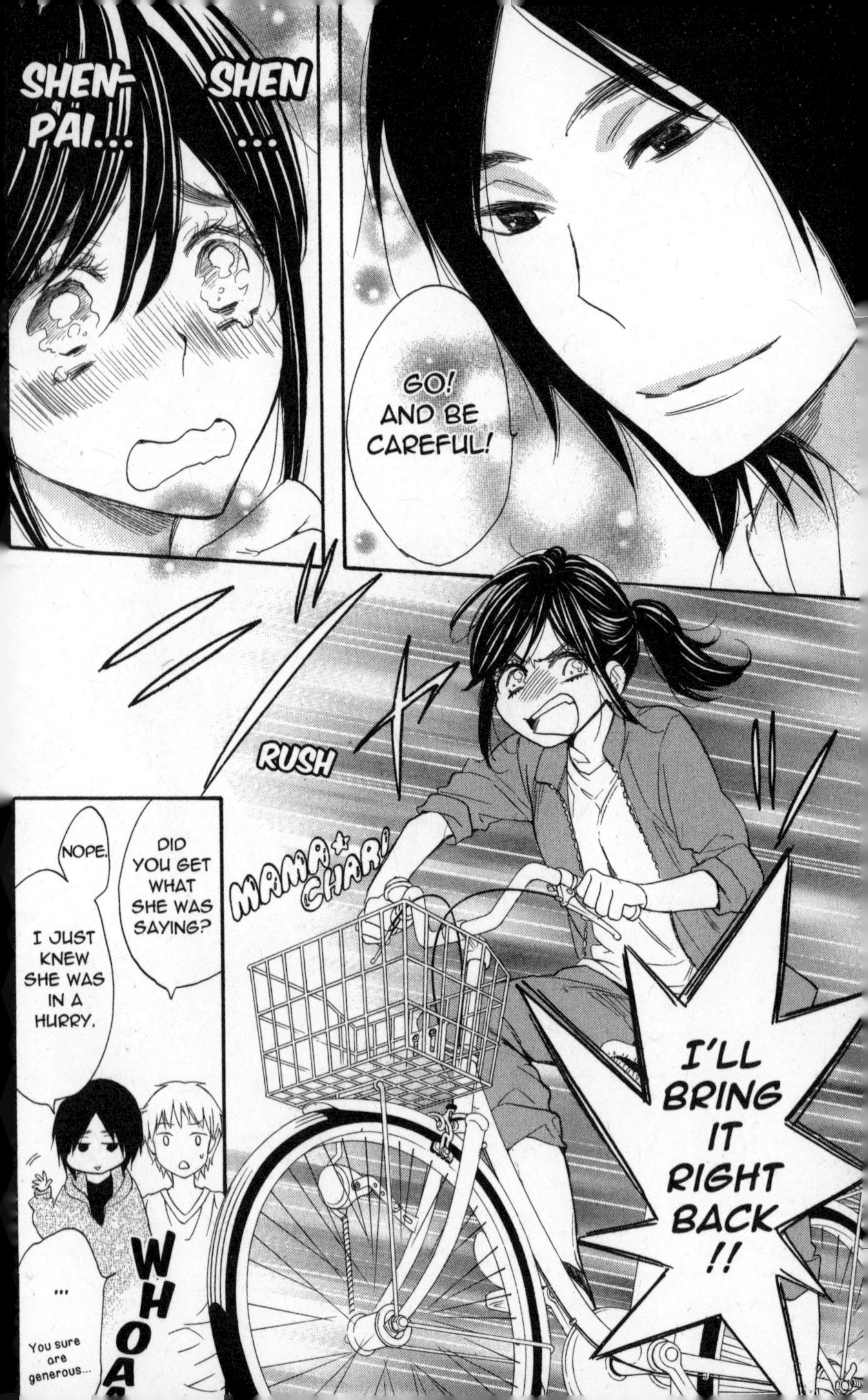
GO! AND BE CAREFUL!
SHEN ...
SHEN-PAI...
RUSH
MAMA★CHARI
I'LL BRING IT RIGHT BACK!!
DID YOU GET WHAT SHE WAS SAYING?
NOPE.
I JUST KNEW SHE WAS IN A HURRY.
WHOA
...
You sure are generous...

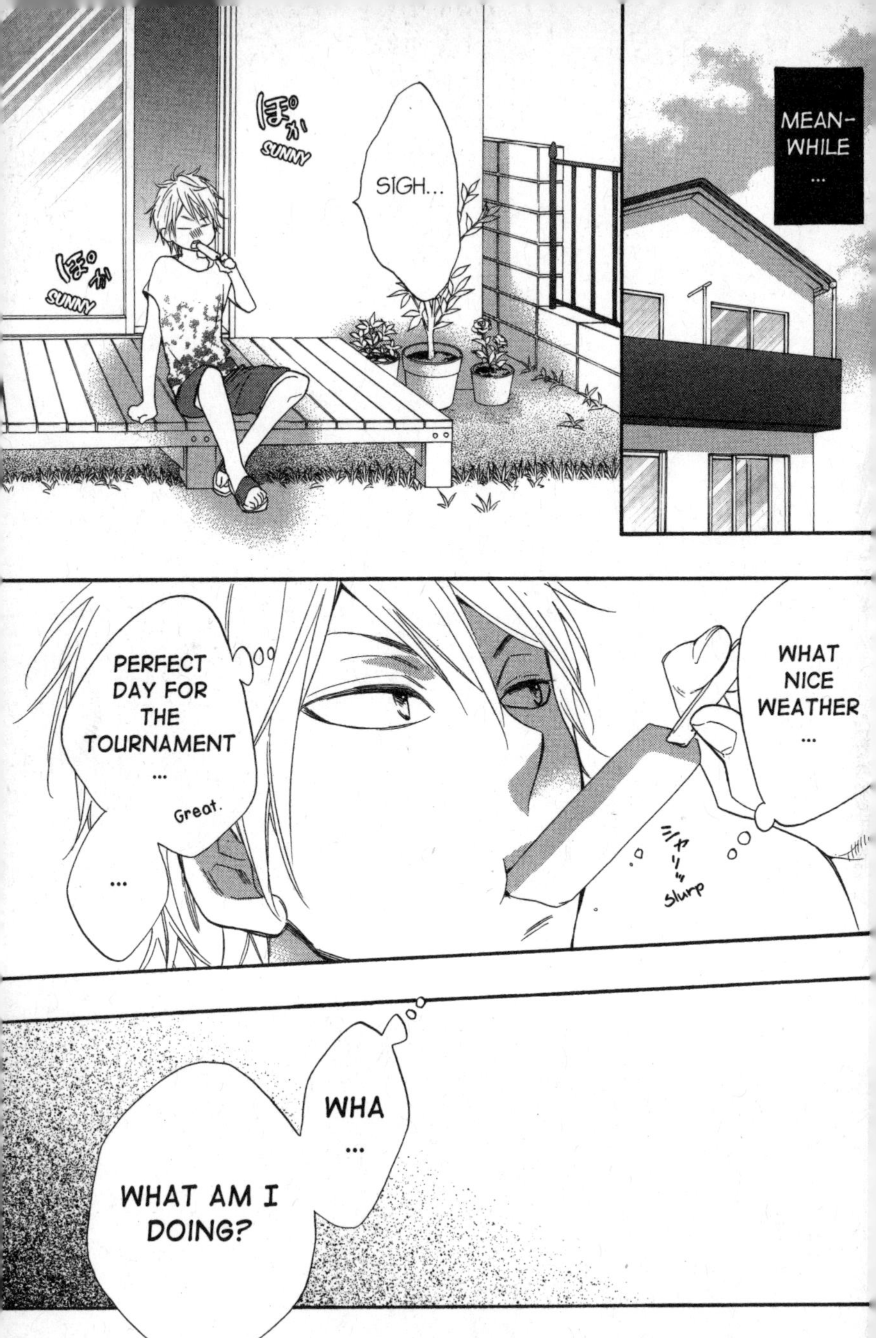
MEAN-WHILE ...
ぽか
SUNNY
ぽか
SUNNY
SIGH...
WHAT NICE WEATHER ...
Slurp
PERFECT DAY FOR THE TOURNAMENT ...
Great.
...
WHA ...
WHAT AM I DOING?

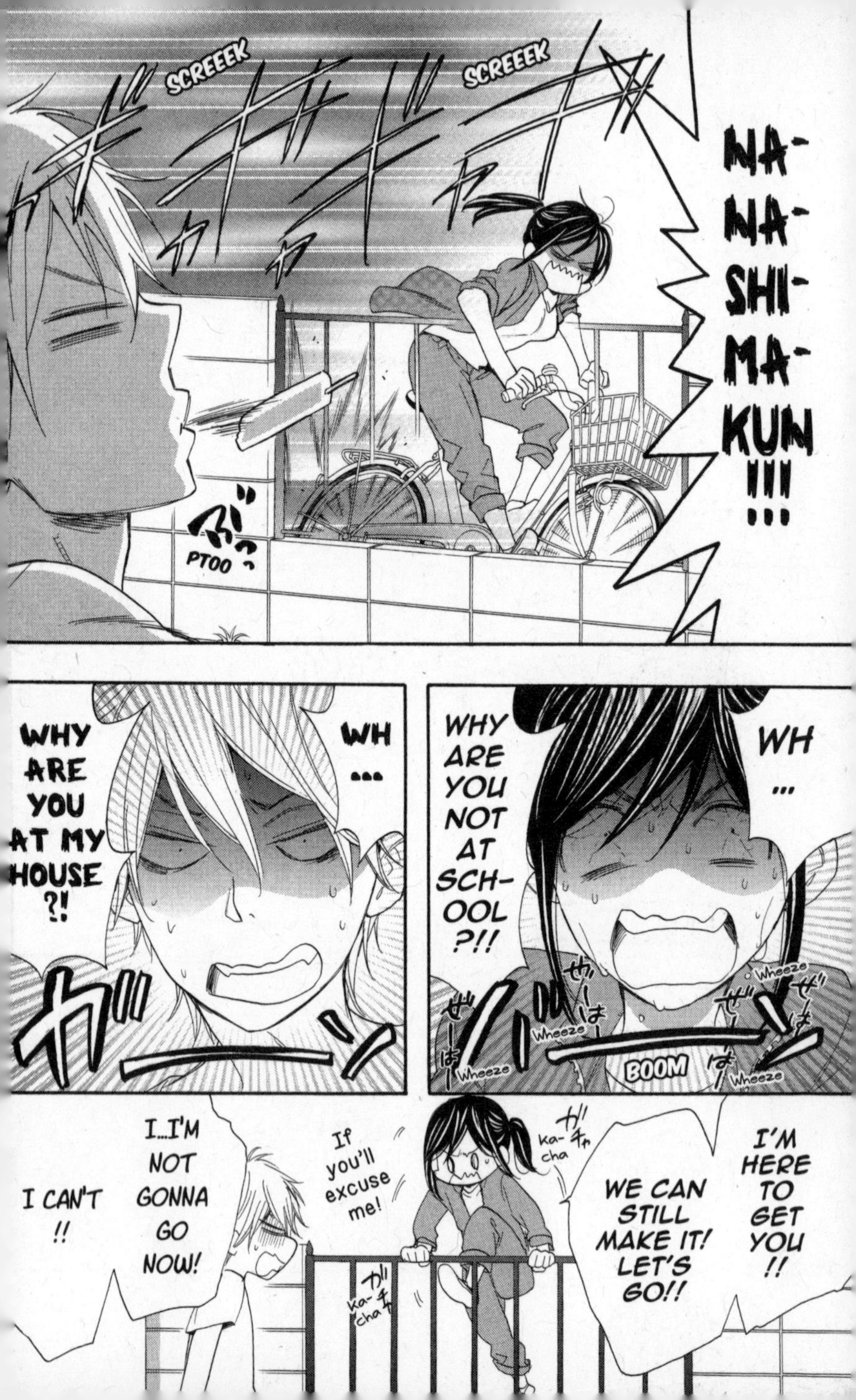

SCREEEK
NA-NA-SHI-MA-KUN!!!
SCREEEK
PTOO
WH...
WHY ARE YOU NOT AT SCH-OOL?!!
Wheeze
Wheeze
Wheeze
Wheeze
BOOM
WH...
WHY ARE YOU AT MY HOUSE?!
I'M HERE TO GET YOU!!
WE CAN STILL MAKE IT! LET'S GO!!
ka-cha
If you'll excuse me!
ka-cha
I...I'M NOT GONNA GO NOW!
I CAN'T!!

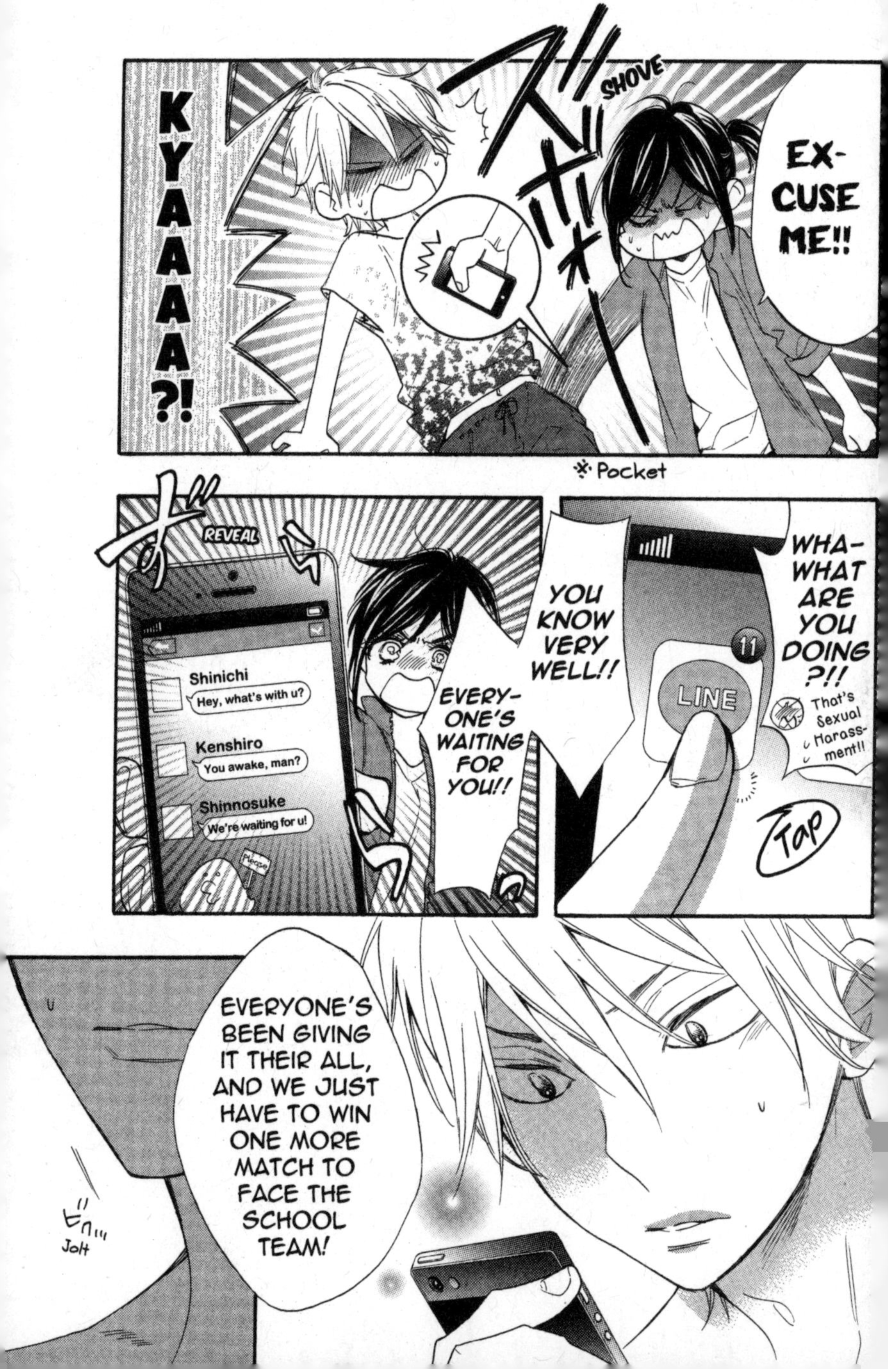

EX-CUSE ME!!
SHOVE
KYAAAAA?!
※Pocket
WHA-WHAT ARE YOU DOING?!!
That's Sexual Harassment!!
LINE
11
Tap
YOU KNOW VERY WELL!!
REVEAL
EVERY-ONE'S WAITING FOR YOU!!
Shinichi
Hey, what's with u?
Kenshiro
You awake, man?
Shinnosuke
We're waiting for u!
Please
EVERYONE'S BEEN GIVING IT THEIR ALL, AND WE JUST HAVE TO WIN ONE MORE MATCH TO FACE THE SCHOOL TEAM!
Jolt

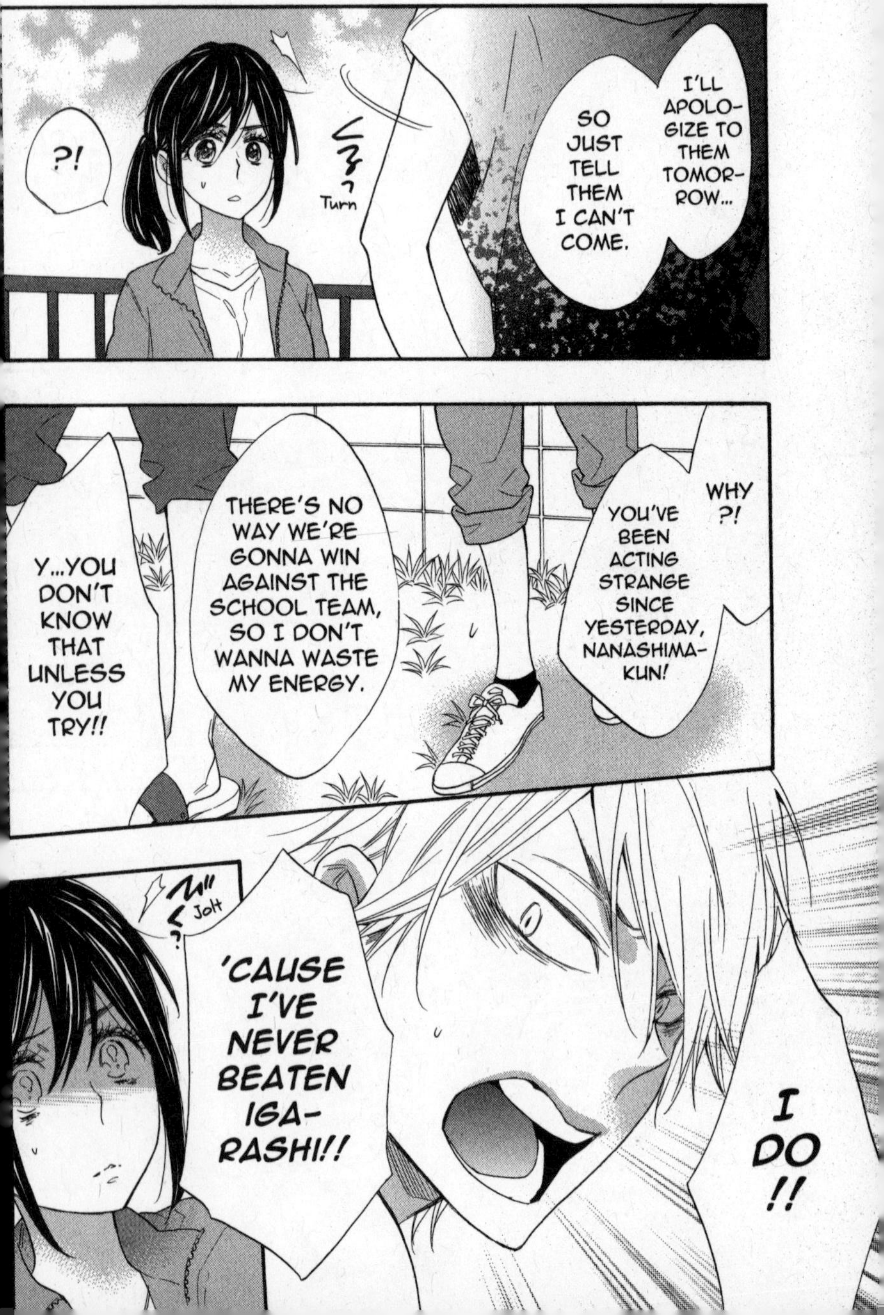
I'LL APOLOGIZE TO THEM TOMORROW...
SO JUST TELL THEM I CAN'T COME.
Turn
?!
WHY?!
YOU'VE BEEN ACTING STRANGE SINCE YESTERDAY, NANASHIMA-KUN!
THERE'S NO WAY WE'RE GONNA WIN AGAINST THE SCHOOL TEAM, SO I DON'T WANNA WASTE MY ENERGY.
Y...YOU DON'T KNOW THAT UNLESS YOU TRY!!
I DO!!
'CAUSE I'VE NEVER BEATEN IGARASHI!!
Jolt

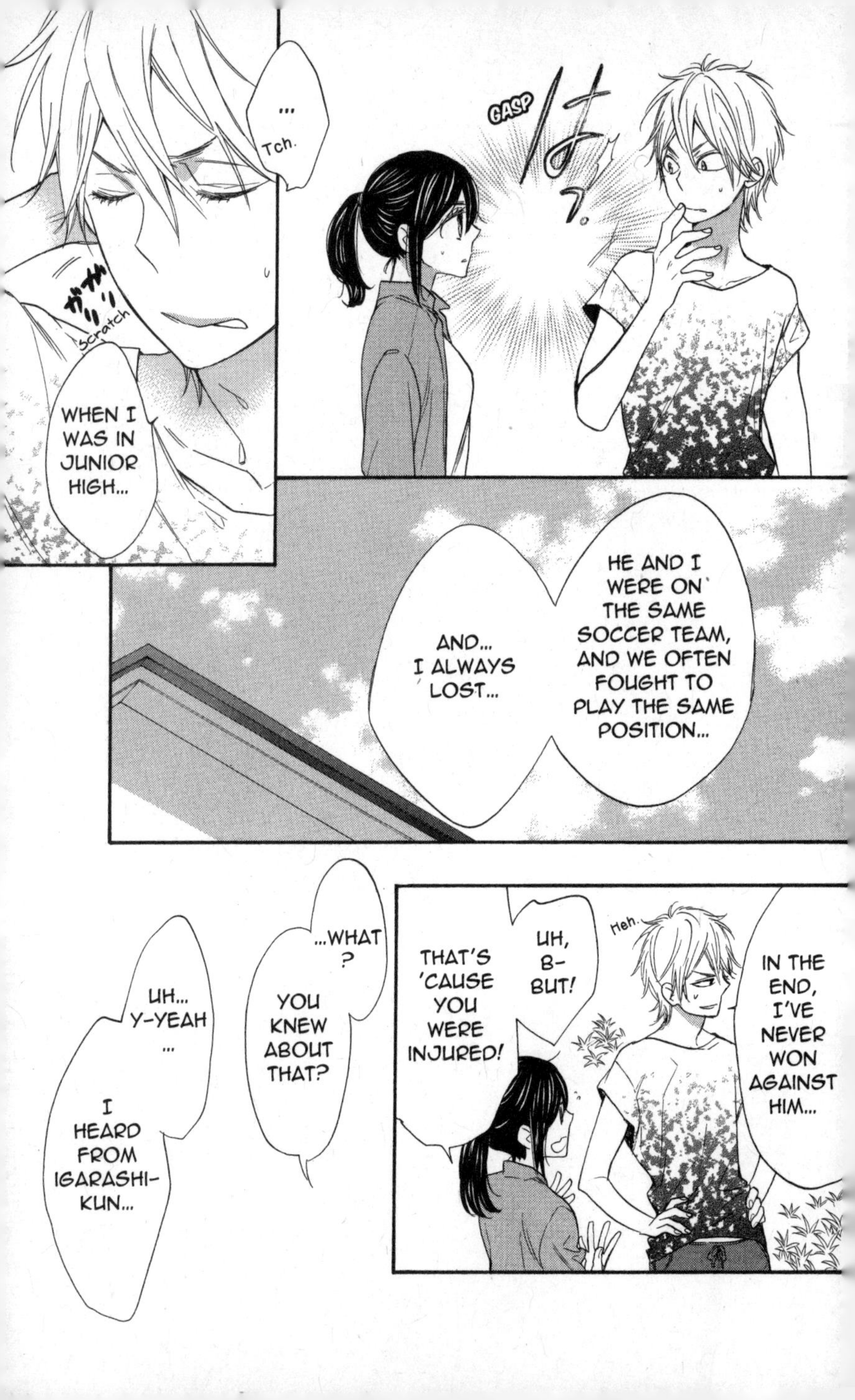
GASP
はっ
...
Tch.
ガリ
scratch
WHEN I WAS IN JUNIOR HIGH...
HE AND I WERE ON THE SAME SOCCER TEAM, AND WE OFTEN FOUGHT TO PLAY THE SAME POSITION...
AND... I ALWAYS LOST...
IN THE END, I'VE NEVER WON AGAINST HIM...
Heh.
UH, B-BUT!
THAT'S 'CAUSE YOU WERE INJURED!
...WHAT?
YOU KNEW ABOUT THAT?
UH... Y-YEAH...
I HEARD FROM IGARASHI-KUN...

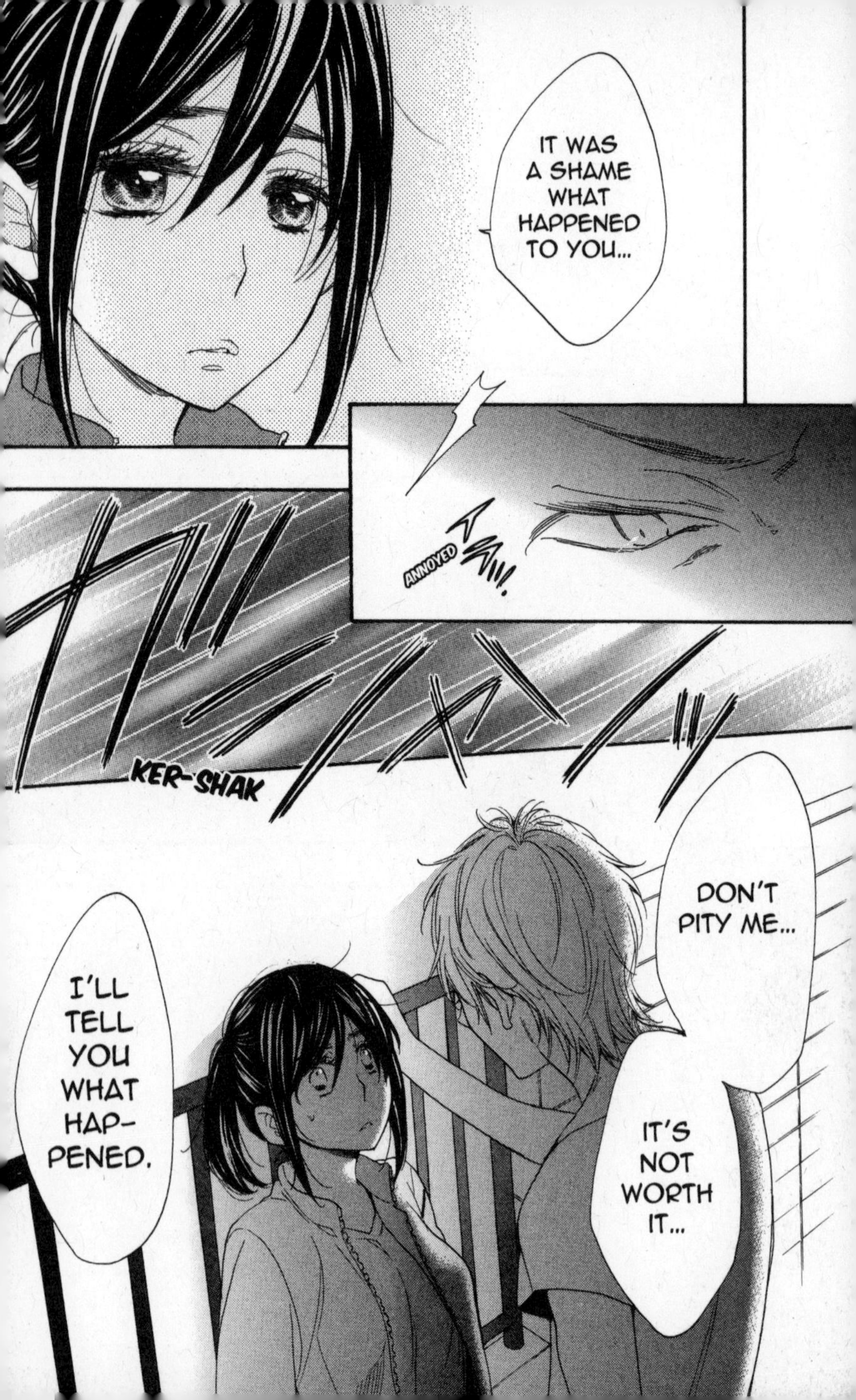
IT WAS A SHAME WHAT HAPPENED TO YOU...
ANNOYED
KER-SHAK
DON'T PITY ME...
IT'S NOT WORTH IT...
I'LL TELL YOU WHAT HAP-PENED.

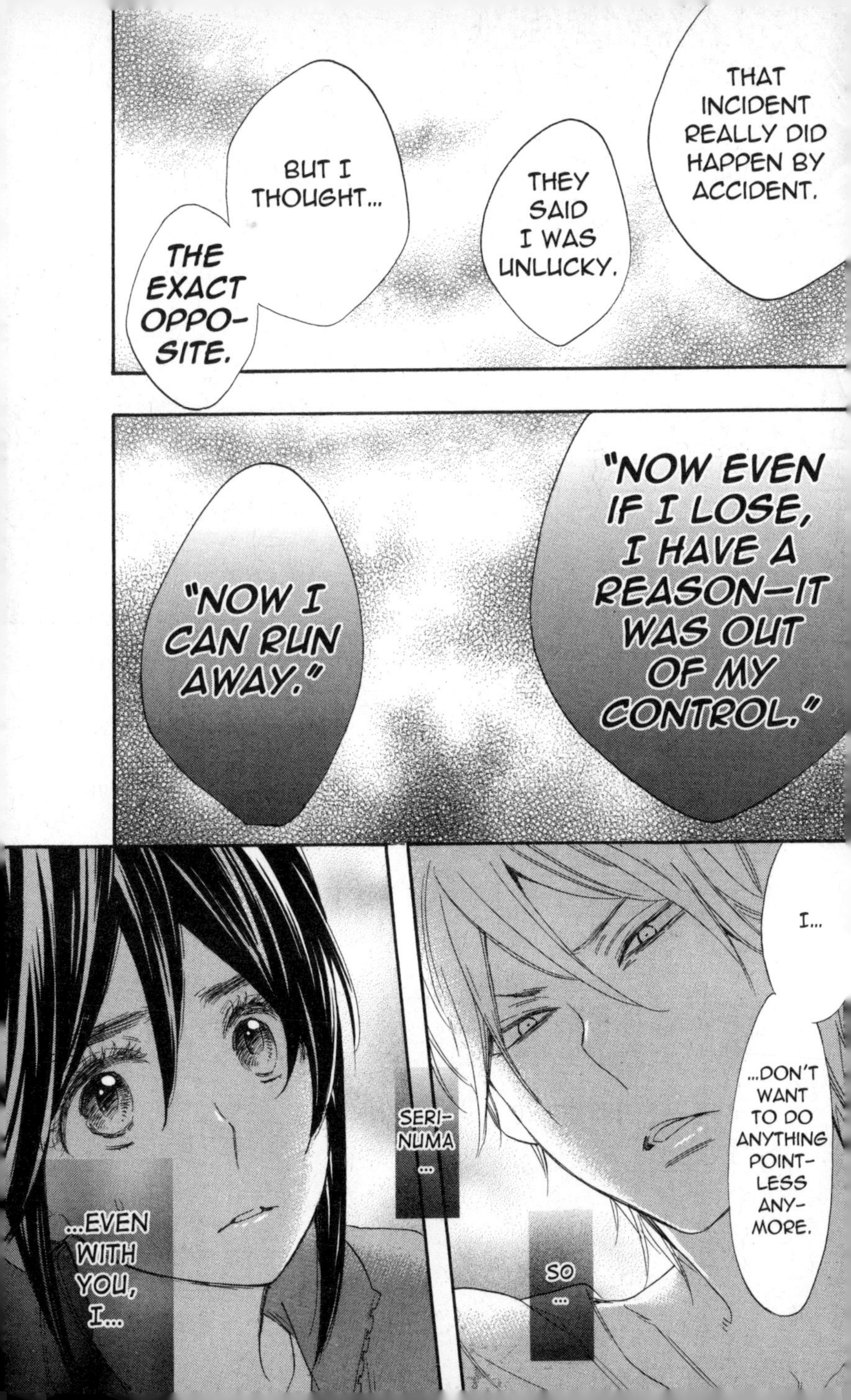
THAT INCIDENT REALLY DID HAPPEN BY ACCIDENT.
THEY SAID I WAS UNLUCKY.
BUT I THOUGHT...
THE EXACT OPPO-SITE.
"NOW EVEN IF I LOSE, I HAVE A REASON—IT WAS OUT OF MY CONTROL."
"NOW I CAN RUN AWAY."
I...
...DON'T WANT TO DO ANYTHING POINT-LESS ANY-MORE.
SO...
SERI-NUMA...
...EVEN WITH YOU, I...

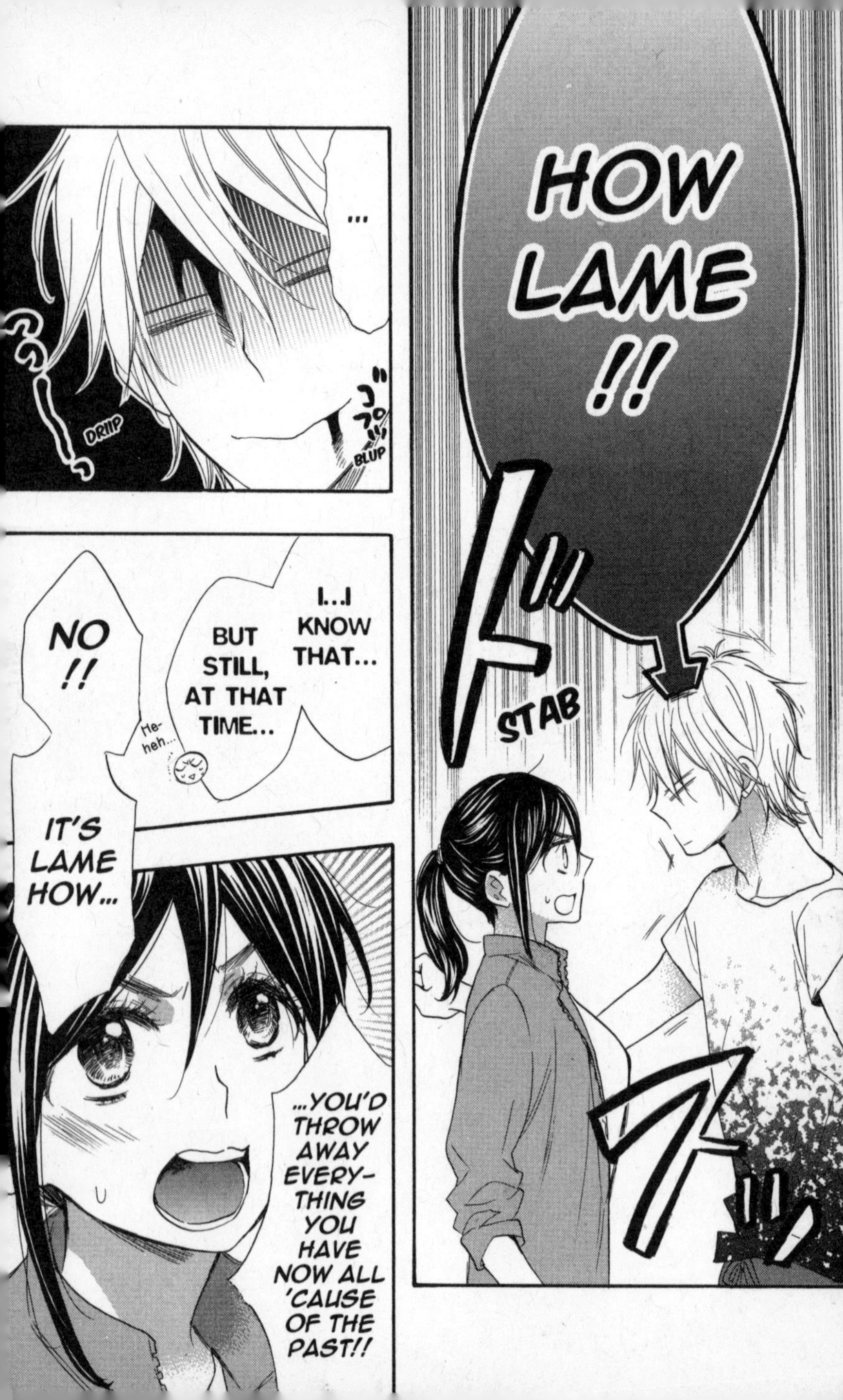
HOW LAME!!
STAB
...
DRIIP
BLUP
I...I KNOW THAT...
BUT STILL, AT THAT TIME...
He-heh...
NO!!
IT'S LAME HOW...
...YOU'D THROW AWAY EVERYTHING YOU HAVE NOW ALL 'CAUSE OF THE PAST!!

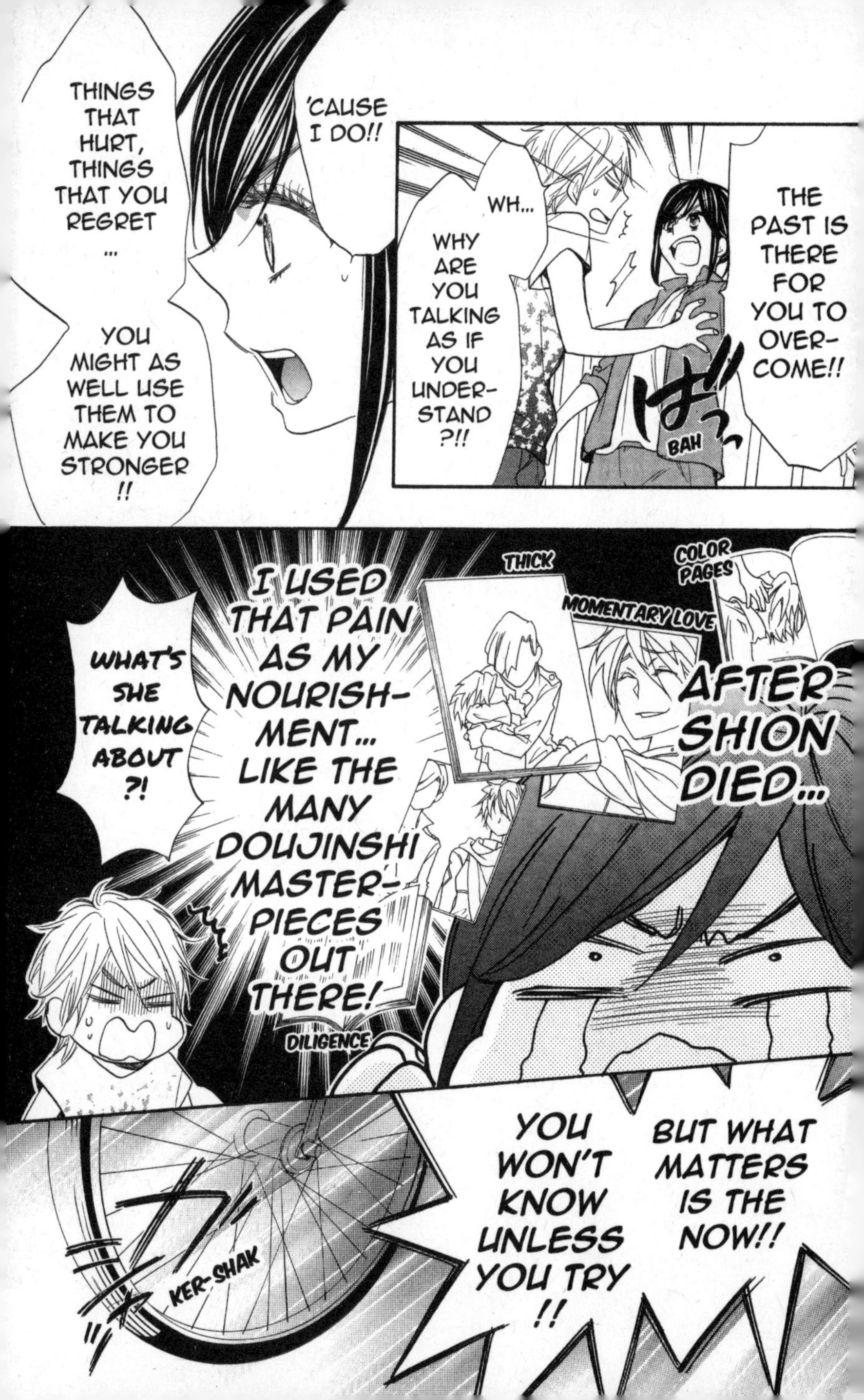
THE PAST IS THERE FOR YOU TO OVERCOME!!
BAH
WH... WHY ARE YOU TALKING AS IF YOU UNDERSTAND ?!!
'CAUSE I DO!!
THINGS THAT HURT, THINGS THAT YOU REGRET ...
YOU MIGHT AS WELL USE THEM TO MAKE YOU STRONGER !!
COLOR PAGES
THICK
MOMENTARY LOVE
AFTER SHION DIED...
I USED THAT PAIN AS MY NOURISH-MENT... LIKE THE MANY DOUJINSHI MASTER-PIECES OUT THERE!
DILIGENCE
WHAT'S SHE TALKING ABOUT ?!
BUT WHAT MATTERS IS THE NOW!!
YOU WON'T KNOW UNLESS YOU TRY !!
KER-SHAK

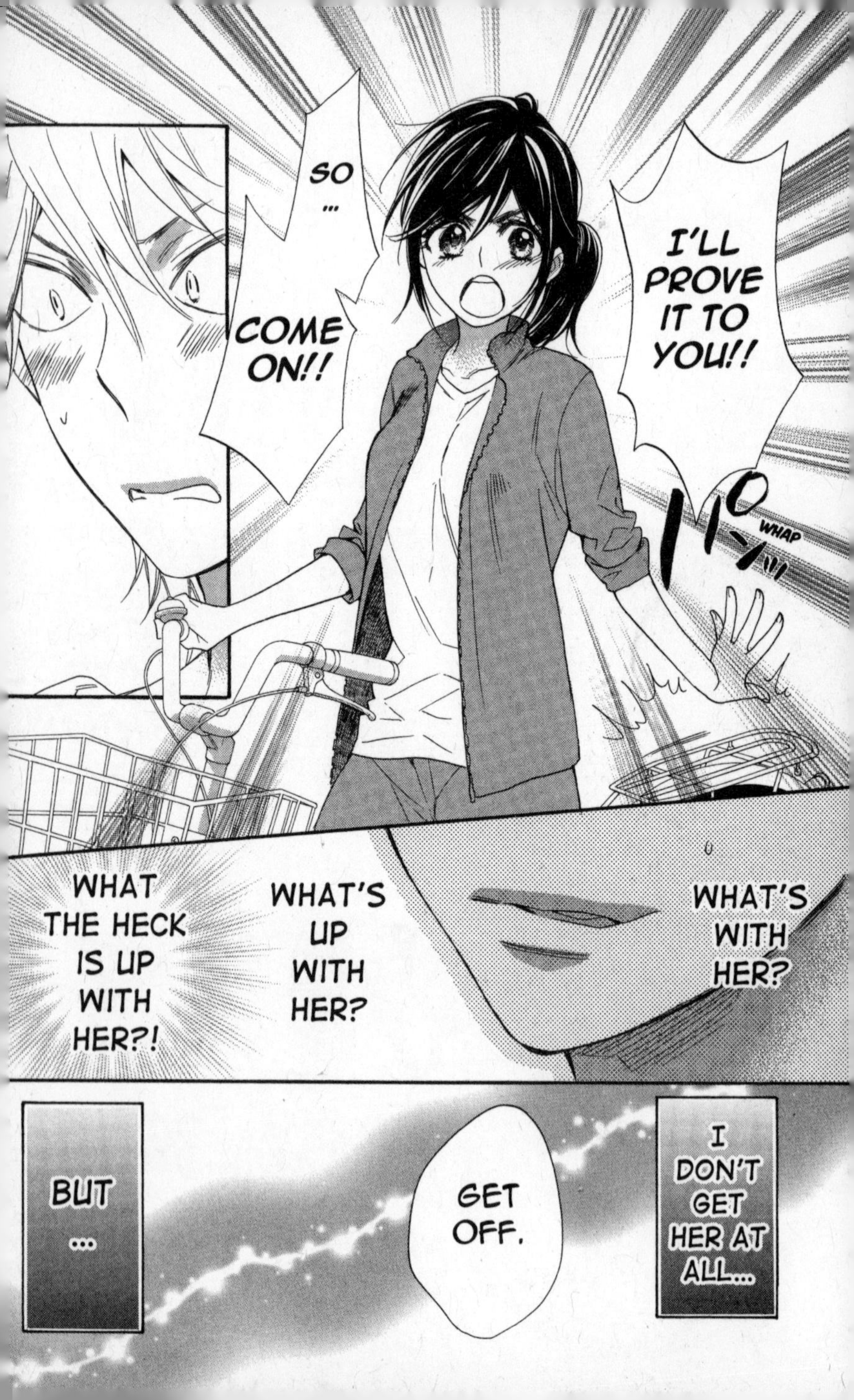
I'LL PROVE IT TO YOU!!
WHAP
SO ...
COME ON!!
WHAT'S WITH HER?
WHAT'S UP WITH HER?
WHAT THE HECK IS UP WITH HER?!
I DON'T GET HER AT ALL...
GET OFF.
BUT ...

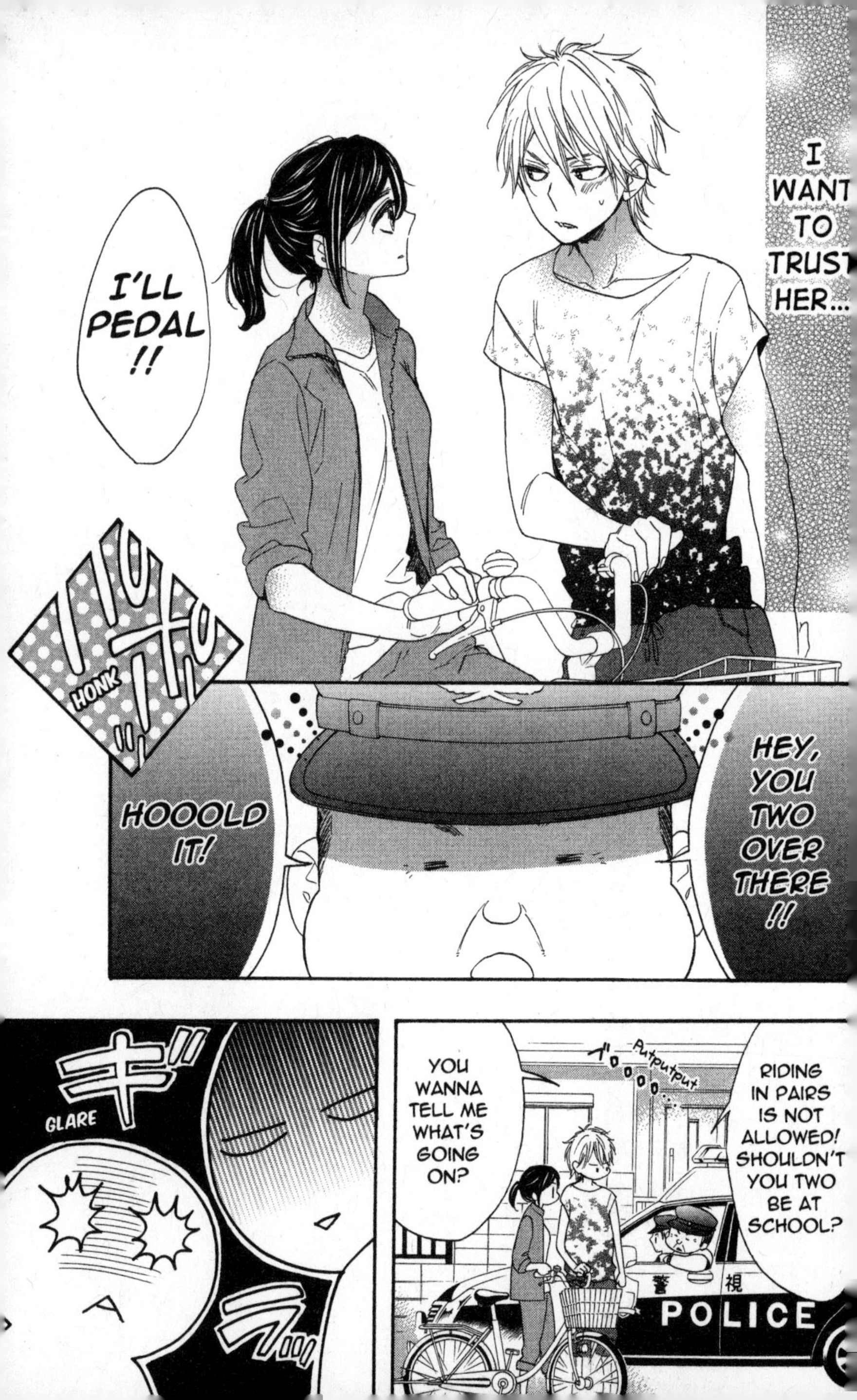
I WANT TO TRUST HER...
I'LL PEDAL!!
HONK
HEY, YOU TWO OVER THERE!!
HOOOLD IT!
RIDING IN PAIRS IS NOT ALLOWED! SHOULDN'T YOU TWO BE AT SCHOOL?
Putputput
YOU WANNA TELL ME WHAT'S GOING ON?
警 視
POLICE
GLARE

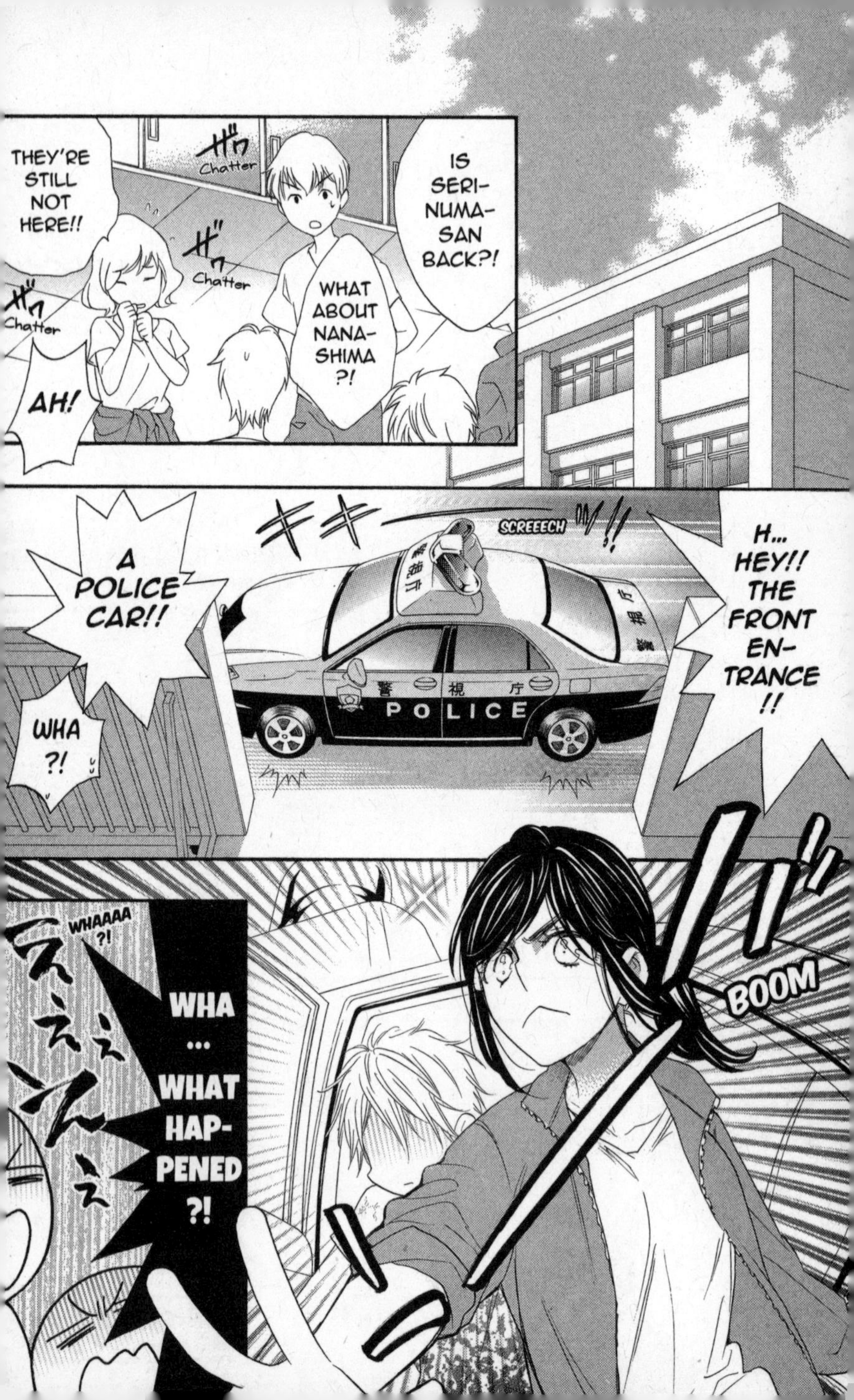
IS SERI-NUMA-SAN BACK?!
WHAT ABOUT NANA-SHIMA?!
Chatter
Chatter
THEY'RE STILL NOT HERE!!
Chatter
AH!
H... HEY!! THE FRONT EN-TRANCE!!
SCREEECH
警視庁
POLICE
A POLICE CAR!!
WHA?!
BOOM
WHA... WHAT HAP-PENED?!
WHAAAA?!

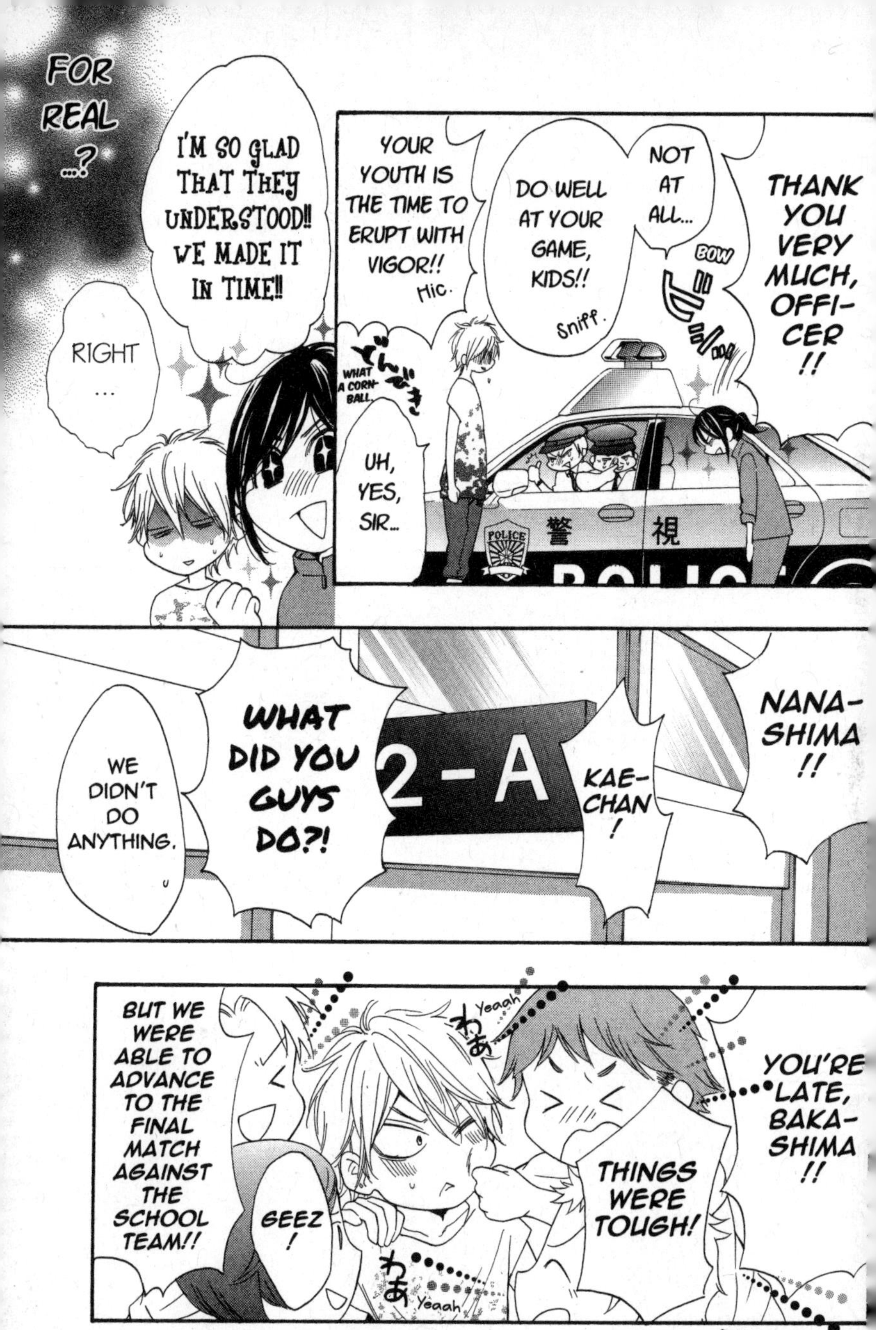
THANK YOU VERY MUCH, OFFICER!!
BOW
NOT AT ALL...
DO WELL AT YOUR GAME, KIDS!!
Sniff.
YOUR YOUTH IS THE TIME TO ERUPT WITH VIGOR!!
Hic.
WHAT A CORNBALL
UH, YES, SIR...
POLICE
I'M SO GLAD THAT THEY UNDERSTOOD!! WE MADE IT IN TIME!!
FOR REAL ...?
RIGHT ...
NANA-SHIMA!!
KAE-CHAN!
2-A
WHAT DID YOU GUYS DO?!
WE DIDN'T DO ANYTHING.
YOU'RE LATE, BAKA-SHIMA!!
THINGS WERE TOUGH!
Yeaah
BUT WE WERE ABLE TO ADVANCE TO THE FINAL MATCH AGAINST THE SCHOOL TEAM!!
GEEZ!
Yeaah

*BAKA = IDIOT

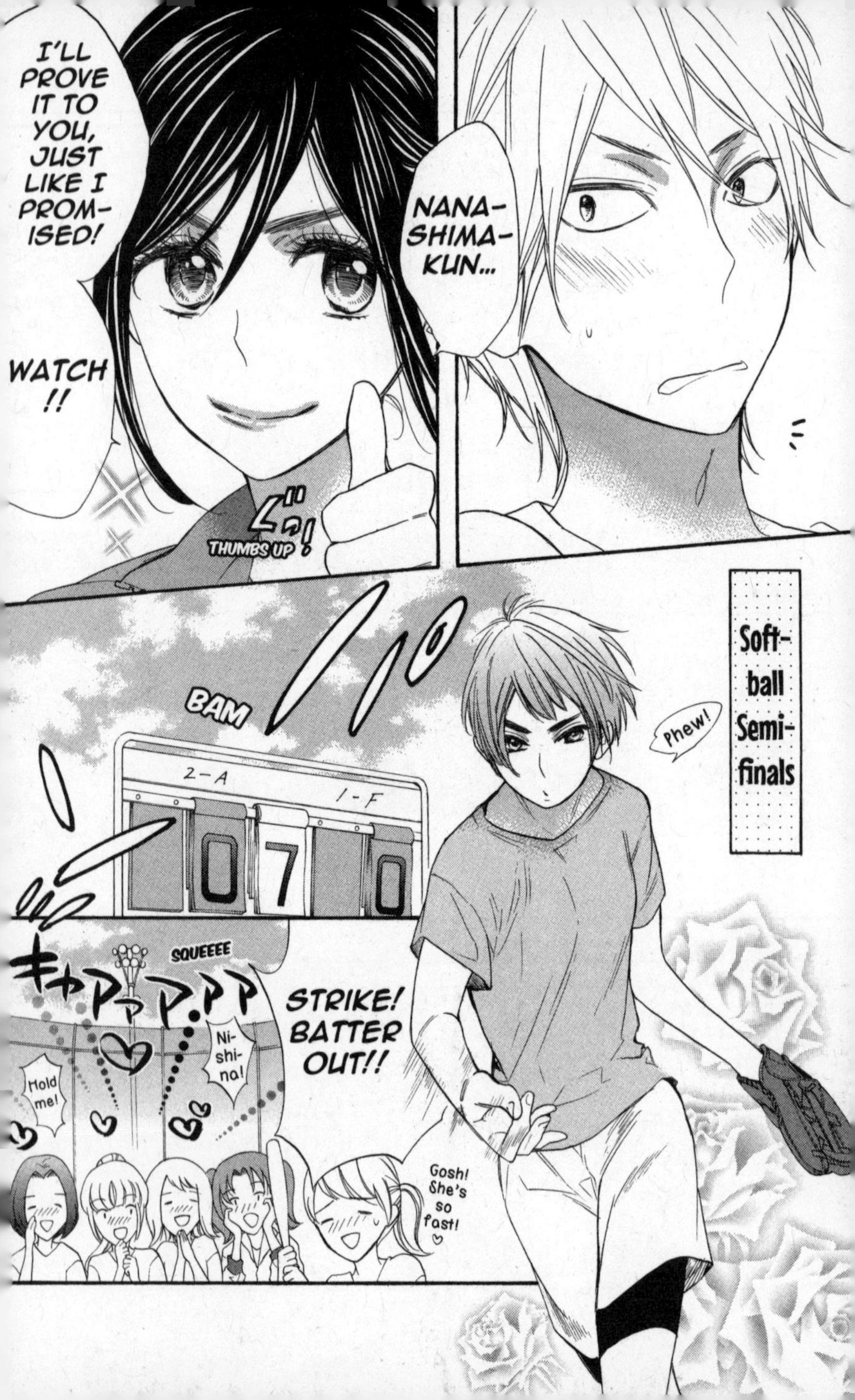
NANA-SHIMA-KUN...
I'LL PROVE IT TO YOU, JUST LIKE I PROMISED!
WATCH!!
THUMBS UP
Soft-ball Semi-finals
Phew!
BAM
2-A
1-F
0
7
0
SQUEEEE
STRIKE! BATTER OUT!!
Ni-shi-na!
Hold me!
Gosh! She's so fast!

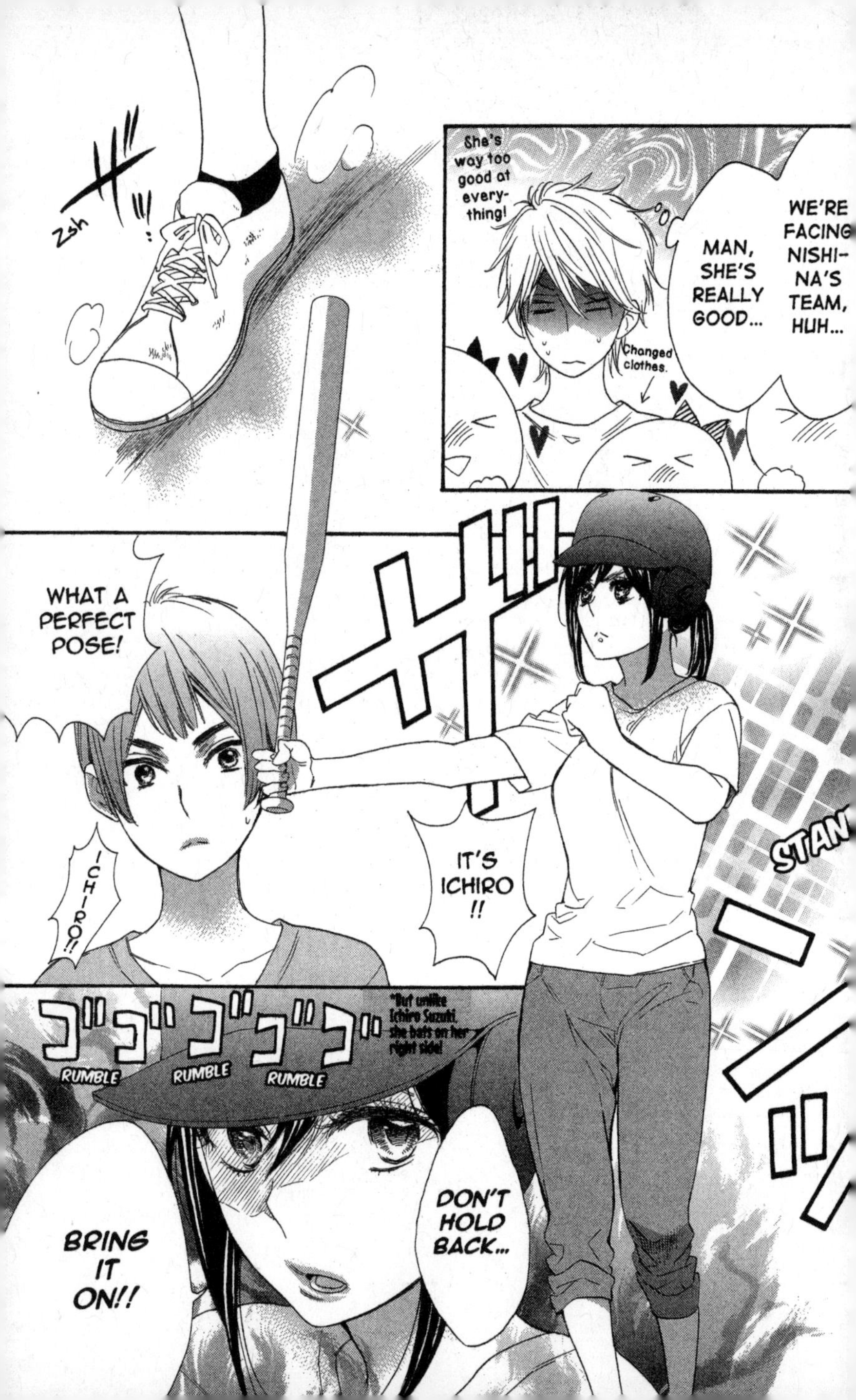

WE'RE FACING NISHINA'S TEAM, HUH...
MAN, SHE'S REALLY GOOD...
She's way too good at everything!
Changed clothes.
Zsh
STAN
IT'S ICHIRO !!
ICHIRO!!
WHAT A PERFECT POSE!
RUMBLE RUMBLE RUMBLE
*But unlike Ichiro Suzuki, she bats on her right side!
DON'T HOLD BACK...
BRING IT ON!!

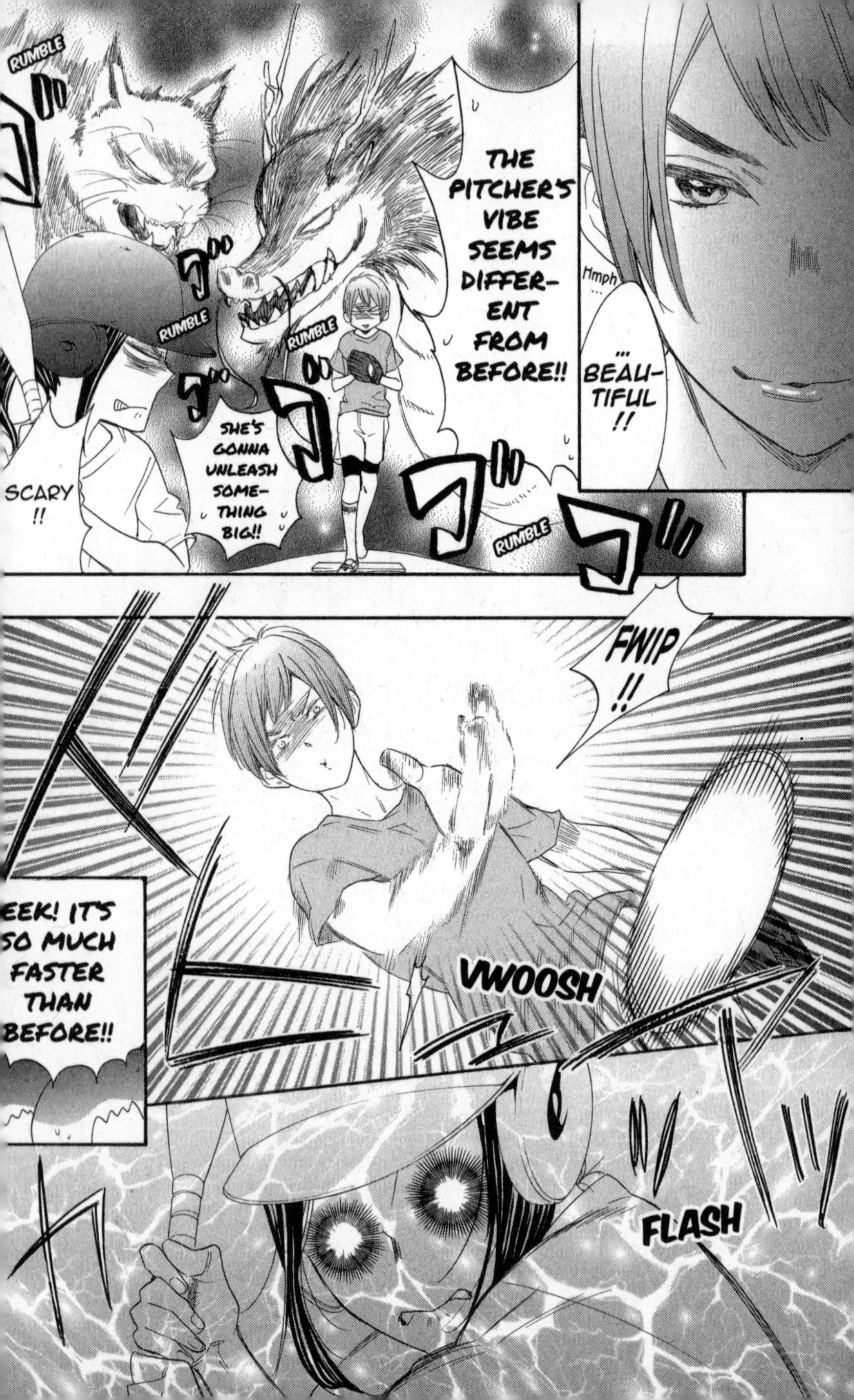
Hmph ...
... BEAUTIFUL !!
THE PITCHER'S VIBE SEEMS DIFFERENT FROM BEFORE!!
RUMBLE
RUMBLE
RUMBLE
RUMBLE
SHE'S GONNA UNLEASH SOMETHING BIG!!
SCARY !!
FWIP !!
VWOOSH
EEK! IT'S SO MUCH FASTER THAN BEFORE!!
FLASH

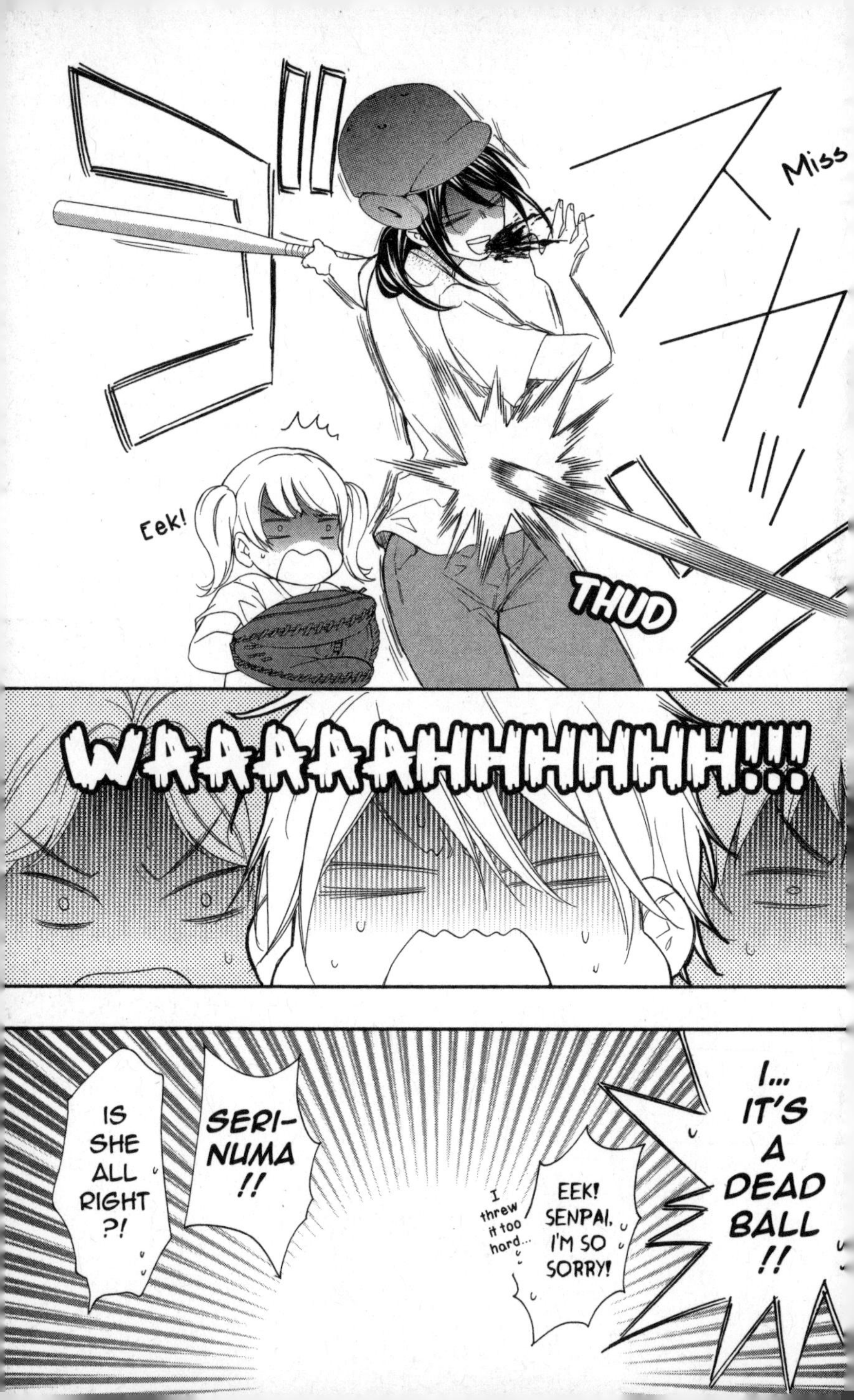
Miss
THUD
Eek!
WAAAAAAHHHHHHH!!!
I... IT'S A DEAD BALL!!
EEK! SENPAI, I'M SO SORRY!
I threw it too hard...
SERI-NUMA!!
IS SHE ALL RIGHT?!

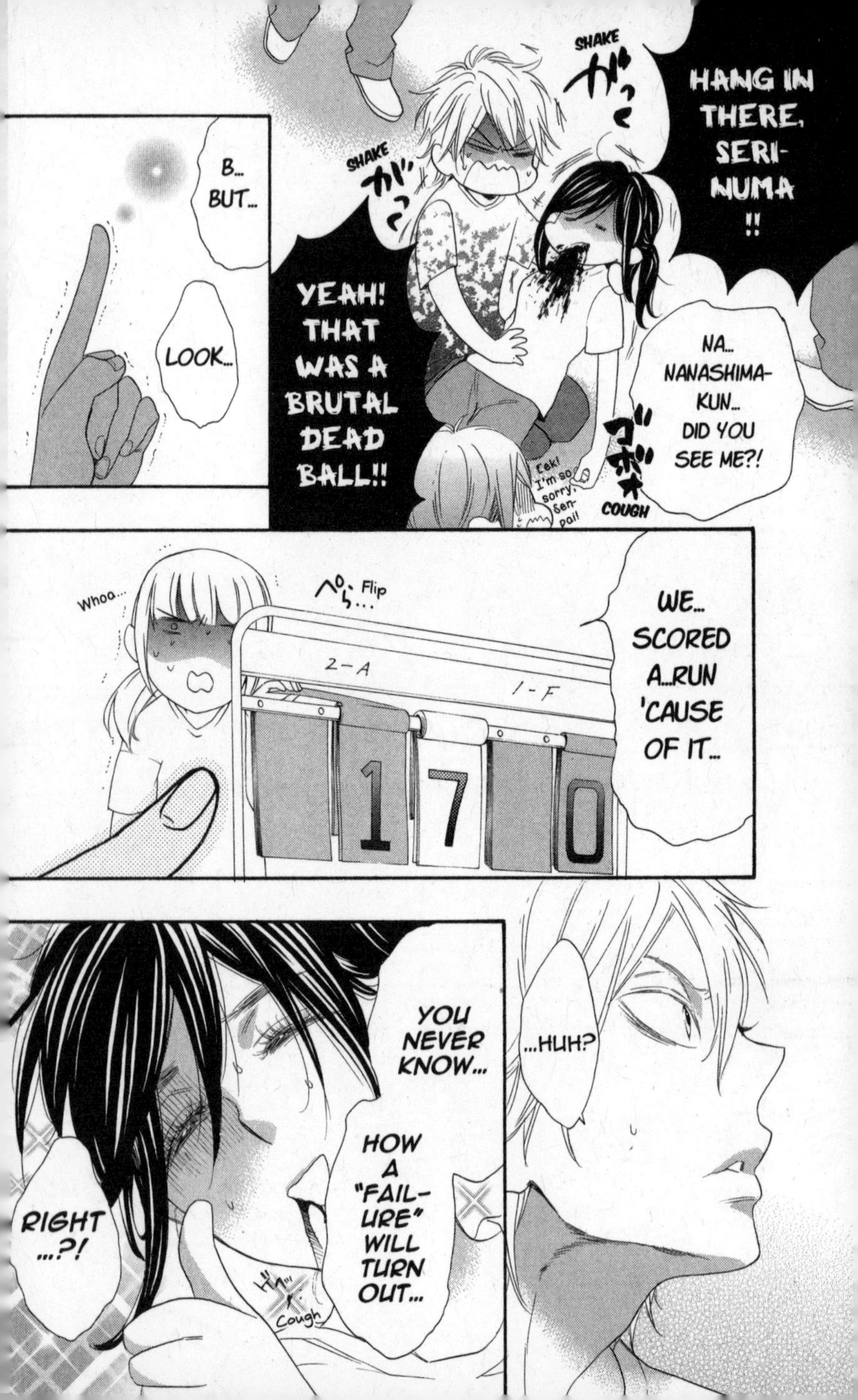
SHAKE
HANG IN THERE, SERI-NUMA!!
SHAKE
YEAH! THAT WAS A BRUTAL DEAD BALL!!
NA... NANASHIMA-KUN... DID YOU SEE ME?!
COUGH
Eek! I'm so sorry, Sen-pai!
B... BUT...
LOOK...
WE... SCORED A...RUN 'CAUSE OF IT...
Flip
Whoa...
2-A
1-F
1
7
0
...HUH?
YOU NEVER KNOW...
HOW A "FAIL-URE" WILL TURN OUT...
Cough
RIGHT ...?!

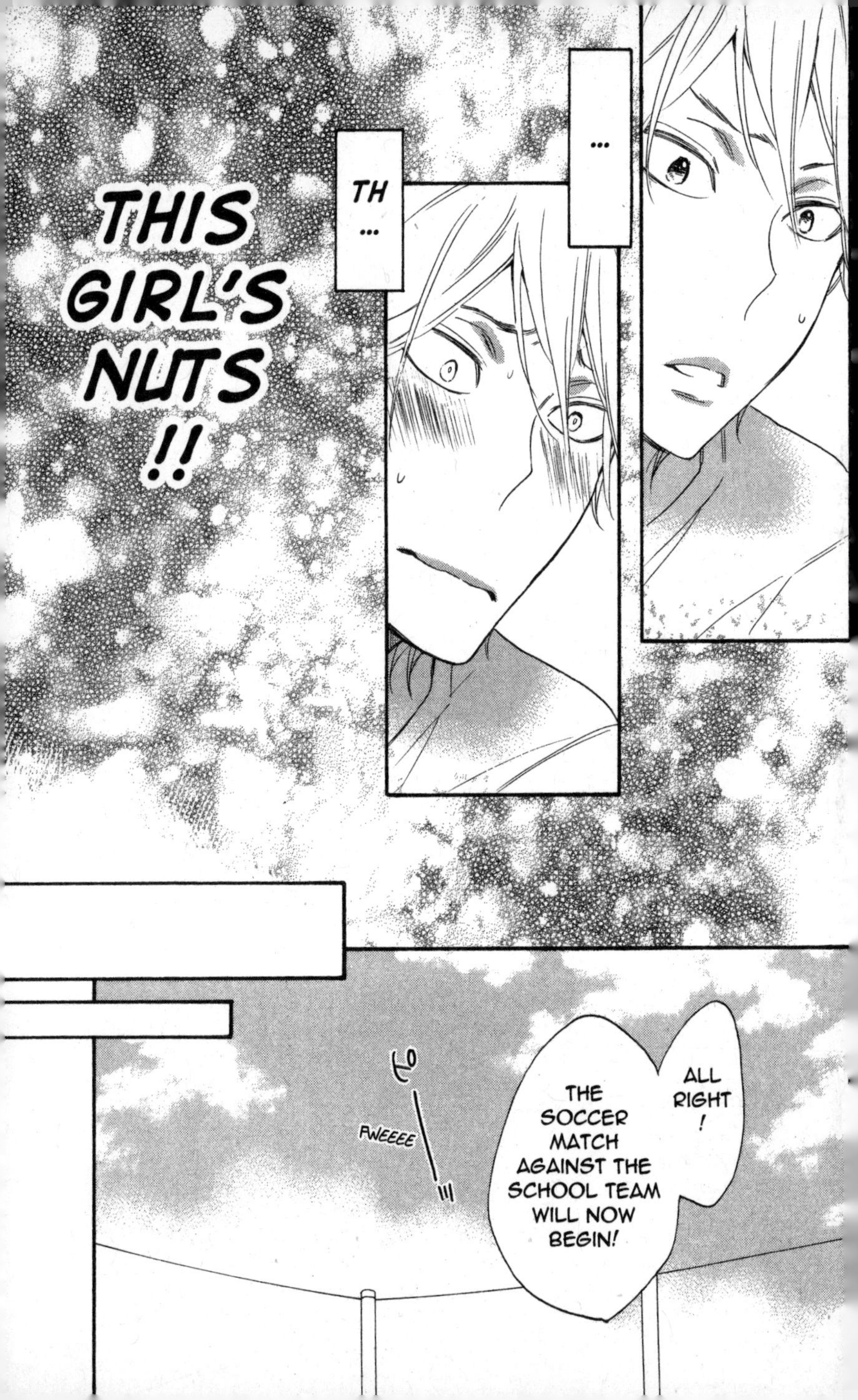
...
TH...
THIS GIRL'S NUTS!!
ALL RIGHT!
THE SOCCER MATCH AGAINST THE SCHOOL TEAM WILL NOW BEGIN!
FWEEEE

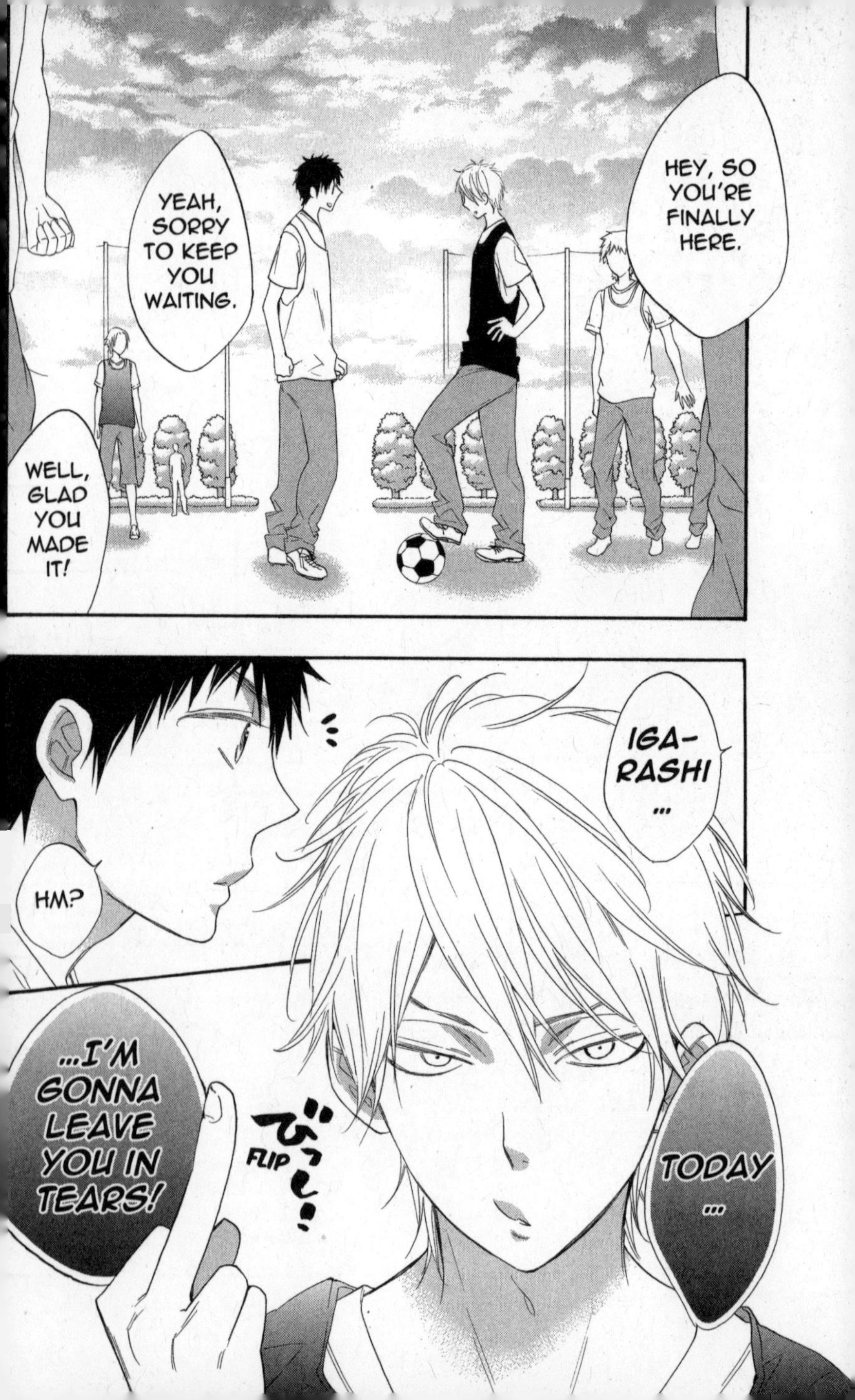
HEY, SO YOU'RE FINALLY HERE.
YEAH, SORRY TO KEEP YOU WAITING.
WELL, GLAD YOU MADE IT!
IGA-RASHI...
HM?
TODAY...
FLIP
...I'M GONNA LEAVE YOU IN TEARS!

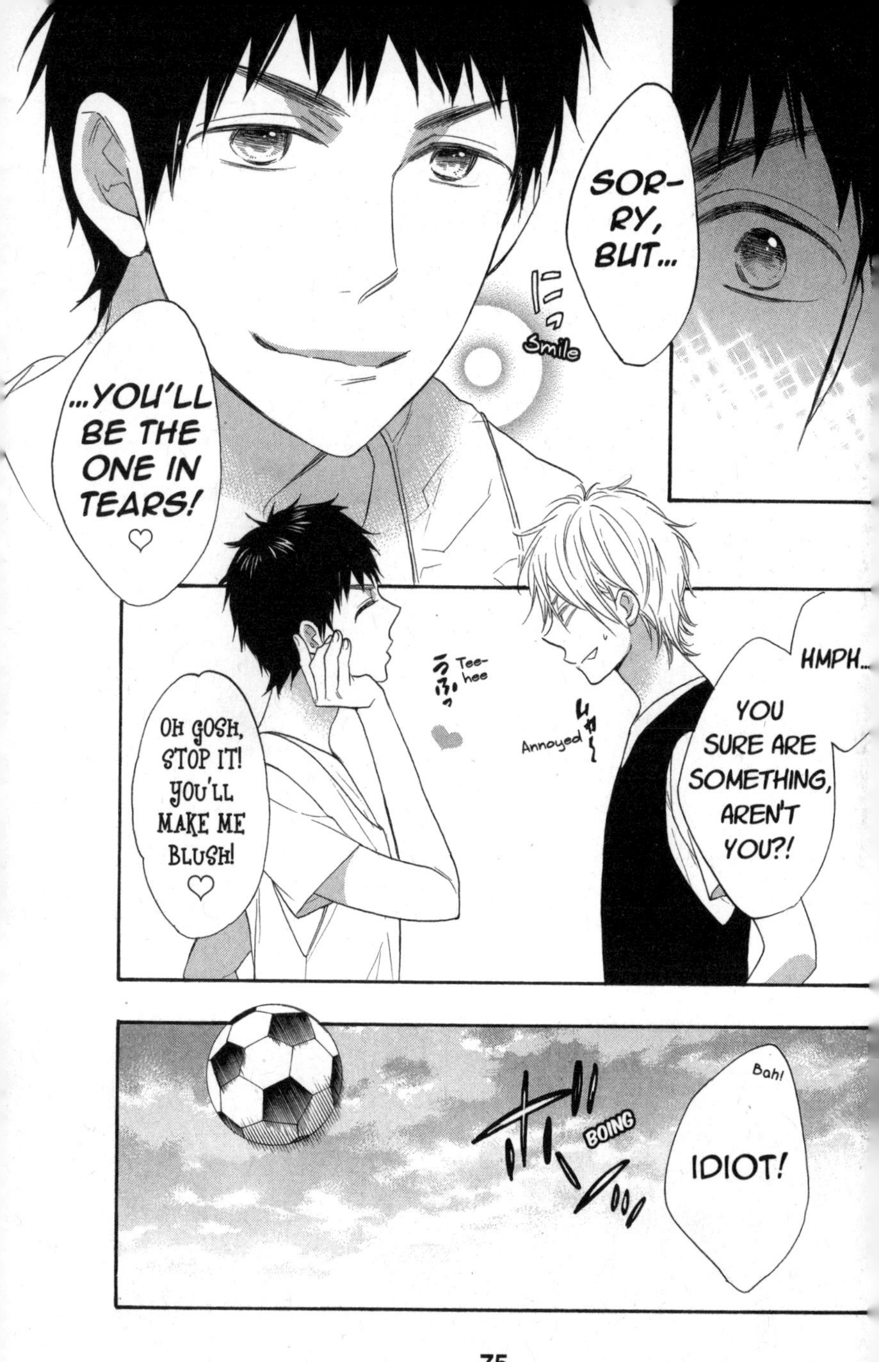
SOR-RY, BUT...
Smile
...YOU'LL BE THE ONE IN TEARS! ♡
HMPH... YOU SURE ARE SOMETHING, AREN'T YOU?!
Annoyed
Tee-hee
OH GOSH, STOP IT! YOU'LL MAKE ME BLUSH! ♡
Bah!
IDIOT!
BOING

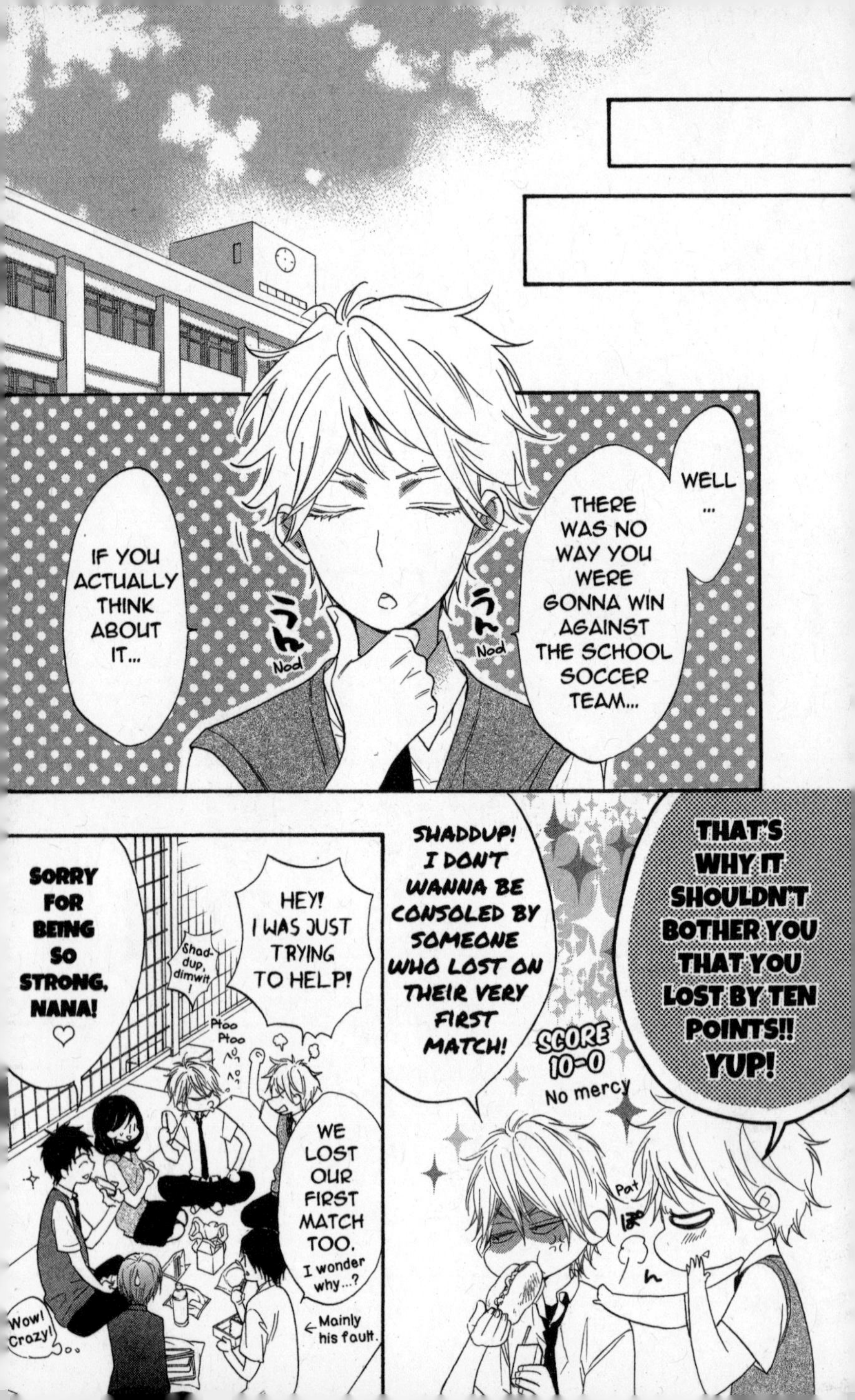
WELL...
THERE WAS NO WAY YOU WERE GONNA WIN AGAINST THE SCHOOL SOCCER TEAM...
うん Nod
うん Nod
IF YOU ACTUALLY THINK ABOUT IT...
THAT'S WHY IT SHOULDN'T BOTHER YOU THAT YOU LOST BY TEN POINTS!! YUP!
SHADDUP! I DON'T WANNA BE CONSOLED BY SOMEONE WHO LOST ON THEIR VERY FIRST MATCH!
SCORE 10-0
No mercy
Pat
ぽん
HEY! I WAS JUST TRYING TO HELP!
Shad-dup, dimwit!
SORRY FOR BEING SO STRONG, NANA! ♡
Ptoo Ptoo
WE LOST OUR FIRST MATCH TOO. I wonder why...?
← Mainly his fault.
Wow! Crazy!

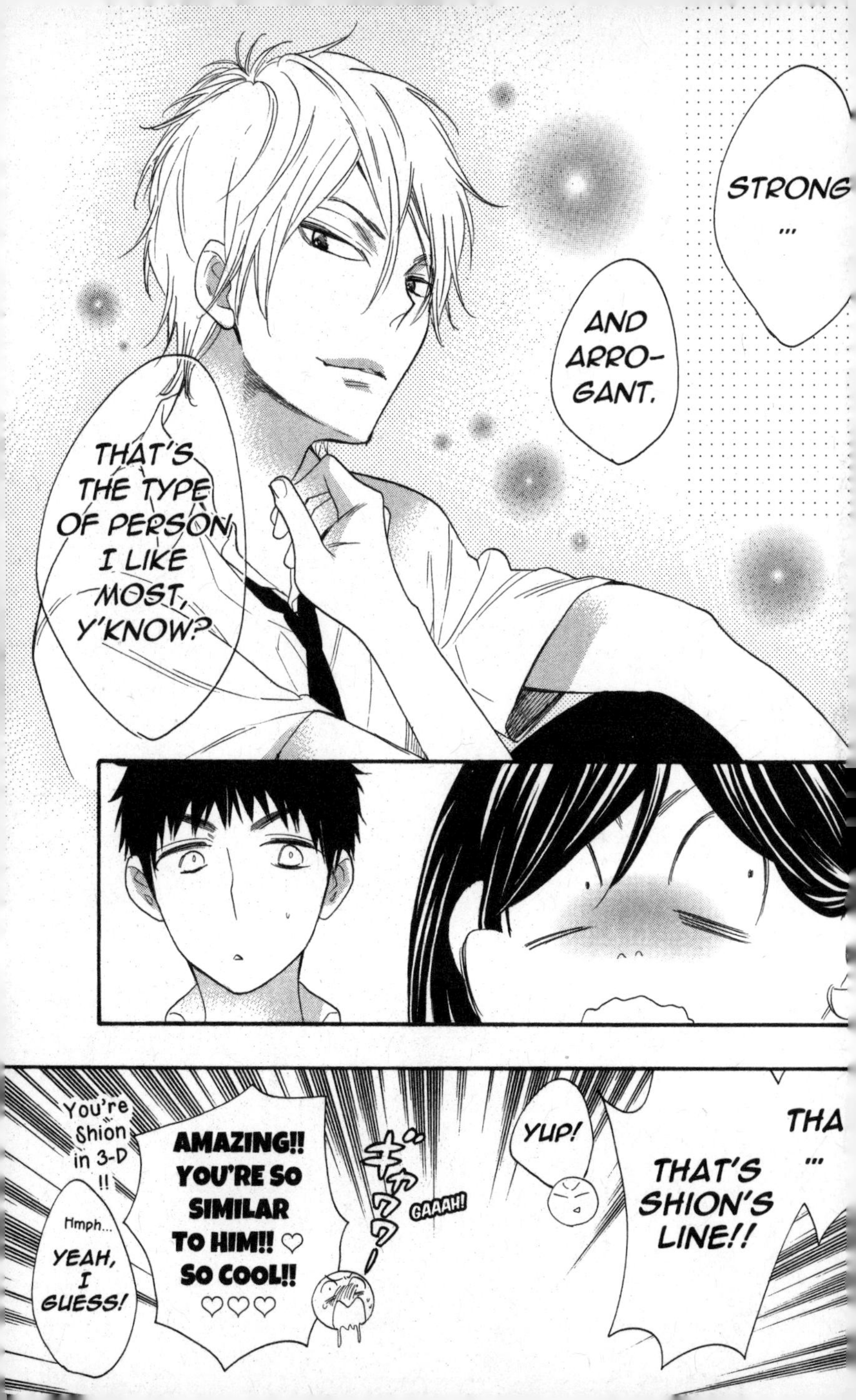
STRONG ...
AND ARRO-GANT.
THAT'S THE TYPE OF PERSON I LIKE MOST, Y'KNOW?
THA ...
THAT'S SHION'S LINE!!
YUP!
GAAAH!
AMAZING!! YOU'RE SO SIMILAR TO HIM!! ♡ SO COOL!! ♡♡♡
You're Shion in 3-D !!
Hmph... YEAH, I GUESS!

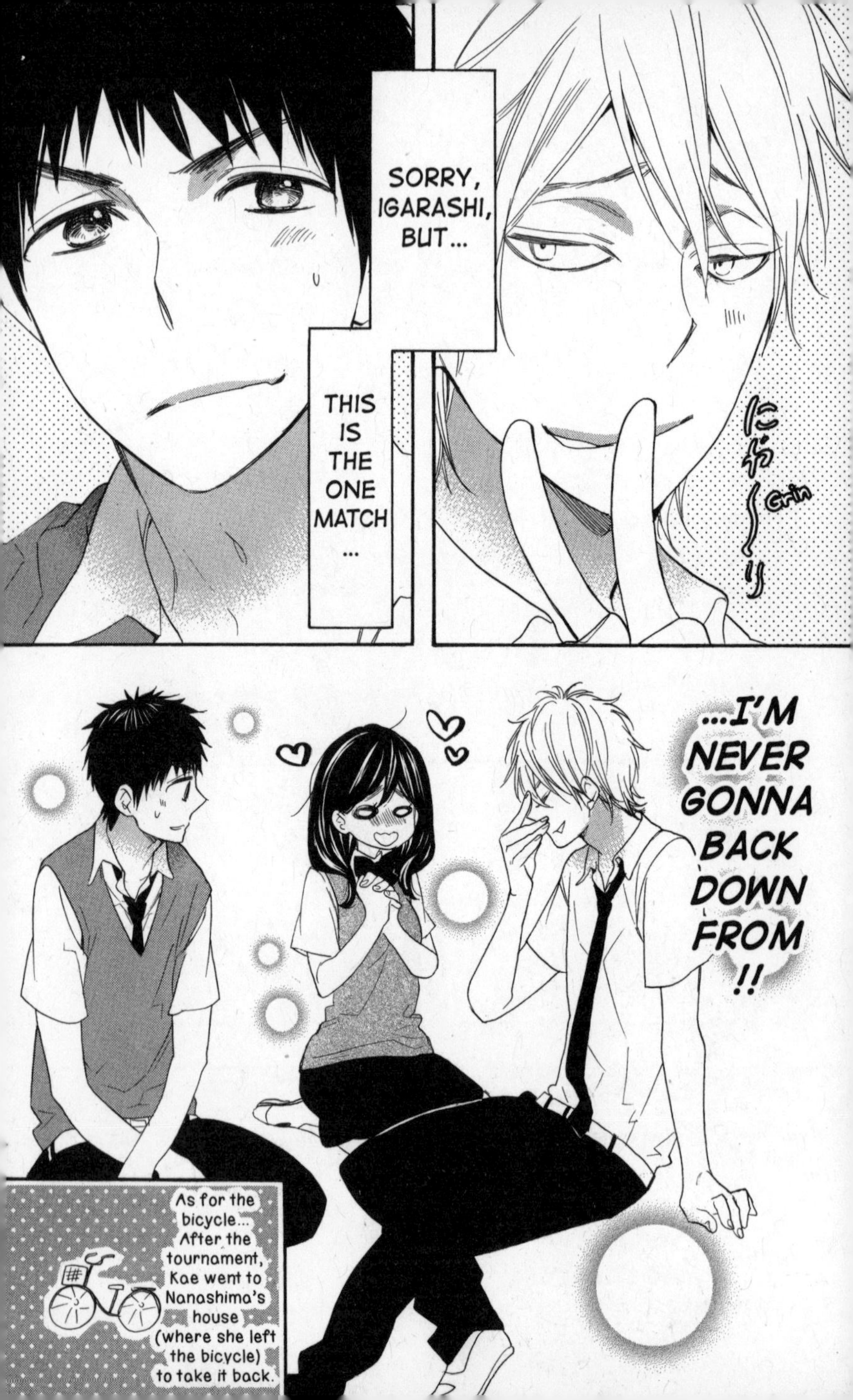
SORRY, IGARASHI, BUT...
THIS IS THE ONE MATCH...
にや～り
Grin
...I'M NEVER GONNA BACK DOWN FROM!!
As for the bicycle... After the tournament, Kae went to Nanashima's house (where she left the bicycle) to take it back.

KiSS HiM, NOT ME!

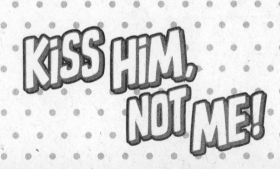

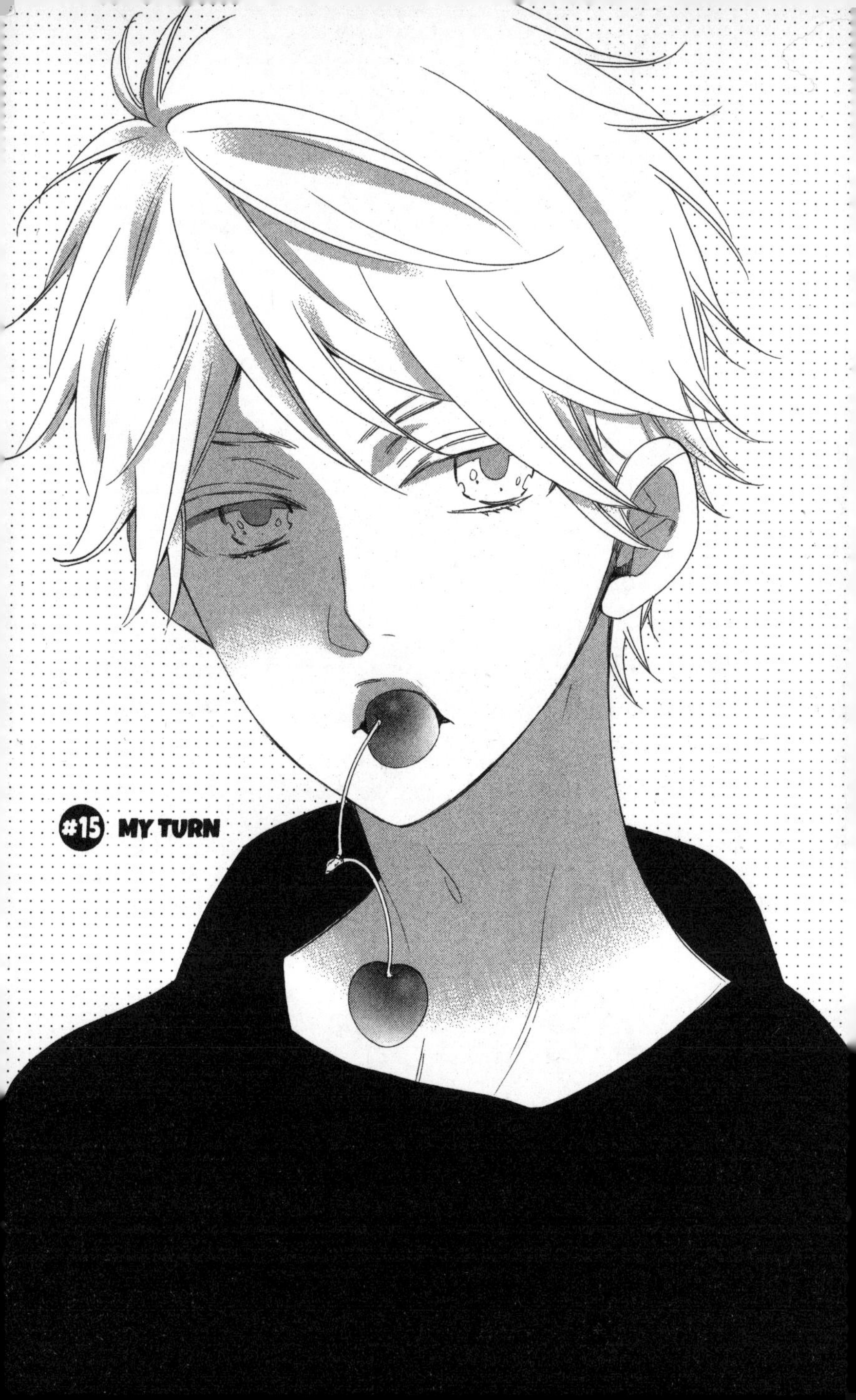
#15 MY TURN

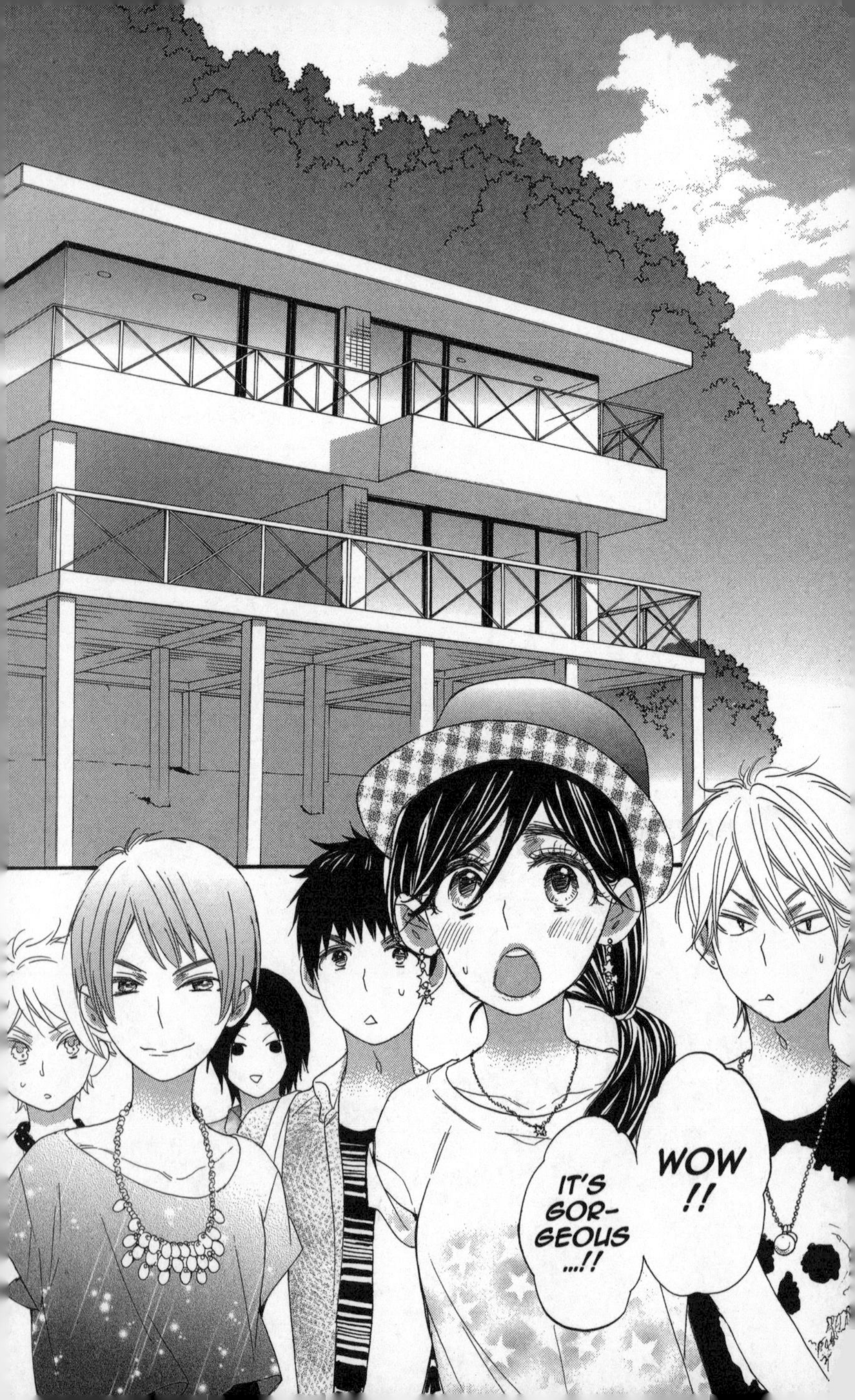
WOW !!
IT'S GOR-GEOUS ...!!

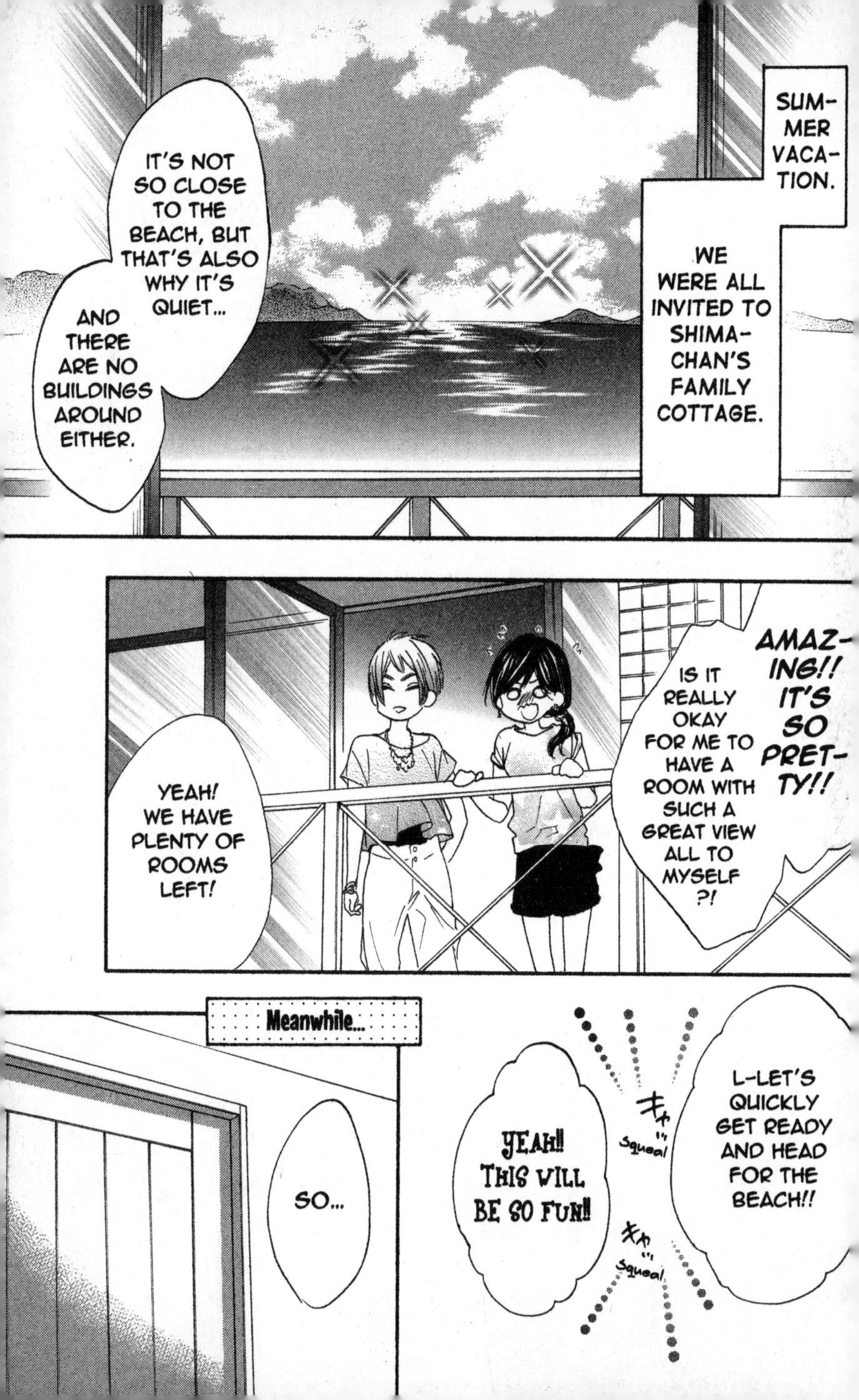
SUMMER VACATION.
WE WERE ALL INVITED TO SHIMA-CHAN'S FAMILY COTTAGE.
IT'S NOT SO CLOSE TO THE BEACH, BUT THAT'S ALSO WHY IT'S QUIET...
AND THERE ARE NO BUILDINGS AROUND EITHER.
AMAZING!! IT'S SO PRETTY!!
IS IT REALLY OKAY FOR ME TO HAVE A ROOM WITH SUCH A GREAT VIEW ALL TO MYSELF?!
YEAH! WE HAVE PLENTY OF ROOMS LEFT!
L-LET'S QUICKLY GET READY AND HEAD FOR THE BEACH!!
Squeal
YEAH!! THIS WILL BE SO FUN!!
Squeal
Meanwhile...
SO...

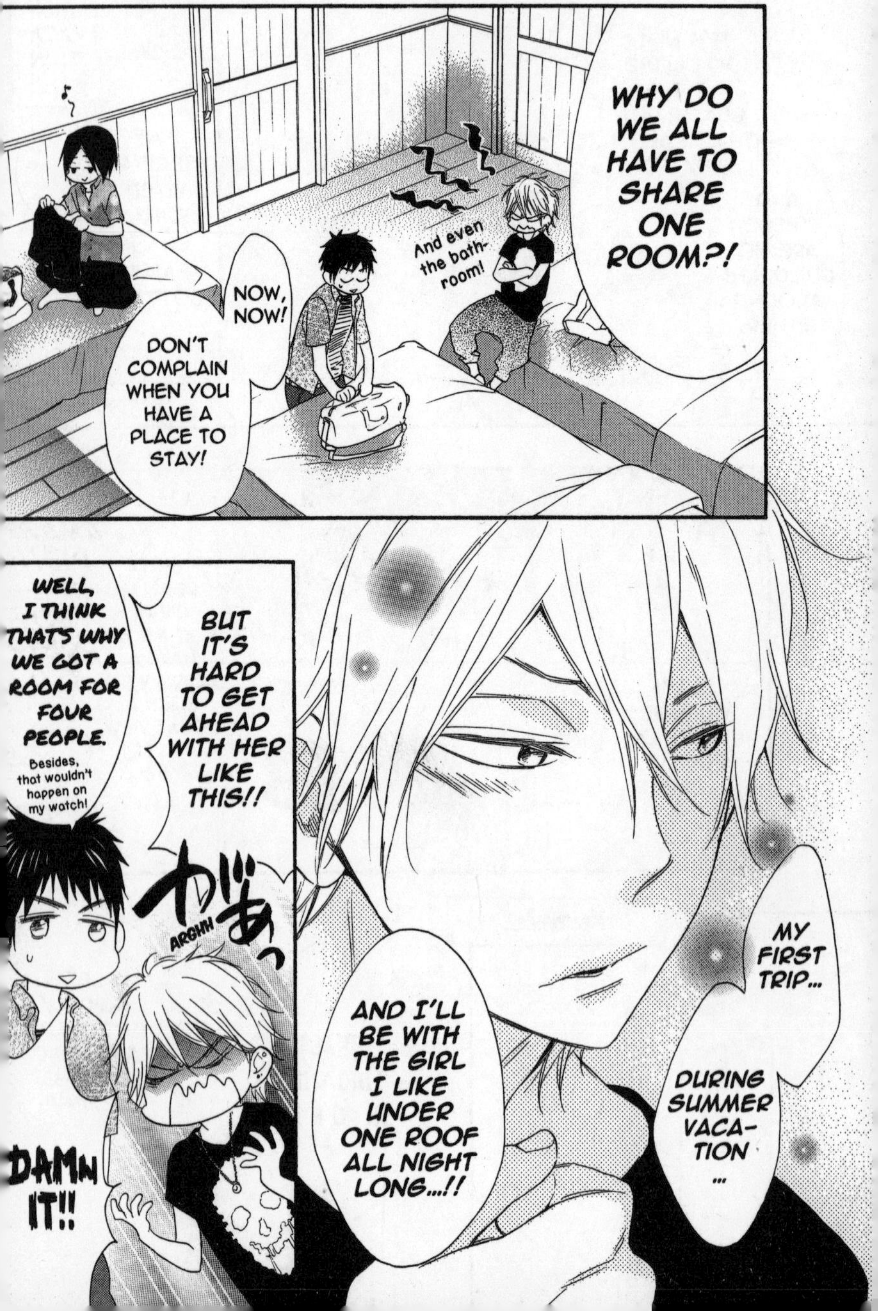
WHY DO WE ALL HAVE TO SHARE ONE ROOM?!
And even the bath-room!
NOW, NOW!
DON'T COMPLAIN WHEN YOU HAVE A PLACE TO STAY!
MY FIRST TRIP...
DURING SUMMER VACA-TION...
AND I'LL BE WITH THE GIRL I LIKE UNDER ONE ROOF ALL NIGHT LONG...!!
BUT IT'S HARD TO GET AHEAD WITH HER LIKE THIS!!
WELL, I THINK THAT'S WHY WE GOT A ROOM FOR FOUR PEOPLE.
Besides, that wouldn't happen on my watch!
ARGHH
DAMN IT!!

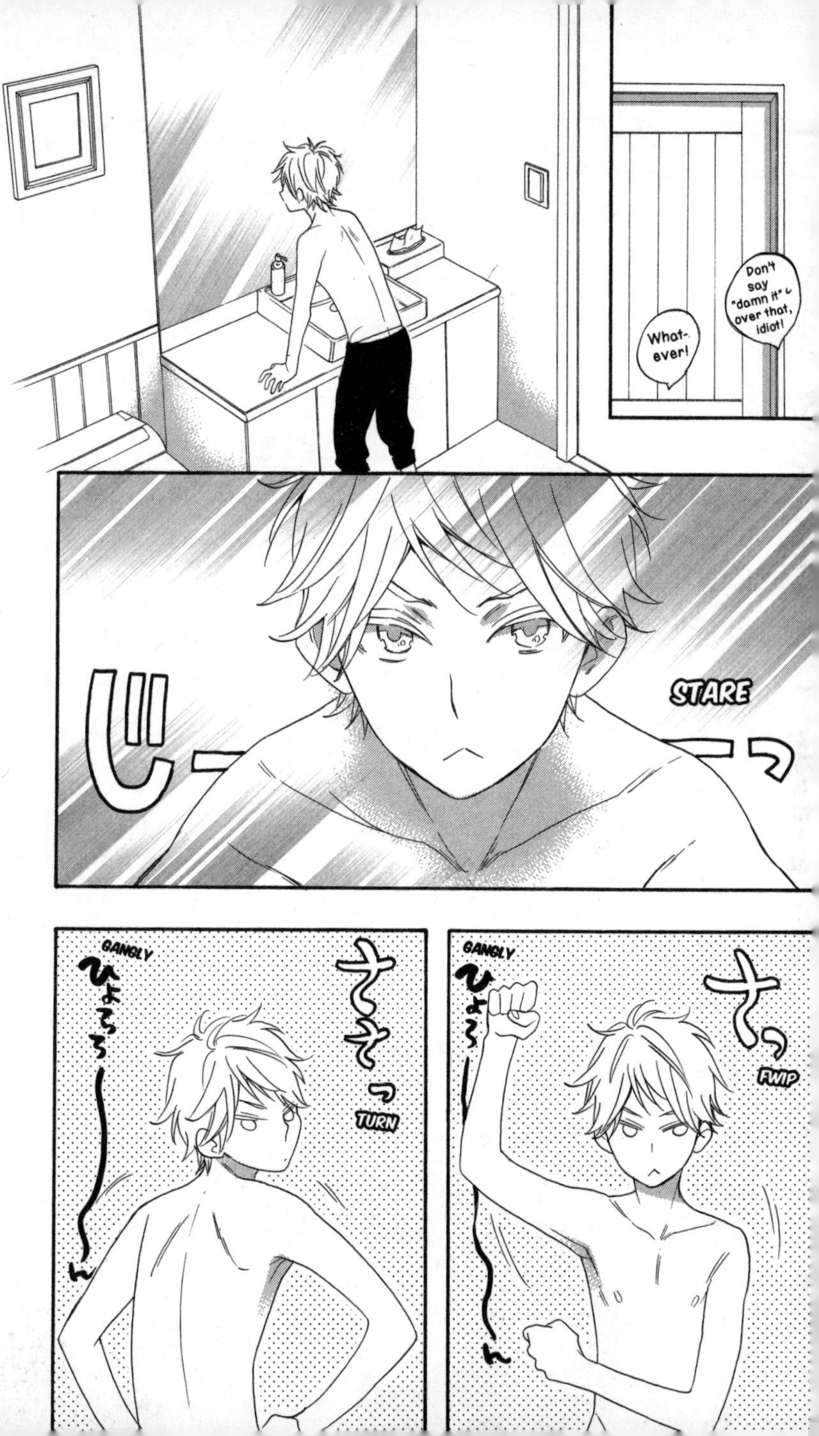

Don't say "damn it" over that, idiot!
What-ever!
じーーっ
STARE
さっ
FWIP
ひょろーーん
GANGLY
そそっ
TURN
ひょろろーーん
GANGLY

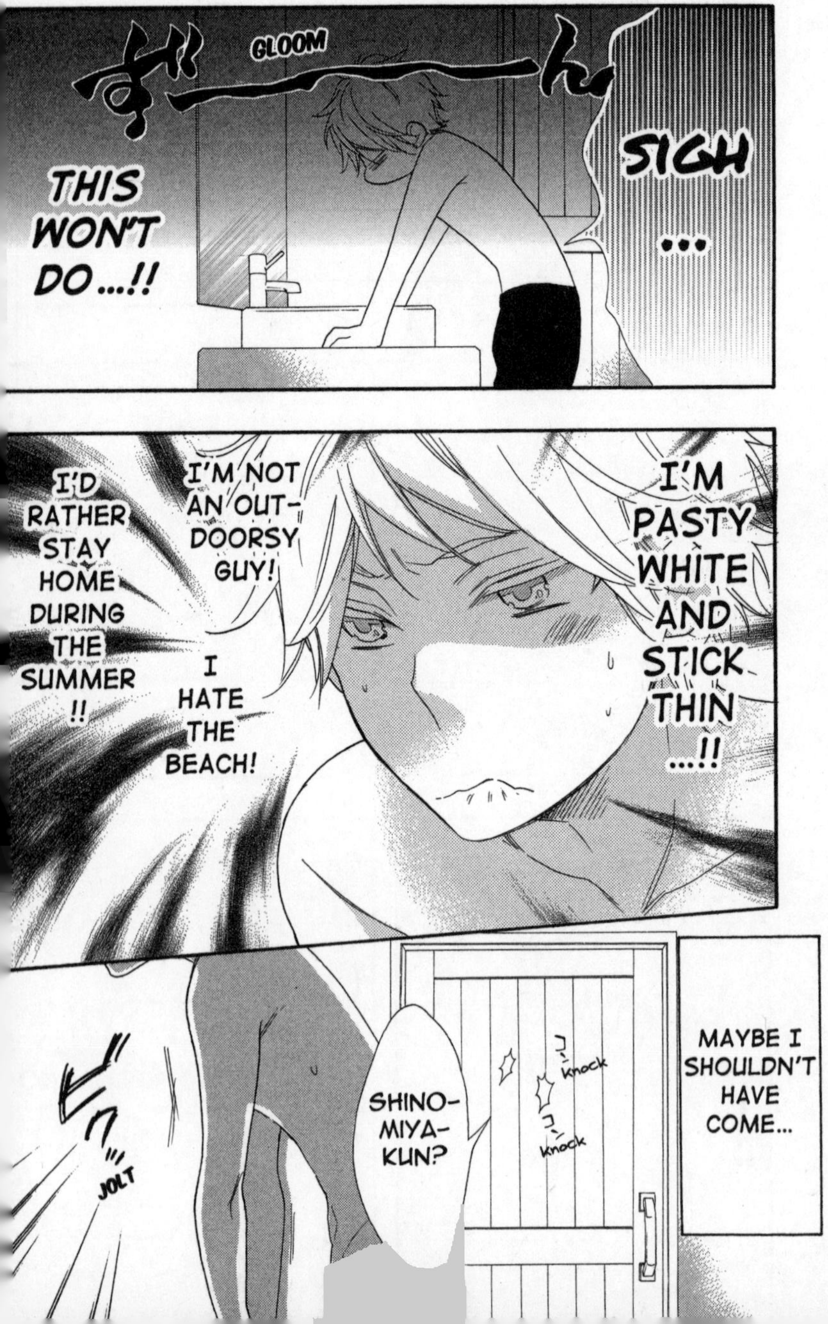
SIGH ...
GLOOM
THIS WON'T DO...!!
I'M PASTY WHITE AND STICK THIN ...!!
I'M NOT AN OUT-DOORSY GUY!
I HATE THE BEACH!
I'D RATHER STAY HOME DURING THE SUMMER !!
MAYBE I SHOULDN'T HAVE COME...
knock
knock
SHINO-MIYA-KUN?
JOLT

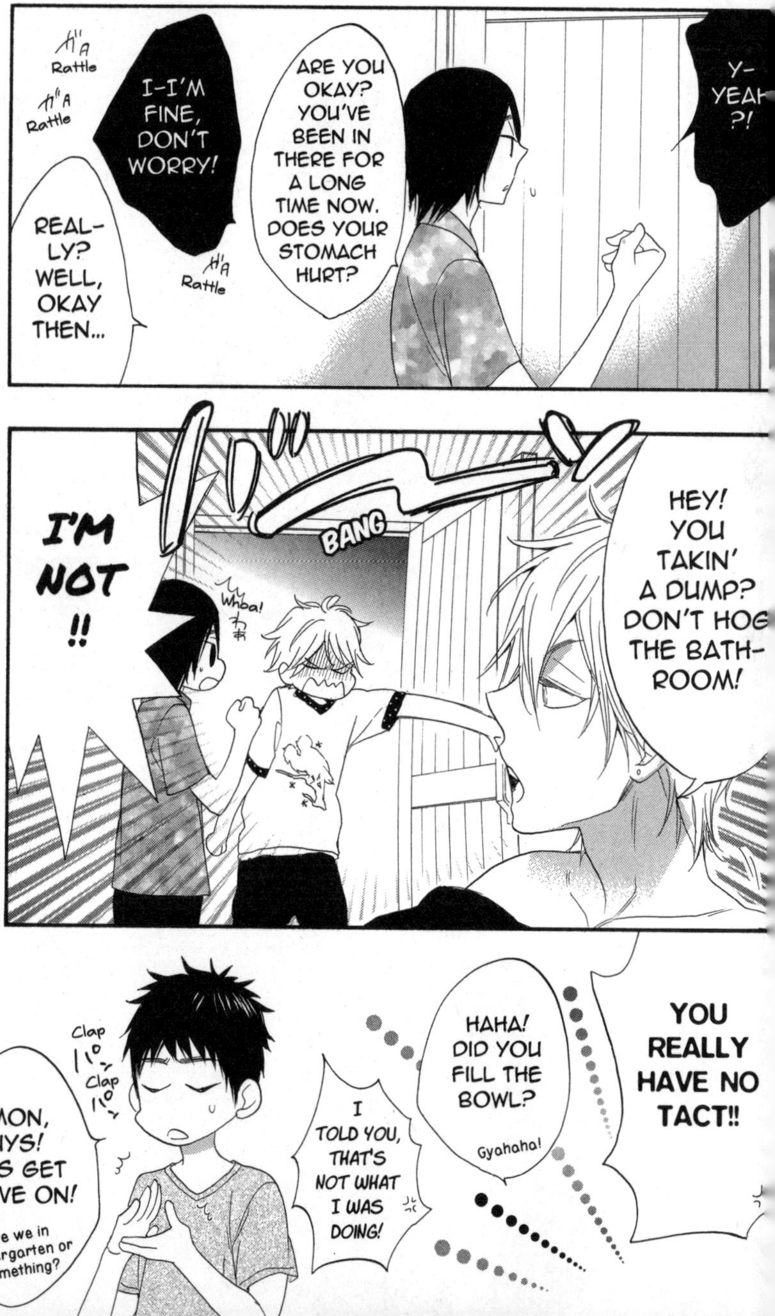
Y-YEAH?!
ARE YOU OKAY? YOU'VE BEEN IN THERE FOR A LONG TIME NOW. DOES YOUR STOMACH HURT?
I-I'M FINE, DON'T WORRY!
Rattle
Rattle
Rattle
REAL-LY? WELL, OKAY THEN...
BANG
HEY! YOU TAKIN' A DUMP? DON'T HOG THE BATH-ROOM!
Whoa!
I'M NOT!!
YOU REALLY HAVE NO TACT!!
HAHA! DID YOU FILL THE BOWL?
Gyahaha!
I TOLD YOU, THAT'S NOT WHAT I WAS DOING!
Clap
Clap
C'MON, GUYS! LET'S GET A MOVE ON!
Are we in kindergarten or something?

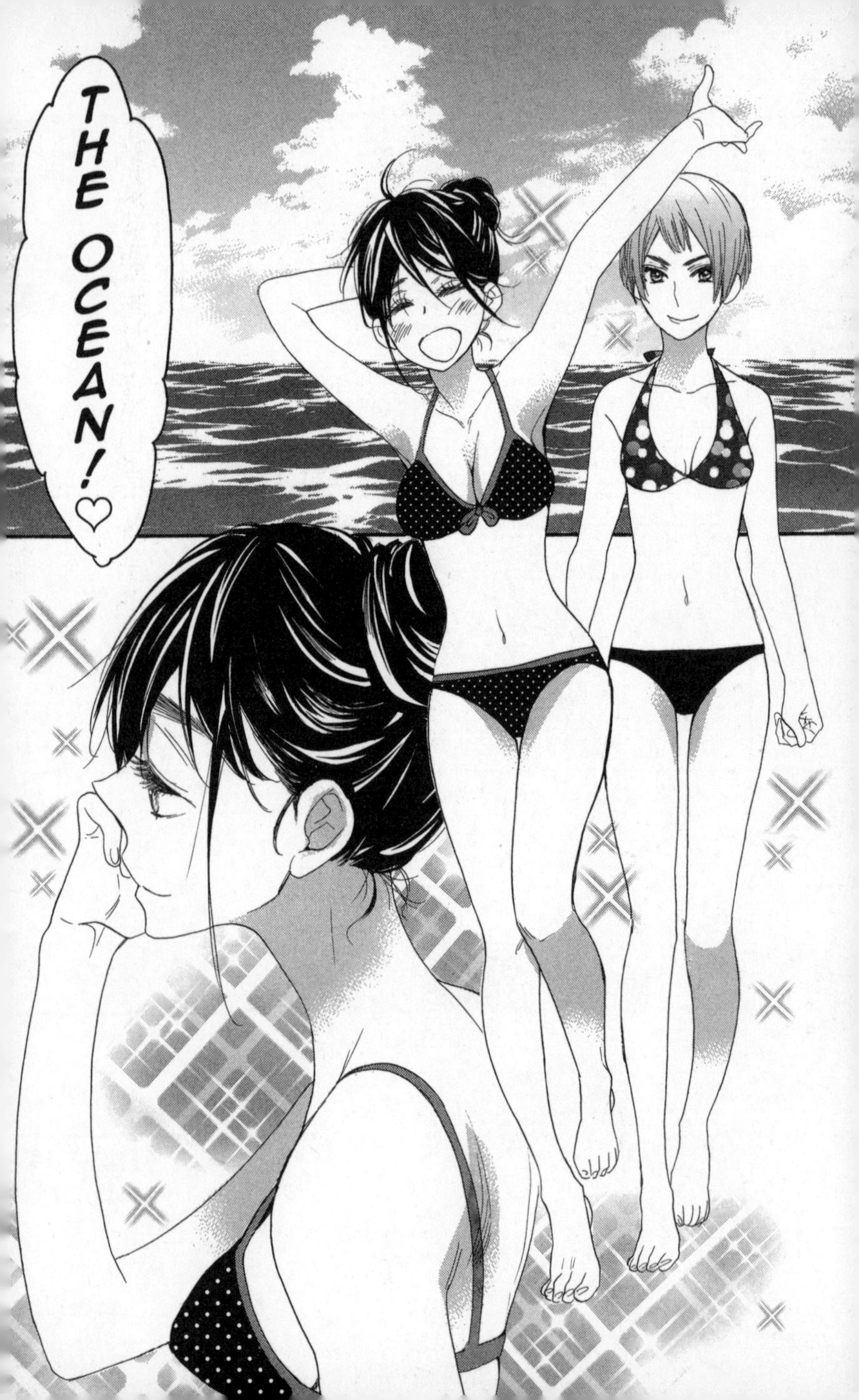
THE OCEAN!♡

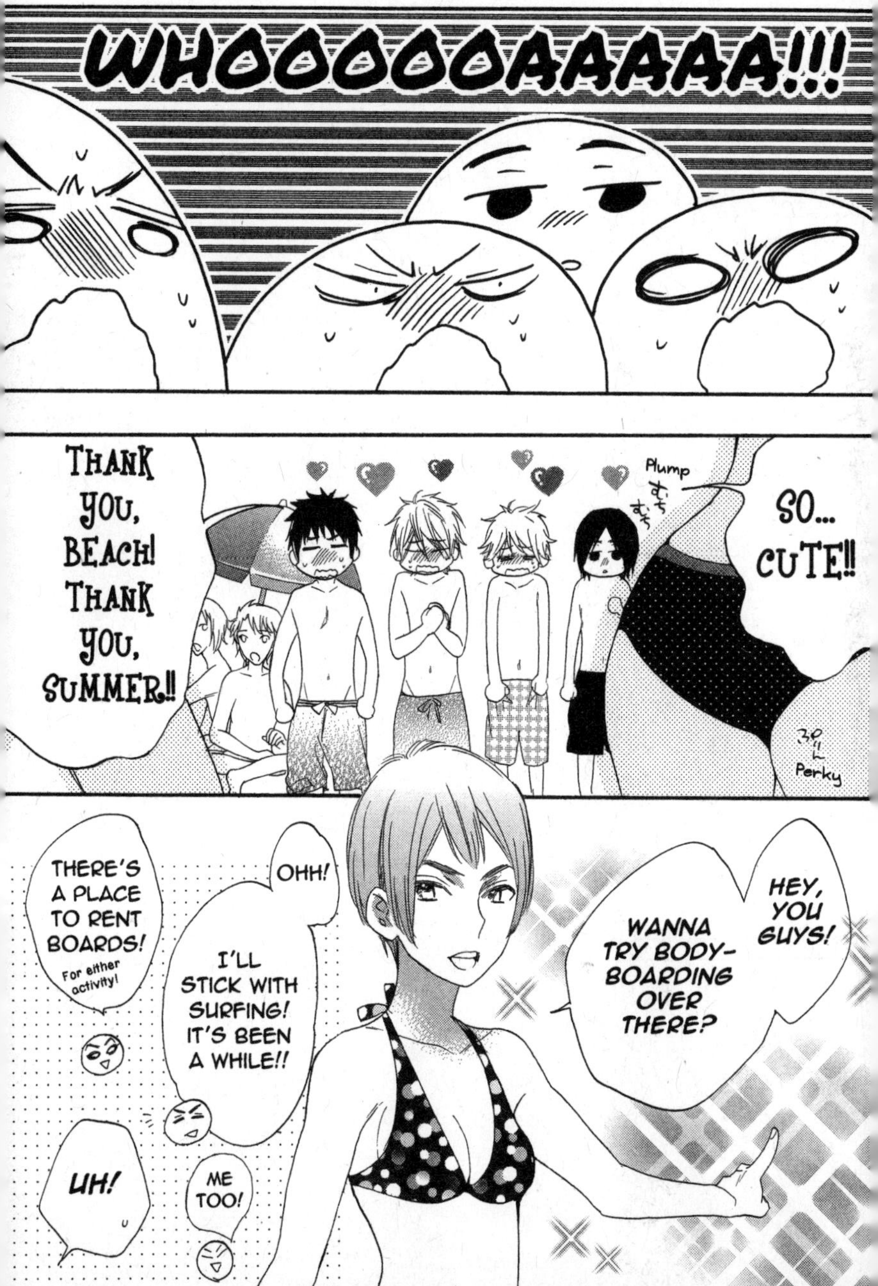
WHOOOOOAAAAA!!!
SO... CUTE!!
Plump
Perky
THANK YOU, BEACH! THANK YOU, SUMMER!!
HEY, YOU GUYS!
WANNA TRY BODY-BOARDING OVER THERE?
OHH!
I'LL STICK WITH SURFING! IT'S BEEN A WHILE!!
THERE'S A PLACE TO RENT BOARDS!
For either activity!
ME TOO!
UH!

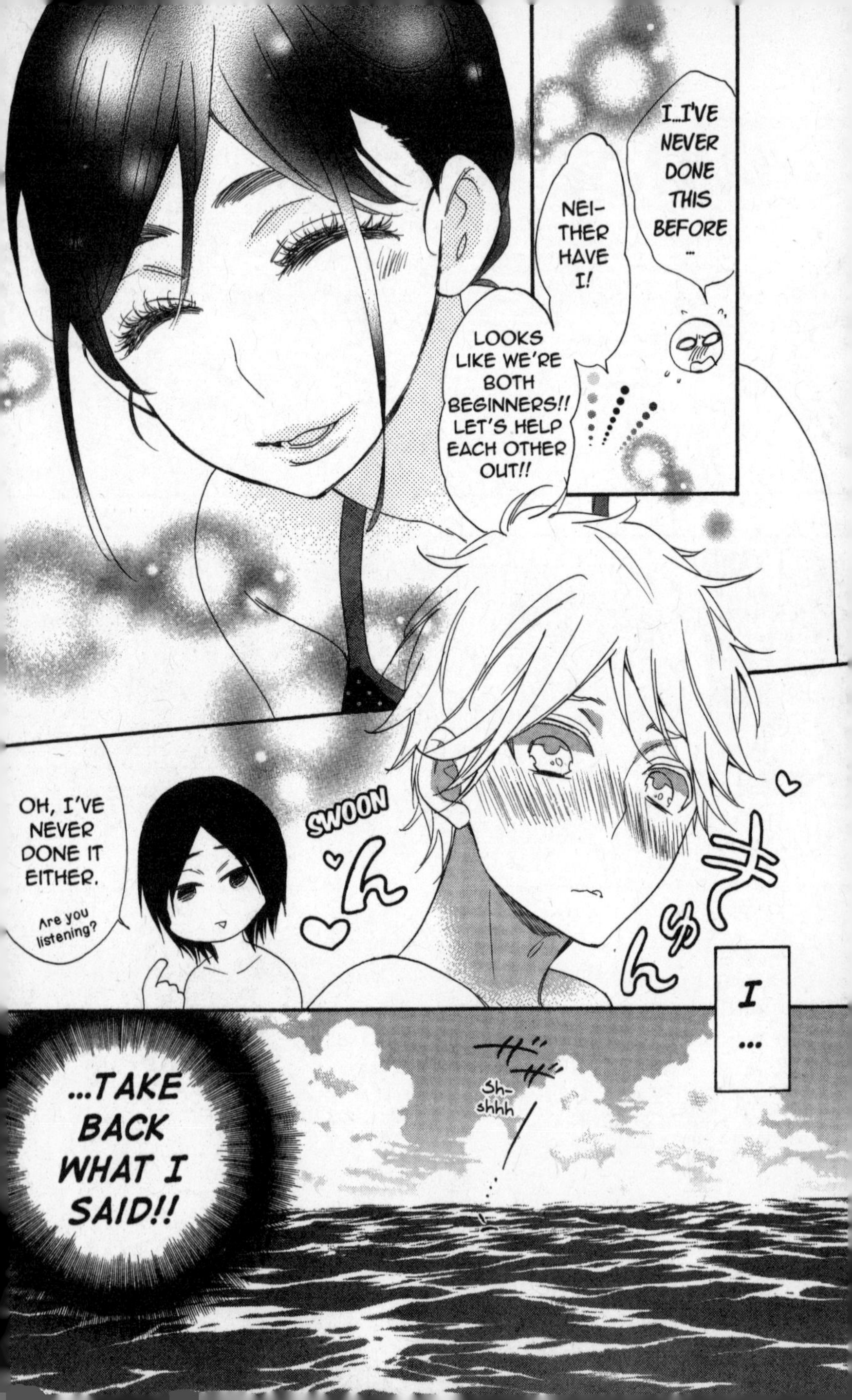
I...I'VE NEVER DONE THIS BEFORE ...
NEI-THER HAVE I!
LOOKS LIKE WE'RE BOTH BEGINNERS!! LET'S HELP EACH OTHER OUT!!
きゅん
SWOON
ん
OH, I'VE NEVER DONE IT EITHER.
Are you listening?
I ...
...TAKE BACK WHAT I SAID!!
ザザ
Sh-shhh

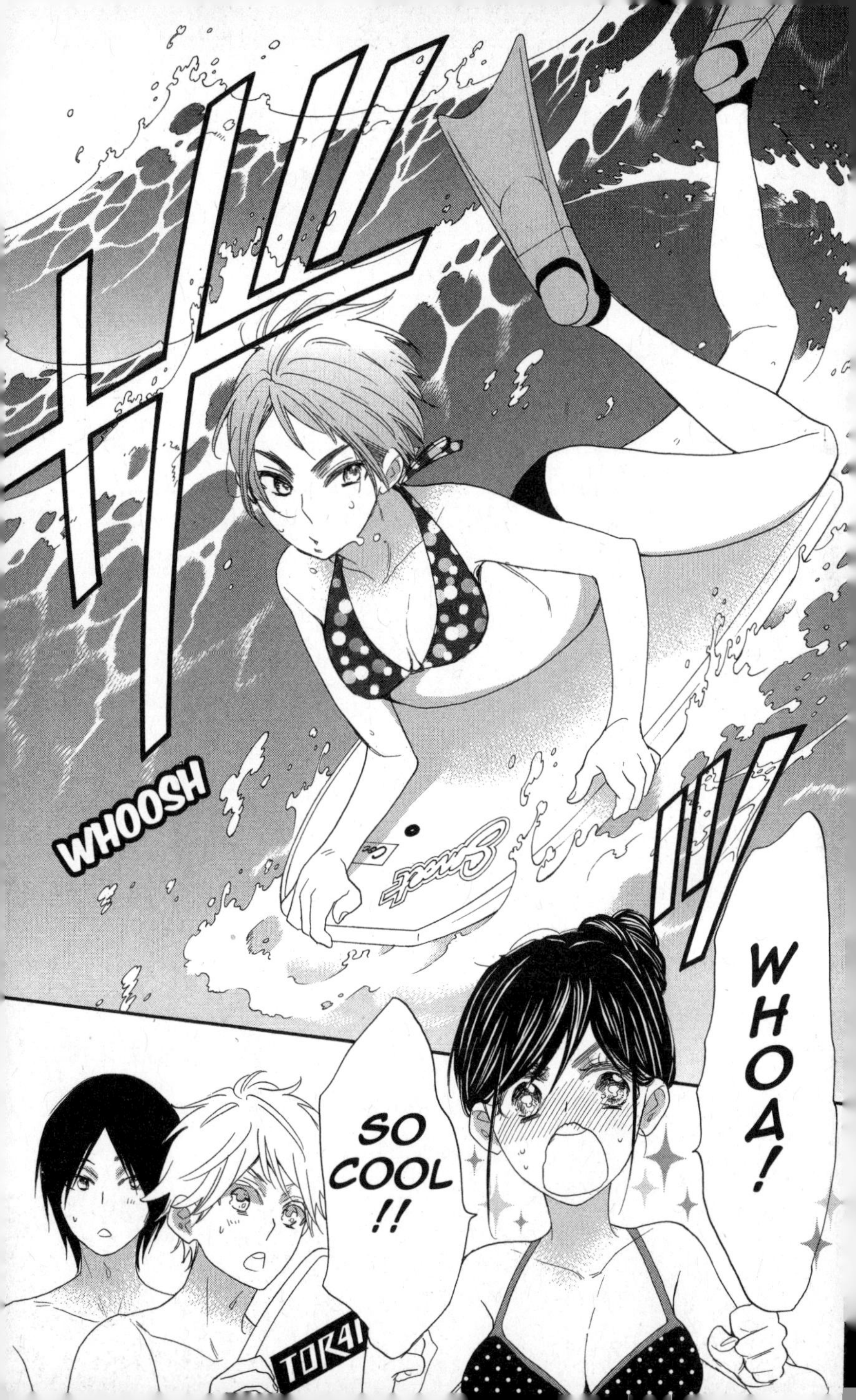
WHOOSH
WHOA!
SO COOL!!

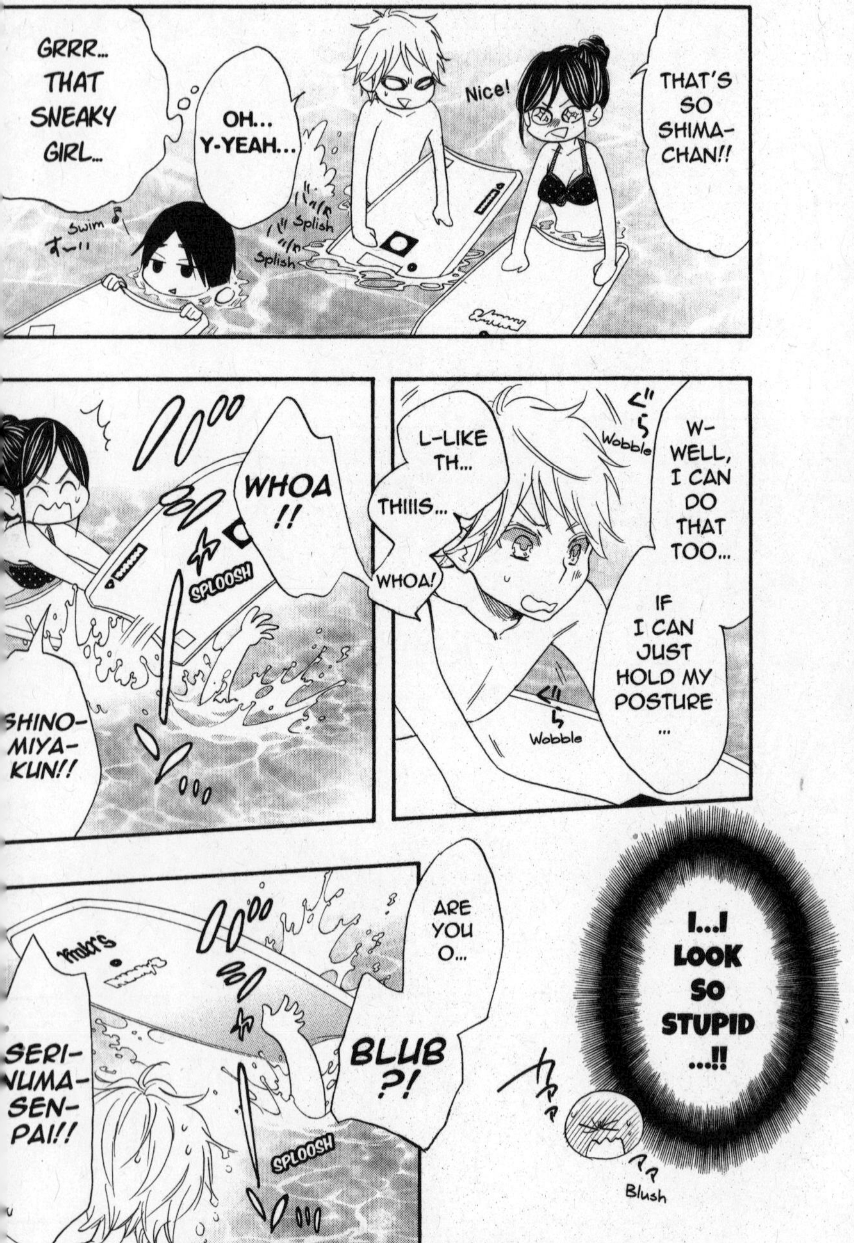
THAT'S SO SHIMA-CHAN!!
Nice!
OH... Y-YEAH...
Splish
Splish
GRRR... THAT SNEAKY GIRL...
Swim
W-WELL, I CAN DO THAT TOO...
Wobble
IF I CAN JUST HOLD MY POSTURE ...
Wobble
L-LIKE TH...
THIIIS...
WHOA!
WHOA !!
SPLOOSH
SHINO-MIYA-KUN!!
I...I LOOK SO STUPID ...!!
Blush
ARE YOU O...
BLUB ?!
SPLOOSH
SERI-NUMA-SEN-PAI!!

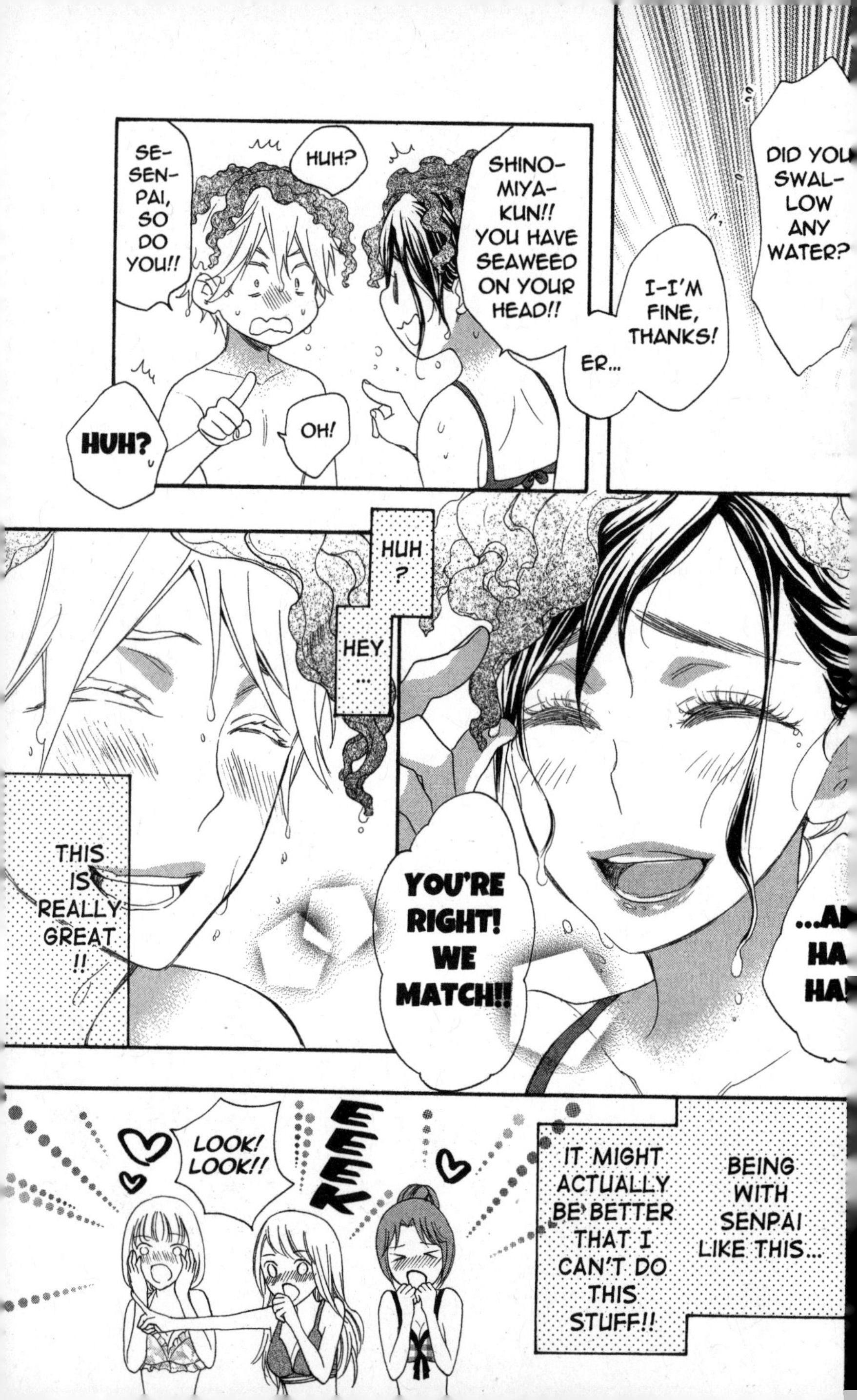
DID YOU SWALLOW ANY WATER?
I-I'M FINE, THANKS!
ER...
SHINOMIYA-KUN!! YOU HAVE SEAWEED ON YOUR HEAD!!
HUH?
SE-SENPAI, SO DO YOU!!
OH!
HUH?
...A HA HA
YOU'RE RIGHT! WE MATCH!!
HUH?
HEY...
THIS IS REALLY GREAT!!
BEING WITH SENPAI LIKE THIS...
IT MIGHT ACTUALLY BE BETTER THAT I CAN'T DO THIS STUFF!!
EEEK
LOOK! LOOK!!

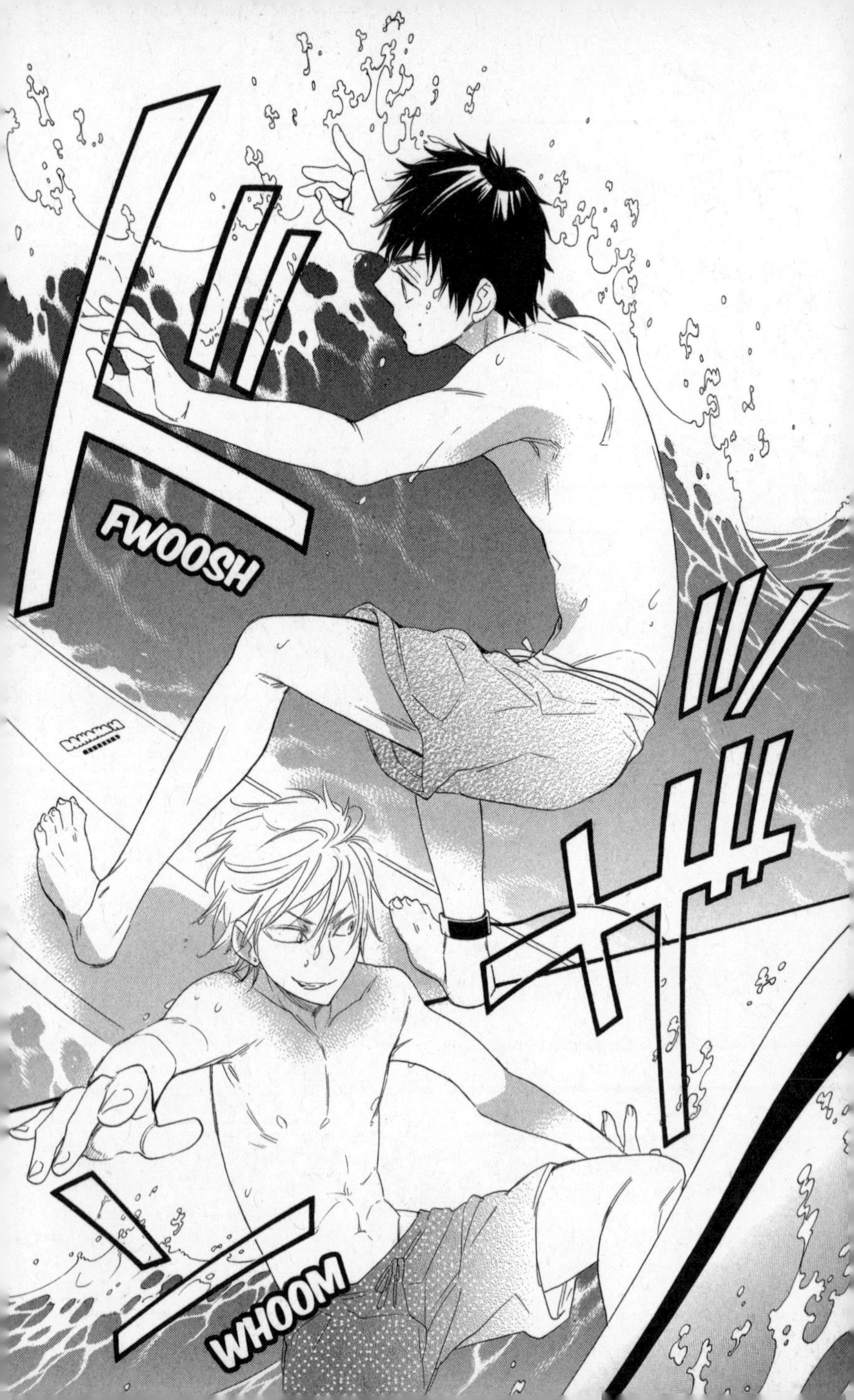
FWOOSH
WHOOM

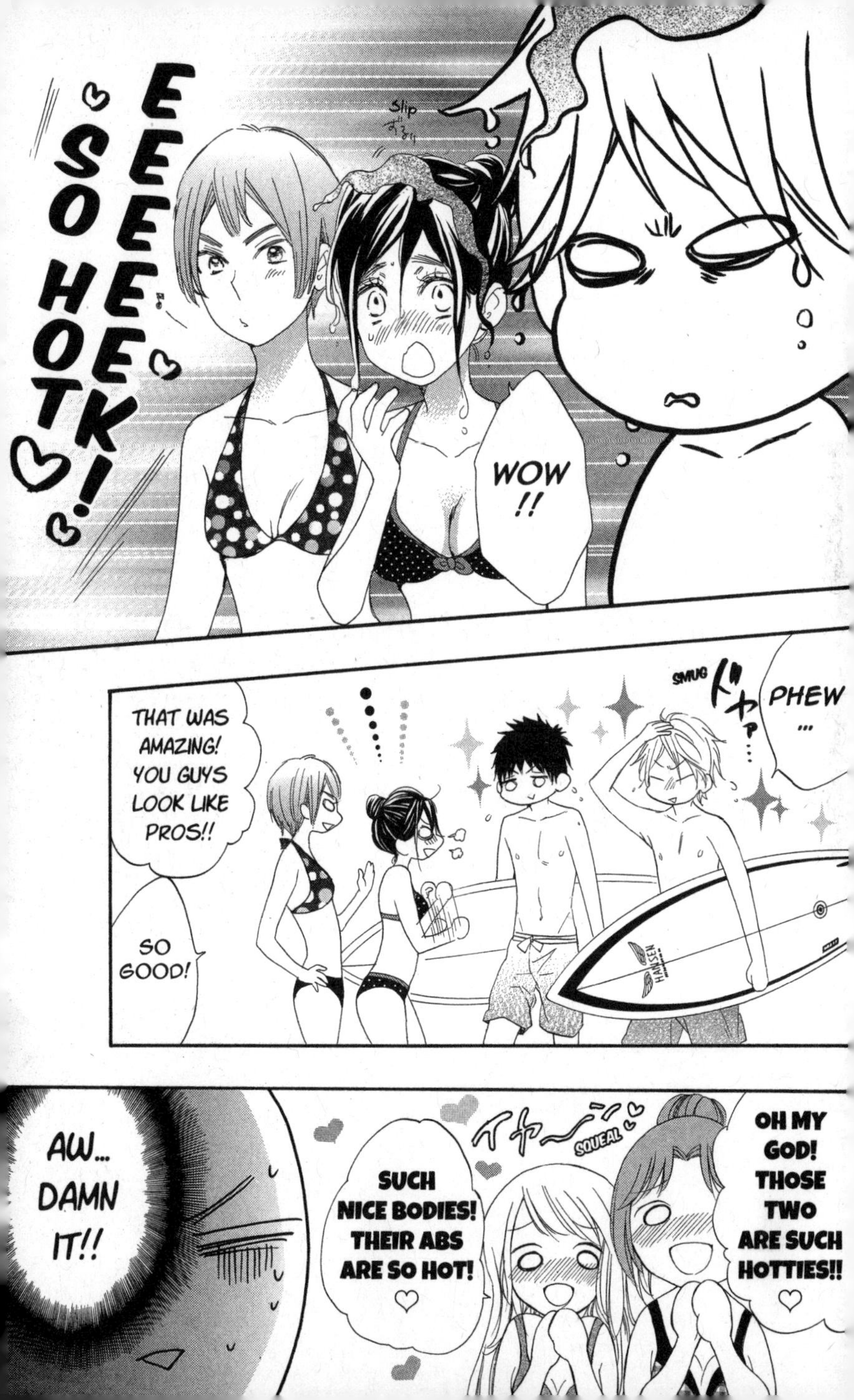
Slip
WOW!!
EEEEEEEK!
SO HOT!
SMUG
PHEW...
THAT WAS AMAZING! YOU GUYS LOOK LIKE PROS!!
SO GOOD!
OH MY GOD! THOSE TWO ARE SUCH HOTTIES!!
SQUEAL
SUCH NICE BODIES! THEIR ABS ARE SO HOT!
AW... DAMN IT!!

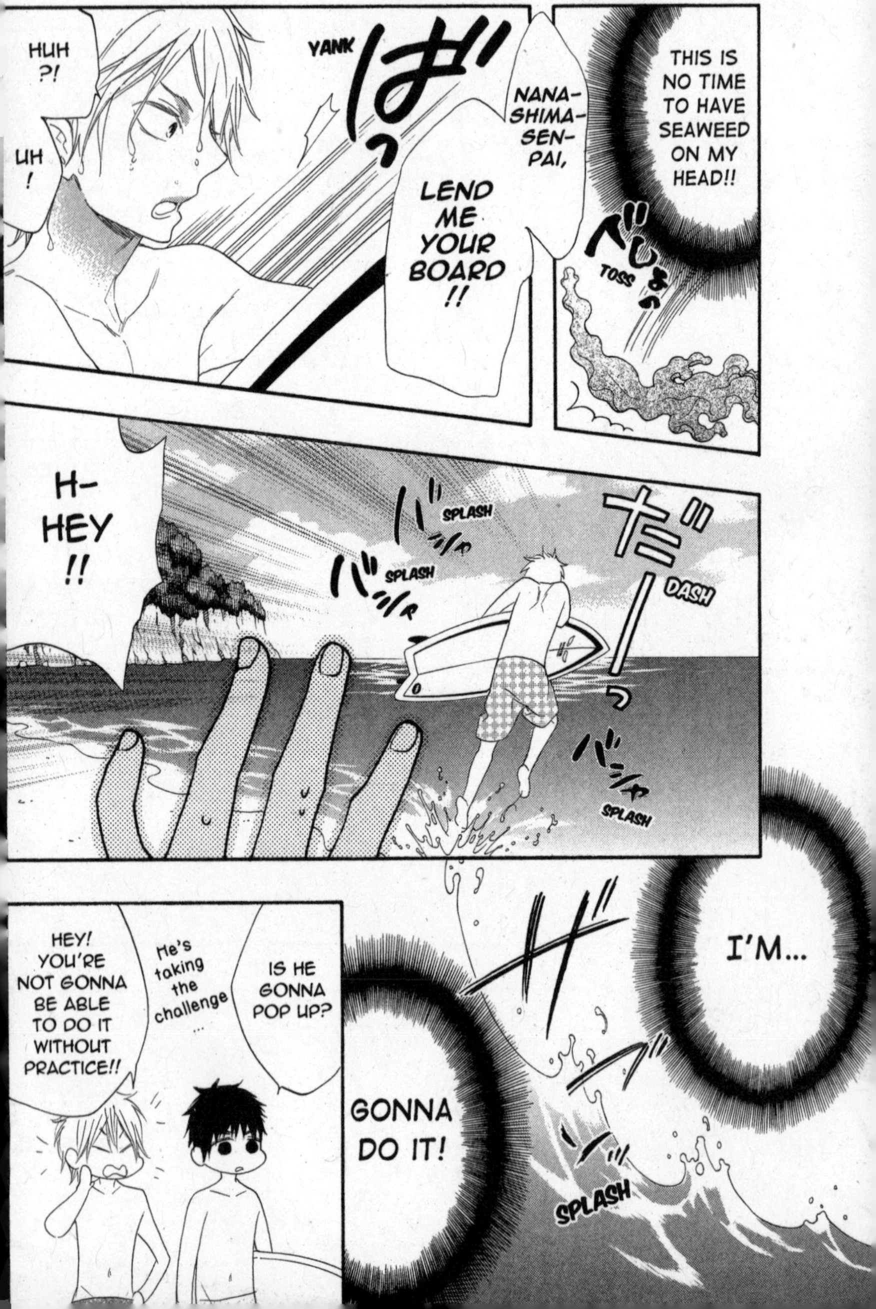
THIS IS NO TIME TO HAVE SEAWEED ON MY HEAD!!
TOSS
NANA-SHIMA-SENPAI,
LEND ME YOUR BOARD!!
YANK
HUH?!
UH!
DASH
SPLASH
SPLASH
SPLASH
H-HEY!!
I'M...
GONNA DO IT!
SPLASH
IS HE GONNA POP UP?
He's taking the challenge...
HEY! YOU'RE NOT GONNA BE ABLE TO DO IT WITHOUT PRACTICE!!

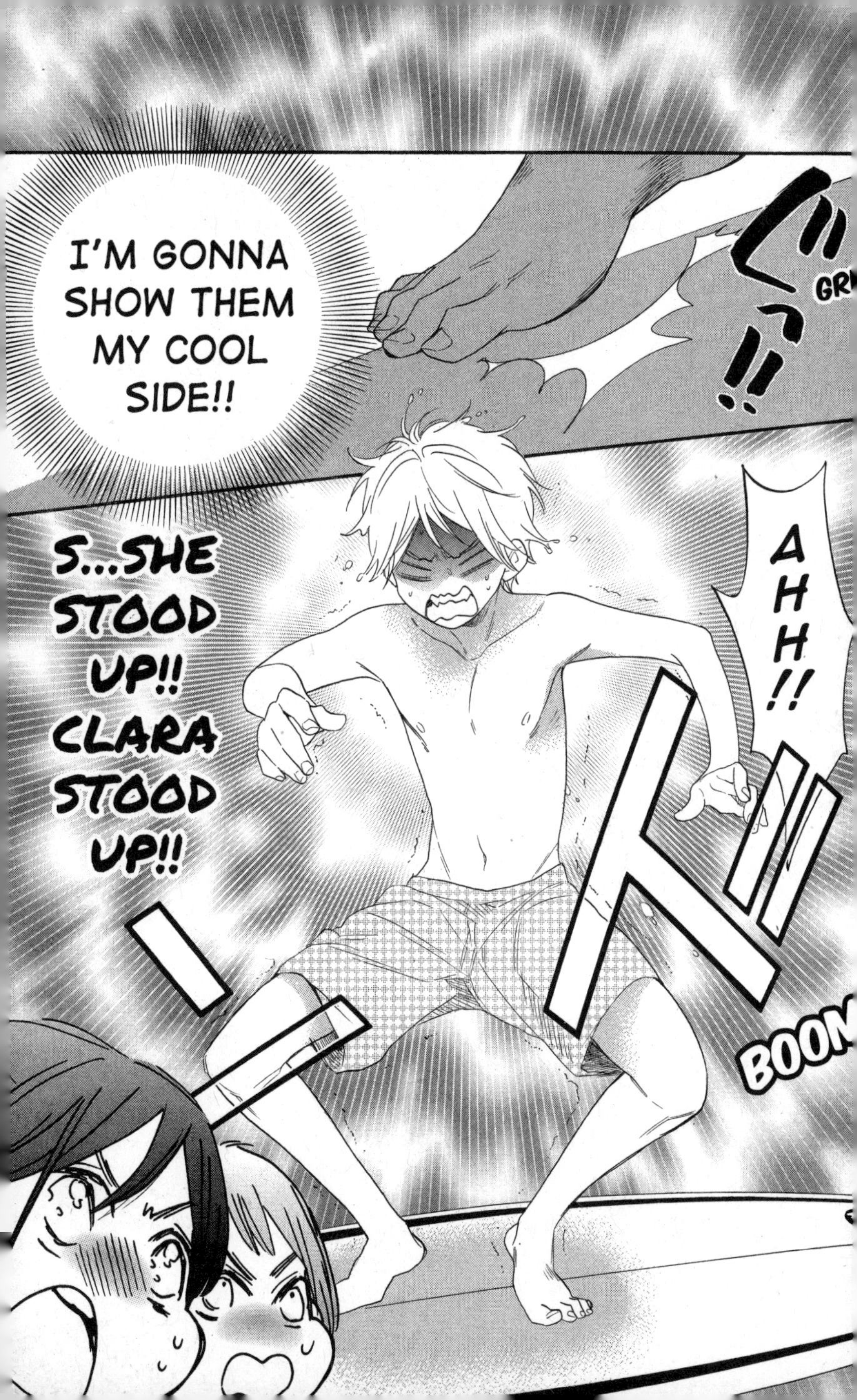
GR
I'M GONNA SHOW THEM MY COOL SIDE!!
AHH!!
S...SHE STOOD UP!! CLARA STOOD UP!!
BOOM

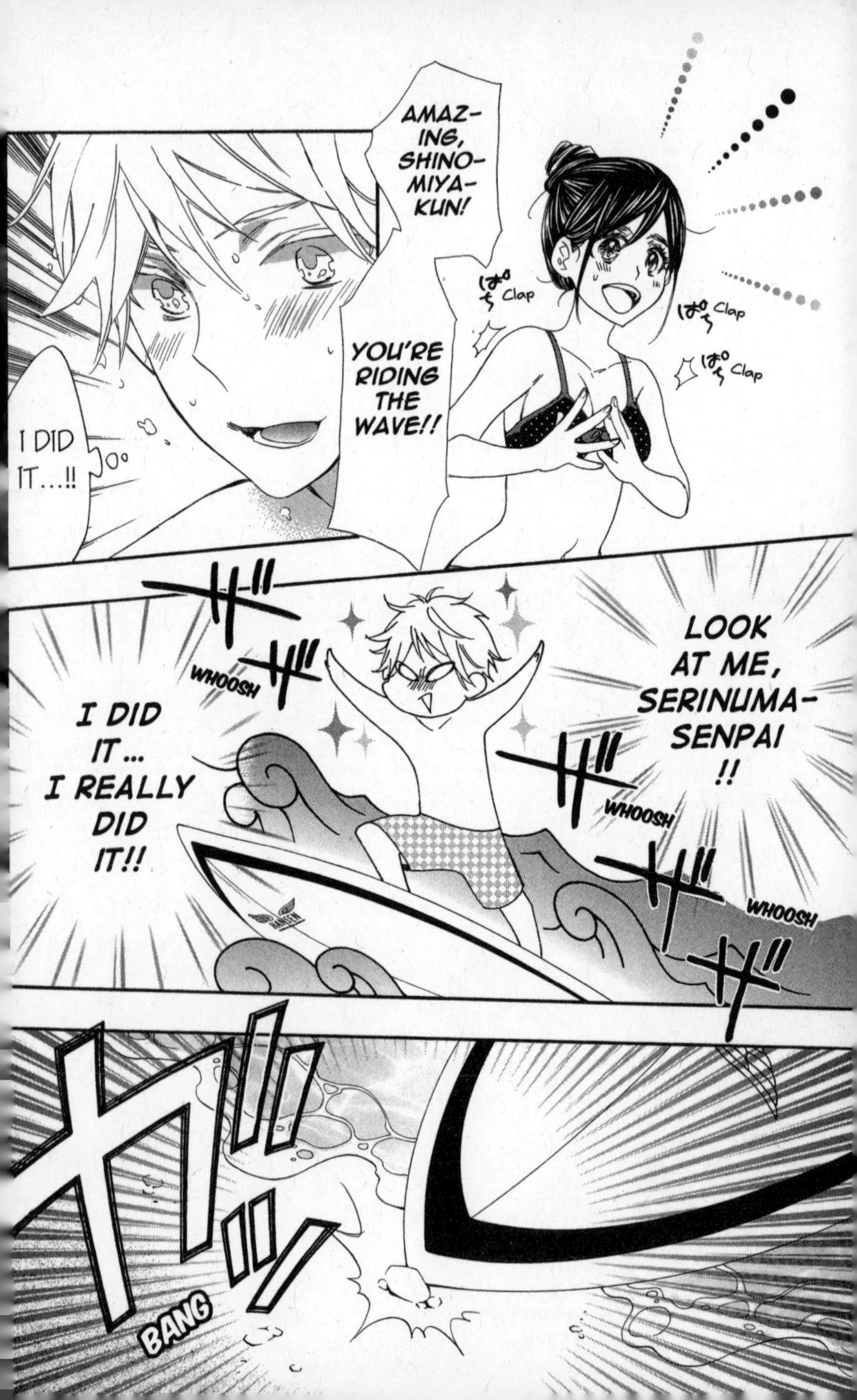
AMAZ-
ING,
SHINO-
MIYA-
KUN!
YOU'RE
RIDING
THE
WAVE!!
Clap
Clap
Clap
I DID
IT...!!
LOOK
AT ME,
SERINUMA-
SENPAI
!!
WHOOSH
WHOOSH
WHOOSH
I DID
IT...
I REALLY
DID
IT!!
BANG

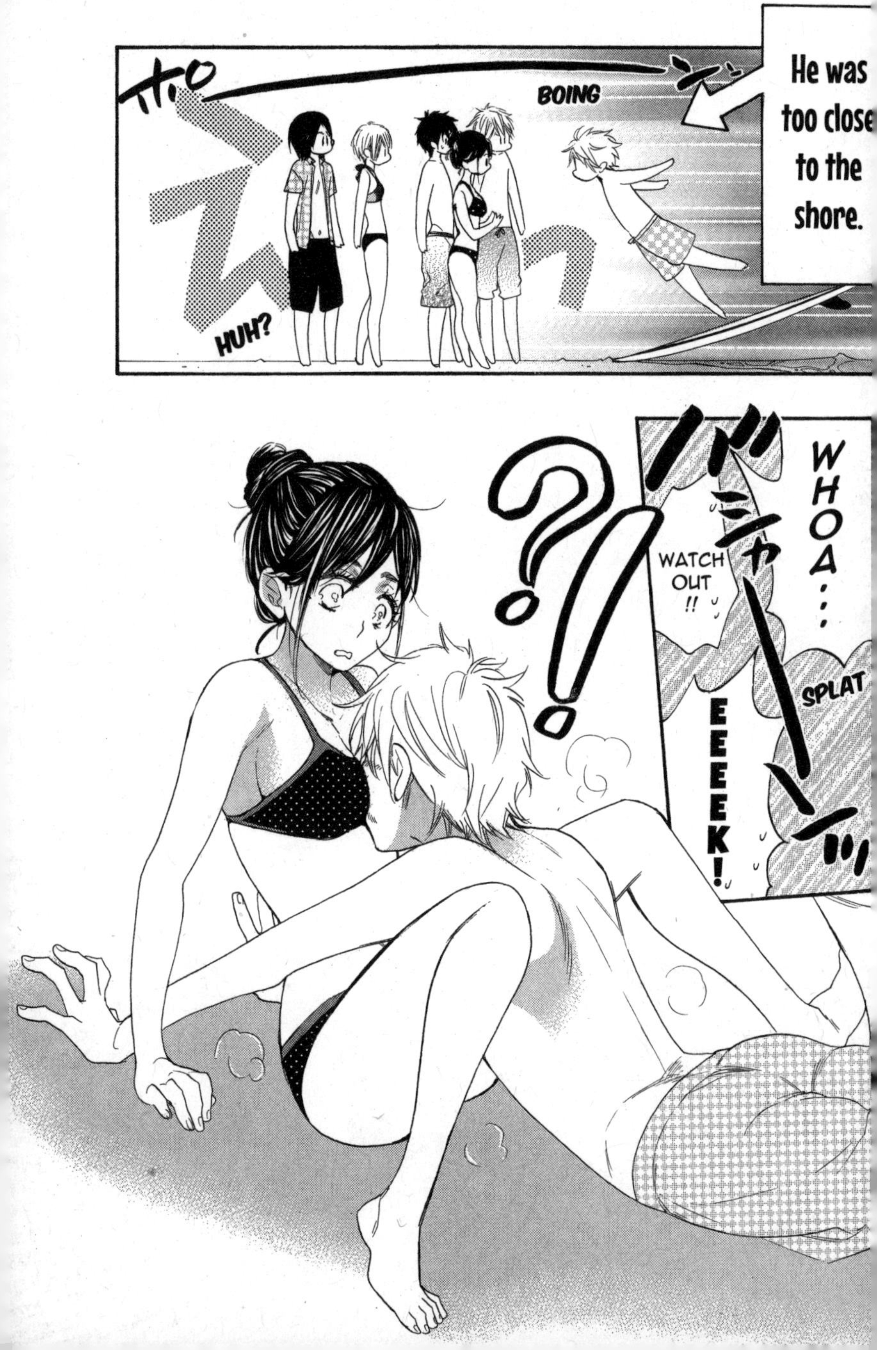
He was too close to the shore.
BOING
HUH?
WHOA...
SPLAT
WATCH OUT!!
EEEEEK!
?!

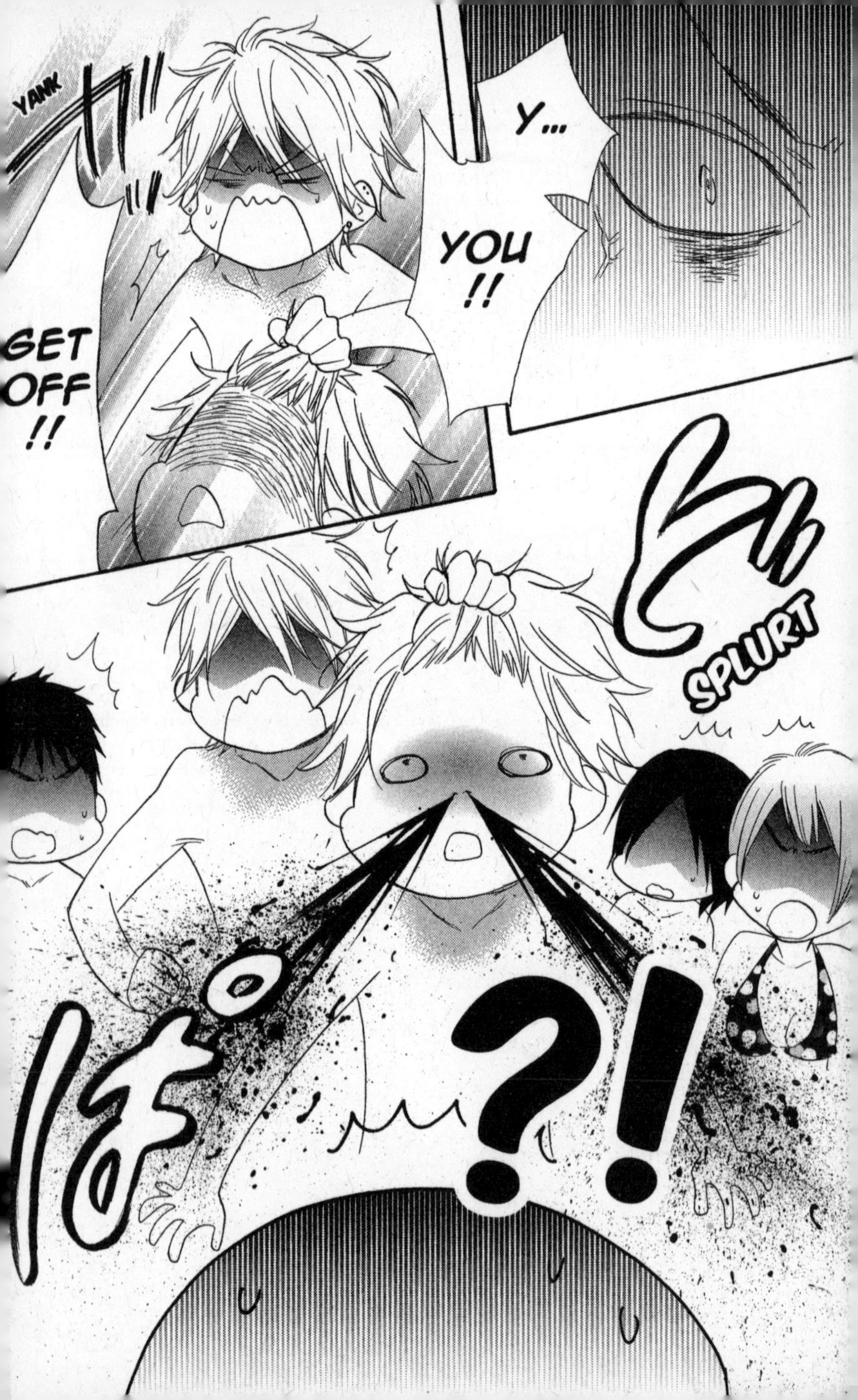
Y...
YOU !!
YANK
GET OFF !!
SPLURT
?!

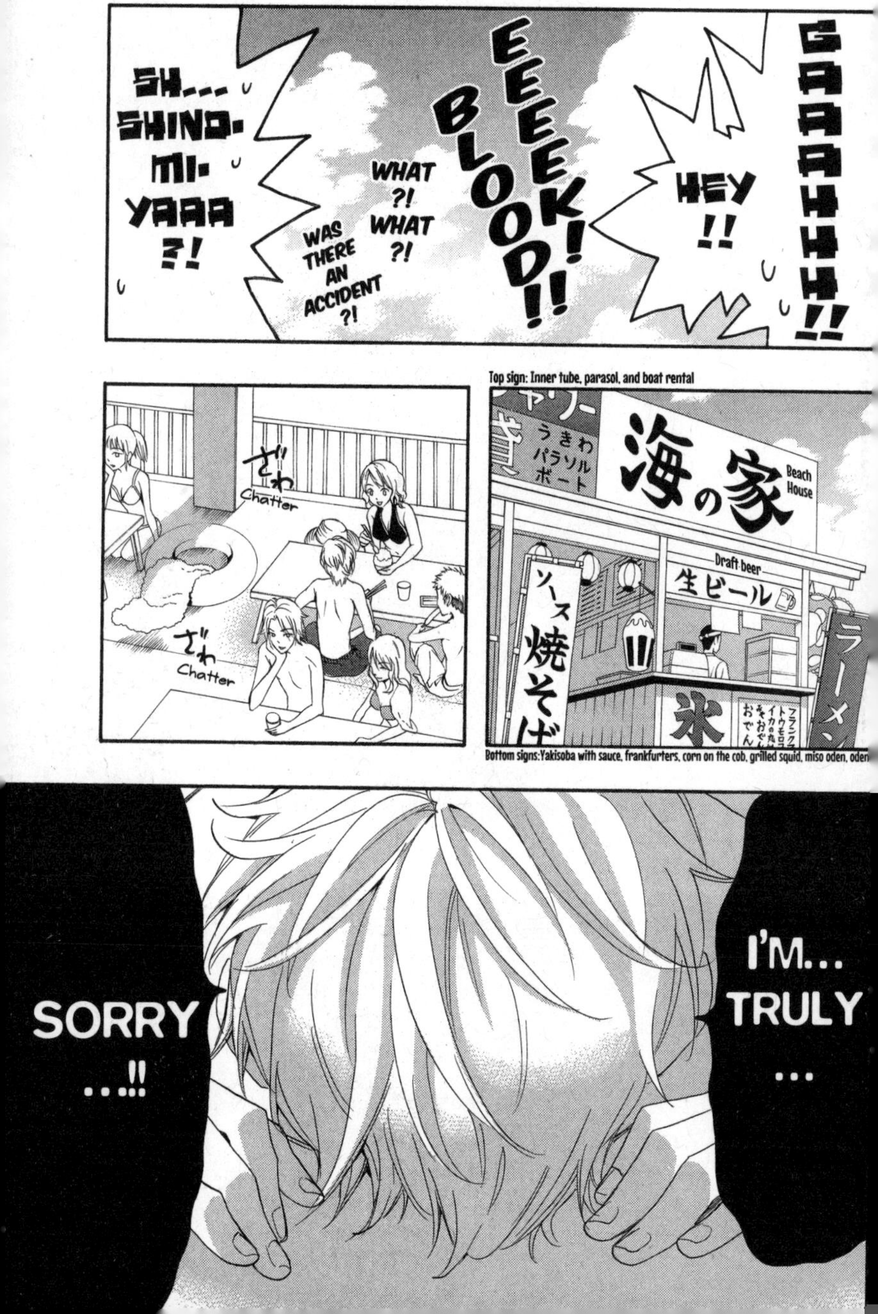
GAAAHHHH!!
HEY!!
EEEEEK! BLOOD!!
WHAT?! WHAT?!
WAS THERE AN ACCIDENT?!
SH... SHINO-MI-YAAA?!
Top sign: Inner tube, parasol, and boat rental
うきわ パラソル ボート
海の家
Beach House
Draft beer
生ビール
ソース焼そば
氷
フランク トウモロコシ イカの丸焼 みそおでん おでん
ラーメン
Bottom signs: Yakisoba with sauce, frankfurters, corn on the cob, grilled squid, miso oden, oden
ざわ
Chatter
ざわ
Chatter
I'M... TRULY...
SORRY...!!

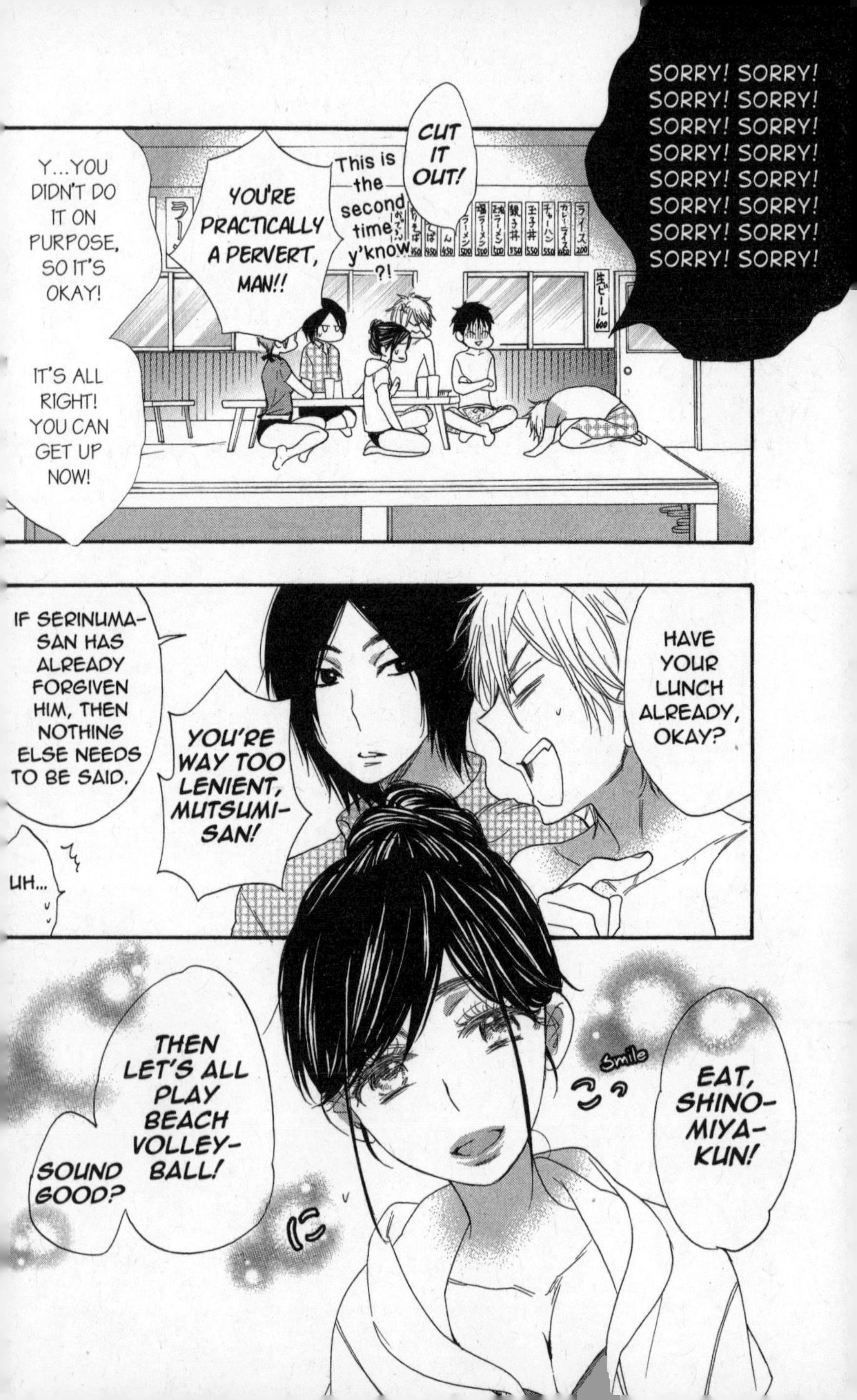
SORRY! SORRY! SORRY! SORRY! SORRY! SORRY! SORRY! SORRY! SORRY! SORRY! SORRY! SORRY! SORRY! SORRY! SORRY! SORRY!
CUT IT OUT!
This is the second time y'know?!
YOU'RE PRACTICALLY A PERVERT, MAN!!
Y...YOU DIDN'T DO IT ON PURPOSE, SO IT'S OKAY!
IT'S ALL RIGHT! YOU CAN GET UP NOW!
HAVE YOUR LUNCH ALREADY, OKAY?
YOU'RE WAY TOO LENIENT, MUTSUMI-SAN!
IF SERINUMA-SAN HAS ALREADY FORGIVEN HIM, THEN NOTHING ELSE NEEDS TO BE SAID.
UH...
EAT, SHINOMIYA-KUN!
Smile
THEN LET'S ALL PLAY BEACH VOLLEYBALL!
SOUND GOOD?

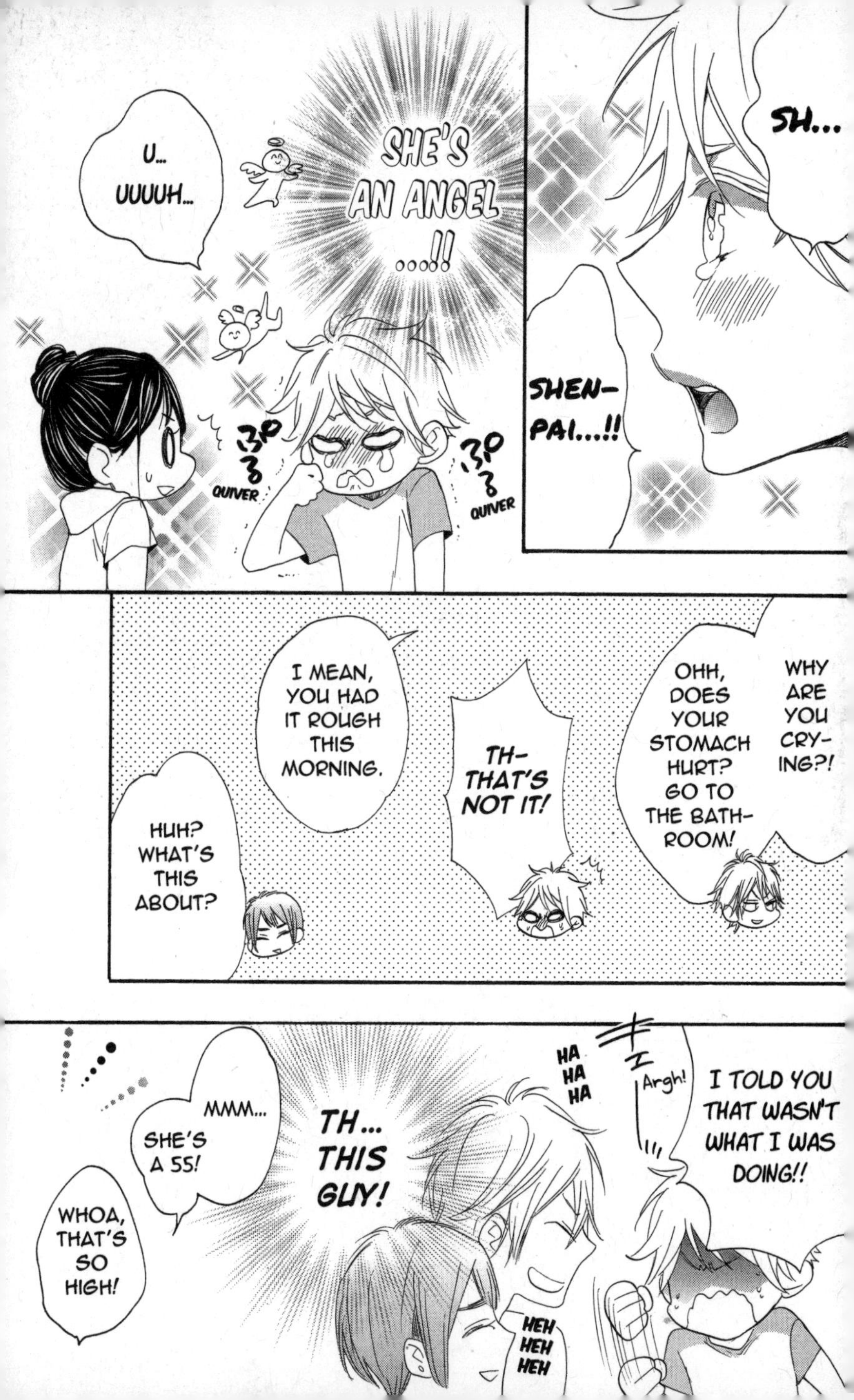
SH...
SHEN-PAI...!!
SHE'S AN ANGEL .....!!
U... UUUUH...
QUIVER
QUIVER
WHY ARE YOU CRY-ING?!
OHH, DOES YOUR STOMACH HURT? GO TO THE BATH-ROOM!
TH- THAT'S NOT IT!
I MEAN, YOU HAD IT ROUGH THIS MORNING.
HUH? WHAT'S THIS ABOUT?
I TOLD YOU THAT WASN'T WHAT I WAS DOING!!
Argh!
HA HA HA
TH... THIS GUY!
MMM... SHE'S A 55!
WHOA, THAT'S SO HIGH!
HEH HEH HEH

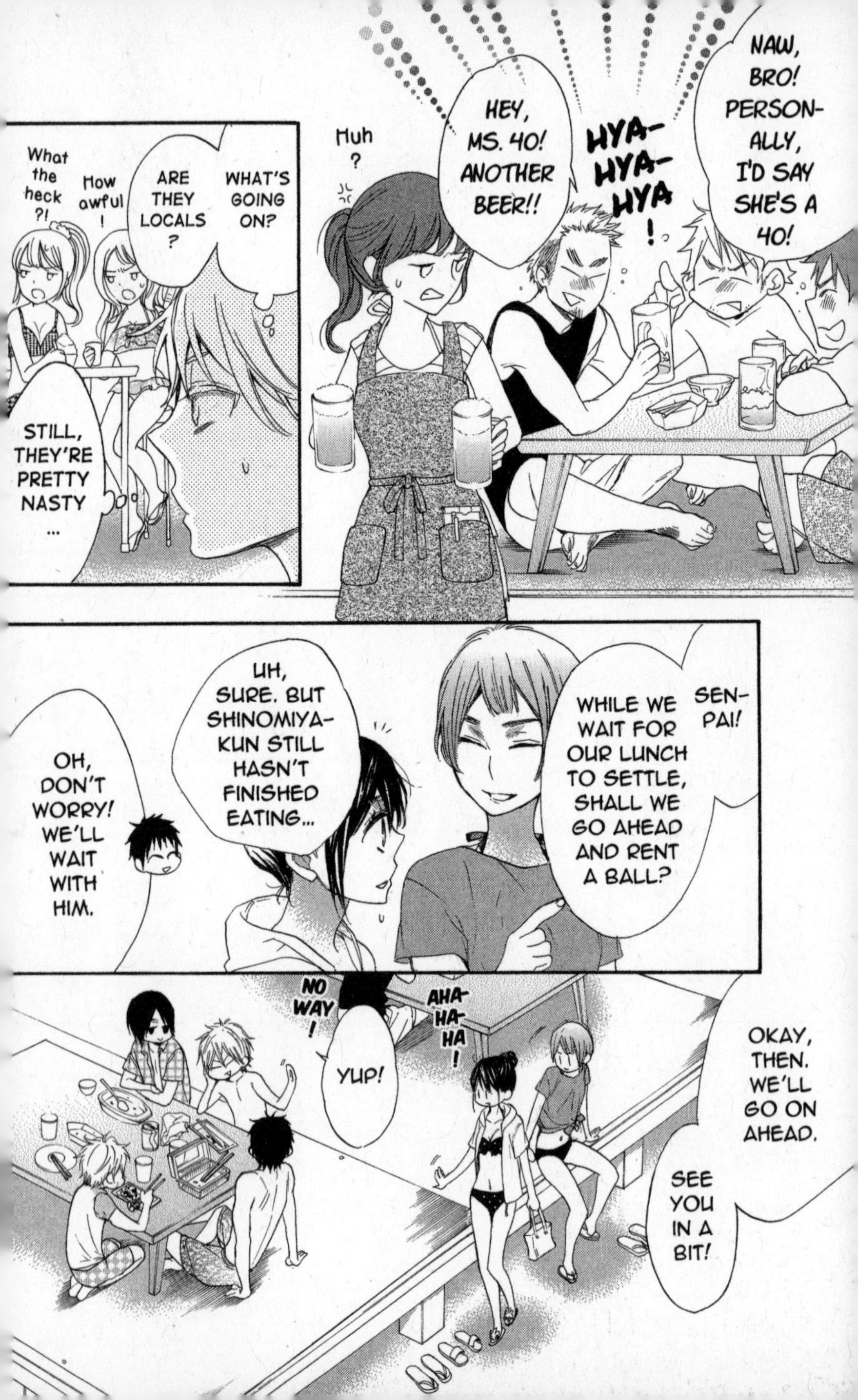
NAW, BRO! PERSON-ALLY, I'D SAY SHE'S A 40!
HYA-HYA-HYA!
HEY, MS. 40! ANOTHER BEER!!
Huh?
WHAT'S GOING ON?
ARE THEY LOCALS?
How awful!
What the heck?!
STILL, THEY'RE PRETTY NASTY...
SEN-PAI!
WHILE WE WAIT FOR OUR LUNCH TO SETTLE, SHALL WE GO AHEAD AND RENT A BALL?
UH, SURE. BUT SHINOMIYA-KUN STILL HASN'T FINISHED EATING...
OH, DON'T WORRY! WE'LL WAIT WITH HIM.
OKAY, THEN. WE'LL GO ON AHEAD.
SEE YOU IN A BIT!
AHA-HA-HA!
YUP!
NO WAY!

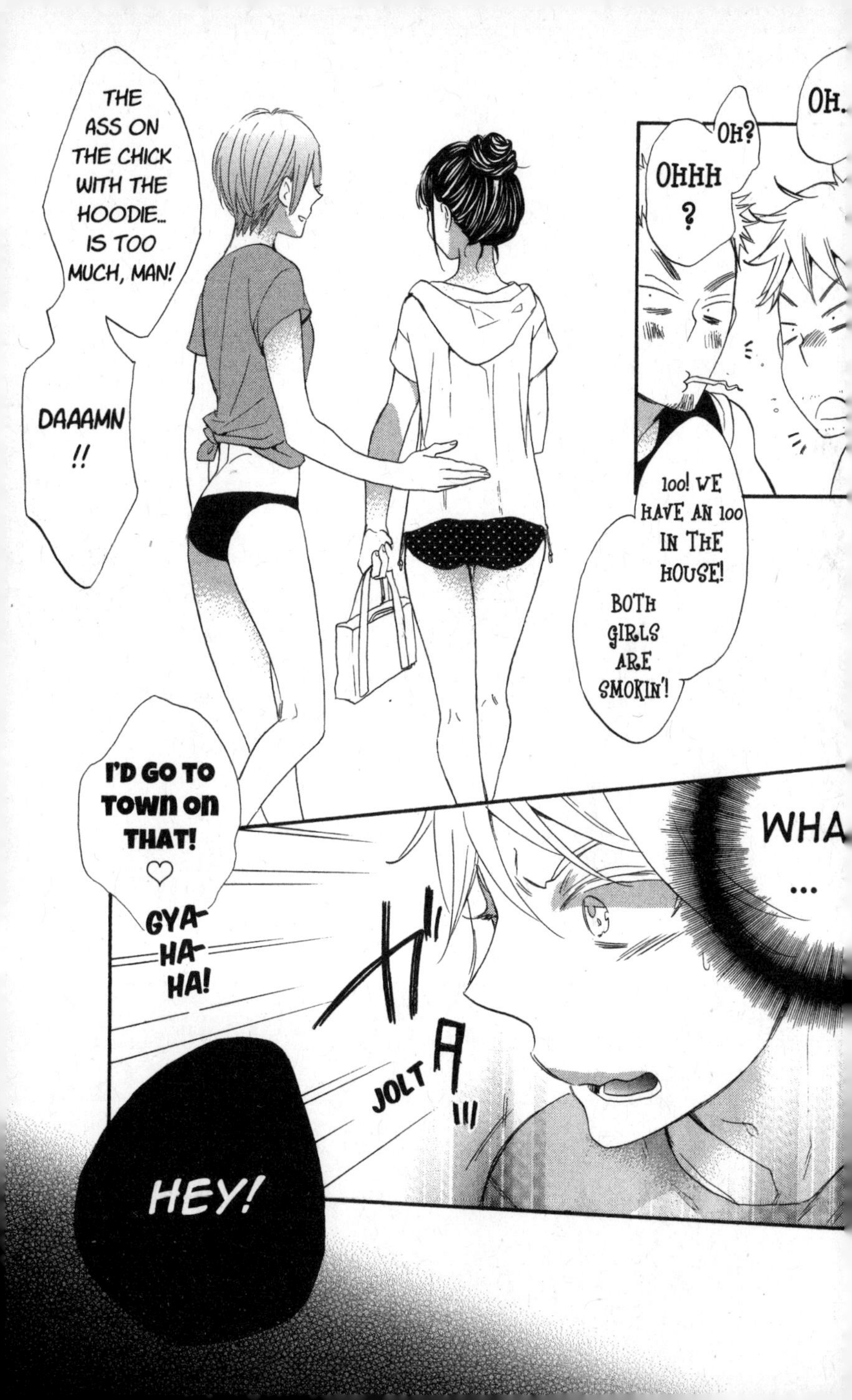
OH.
OH?
OHHH ?
100! WE HAVE AN 100 IN THE HOUSE!
BOTH GIRLS ARE SMOKIN'!
THE ASS ON THE CHICK WITH THE HOODIE... IS TOO MUCH, MAN!
DAAAMN !!
I'D GO TO TOWN ON THAT! ♡
GYA-HA-HA!
WHA ...
JOLT
HEY!

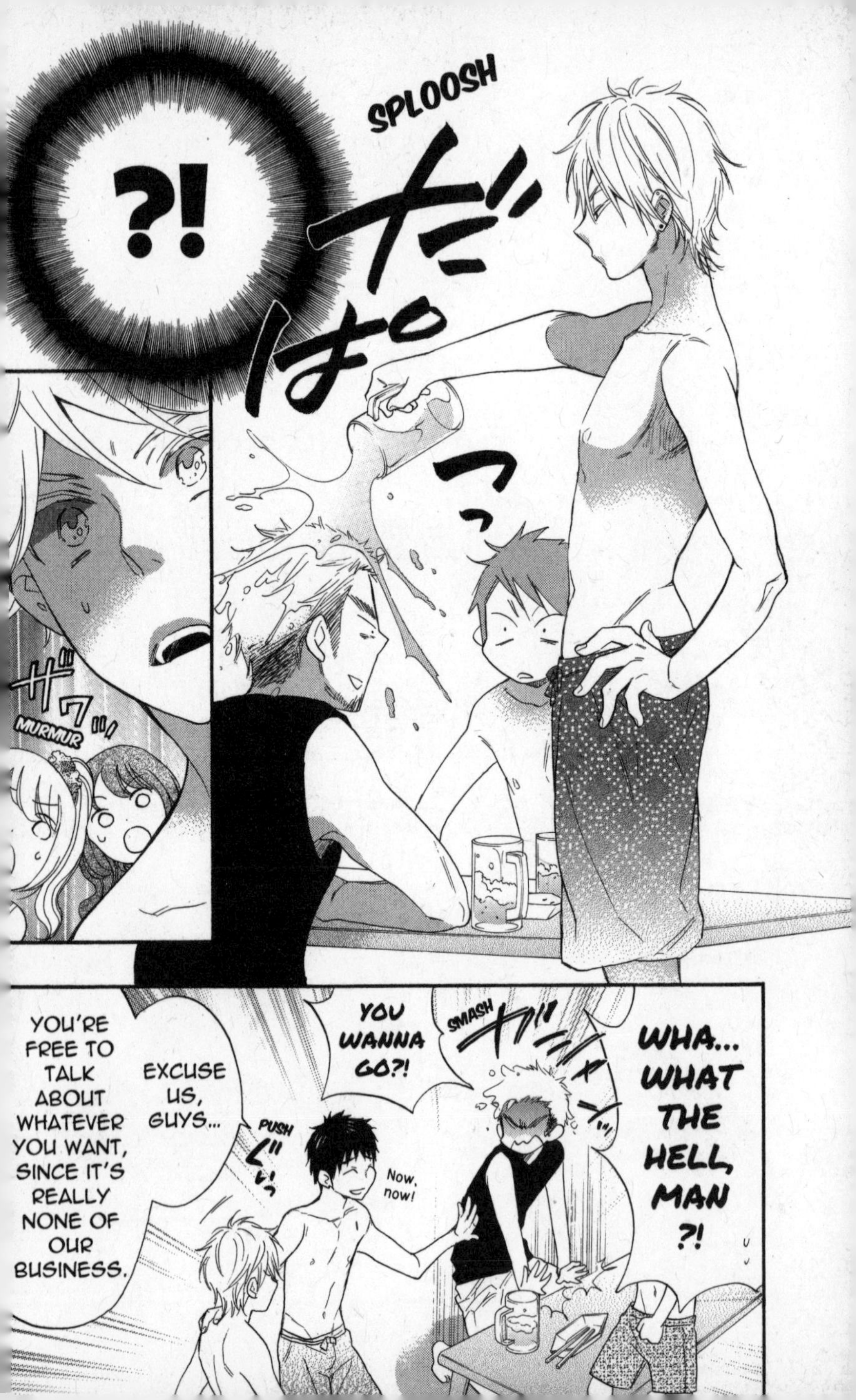
SPLOOSH
?!
MURMUR
WHA... WHAT THE HELL, MAN?!
SMASH
YOU WANNA GO?!
Now, now!
PUSH
EXCUSE US, GUYS...
YOU'RE FREE TO TALK ABOUT WHATEVER YOU WANT, SINCE IT'S REALLY NONE OF OUR BUSINESS.

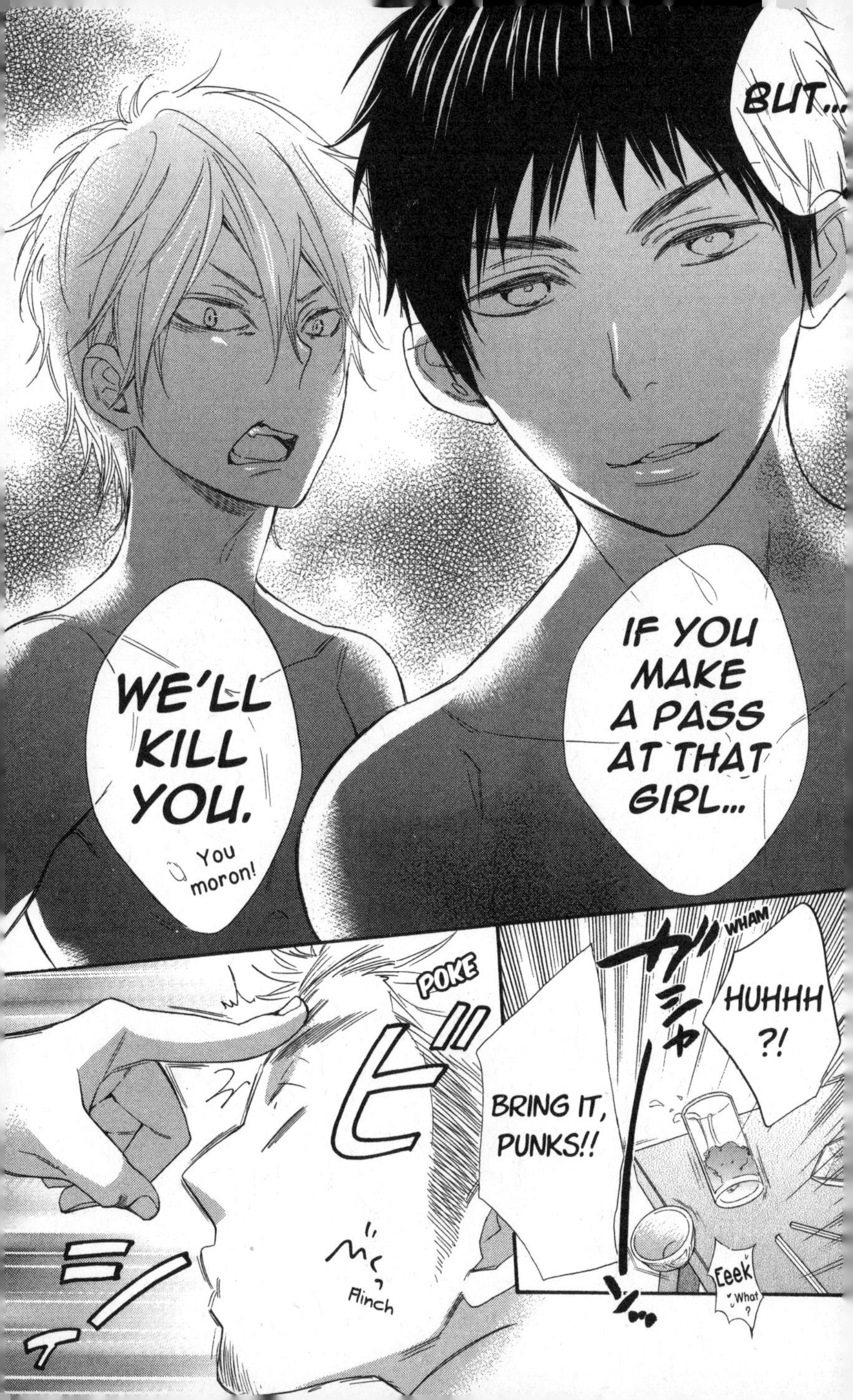
BUT...
IF YOU MAKE A PASS AT THAT GIRL...
WE'LL KILL YOU.
You moron!
WHAM
HUHHH ?!
BRING IT, PUNKS!!
Eeek
What ?
POKE
Flinch

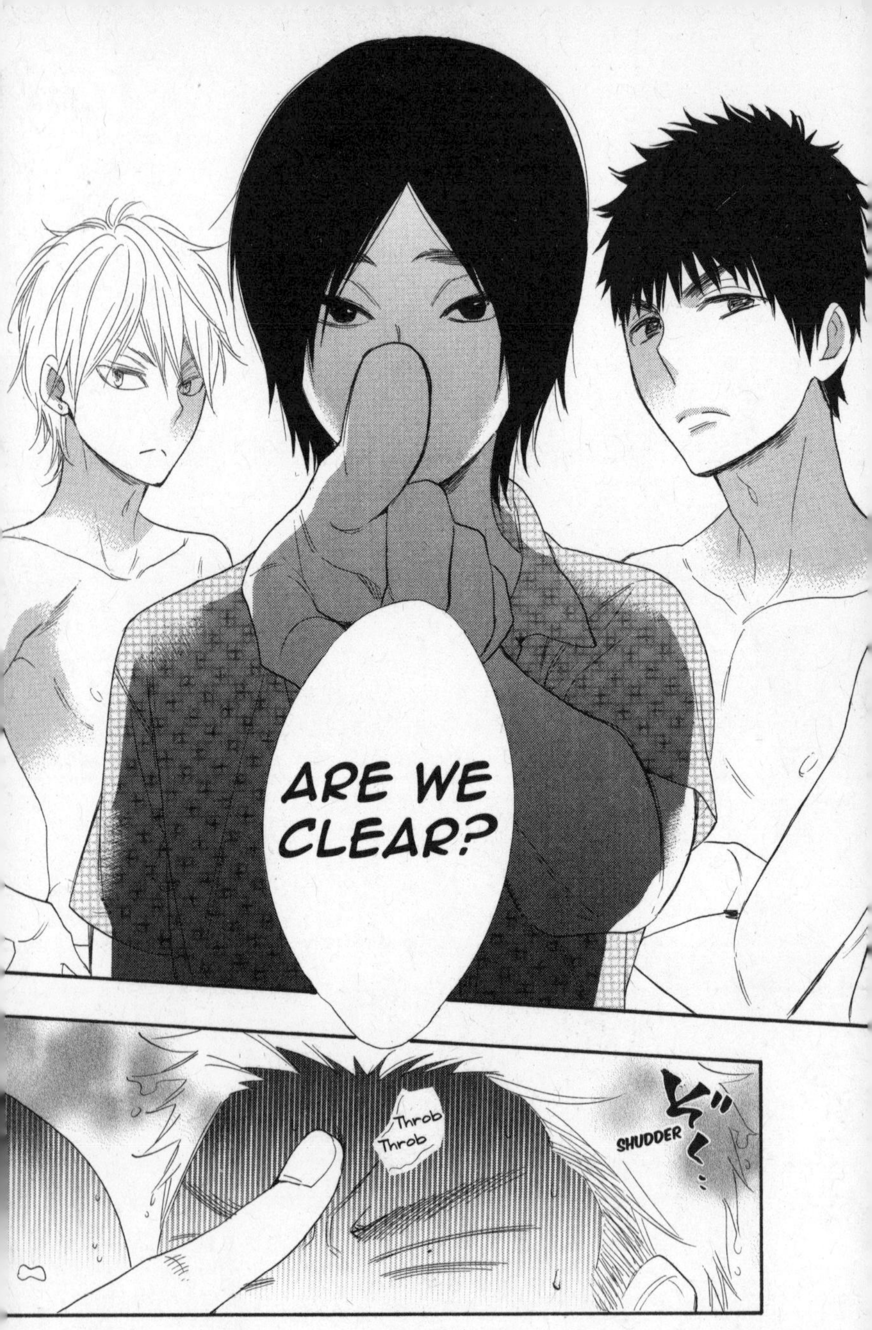
ARE WE CLEAR?
どく…
SHUDDER
Throb Throb

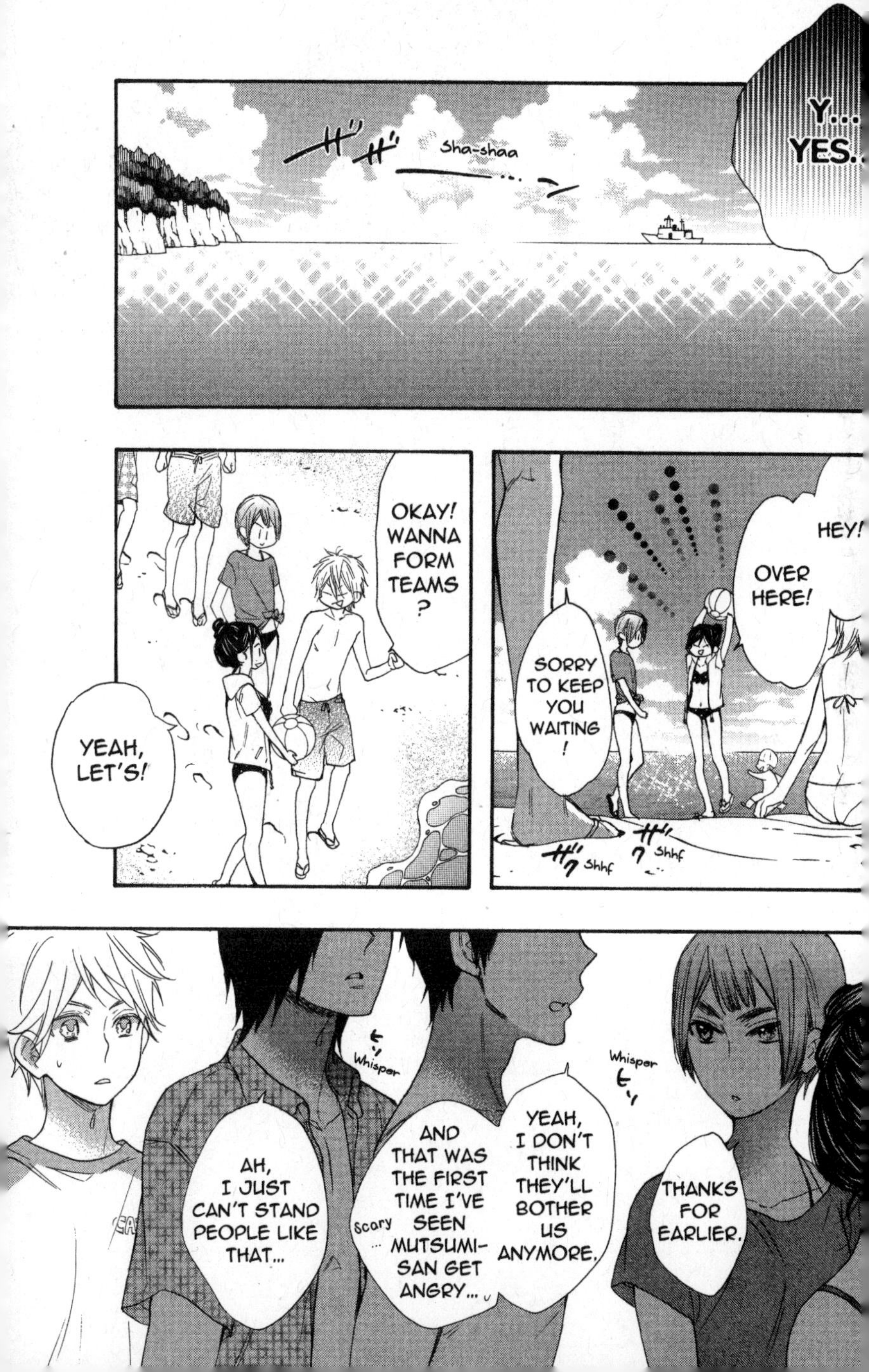
Y... YES...
Sha-shaa
HEY! OVER HERE!
SORRY TO KEEP YOU WAITING!
Shhf
Shhf
OKAY! WANNA FORM TEAMS?
YEAH, LET'S!
THANKS FOR EARLIER.
Whisper
YEAH, I DON'T THINK THEY'LL BOTHER US ANYMORE.
AND THAT WAS THE FIRST TIME I'VE SEEN MUTSUMI-SAN GET ANGRY...
Scary...
Whisper
AH, I JUST CAN'T STAND PEOPLE LIKE THAT...

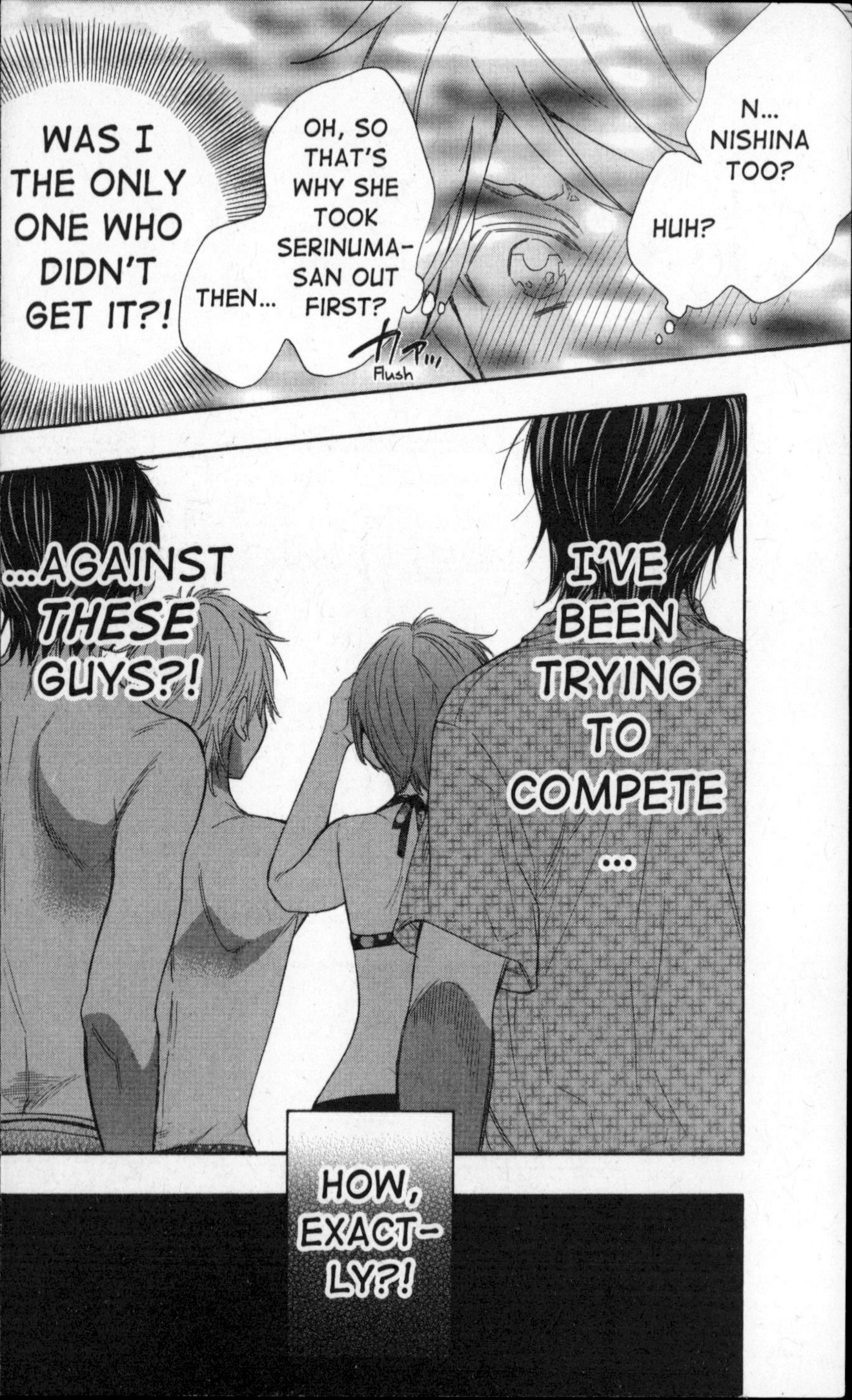
N... NISHINA TOO?
HUH?
OH, SO THAT'S WHY SHE TOOK SERINUMA-SAN OUT FIRST?
THEN...
Flush
WAS I THE ONLY ONE WHO DIDN'T GET IT?!
I'VE BEEN TRYING TO COMPETE...
...AGAINST *THESE* GUYS?!
HOW, EXACT-LY?!

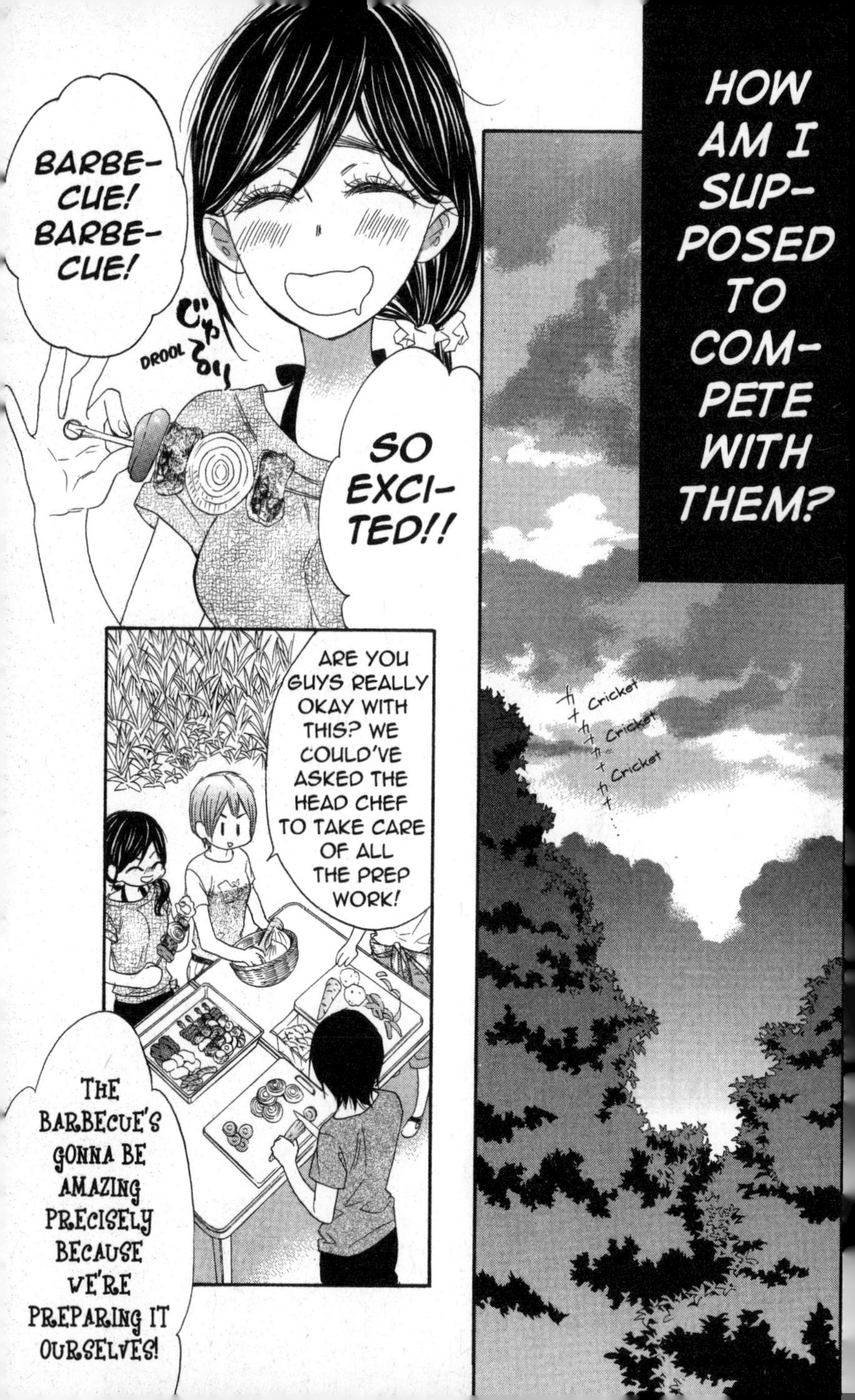
HOW AM I SUPPOSED TO COMPETE WITH THEM?
Cricket Cricket Cricket
BARBECUE! BARBECUE!
DROOL
SO EXCITED!!
ARE YOU GUYS REALLY OKAY WITH THIS? WE COULD'VE ASKED THE HEAD CHEF TO TAKE CARE OF ALL THE PREP WORK!
THE BARBECUE'S GONNA BE AMAZING PRECISELY BECAUSE WE'RE PREPARING IT OURSELVES!

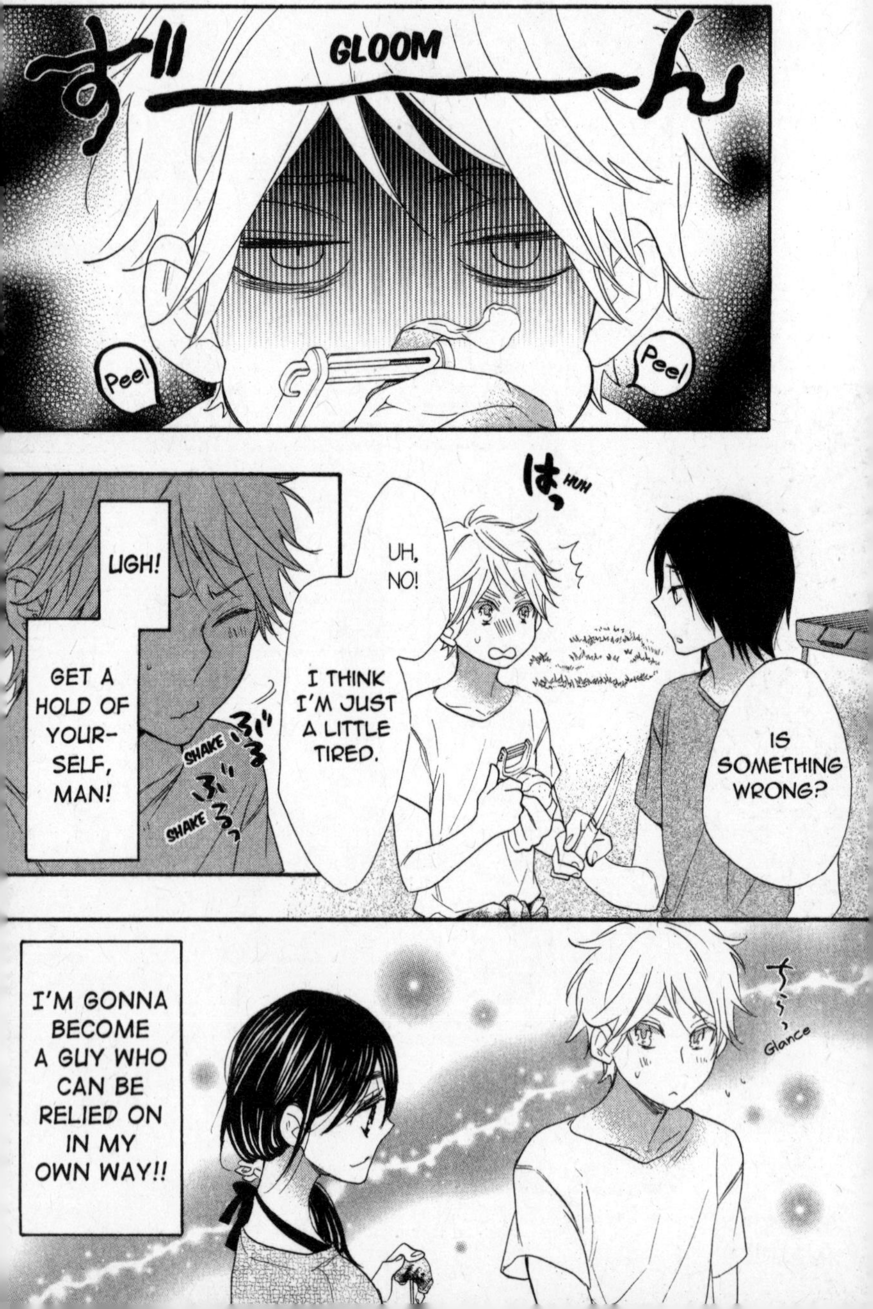
すーーーん
GLOOM
Peel
Peel
はっ
HUH
IS SOMETHING WRONG?
UH, NO!
I THINK I'M JUST A LITTLE TIRED.
UGH!
GET A HOLD OF YOUR-SELF, MAN!
ぶるぶるっ
SHAKE
SHAKE
ちらっ
Glance
I'M GONNA BECOME A GUY WHO CAN BE RELIED ON IN MY OWN WAY!!

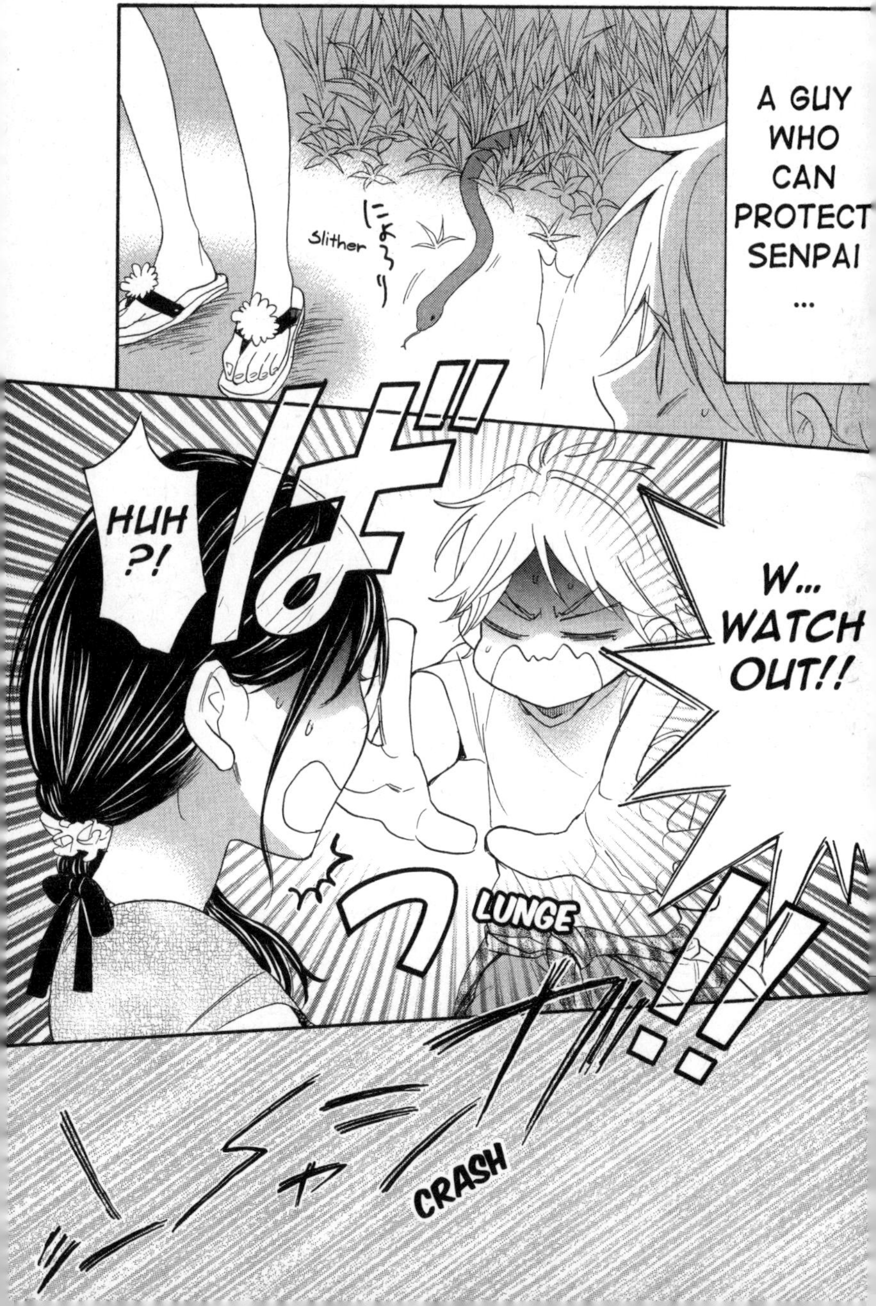
A GUY WHO CAN PROTECT SENPAI ...
にょろり
Slither
W... WATCH OUT!!
HUH ?!
LUNGE
CRASH

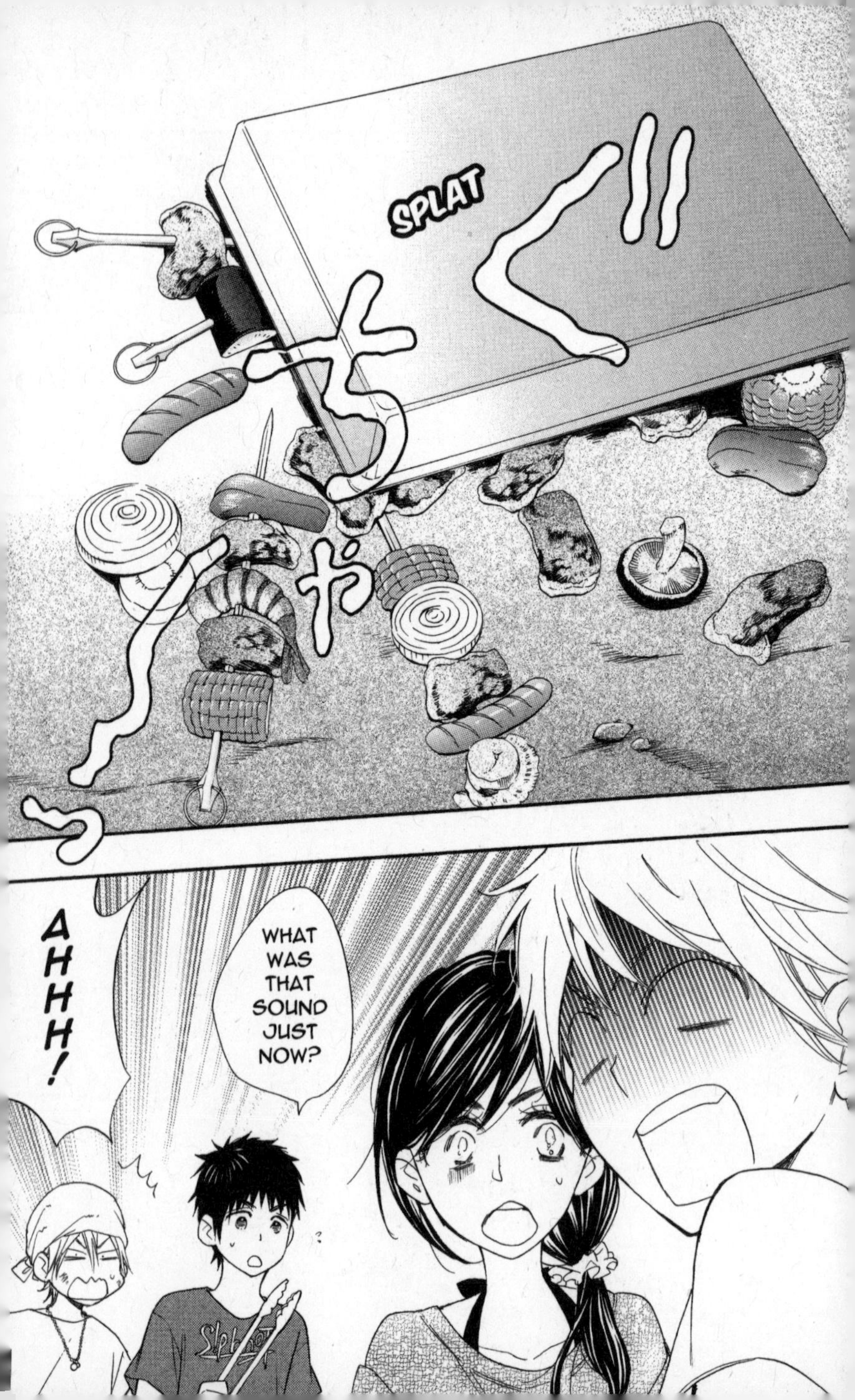
SPLAT
WHAT WAS THAT SOUND JUST NOW?
AHHHH!

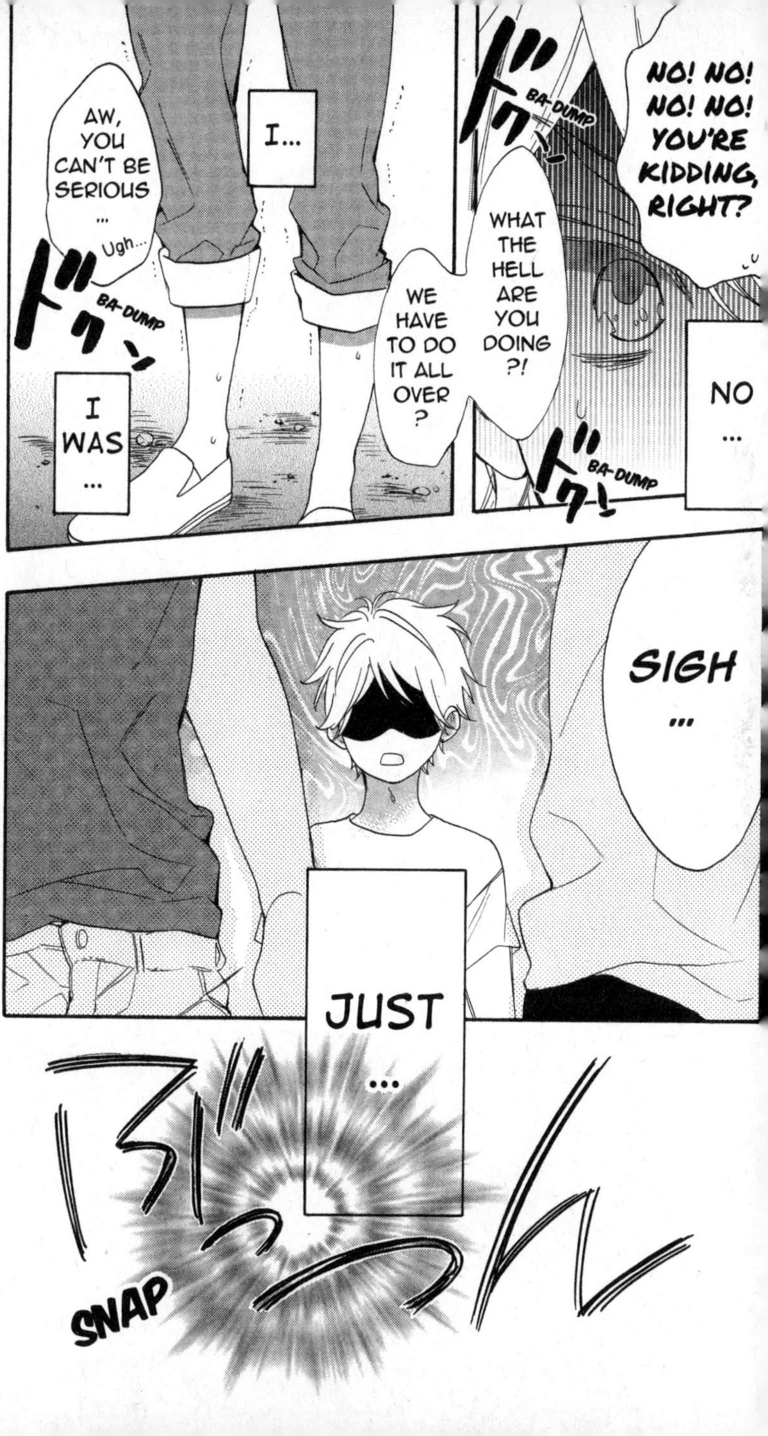
NO! NO! NO! NO! YOU'RE KIDDING, RIGHT?
BA-DUMP
WHAT THE HELL ARE YOU DOING ?!
NO ...
BA-DUMP
WE HAVE TO DO IT ALL OVER ?
I...
AW, YOU CAN'T BE SERIOUS ...
Ugh...
BA-DUMP
I WAS ...
SIGH ...
JUST ...
SNAP

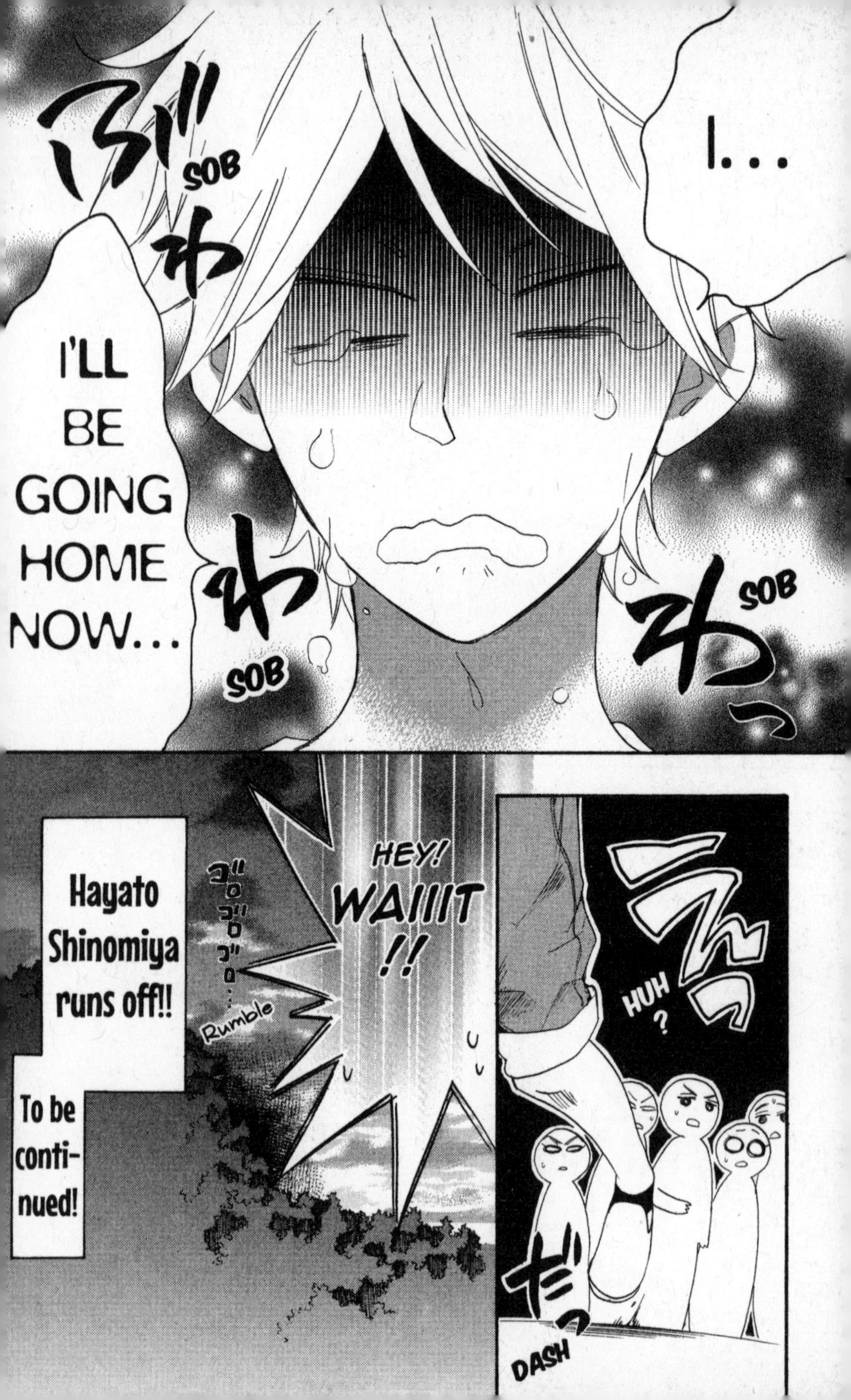
I...
SOB
SOB
I'LL BE GOING HOME NOW...
SOB
HUH?
DASH
HEY! WAIIIT!!
Rumble
Hayato Shinomiya runs off!!
To be continued!

#16 I WILL PROTECT HER!

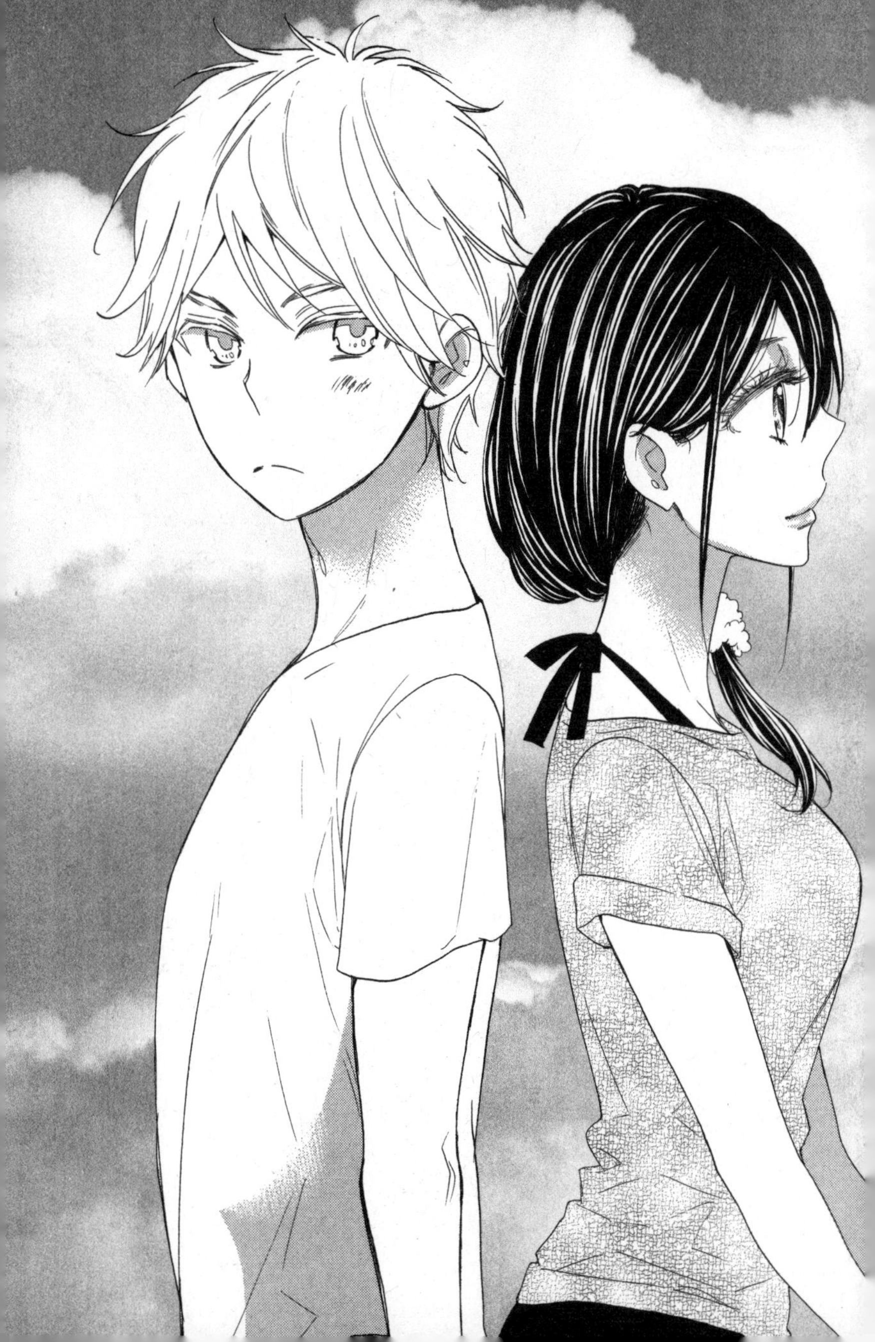

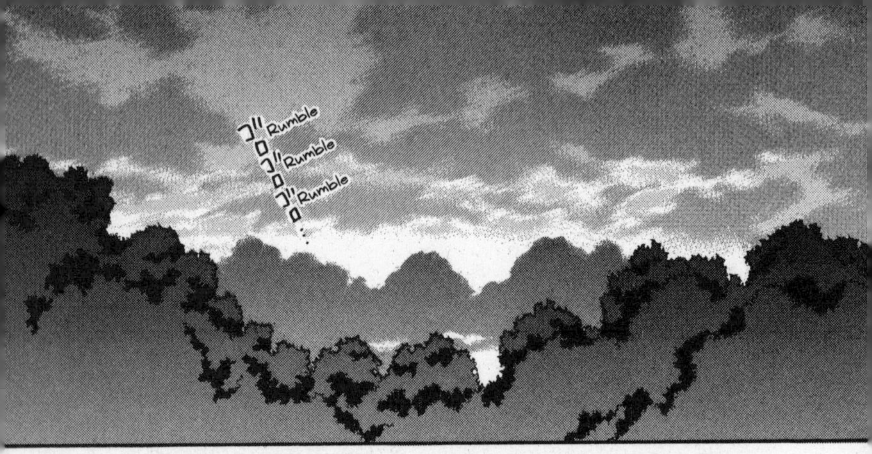
Rumble
Rumble
Rumble

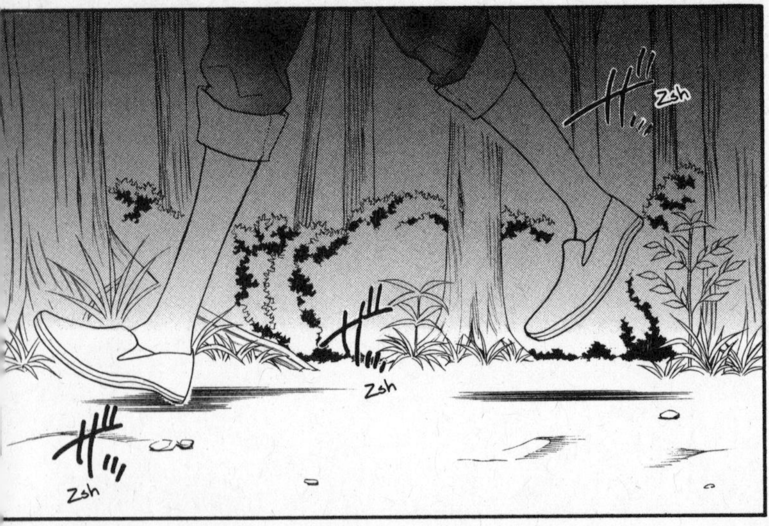
Zsh
Zsh
Zsh

KiSS HiM, NOT ME!

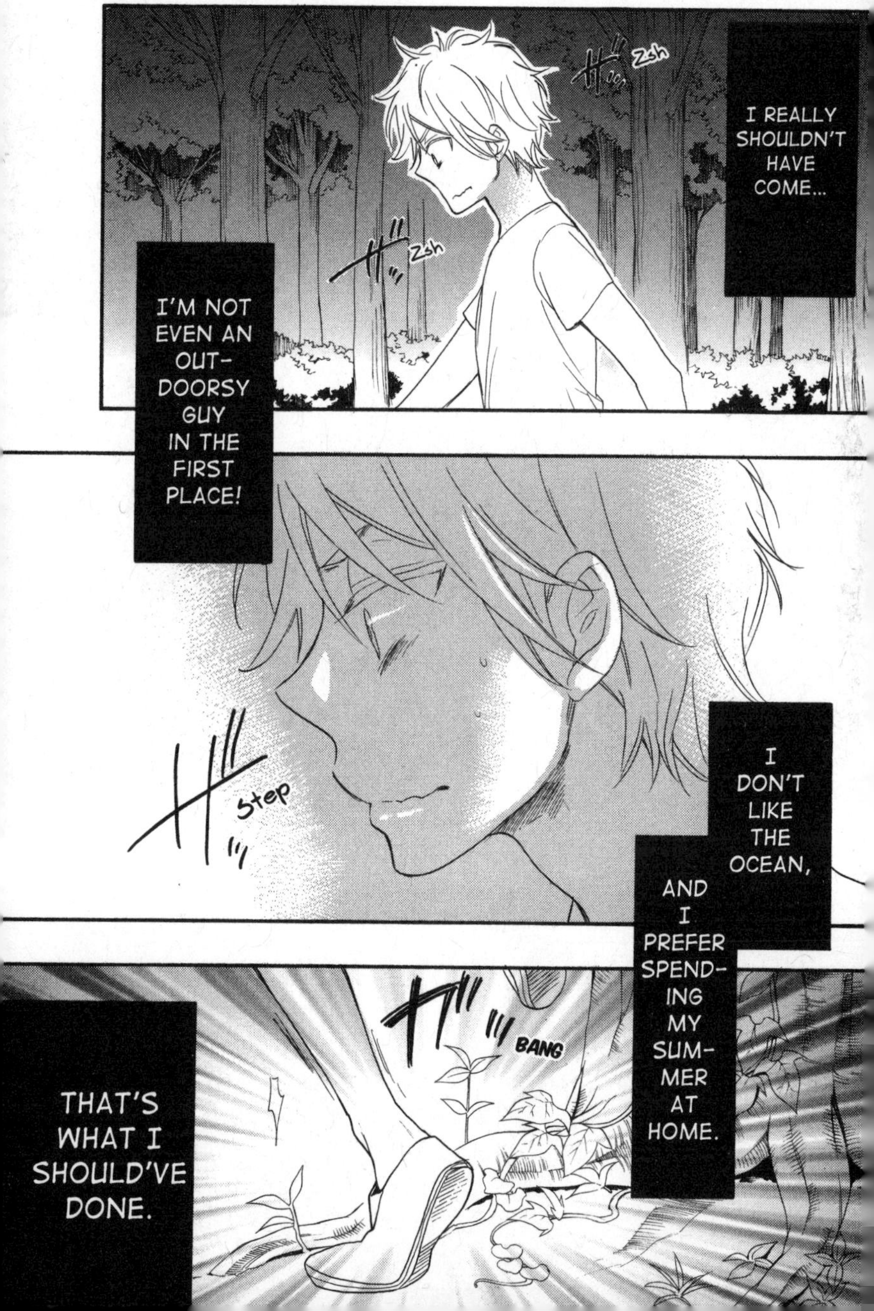
I REALLY SHOULDN'T HAVE COME...
Zsh
Zsh
I'M NOT EVEN AN OUT-DOORSY GUY IN THE FIRST PLACE!
I DON'T LIKE THE OCEAN,
AND I PREFER SPEND-ING MY SUM-MER AT HOME.
Step
BANG
THAT'S WHAT I SHOULD'VE DONE.

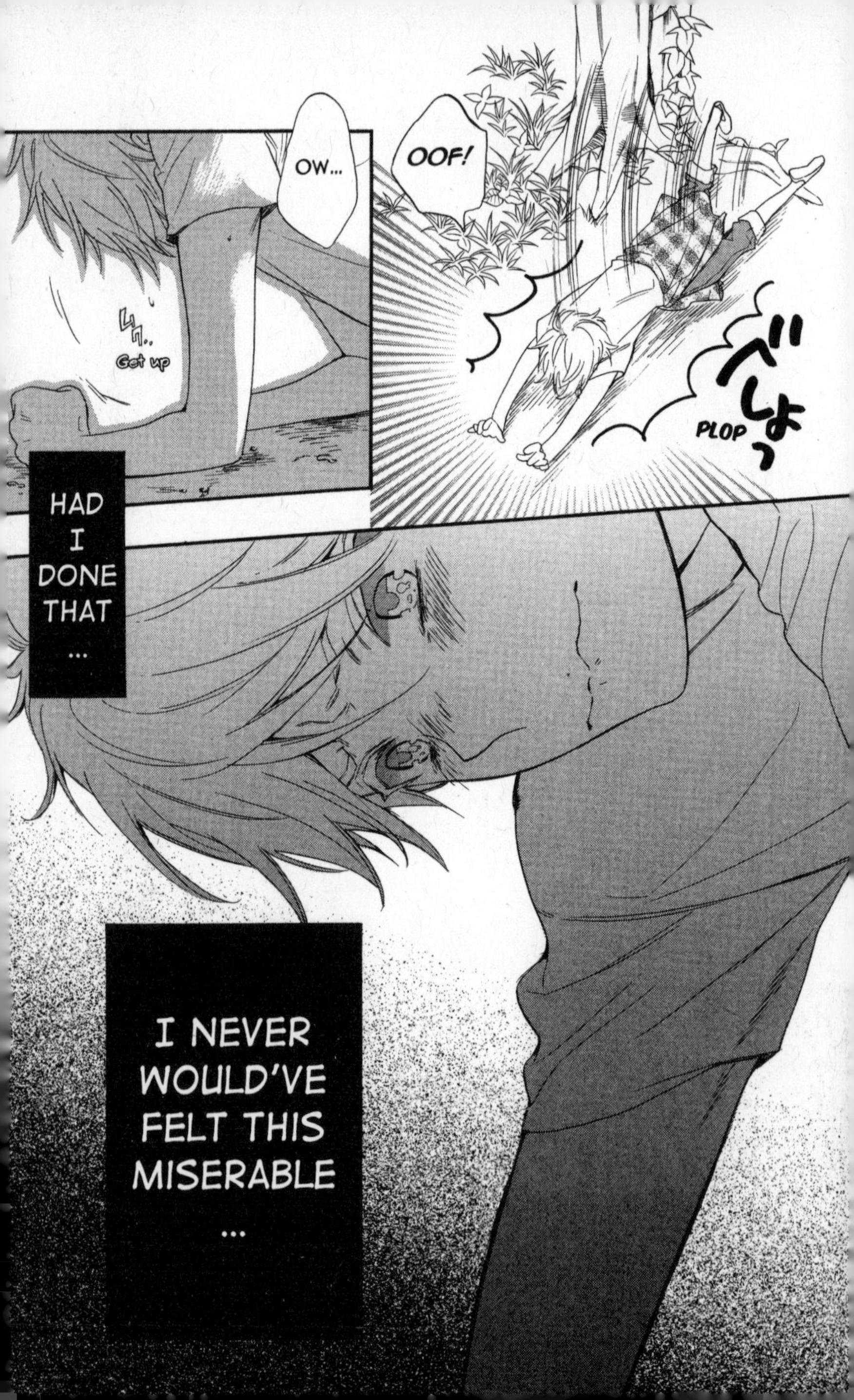
OOF!
べしょっ
PLOP
OW...
Get up
HAD I DONE THAT ...
I NEVER WOULD'VE FELT THIS MISERABLE ...

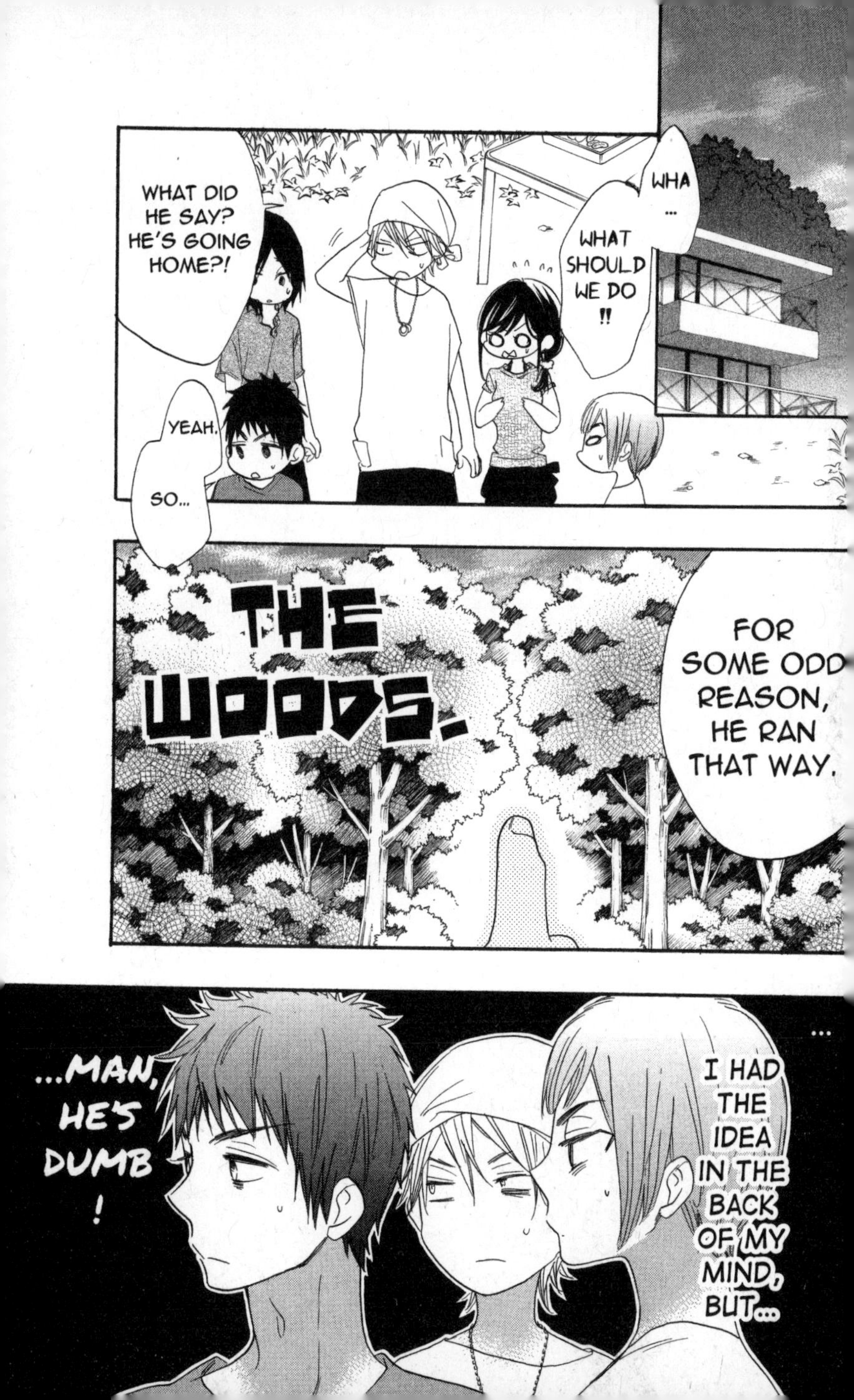
WHA ... WHAT SHOULD WE DO !!
WHAT DID HE SAY? HE'S GOING HOME?!
YEAH.
SO...
FOR SOME ODD REASON, HE RAN THAT WAY.
THE WOODS.
... I HAD THE IDEA IN THE BACK OF MY MIND, BUT...
...MAN, HE'S DUMB!

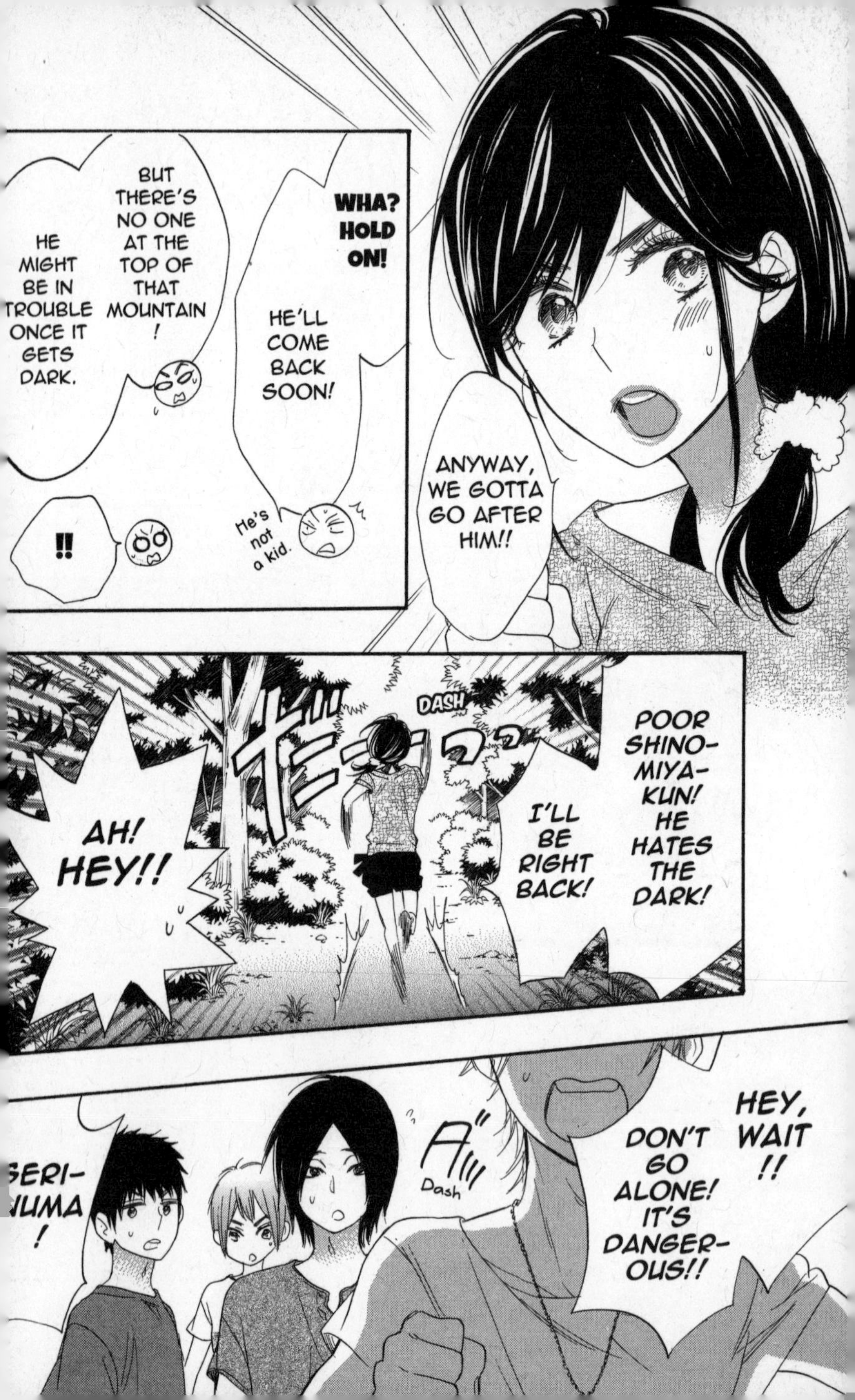
WHA? HOLD ON!
HE'LL COME BACK SOON!
He's not a kid.
BUT THERE'S NO ONE AT THE TOP OF THAT MOUNTAIN!
HE MIGHT BE IN TROUBLE ONCE IT GETS DARK.
!!
ANYWAY, WE GOTTA GO AFTER HIM!!
POOR SHINOMIYA-KUN! HE HATES THE DARK!
I'LL BE RIGHT BACK!
DASH
AH! HEY!!
HEY, WAIT!!
DON'T GO ALONE! IT'S DANGEROUS!!
A"
Dash
SERI-NUMA!

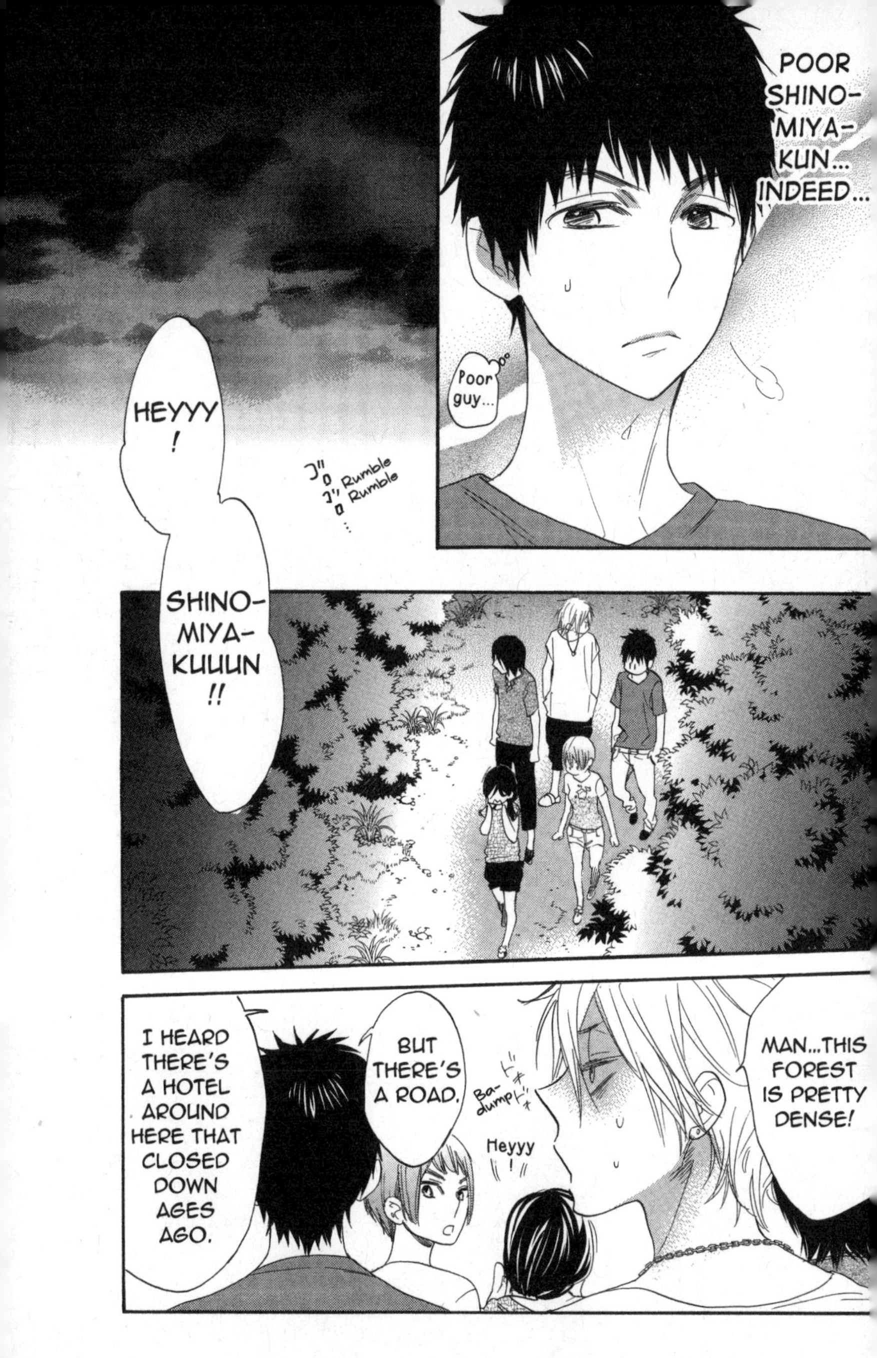
POOR SHINOMIYA-KUN... INDEED...
Poor guy...
HEYYY! SHINOMIYA-KUUUN!!
Rumble Rumble
MAN...THIS FOREST IS PRETTY DENSE!
Ba-dump
Heyyy!
BUT THERE'S A ROAD.
I HEARD THERE'S A HOTEL AROUND HERE THAT CLOSED DOWN AGES AGO.

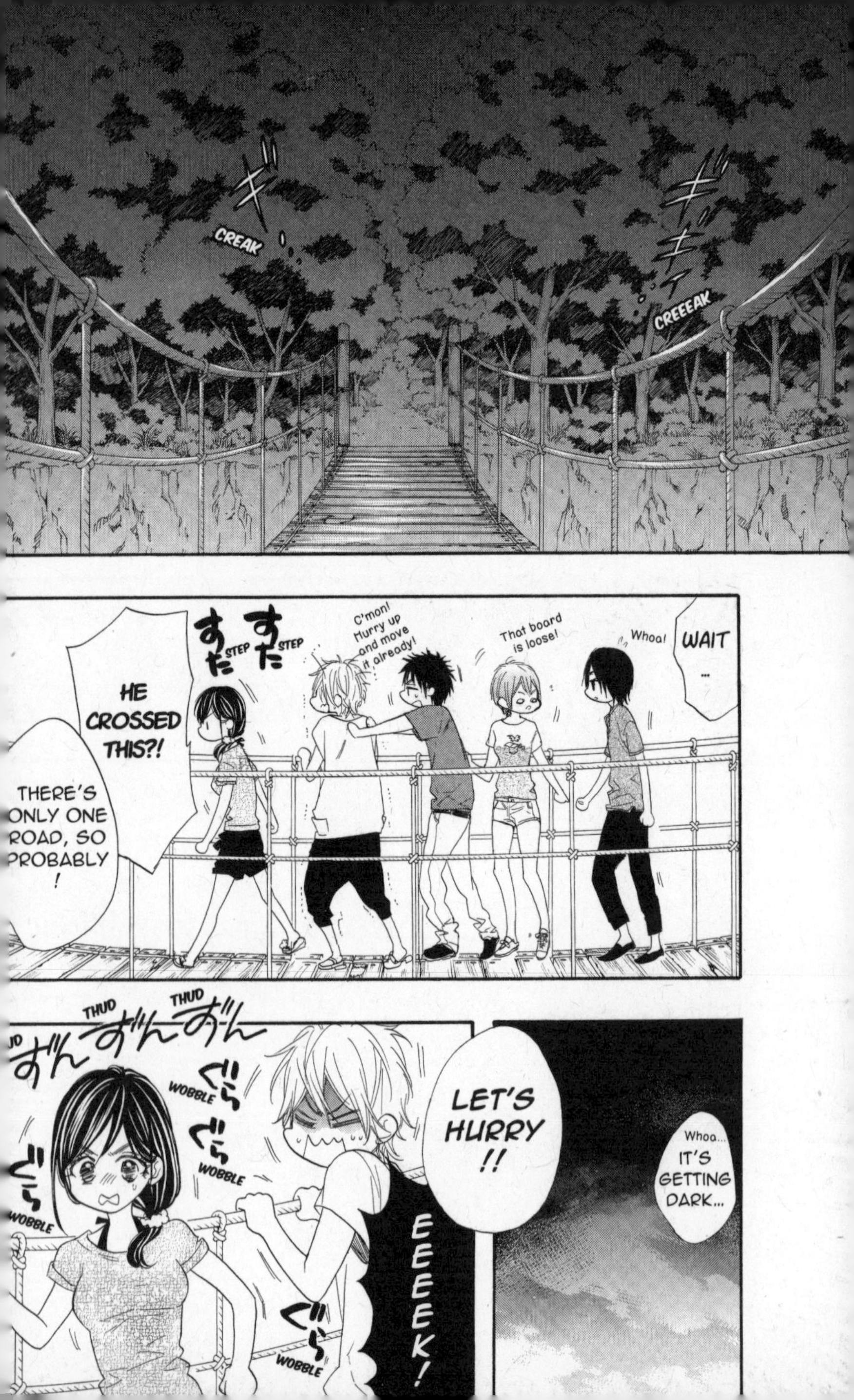
CREEEAK
CREAK
WAIT ...
Whoa!
That board is loose!
C'mon! Hurry up and move it already!
STEP STEP
HE CROSSED THIS?!
THERE'S ONLY ONE ROAD, SO PROBABLY!
Whoa... IT'S GETTING DARK...
LET'S HURRY!!
EEEEEK!
THUD THUD
WOBBLE
WOBBLE
WOBBLE
WOBBLE

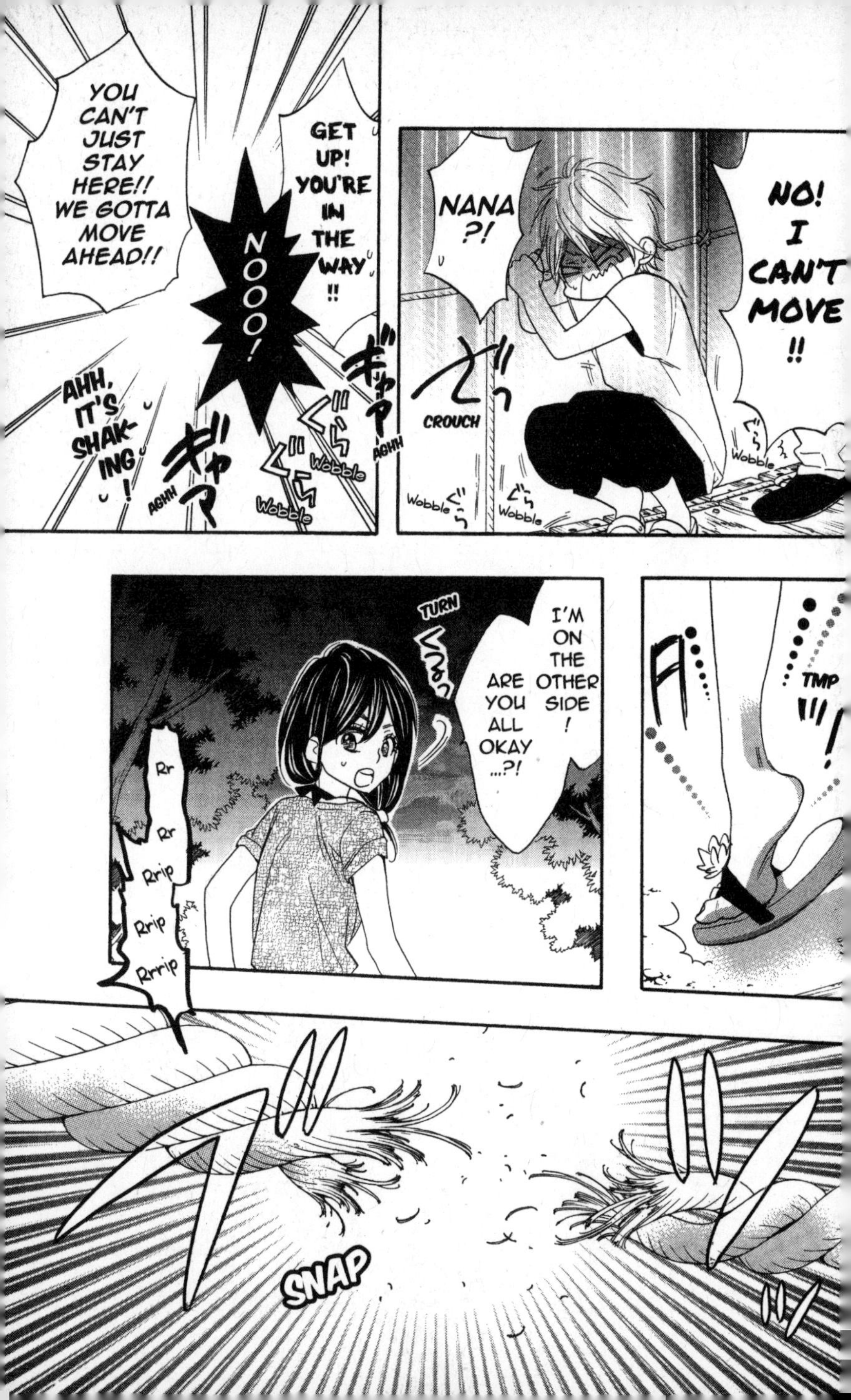

NO! I CAN'T MOVE!!
NANA?!
CROUCH
Wobble
Wobble
Wobble
GET UP! YOU'RE IN THE WAY!!
YOU CAN'T JUST STAY HERE!! WE GOTTA MOVE AHEAD!!
NOOO!
AGHH
Wobble
Wobble
AHH, IT'S SHAKING!
AGHH
TMP
I'M ON THE OTHER SIDE!
ARE YOU ALL OKAY...?!
TURN
Rr
Rr
Rrip
Rrip
Rrrip
SNAP

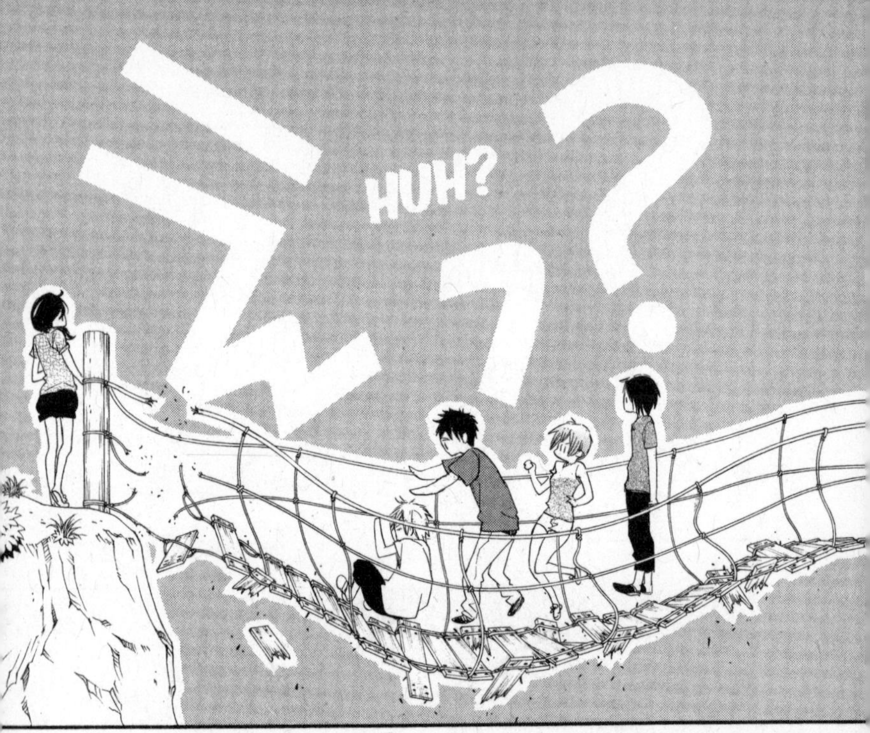
HUH?

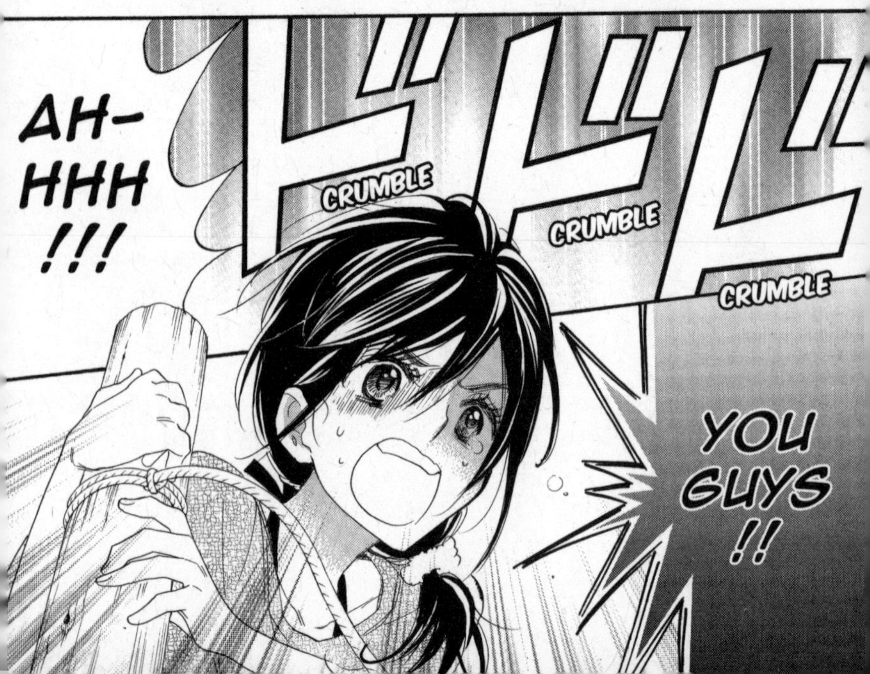
CRUMBLE
CRUMBLE
CRUMBLE
AH-HHH!!!
YOU GUYS!!

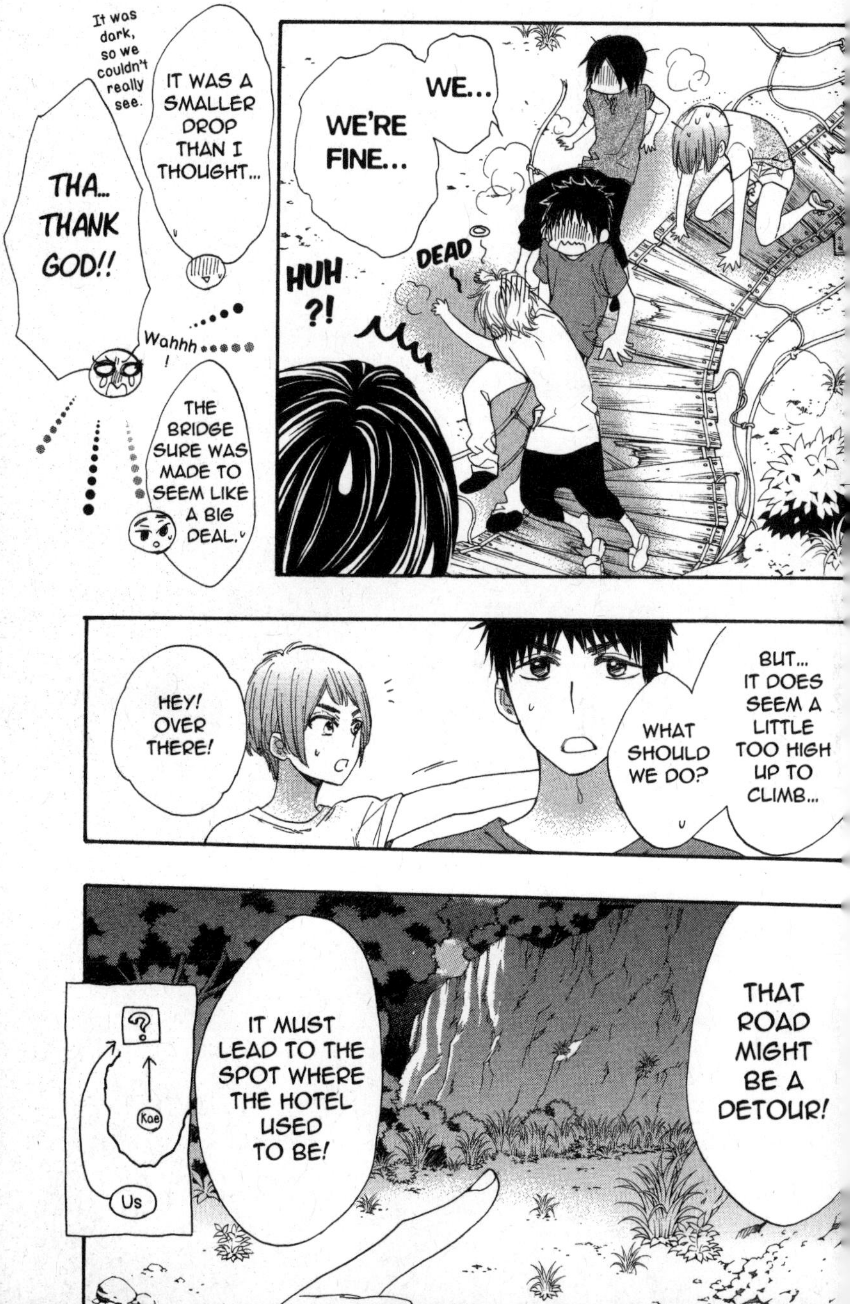
WE... WE'RE FINE...
DEAD
HUH ?!
IT WAS A SMALLER DROP THAN I THOUGHT...
It was dark, so we couldn't really see.
THA... THANK GOD!!
Wahhh!
THE BRIDGE SURE WAS MADE TO SEEM LIKE A BIG DEAL.
BUT... IT DOES SEEM A LITTLE TOO HIGH UP TO CLIMB...
WHAT SHOULD WE DO?
HEY! OVER THERE!
THAT ROAD MIGHT BE A DETOUR!
IT MUST LEAD TO THE SPOT WHERE THE HOTEL USED TO BE!
?
Kae
Us

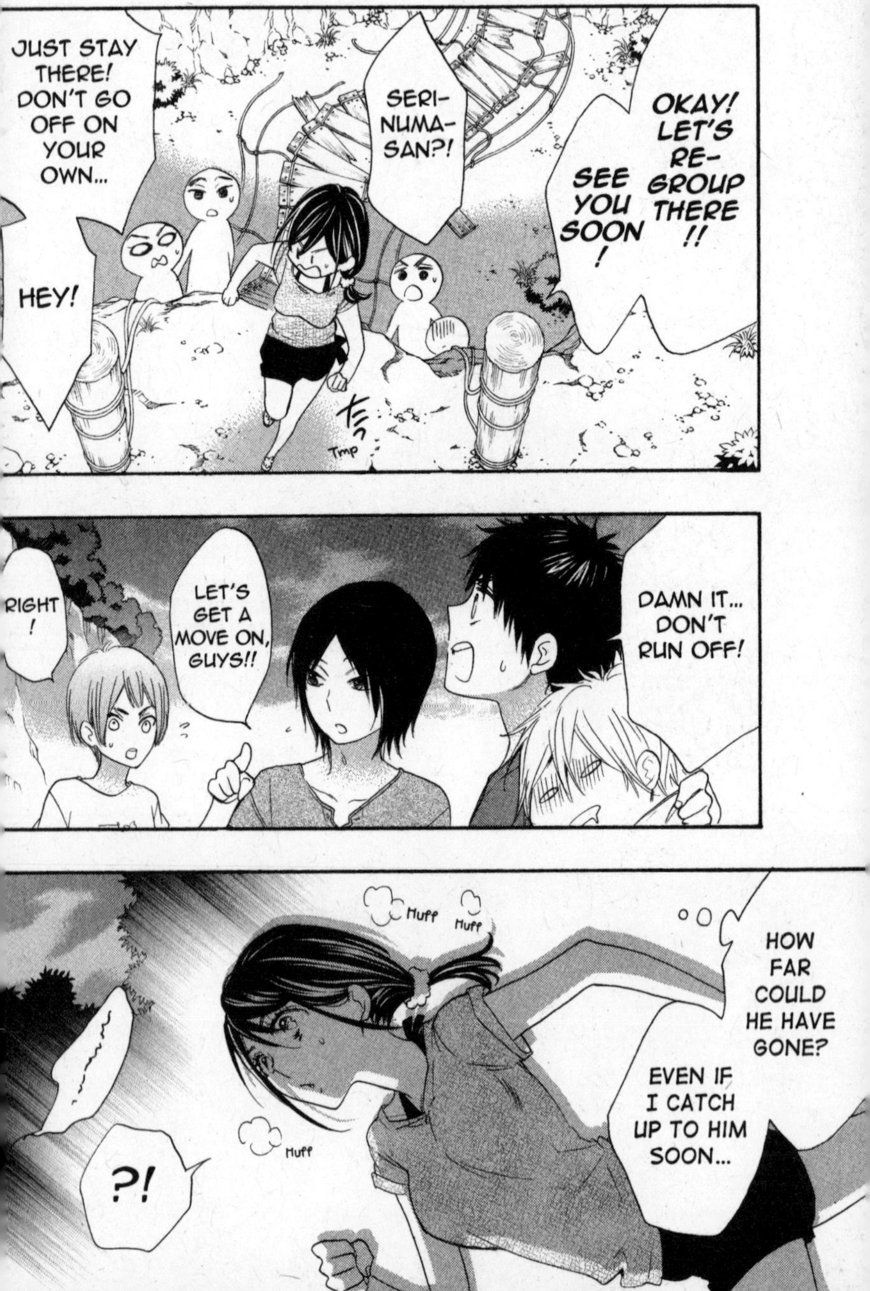
OKAY! LET'S RE-GROUP THERE!!
SEE YOU SOON!
SERI-NUMA-SAN?!
JUST STAY THERE! DON'T GO OFF ON YOUR OWN...
HEY!
Tmp
DAMN IT... DON'T RUN OFF!
LET'S GET A MOVE ON, GUYS!!
RIGHT!
HOW FAR COULD HE HAVE GONE?
EVEN IF I CATCH UP TO HIM SOON...
Huff Huff
Huff
?!

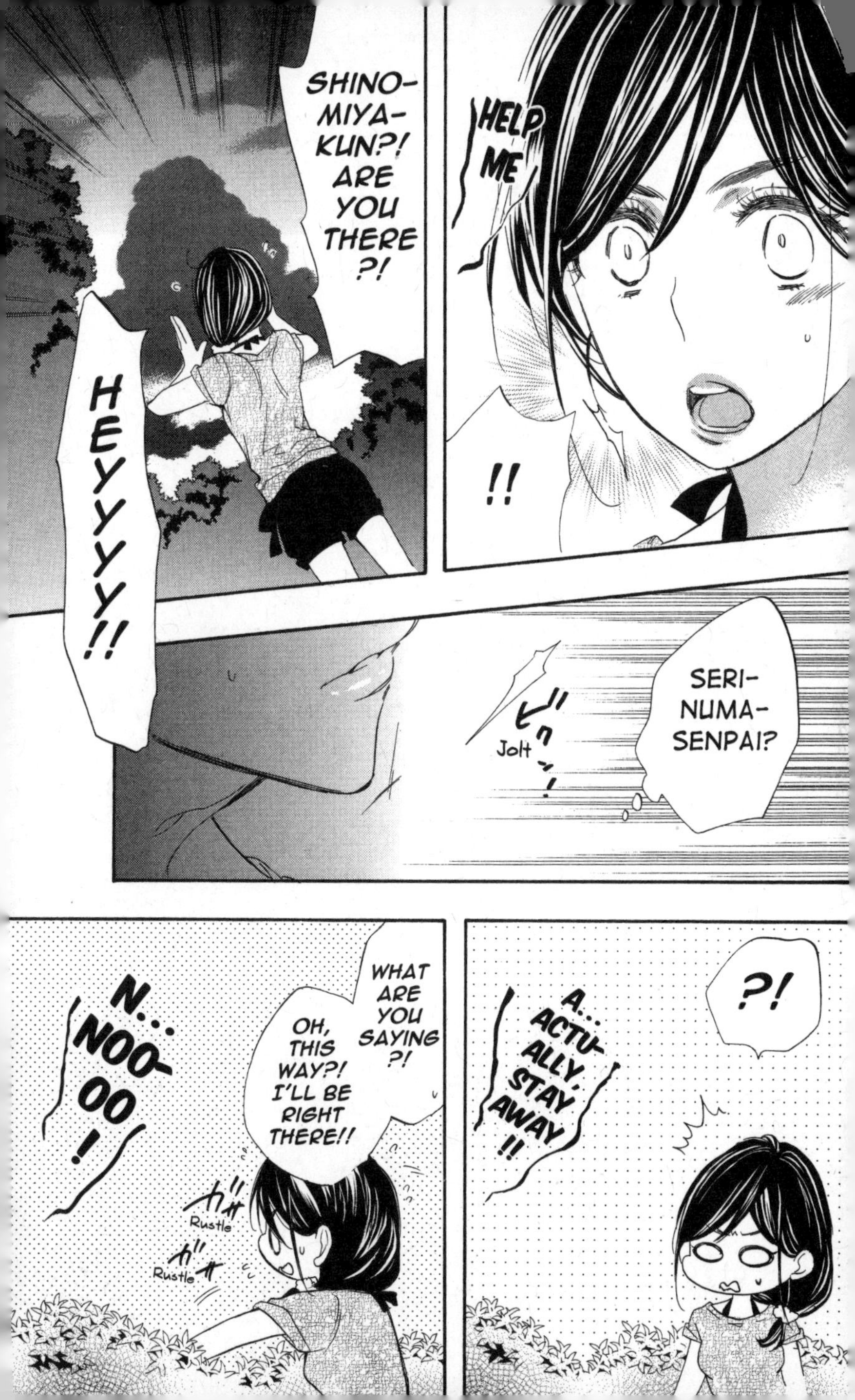
HELP ME
!!
SHINO-MIYA-KUN?! ARE YOU THERE?!
HEYYYYY!!
SERI-NUMA-SENPAI?
Jolt
?!
A... ACTUALLY, STAY AWAY!!
WHAT ARE YOU SAYING?!
OH, THIS WAY?! I'LL BE RIGHT THERE!!
N... NOOOOO!
Rustle
Rustle

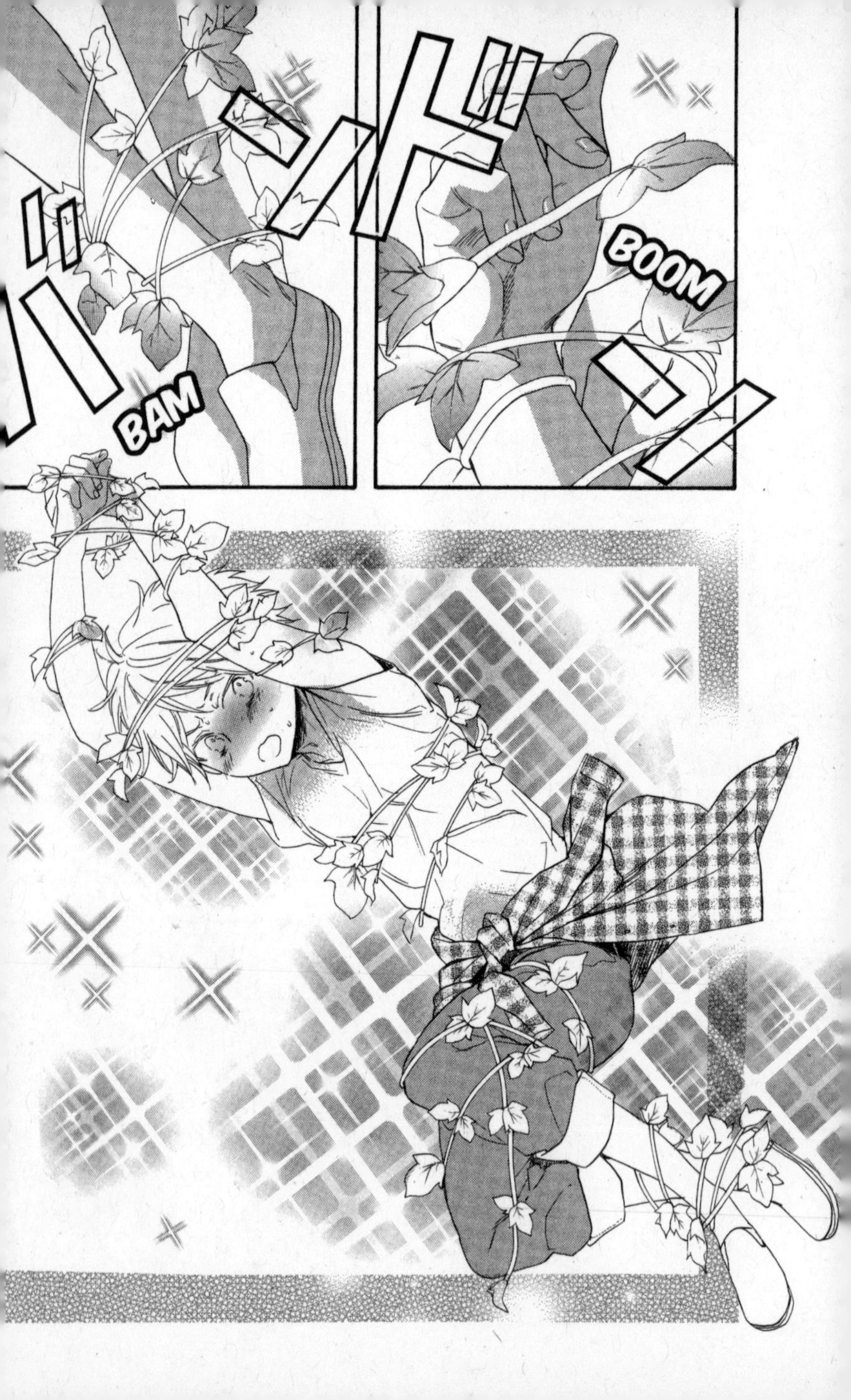
BOOM
BAM

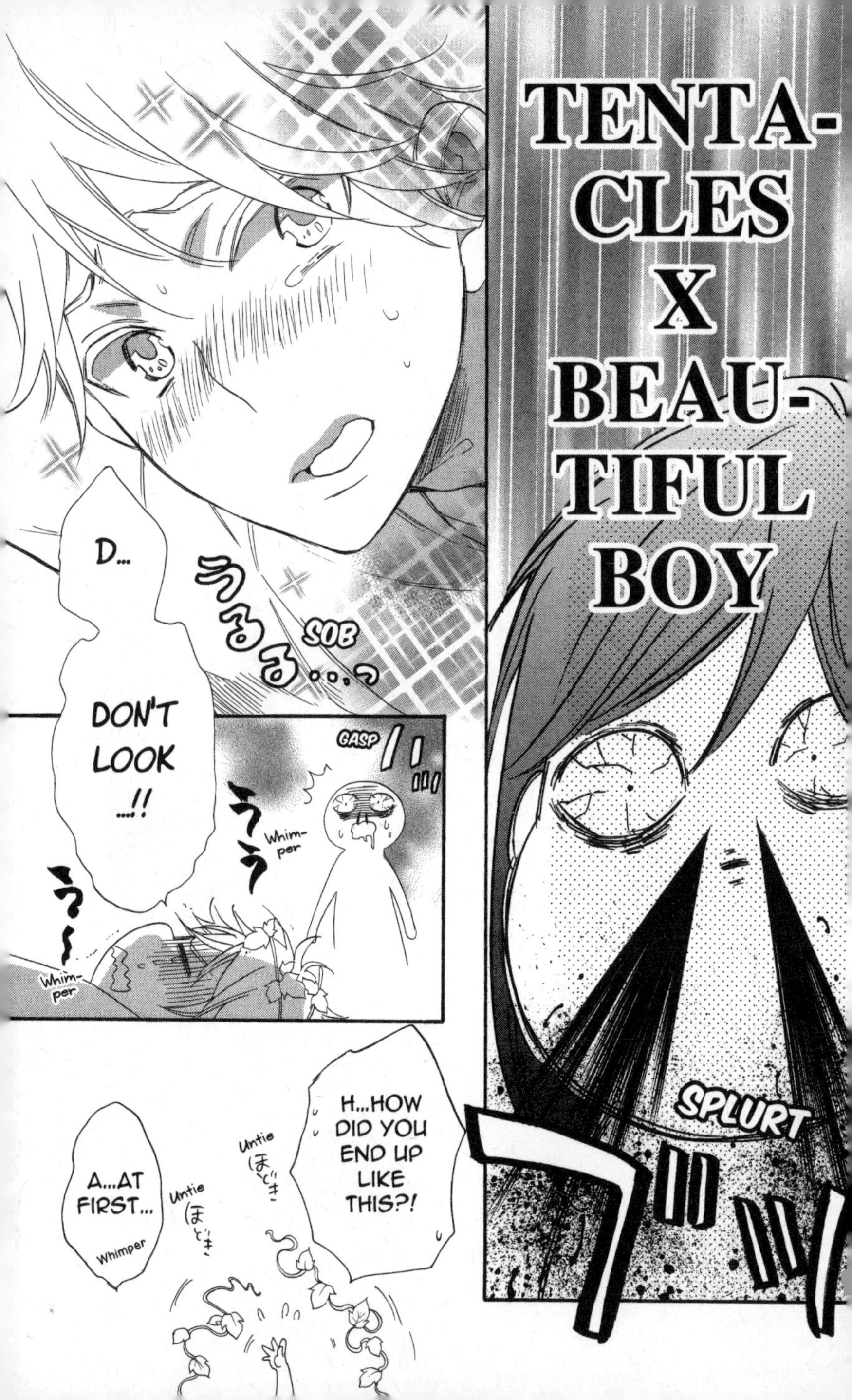
TENTA-
CLES
X
BEAU-
TIFUL
BOY
SPLURT
D...
DON'T LOOK ...!!
うるる…っ
SOB
GASP
うう
Whim-per
うー
Whim-per
H...HOW DID YOU END UP LIKE THIS?!
Untie
ほどき
Untie
ほどき
A...AT FIRST...
Whimper

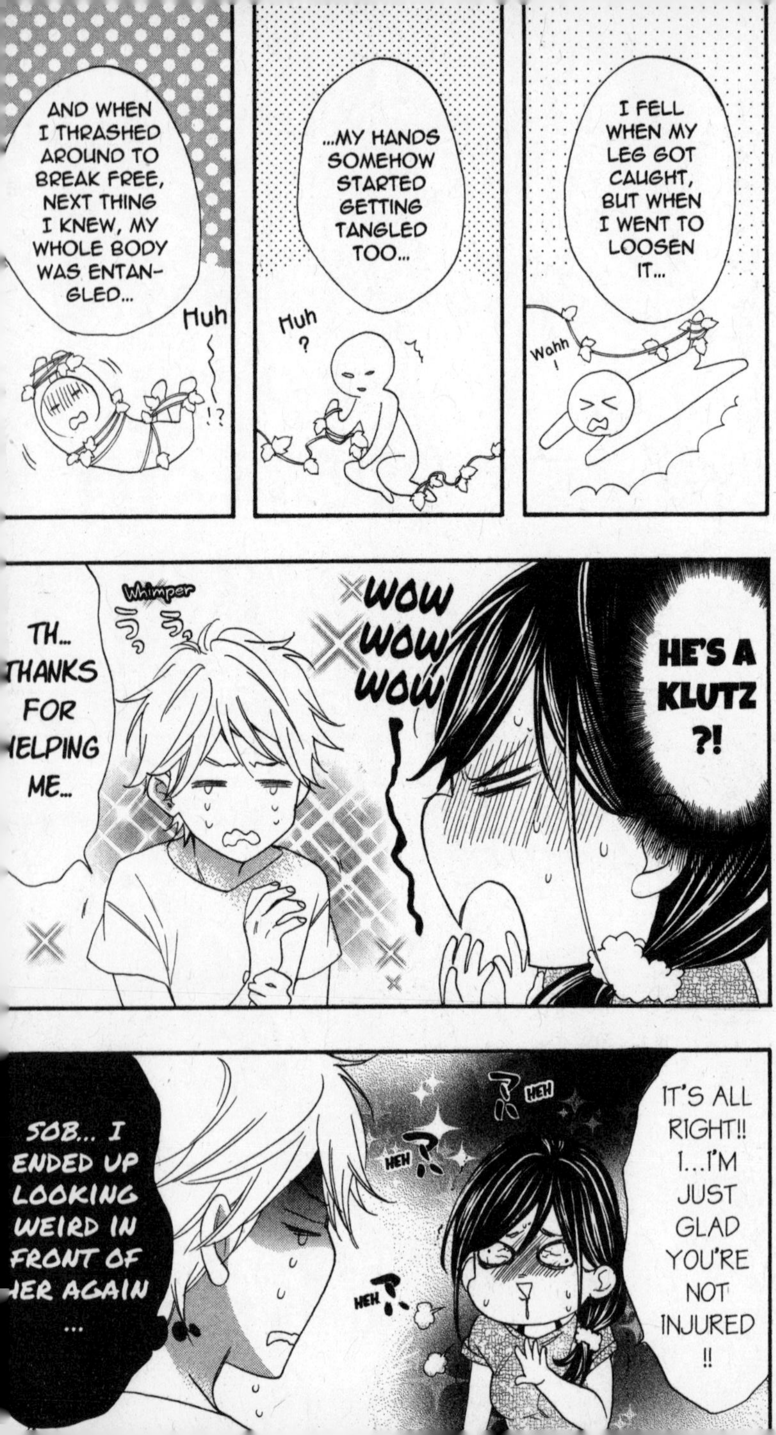
I FELL WHEN MY LEG GOT CAUGHT, BUT WHEN I WENT TO LOOSEN IT...
Wahh !
...MY HANDS SOMEHOW STARTED GETTING TANGLED TOO...
Huh ?
AND WHEN I THRASHED AROUND TO BREAK FREE, NEXT THING I KNEW, MY WHOLE BODY WAS ENTANGLED...
Huh !?
HE'S A KLUTZ ?!
WOW WOW WOW
Whimper
TH... THANKS FOR HELPING ME...
IT'S ALL RIGHT!! I...I'M JUST GLAD YOU'RE NOT INJURED !!
HEH
HEH
HEH
SOB... I ENDED UP LOOKING WEIRD IN FRONT OF HER AGAIN ...

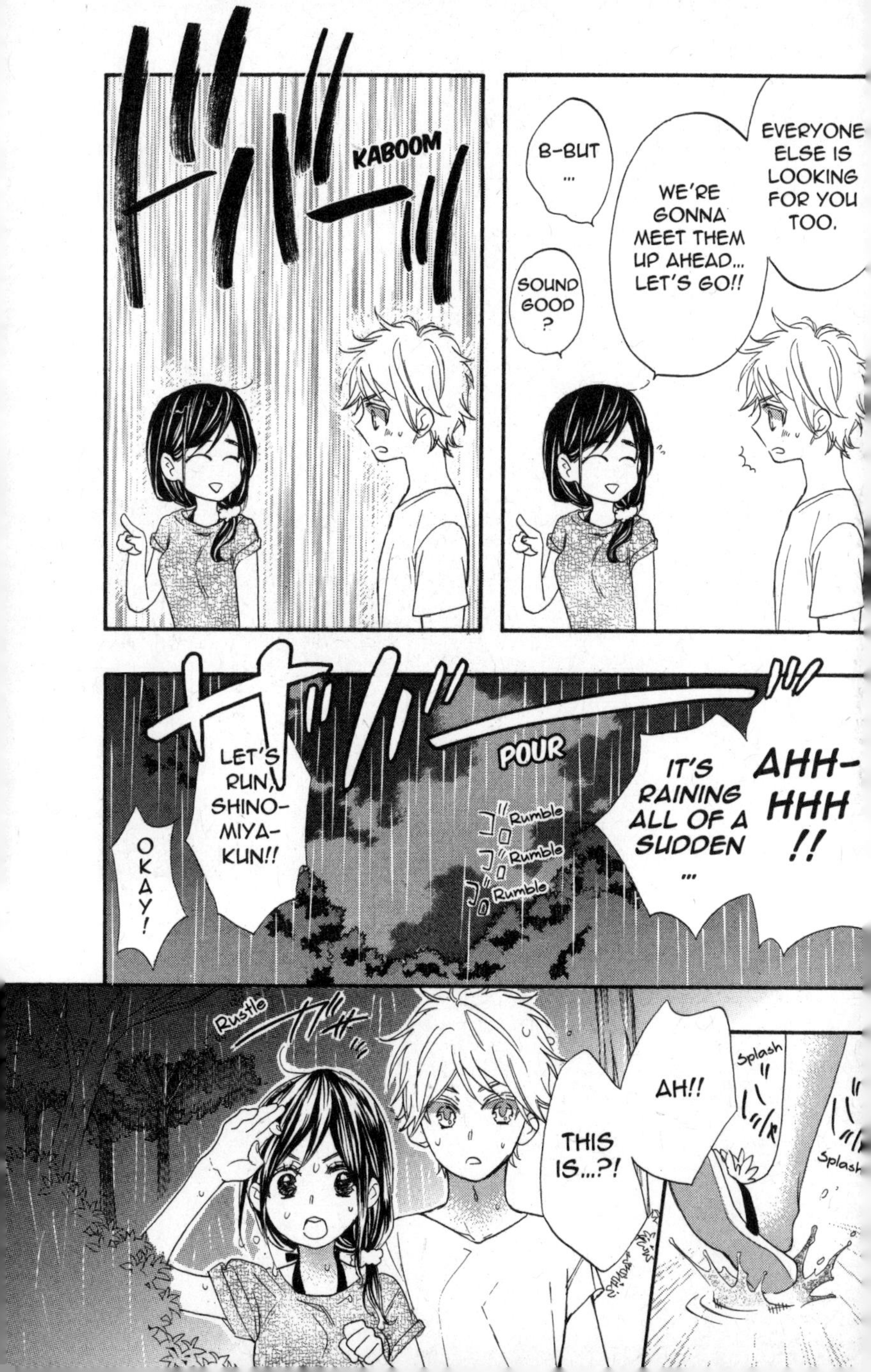
EVERYONE ELSE IS LOOKING FOR YOU TOO.
WE'RE GONNA MEET THEM UP AHEAD... LET'S GO!!
B-BUT ...
SOUND GOOD ?
KABOOM
AHH-HHH!!
IT'S RAINING ALL OF A SUDDEN ...
POUR
Rumble
Rumble
Rumble
LET'S RUN, SHINOMIYA-KUN!!
OKAY!
Splash
Splash
AH!!
THIS IS...?!
Rustle

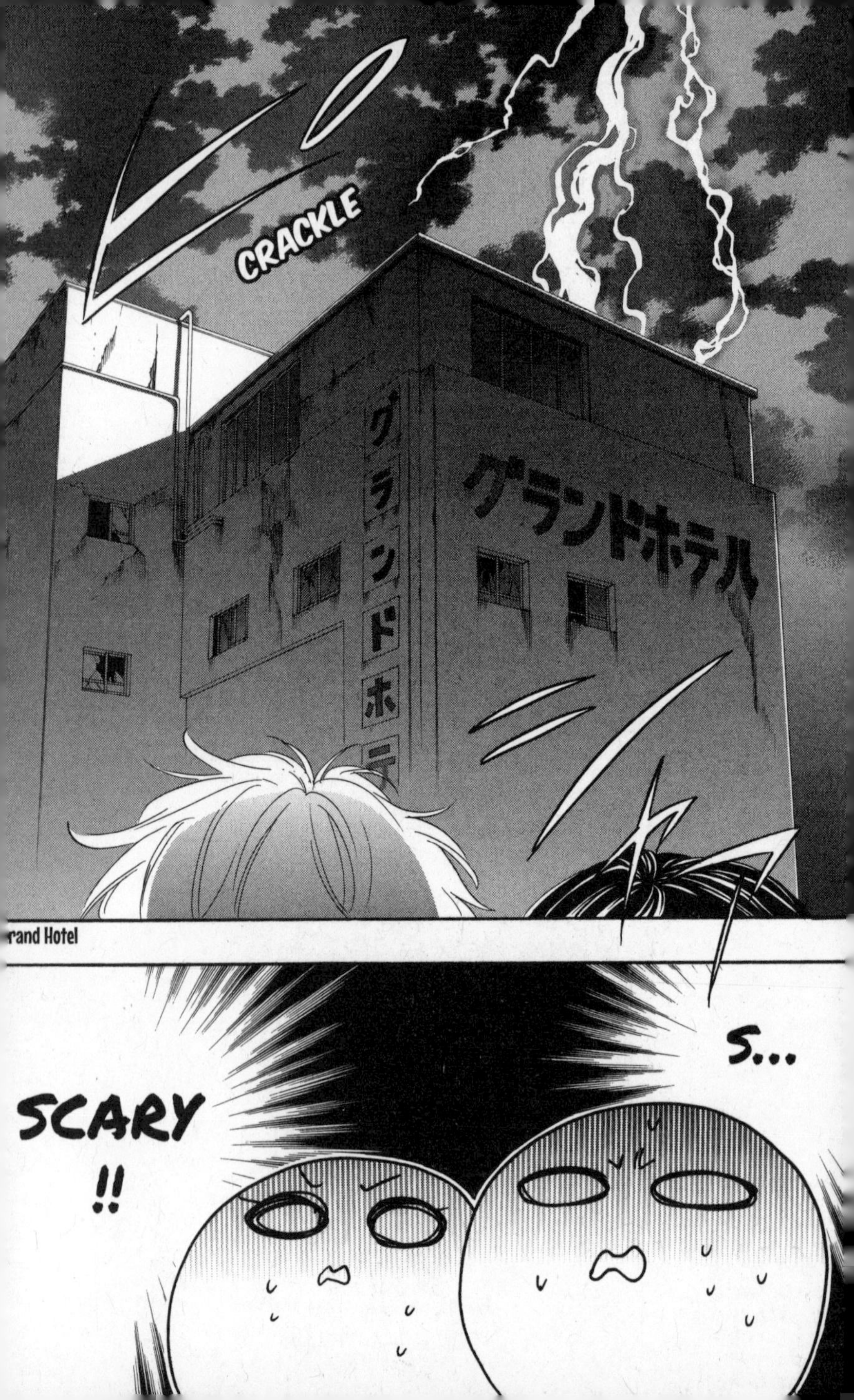
CRACKLE
グランドホテル
グランドホテ
rand Hotel
S...
SCARY !!

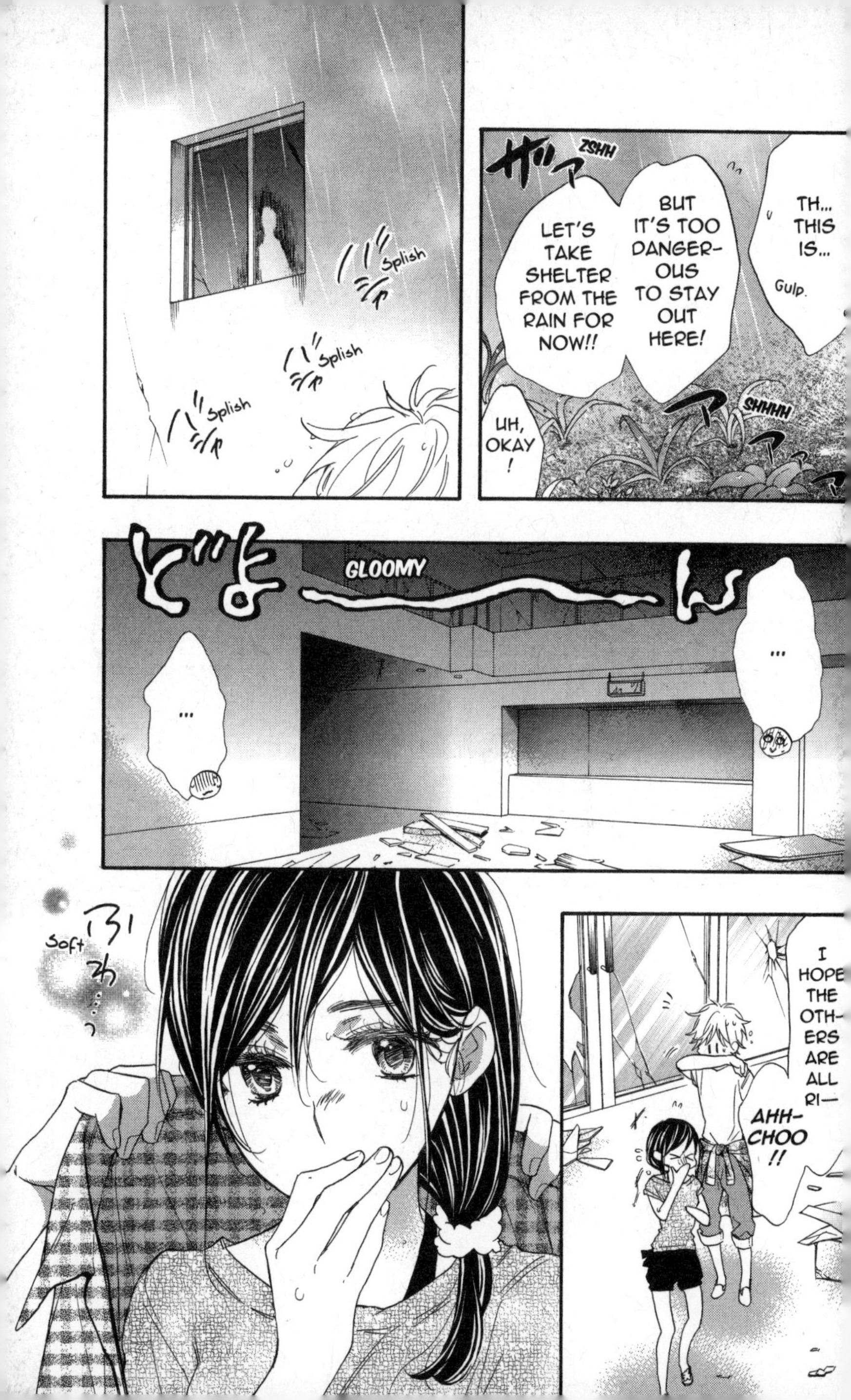
ZSHH
TH... THIS IS...
Gulp.
BUT IT'S TOO DANGER-OUS TO STAY OUT HERE!
LET'S TAKE SHELTER FROM THE RAIN FOR NOW!!
UH, OKAY!
SHHHH
Splish
Splish
Splish
GLOOMY
...
...
I HOPE THE OTH-ERS ARE ALL RI—
AHH-CHOO!!
Soft

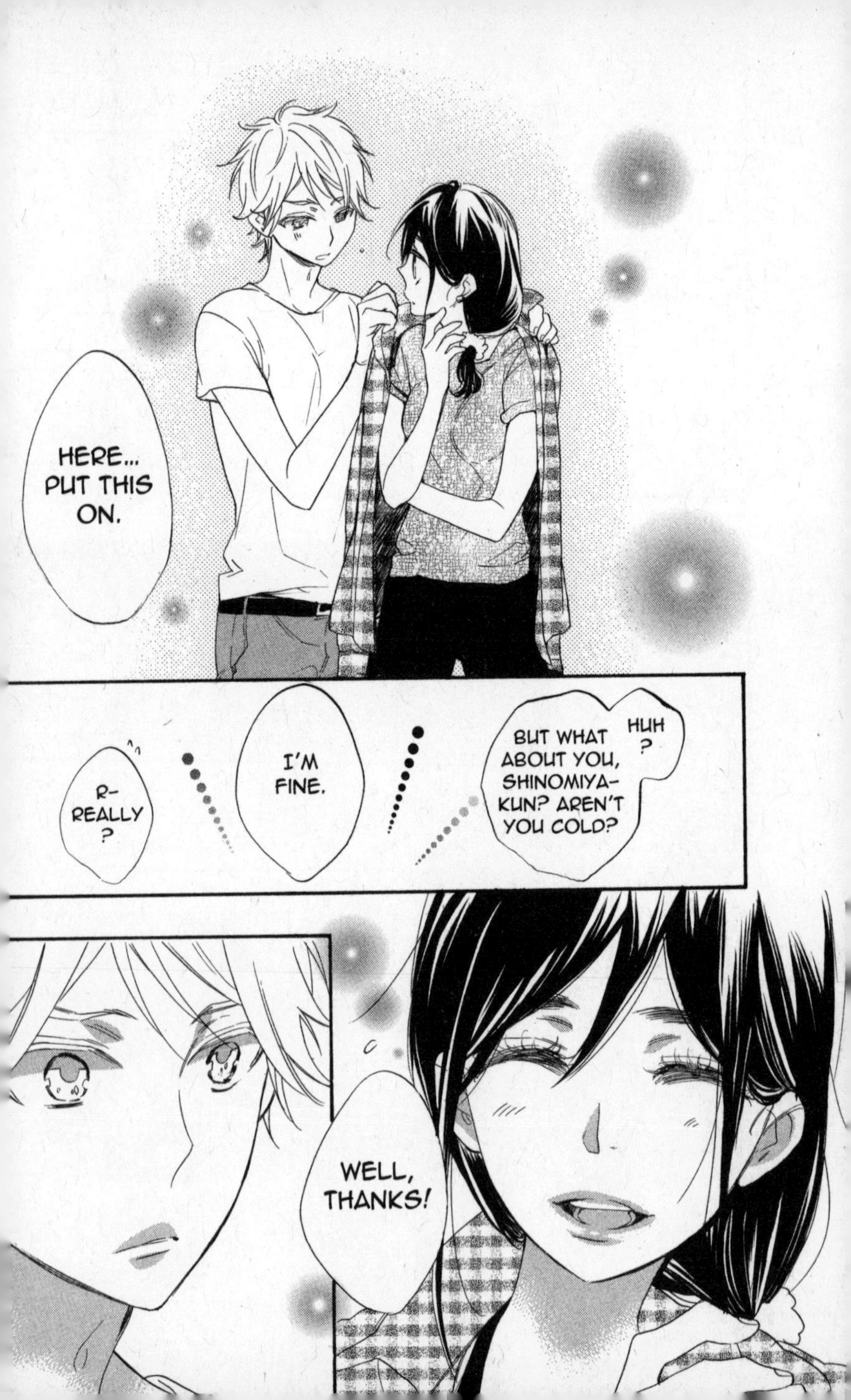
HERE... PUT THIS ON.
HUH?
BUT WHAT ABOUT YOU, SHINOMIYA-KUN? AREN'T YOU COLD?
I'M FINE.
R-REALLY?
WELL, THANKS!

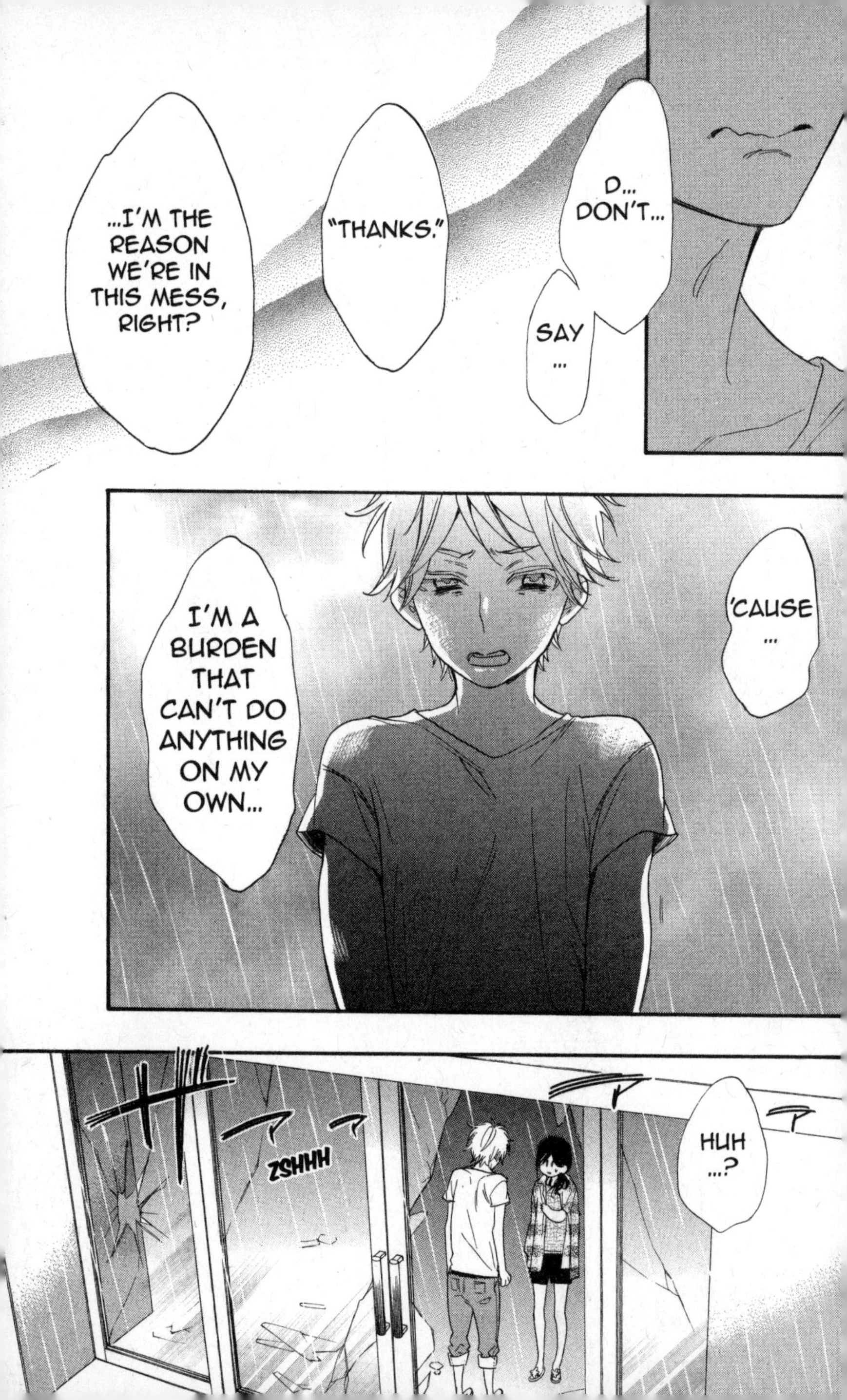
D... DON'T...
SAY ...
"THANKS."
...I'M THE REASON WE'RE IN THIS MESS, RIGHT?
'CAUSE ...
I'M A BURDEN THAT CAN'T DO ANYTHING ON MY OWN...
HUH ...?
ZSHHH

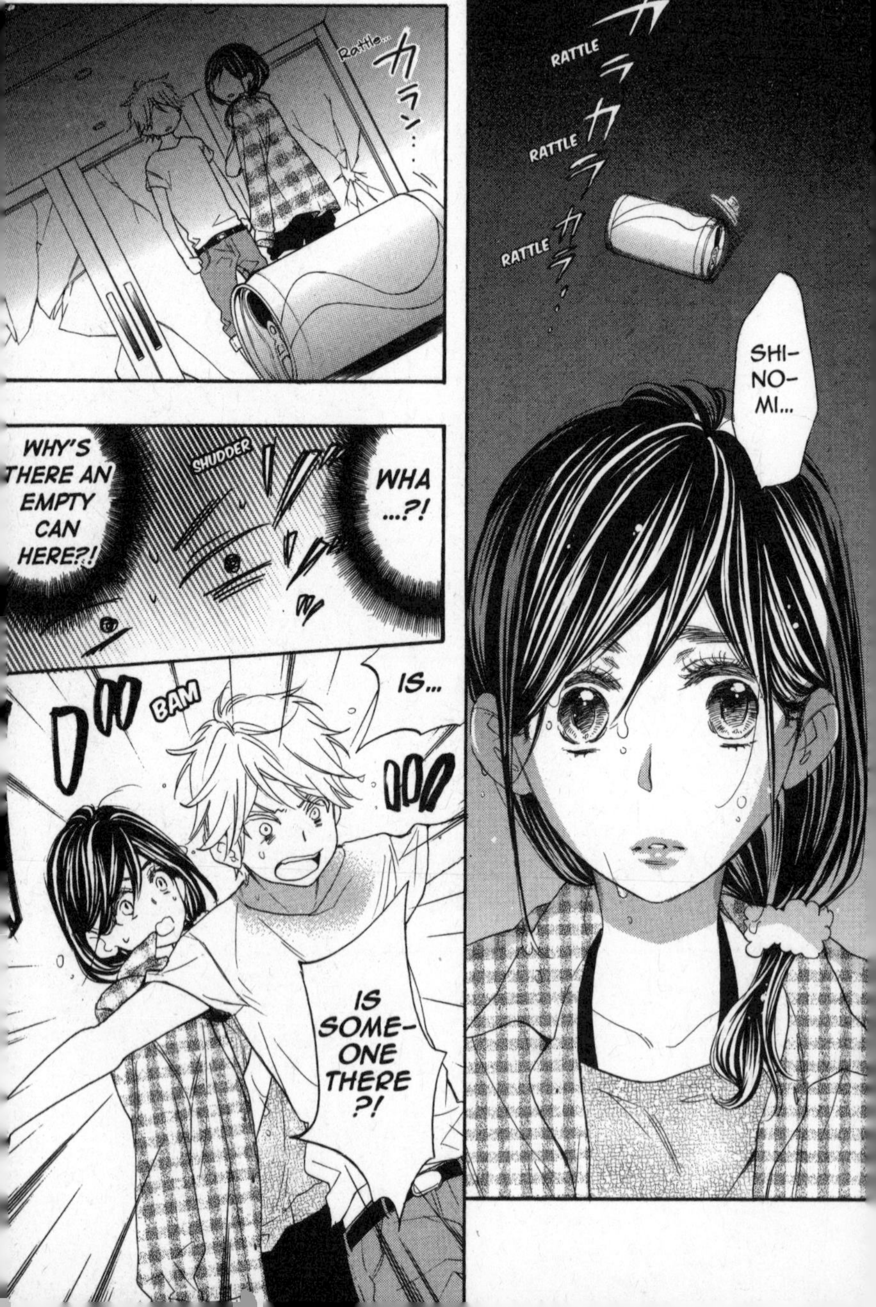
RATTLE
カラカラカラ
RATTLE
RATTLE
SHI-NO-MI...
Rattle...
カラン…
WHA ...?!
SHUDDER
WHY'S THERE AN EMPTY CAN HERE?!
IS...
BAM
IS SOMEONE THERE?!

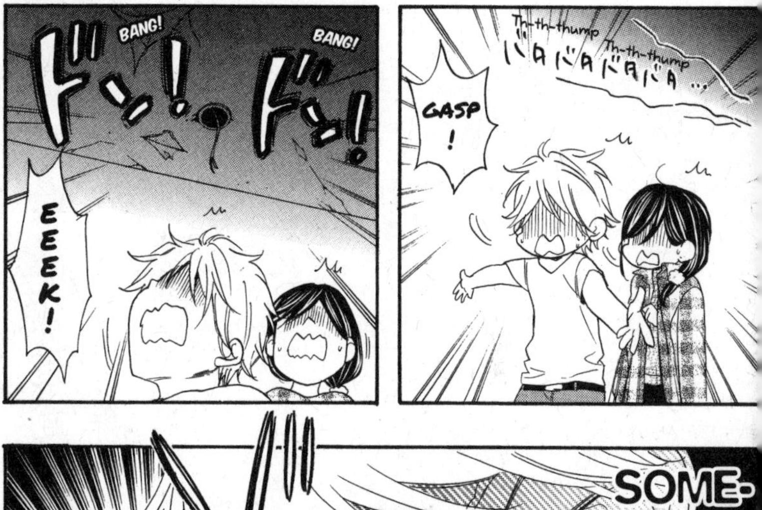
Th-th-thump
Th-th-thump
GASP!
BANG!
BANG!
EEEEK!
SOME-THING...
SOME-THING'S HERE...!!
SHUDDER

*Short for *Namuamidabutsu*, a Buddhist invocation.

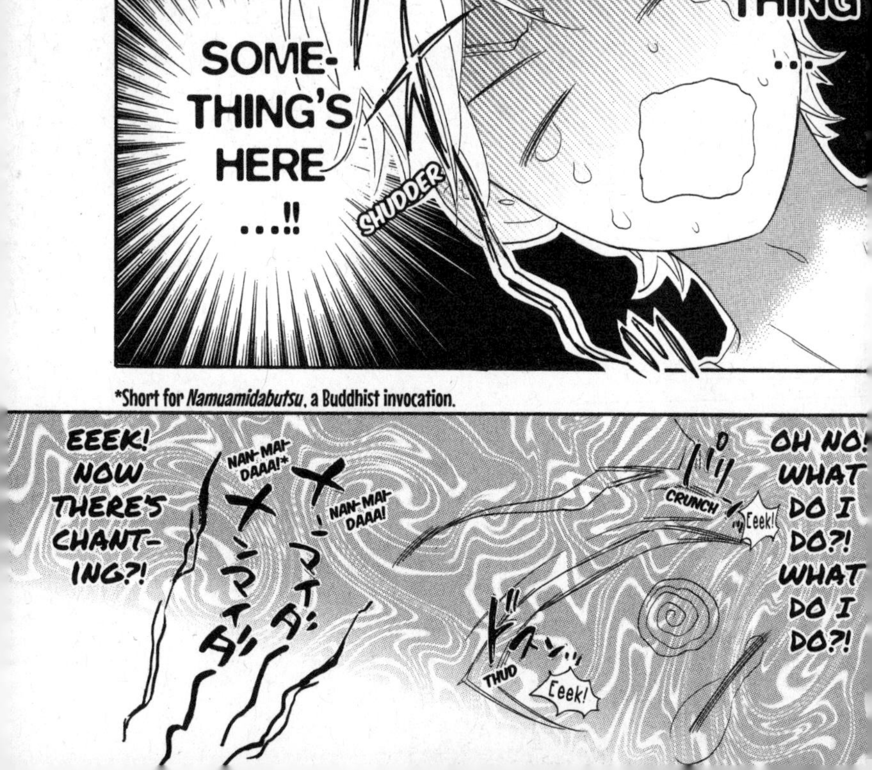
OH NO! WHAT DO I DO?! WHAT DO I DO?!
CRUNCH
Eeek!
THUD
Eeek!
NAN-MAI-DAAA!
NAN-MAI-DAAA!*
EEEK! NOW THERE'S CHANT-ING?!

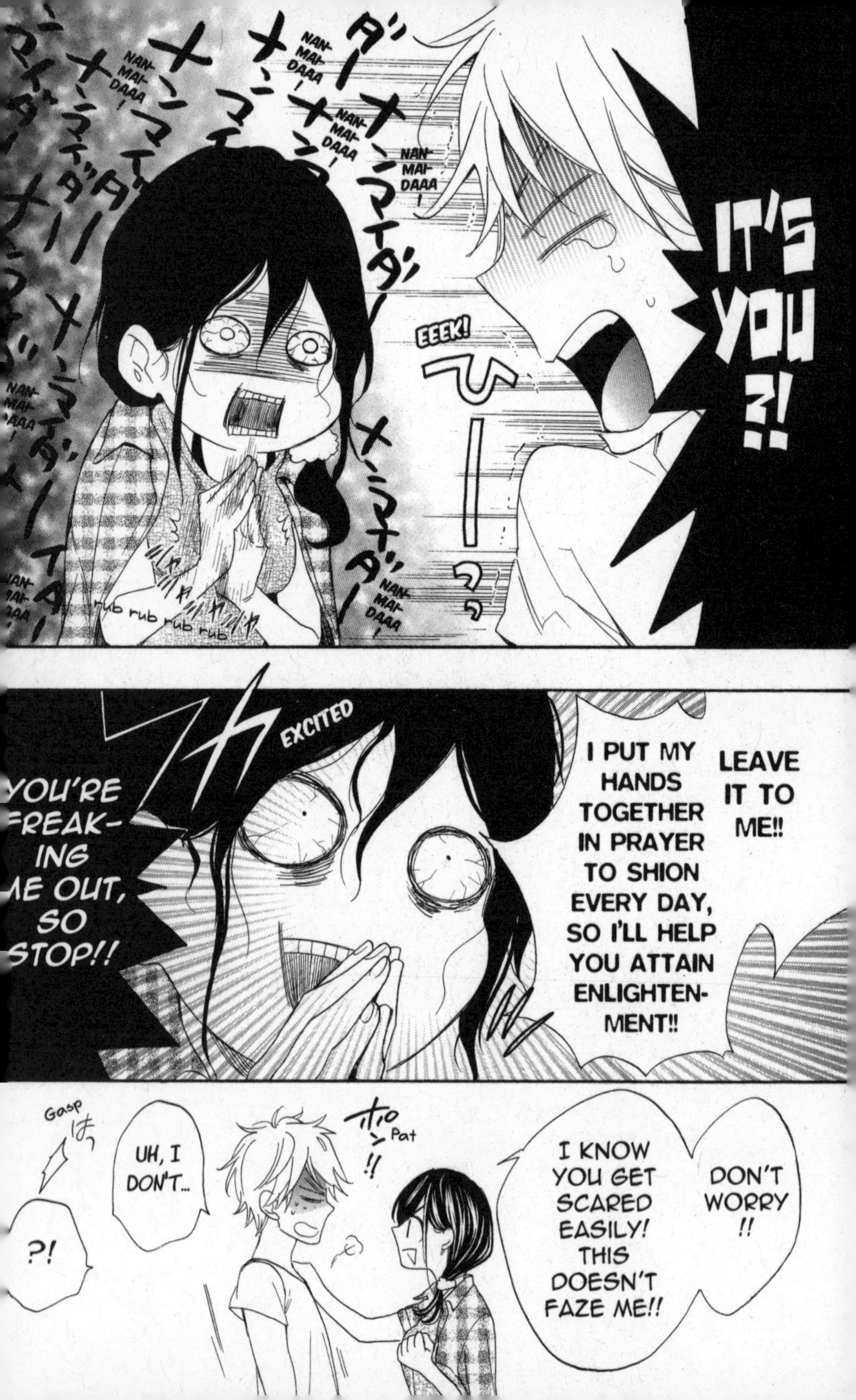
IT'S YOU?!!
EEEK!
NAN-MAI-DAAA!
NAN-MAI-DAAA!
NAN-MAI-DAAA!
NAN-MAI-DAAA!
NAN-MAI-DAAA!
NAN-MAI-DAAA!
NAN-MAI-DAAA!
rub rub rub rub
LEAVE IT TO ME!!
I PUT MY HANDS TOGETHER IN PRAYER TO SHION EVERY DAY, SO I'LL HELP YOU ATTAIN ENLIGHTEN-MENT!!
EXCITED
YOU'RE FREAK-ING ME OUT, SO STOP!!
DON'T WORRY!!
I KNOW YOU GET SCARED EASILY! THIS DOESN'T FAZE ME!!
Pat
UH, I DON'T...
Gasp
?!

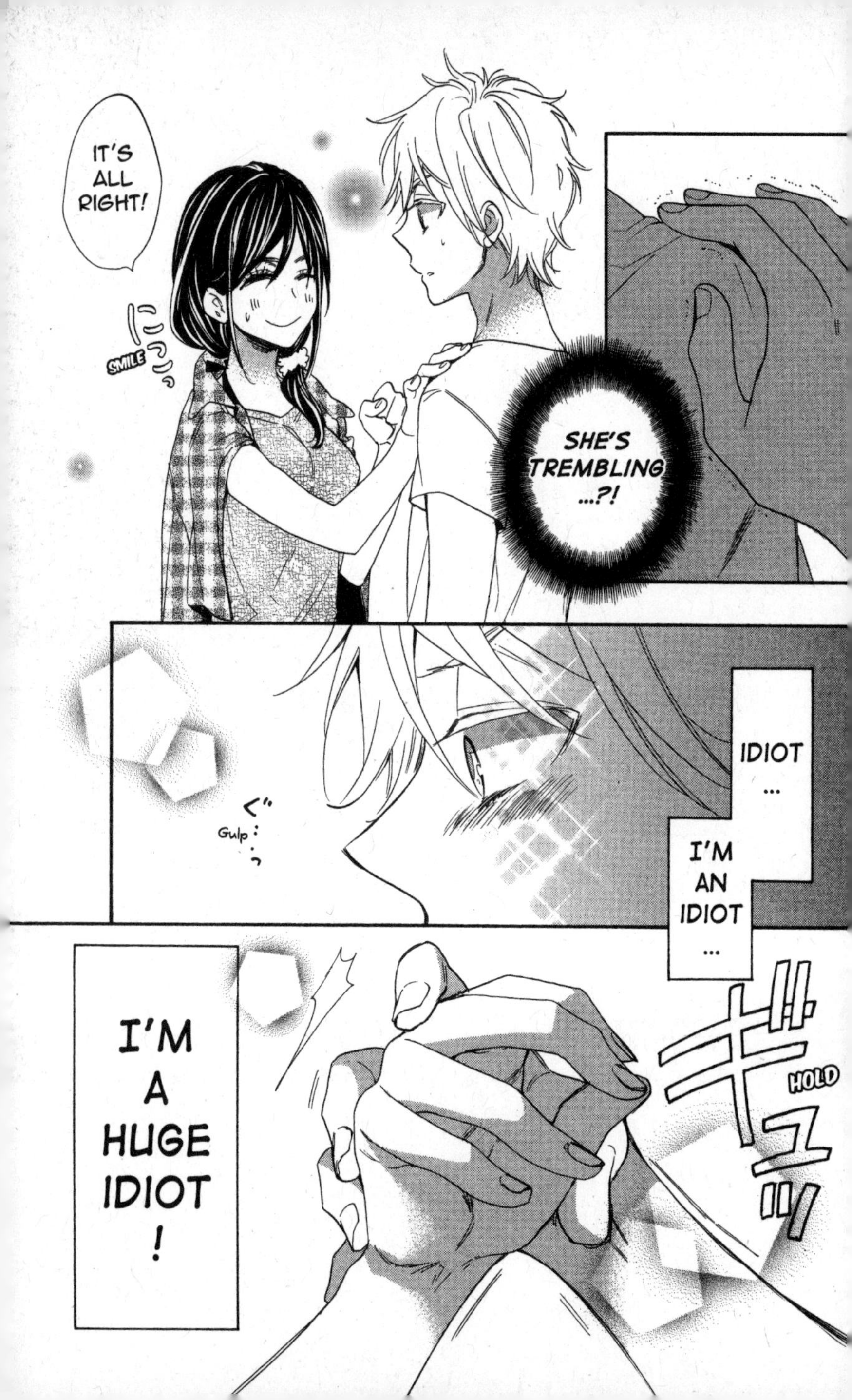
SHE'S TREMBLING ...?!
IT'S ALL RIGHT!
にこっ
SMILE
IDIOT ...
I'M AN IDIOT ...
ぐっ
Gulp
ギュッ
HOLD
I'M A HUGE IDIOT!

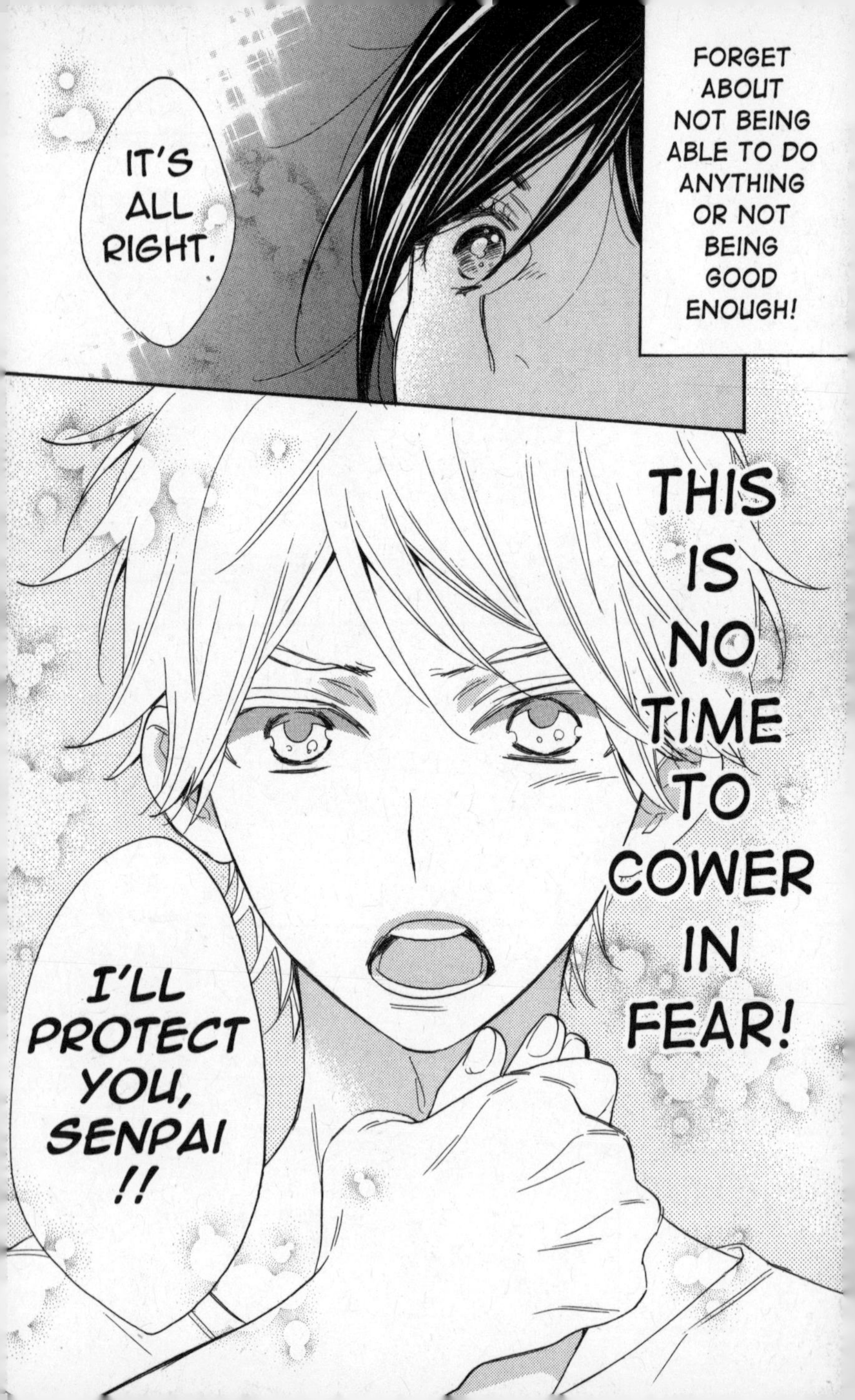
FORGET ABOUT NOT BEING ABLE TO DO ANYTHING OR NOT BEING GOOD ENOUGH!
IT'S ALL RIGHT.
THIS IS NO TIME TO COWER IN FEAR!
I'LL PROTECT YOU, SENPAI!!

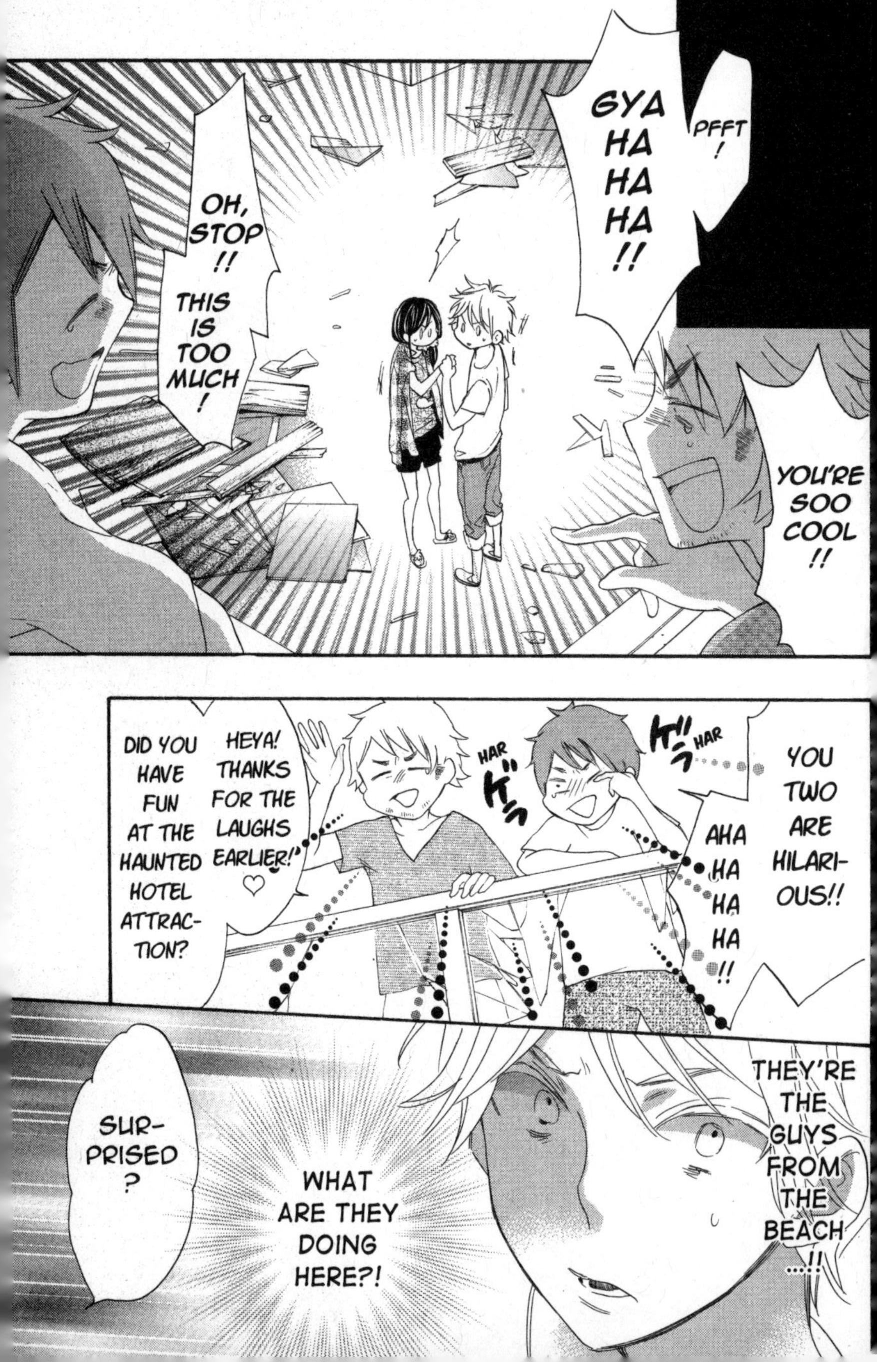
PFFT!
GYA HA HA HA!!
YOU'RE SOO COOL!!
OH, STOP!! THIS IS TOO MUCH!
YOU TWO ARE HILARI-OUS!!
HAR
AHA HA HA HA!!
HAR
HEYA! THANKS FOR THE LAUGHS EARLIER! ♡
DID YOU HAVE FUN AT THE HAUNTED HOTEL ATTRAC-TION?
THEY'RE THE GUYS FROM THE BEACH!!
.....!!
WHAT ARE THEY DOING HERE?!
SUR-PRISED?

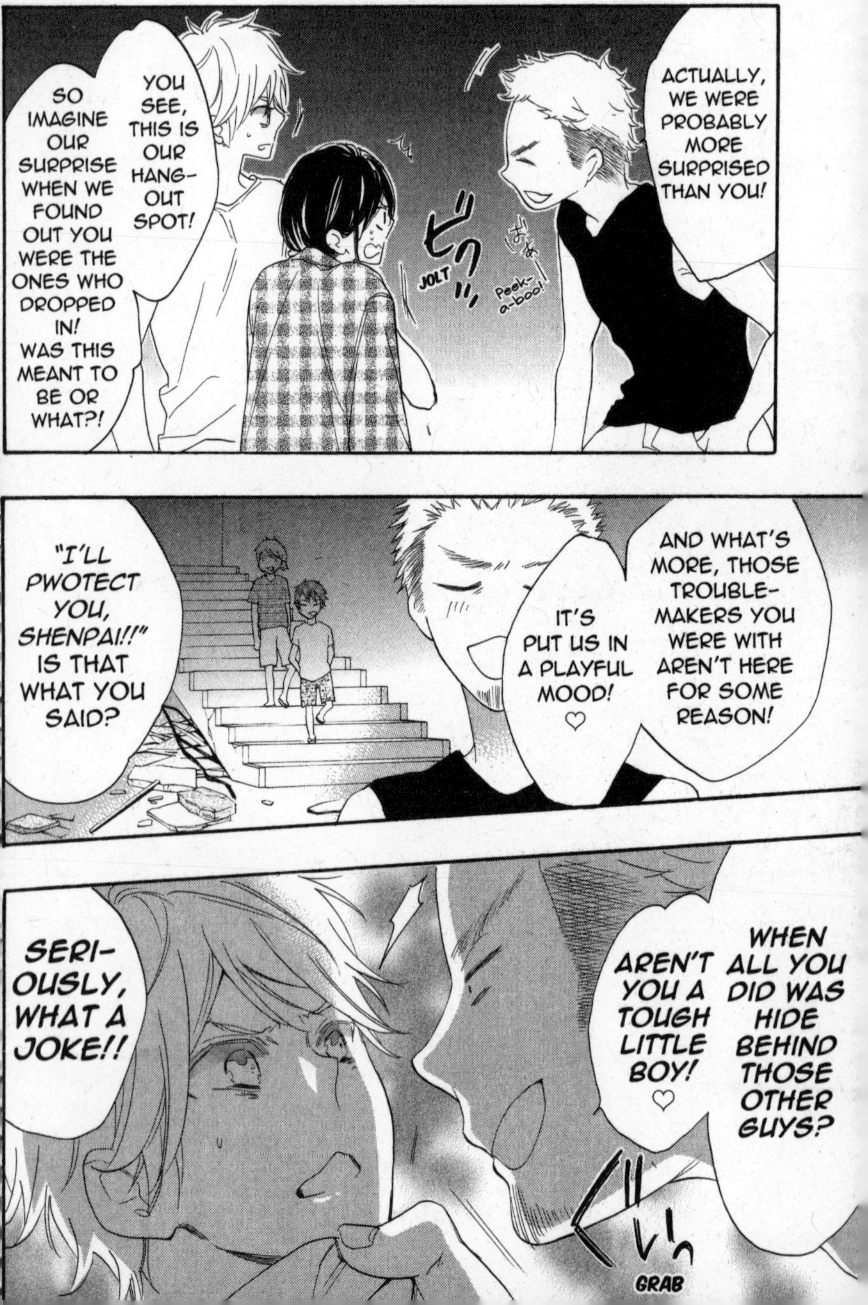
ACTUALLY, WE WERE PROBABLY MORE SURPRISED THAN YOU!
Peek-a-boo!
JOLT
YOU SEE, THIS IS OUR HANG-OUT SPOT!
SO IMAGINE OUR SURPRISE WHEN WE FOUND OUT YOU WERE THE ONES WHO DROPPED IN! WAS THIS MEANT TO BE OR WHAT?!
AND WHAT'S MORE, THOSE TROUBLE-MAKERS YOU WERE WITH AREN'T HERE FOR SOME REASON!
IT'S PUT US IN A PLAYFUL MOOD! ♡
"I'LL PWOTECT YOU, SHENPAI!!" IS THAT WHAT YOU SAID?
WHEN ALL YOU DID WAS HIDE BEHIND THOSE OTHER GUYS?
AREN'T YOU A TOUGH LITTLE BOY! ♡
GRAB
SERI-OUSLY, WHAT A JOKE!!

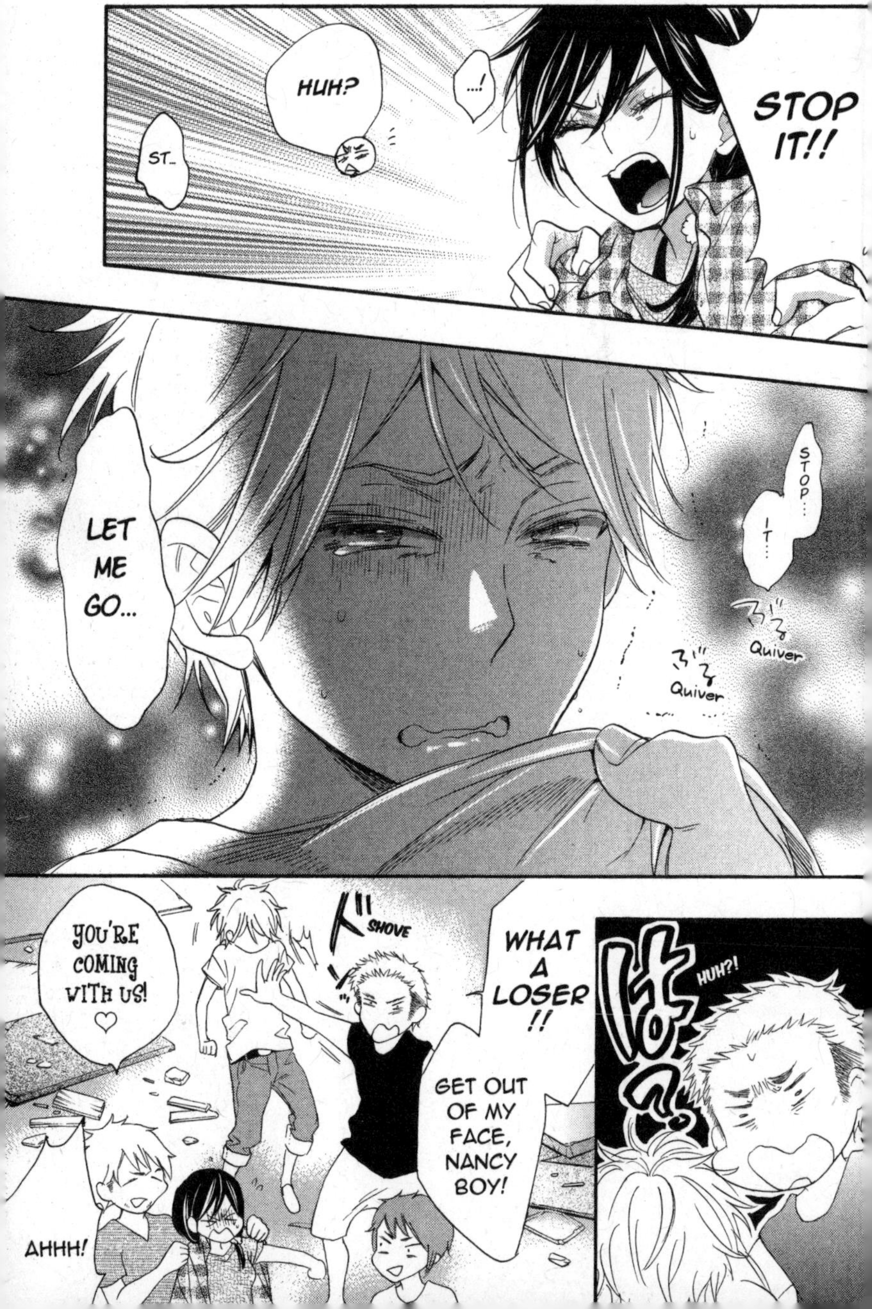
STOP IT!!
...!
HUH?
ST...
STOP... IT...
Quiver
Quiver
LET ME GO...
HUH?!
WHAT A LOSER!!
GET OUT OF MY FACE, NANCY BOY!
SHOVE
YOU'RE COMING WITH US! ♡
AHHH!

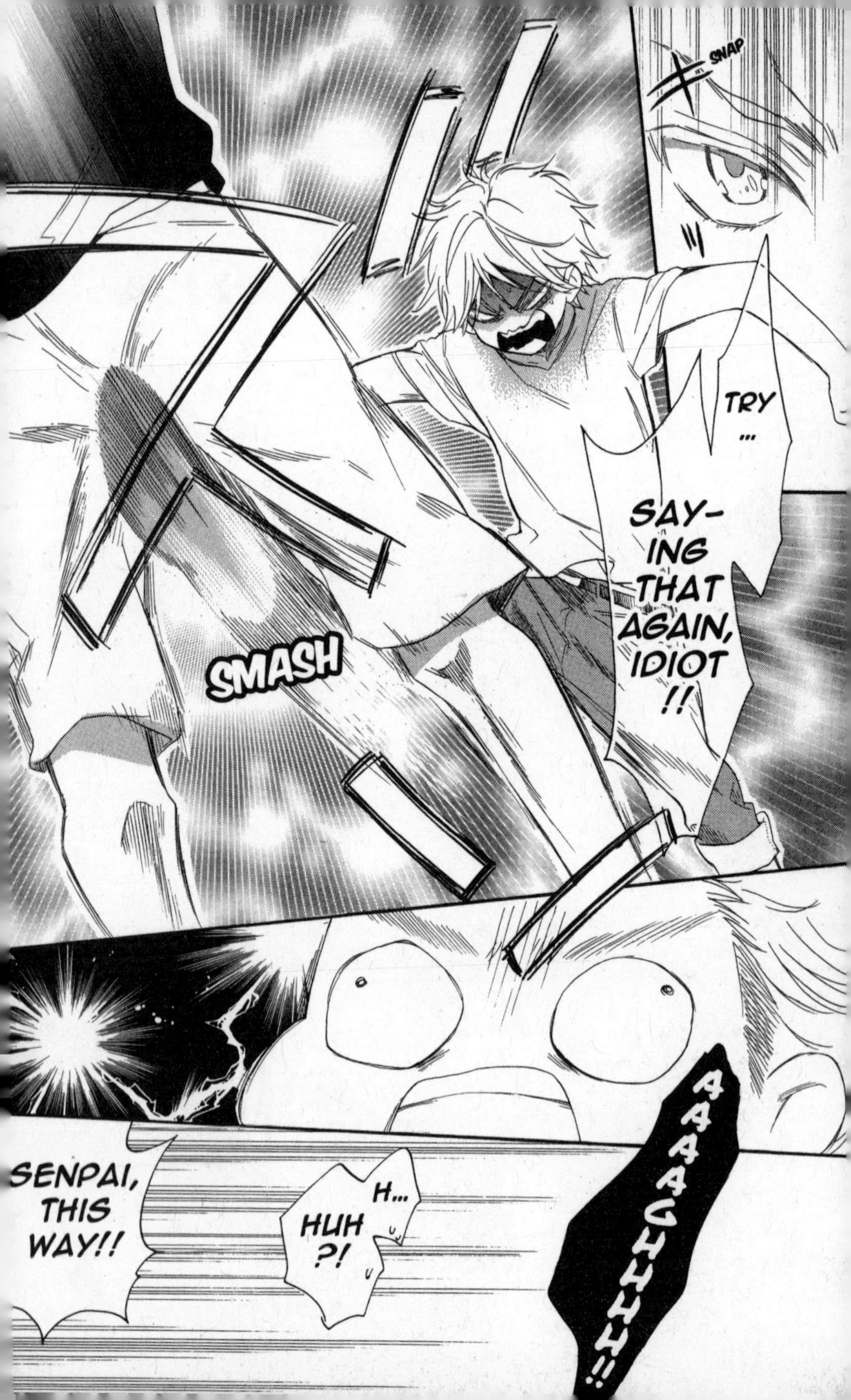
SNAP
TRY ...
SAYING THAT AGAIN, IDIOT!!
SMASH
AAAAGHHHHH!!
H... HUH?!
SENPAI, THIS WAY!!

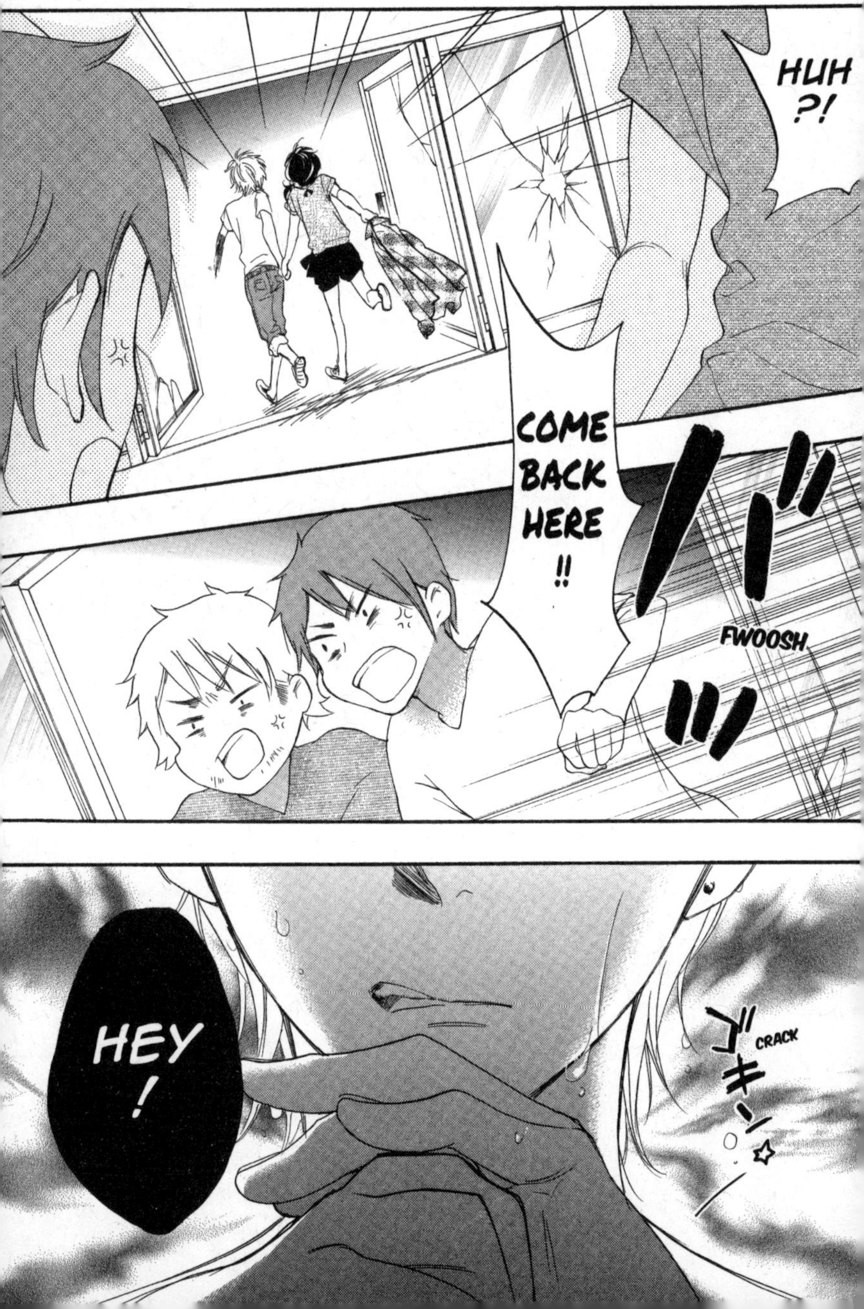
HUH ?!
COME BACK HERE !!
FWOOSH
HEY !
CRACK

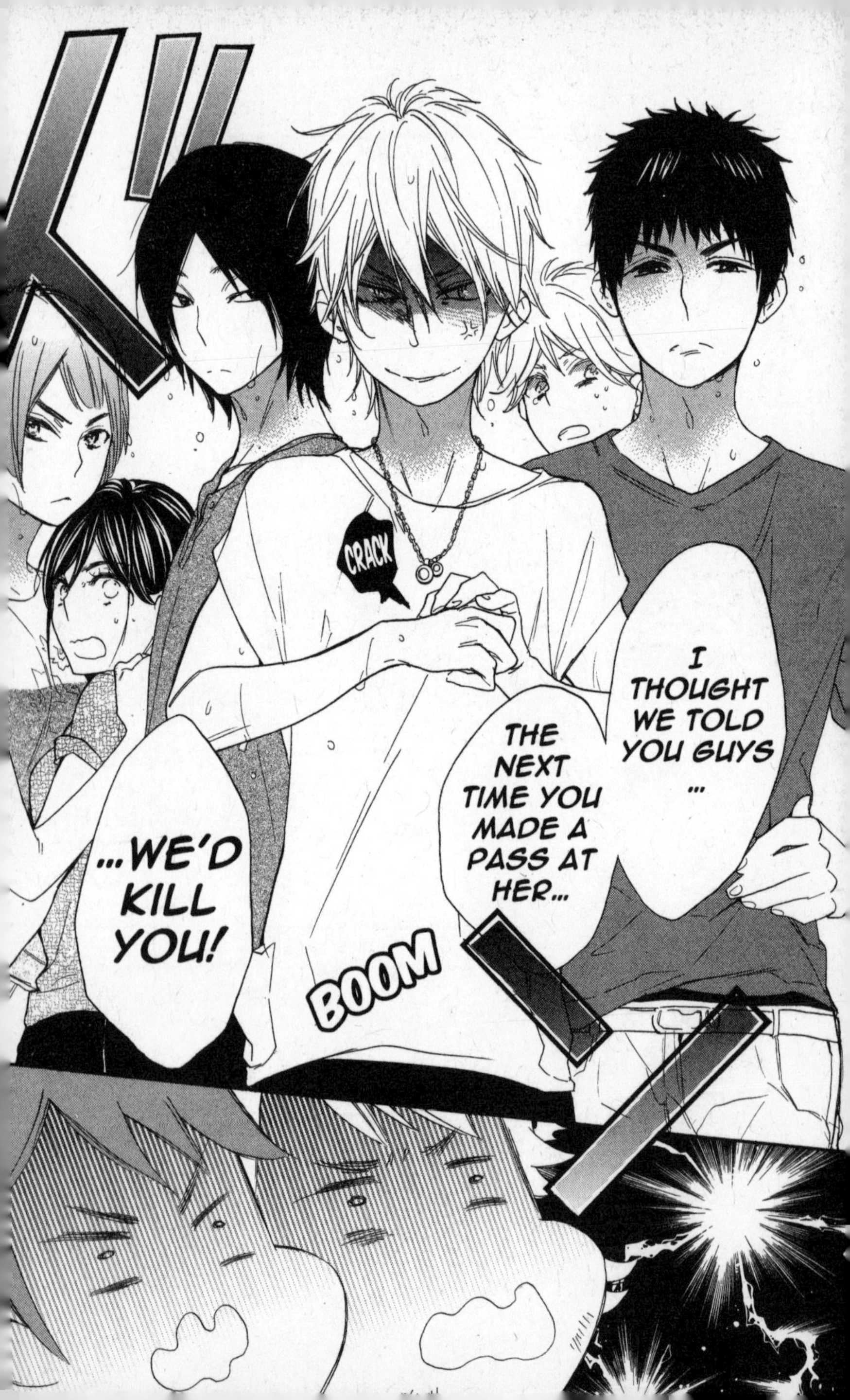

CRACK
I THOUGHT WE TOLD YOU GUYS ...
THE NEXT TIME YOU MADE A PASS AT HER...
...WE'D KILL YOU!
BOOM

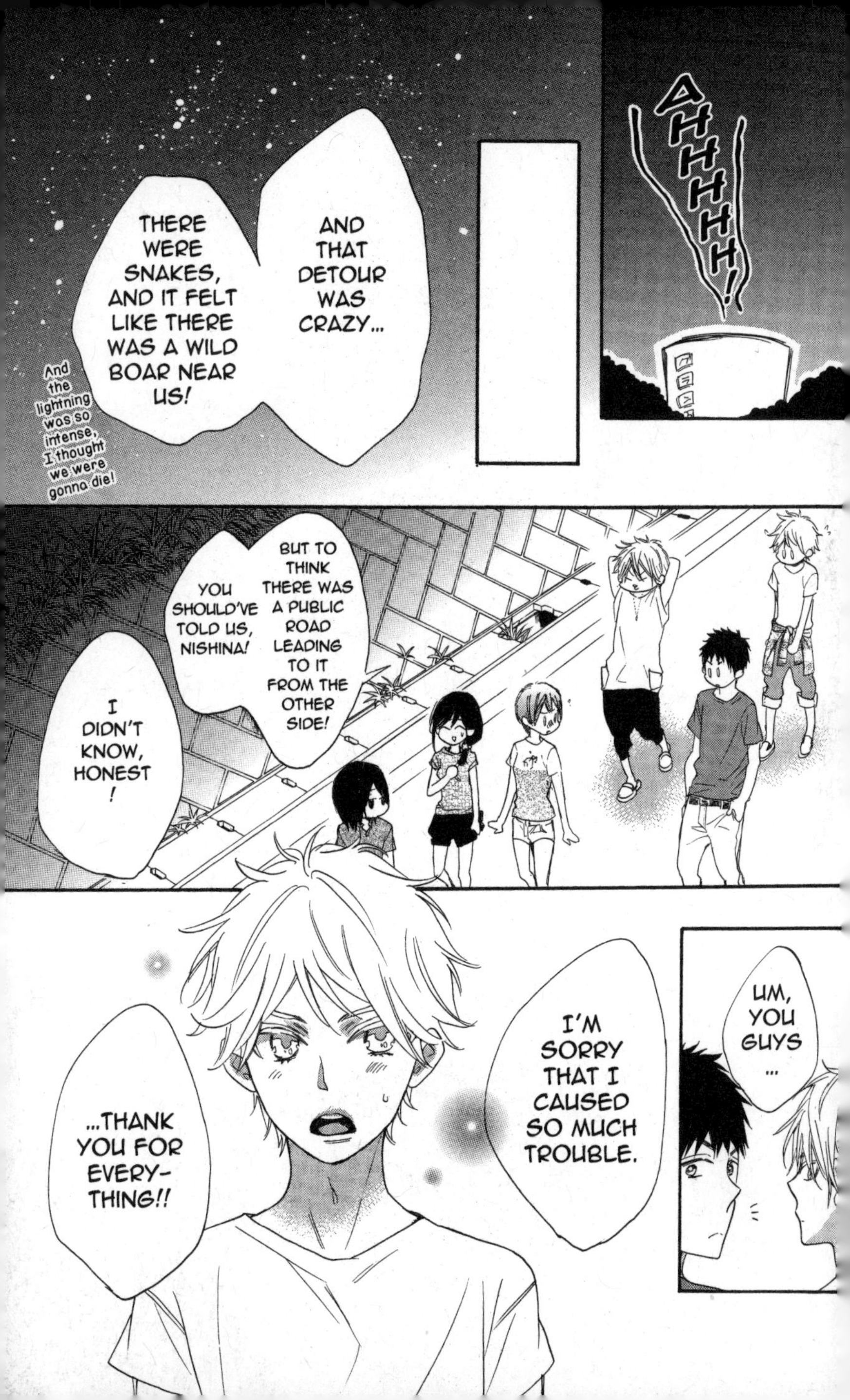
AHHHHH!
AND THAT DETOUR WAS CRAZY...
THERE WERE SNAKES, AND IT FELT LIKE THERE WAS A WILD BOAR NEAR US!
And the lightning was so intense, I thought we were gonna die!
BUT TO THINK THERE WAS A PUBLIC ROAD LEADING TO IT FROM THE OTHER SIDE!
YOU SHOULD'VE TOLD US, NISHINA!
I DIDN'T KNOW, HONEST!
UM, YOU GUYS...
I'M SORRY THAT I CAUSED SO MUCH TROUBLE.
...THANK YOU FOR EVERY-THING!!

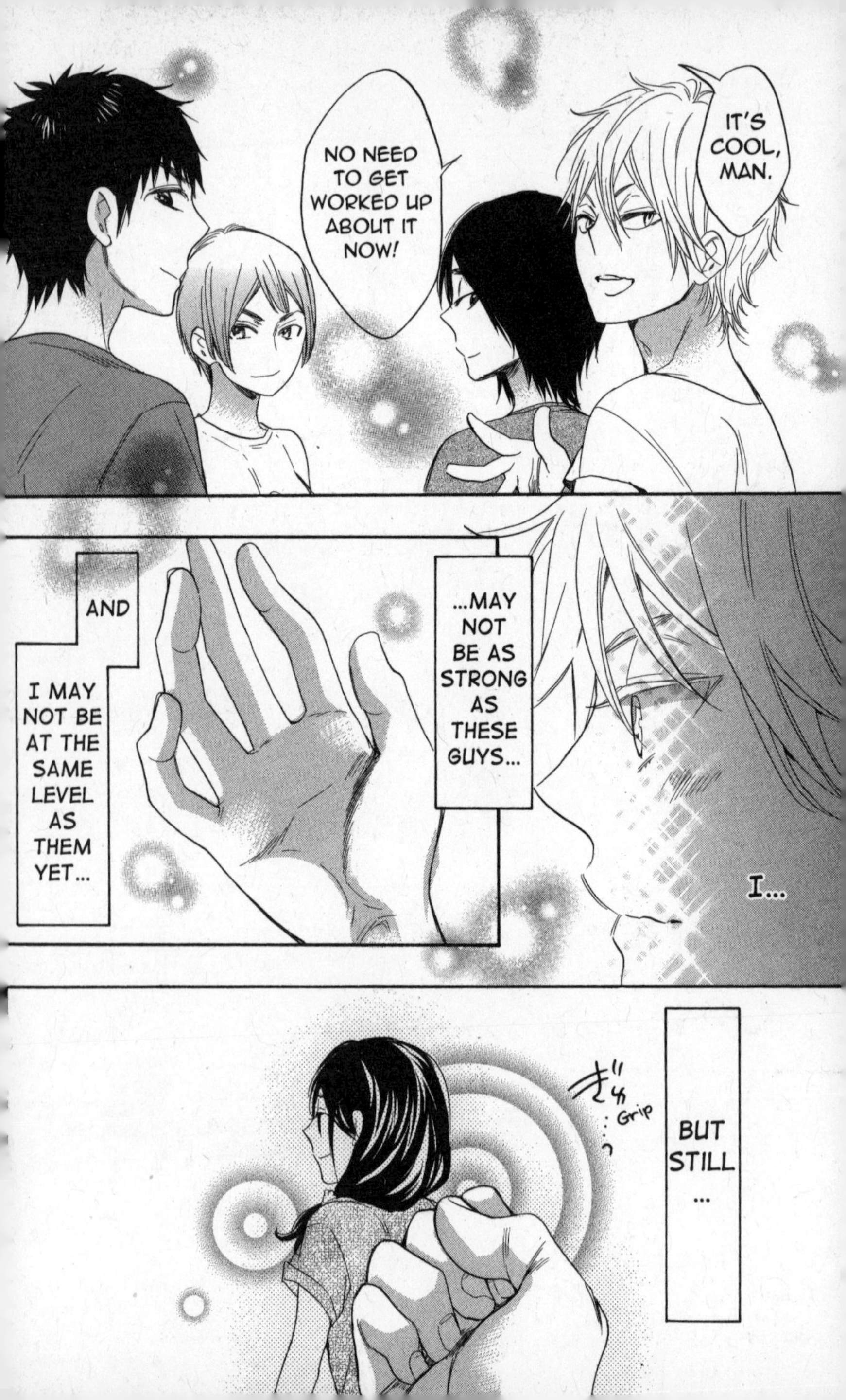
IT'S COOL, MAN.
NO NEED TO GET WORKED UP ABOUT IT NOW!
I...
...MAY NOT BE AS STRONG AS THESE GUYS...
AND
I MAY NOT BE AT THE SAME LEVEL AS THEM YET...
BUT STILL ...
Grip

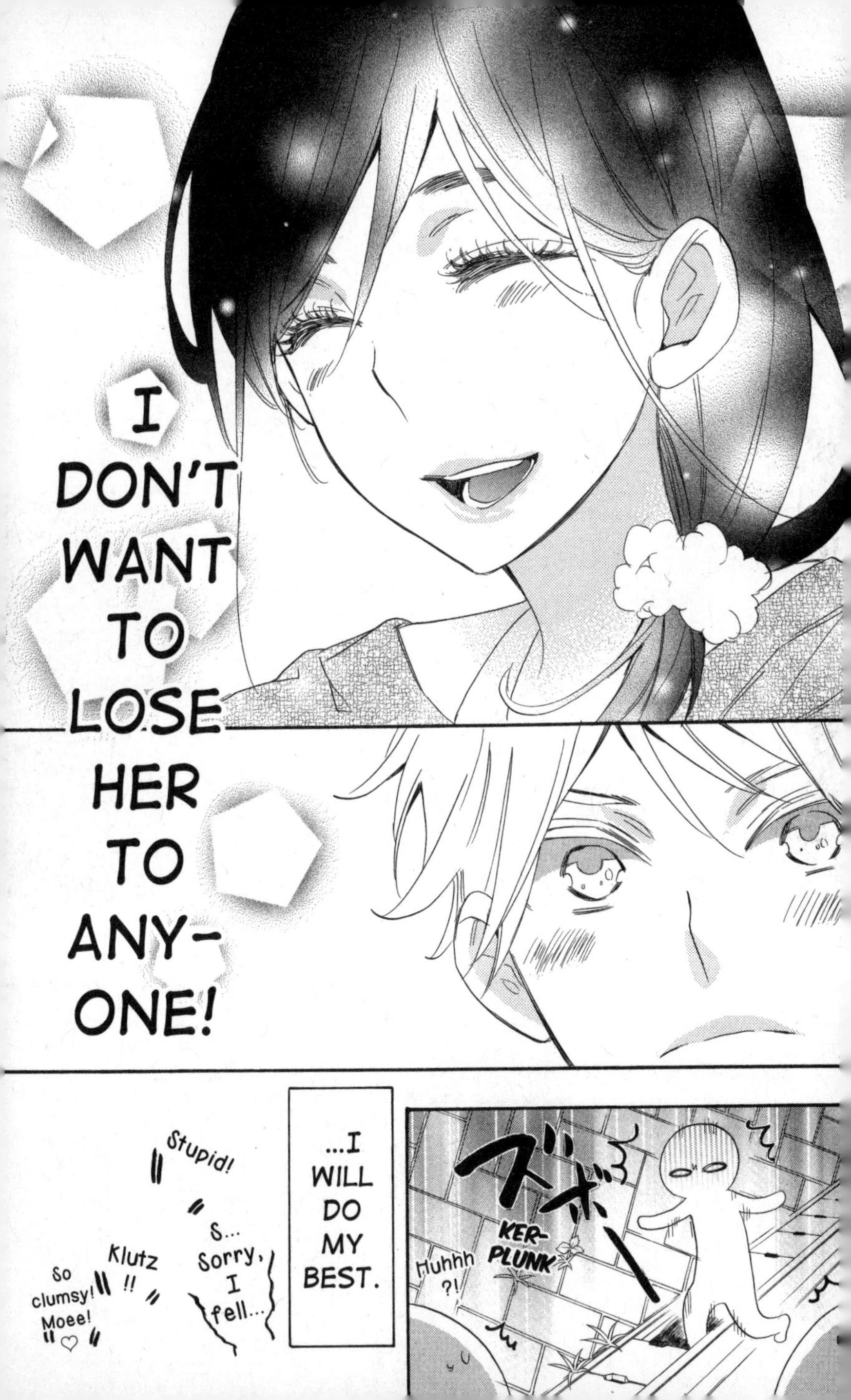

I DON'T WANT TO LOSE HER TO ANY-ONE!
KER-PLUNK
Huhhh ?!
...I WILL DO MY BEST.
S... Sorry, I fell...
Stupid!
Klutz !!
So clumsy! Moee! ♡

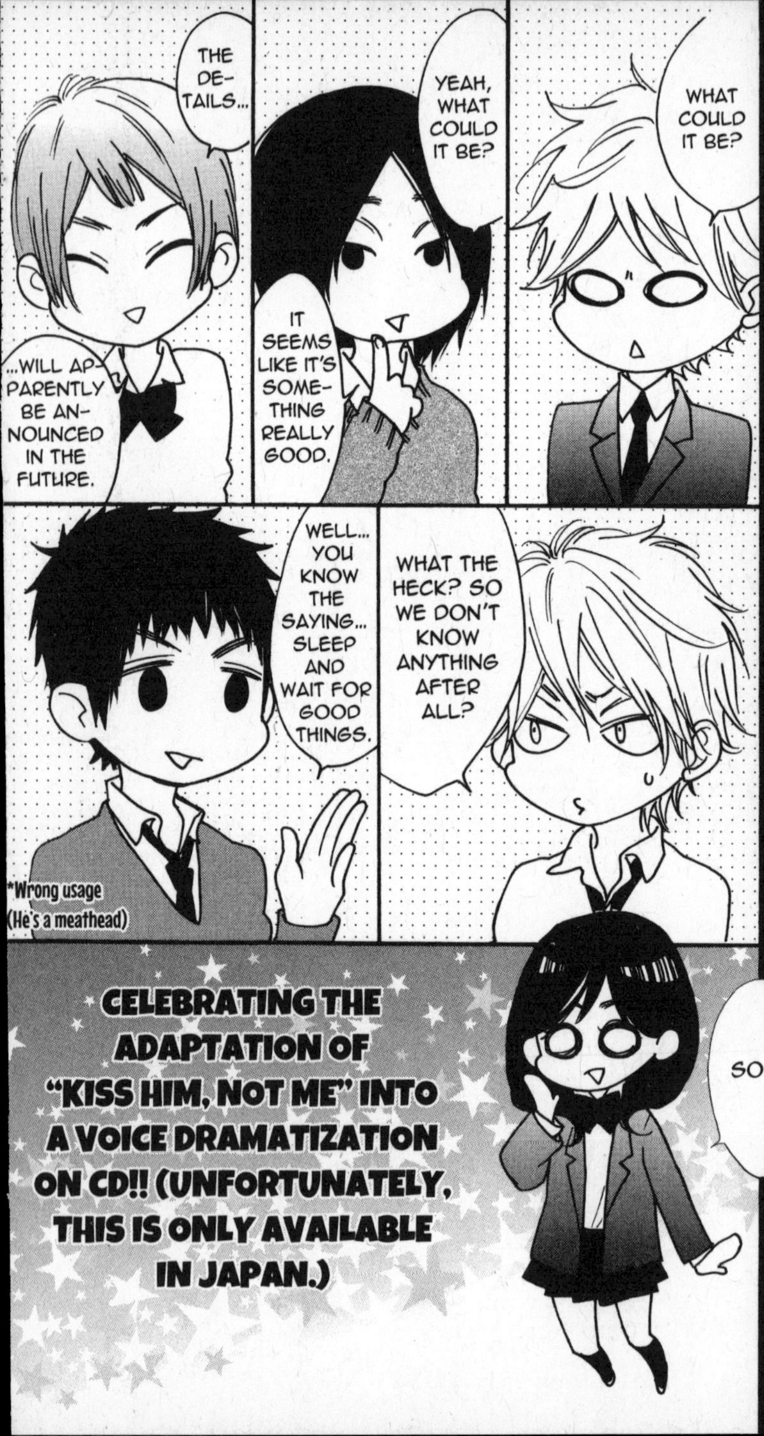

WHAT COULD IT BE?
YEAH, WHAT COULD IT BE?
IT SEEMS LIKE IT'S SOME-THING REALLY GOOD.
THE DE-TAILS...
...WILL AP-PARENTLY BE AN-NOUNCED IN THE FUTURE.
WHAT THE HECK? SO WE DON'T KNOW ANYTHING AFTER ALL?
WELL... YOU KNOW THE SAYING... SLEEP AND WAIT FOR GOOD THINGS.
*Wrong usage (He's a meathead)
SO...
CELEBRATING THE ADAPTATION OF "KISS HIM, NOT ME" INTO A VOICE DRAMATIZATION ON CD!! (UNFORTUNATELY, THIS IS ONLY AVAILABLE IN JAPAN.)

TO BE CONTINUED
IN VOLUME 5 OF

KISS HIM,
NOT ME!

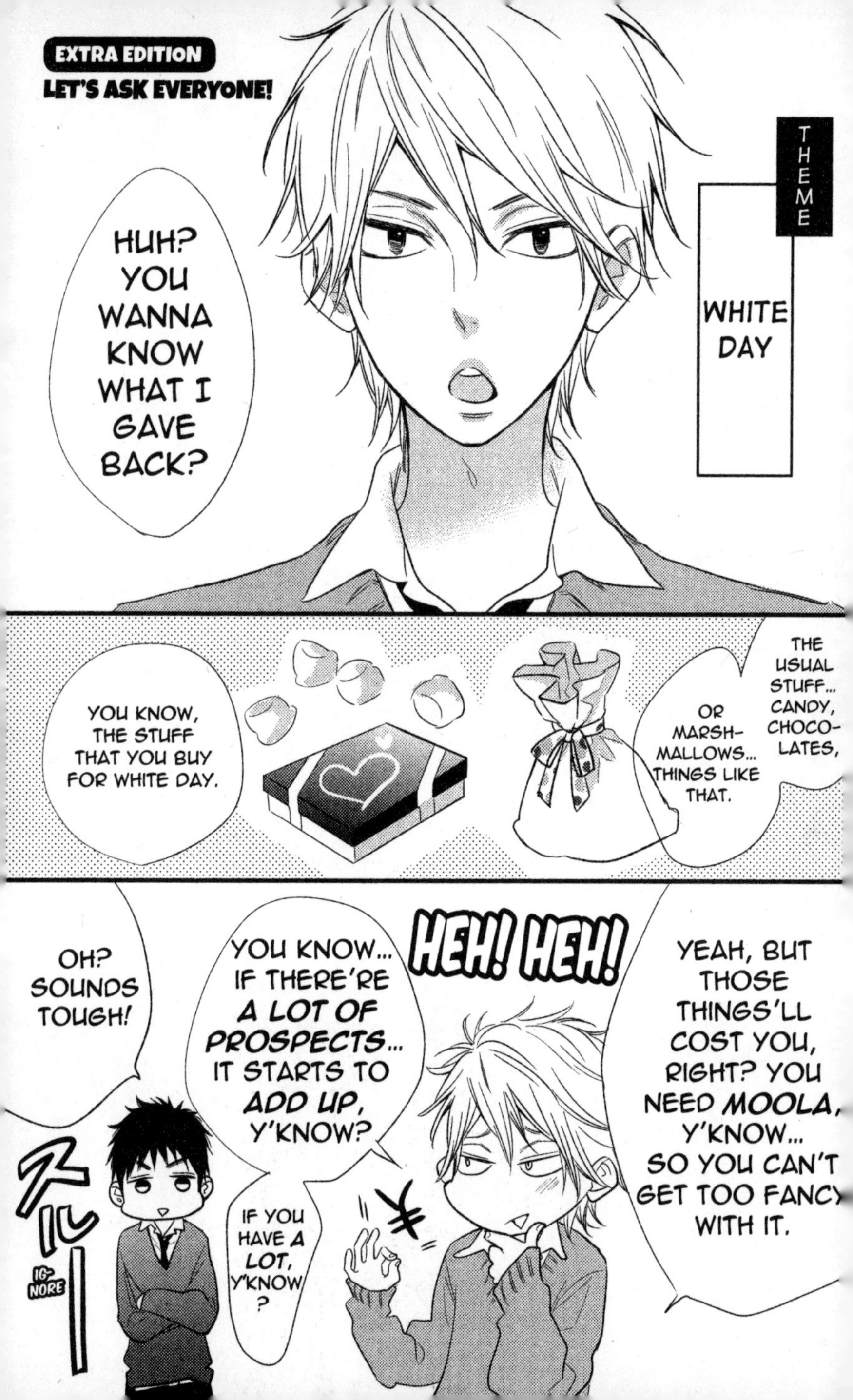
EXTRA EDITION
LET'S ASK EVERYONE!
THEME
WHITE DAY
HUH? YOU WANNA KNOW WHAT I GAVE BACK?
THE USUAL STUFF... CANDY, CHOCOLATES,
OR MARSHMALLOWS... THINGS LIKE THAT.
YOU KNOW, THE STUFF THAT YOU BUY FOR WHITE DAY.
YEAH, BUT THOSE THINGS'LL COST YOU, RIGHT? YOU NEED MOOLA, Y'KNOW... SO YOU CAN'T GET TOO FANCY WITH IT.
HEH! HEH!
YOU KNOW... IF THERE'RE A LOT OF PROSPECTS... IT STARTS TO ADD UP, Y'KNOW?
IF YOU HAVE A LOT, Y'KNOW?
OH? SOUNDS TOUGH!
IG-NORE

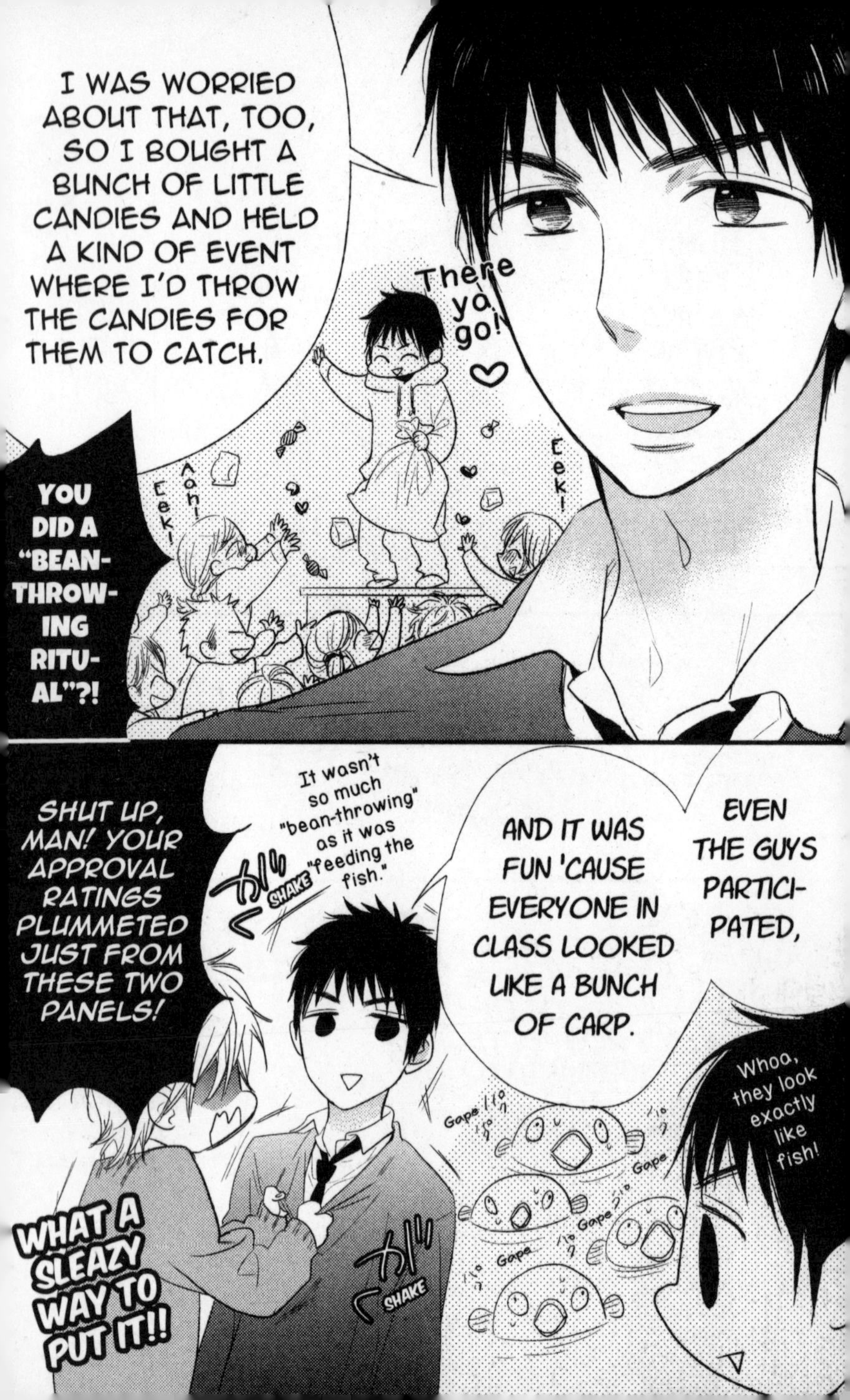
I WAS WORRIED ABOUT THAT, TOO, SO I BOUGHT A BUNCH OF LITTLE CANDIES AND HELD A KIND OF EVENT WHERE I'D THROW THE CANDIES FOR THEM TO CATCH.
There ya go!
Eek!
Aah!
Eek!
YOU DID A "BEAN-THROWING RITUAL"?!
EVEN THE GUYS PARTICIPATED,
AND IT WAS FUN 'CAUSE EVERYONE IN CLASS LOOKED LIKE A BUNCH OF CARP.
Whoa, they look exactly like fish!
Gape
Gape
Gape
Gape
It wasn't so much "bean-throwing" as it was "feeding the fish."
SHAKE
SHUT UP, MAN! YOUR APPROVAL RATINGS PLUMMETED JUST FROM THESE TWO PANELS!
SHAKE
WHAT A SLEAZY WAY TO PUT IT!!

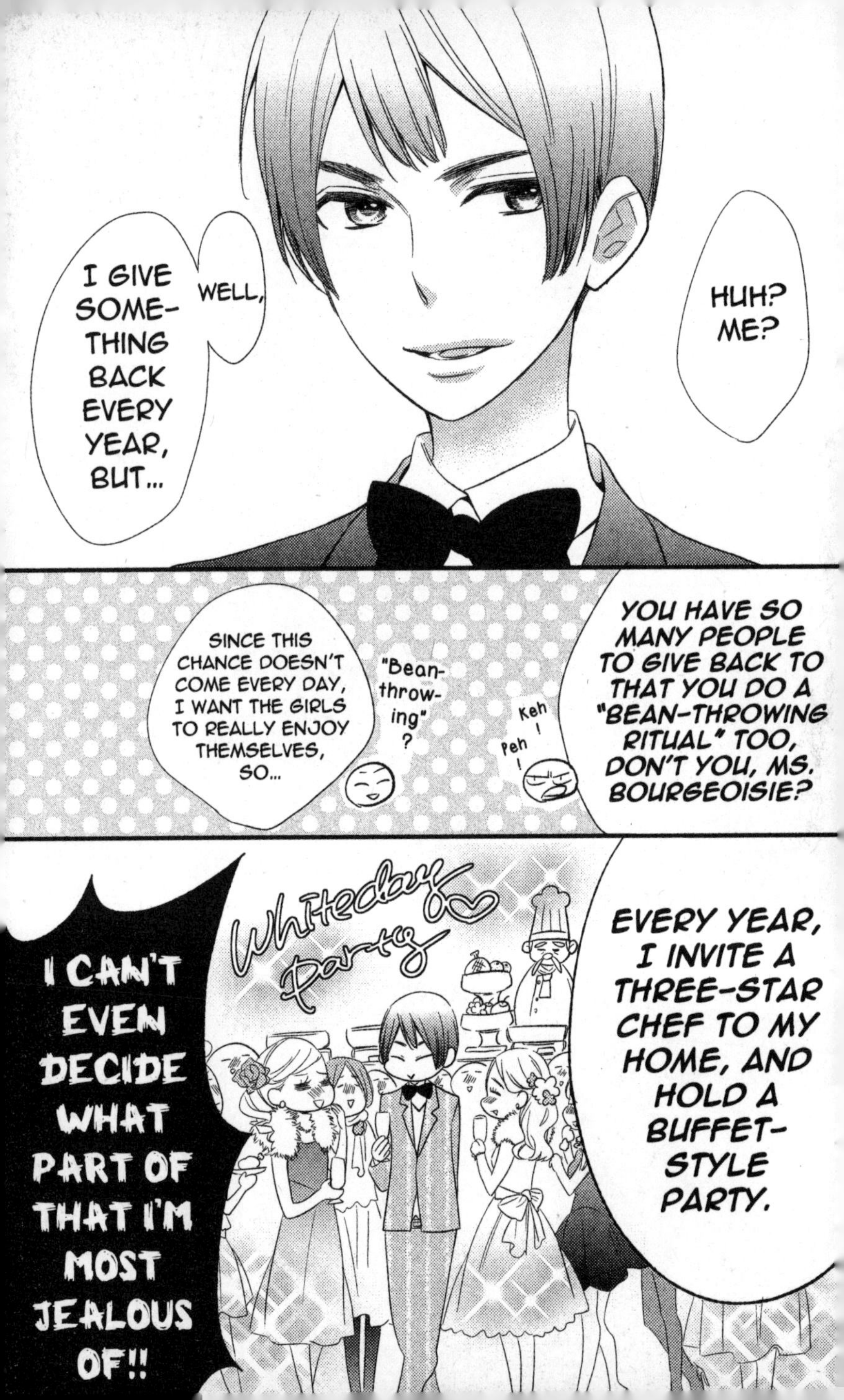
HUH? ME?
WELL,
I GIVE SOMETHING BACK EVERY YEAR, BUT...
YOU HAVE SO MANY PEOPLE TO GIVE BACK TO THAT YOU DO A "BEAN-THROWING RITUAL" TOO, DON'T YOU, MS. BOURGEOISIE?
Keh!
Peh!
"Bean-throwing"?
SINCE THIS CHANCE DOESN'T COME EVERY DAY, I WANT THE GIRLS TO REALLY ENJOY THEMSELVES, SO...
EVERY YEAR, I INVITE A THREE-STAR CHEF TO MY HOME, AND HOLD A BUFFET-STYLE PARTY.
Whiteday Party
I CAN'T EVEN DECIDE WHAT PART OF THAT I'M MOST JEALOUS OF!!

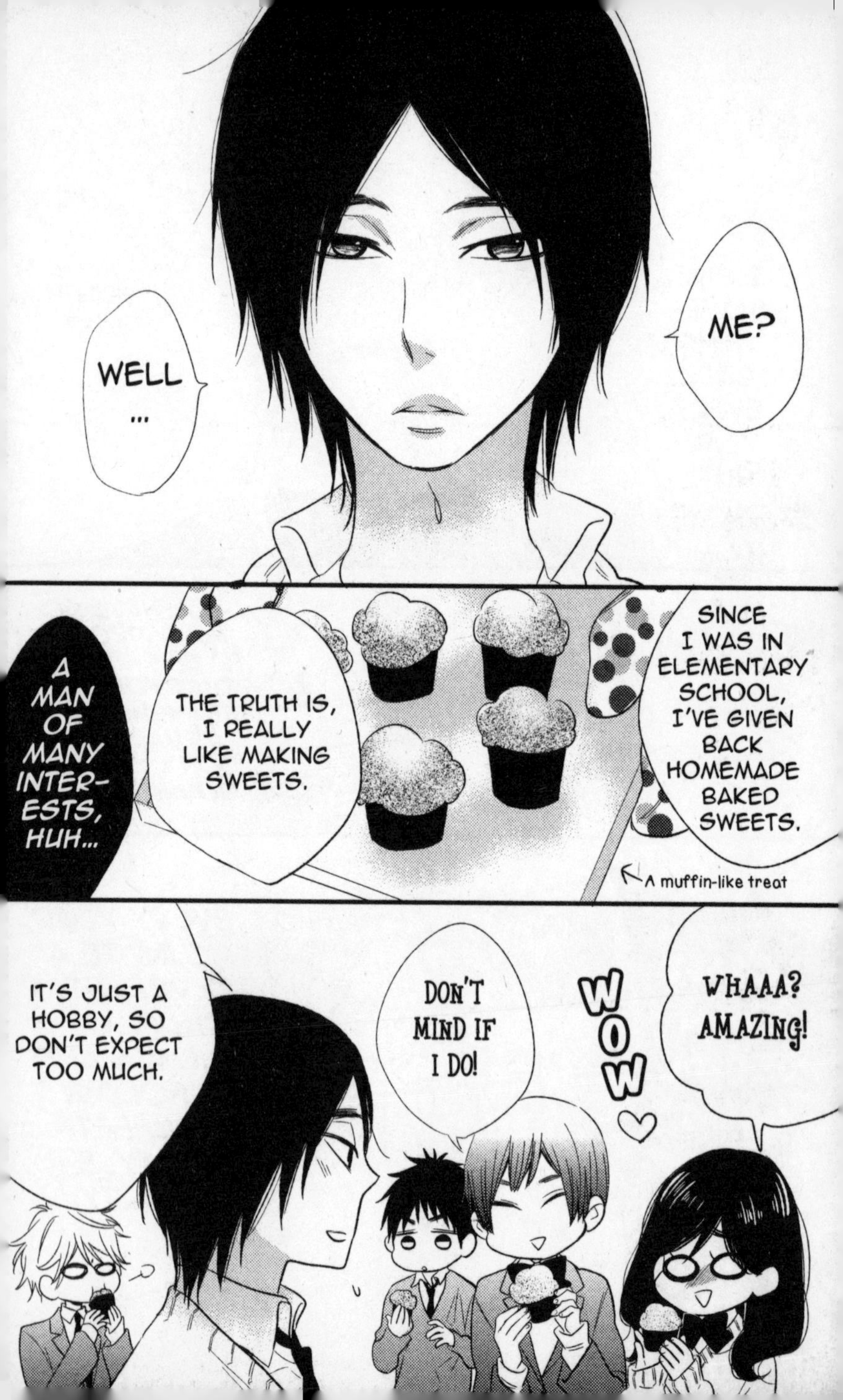
ME?
WELL ...
SINCE I WAS IN ELEMENTARY SCHOOL, I'VE GIVEN BACK HOMEMADE BAKED SWEETS.
A muffin-like treat
THE TRUTH IS, I REALLY LIKE MAKING SWEETS.
A MAN OF MANY INTER-ESTS, HUH...
WHAAA? AMAZING!
WOW ♥
DON'T MIND IF I DO!
IT'S JUST A HOBBY, SO DON'T EXPECT TOO MUCH.

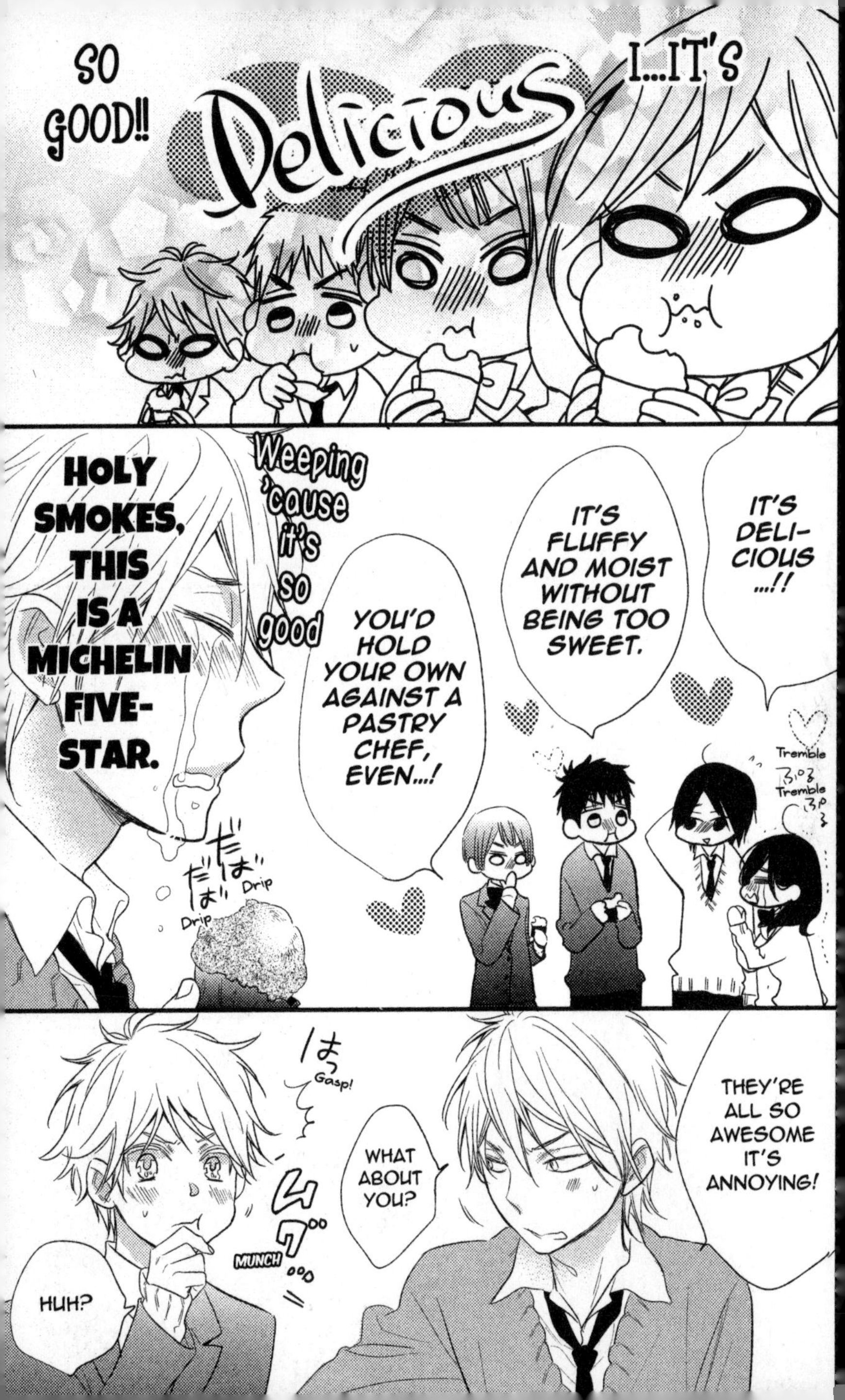
I...IT'S
Delicious
SO GOOD!!
IT'S DELICIOUS...!!
Tremble
Tremble
IT'S FLUFFY AND MOIST WITHOUT BEING TOO SWEET.
YOU'D HOLD YOUR OWN AGAINST A PASTRY CHEF, EVEN...!
Weeping 'cause it's so good
Drip
Drip
HOLY SMOKES, THIS IS A MICHELIN FIVE-STAR.
THEY'RE ALL SO AWESOME IT'S ANNOYING!
WHAT ABOUT YOU?
Gasp!
MUNCH
HUH?

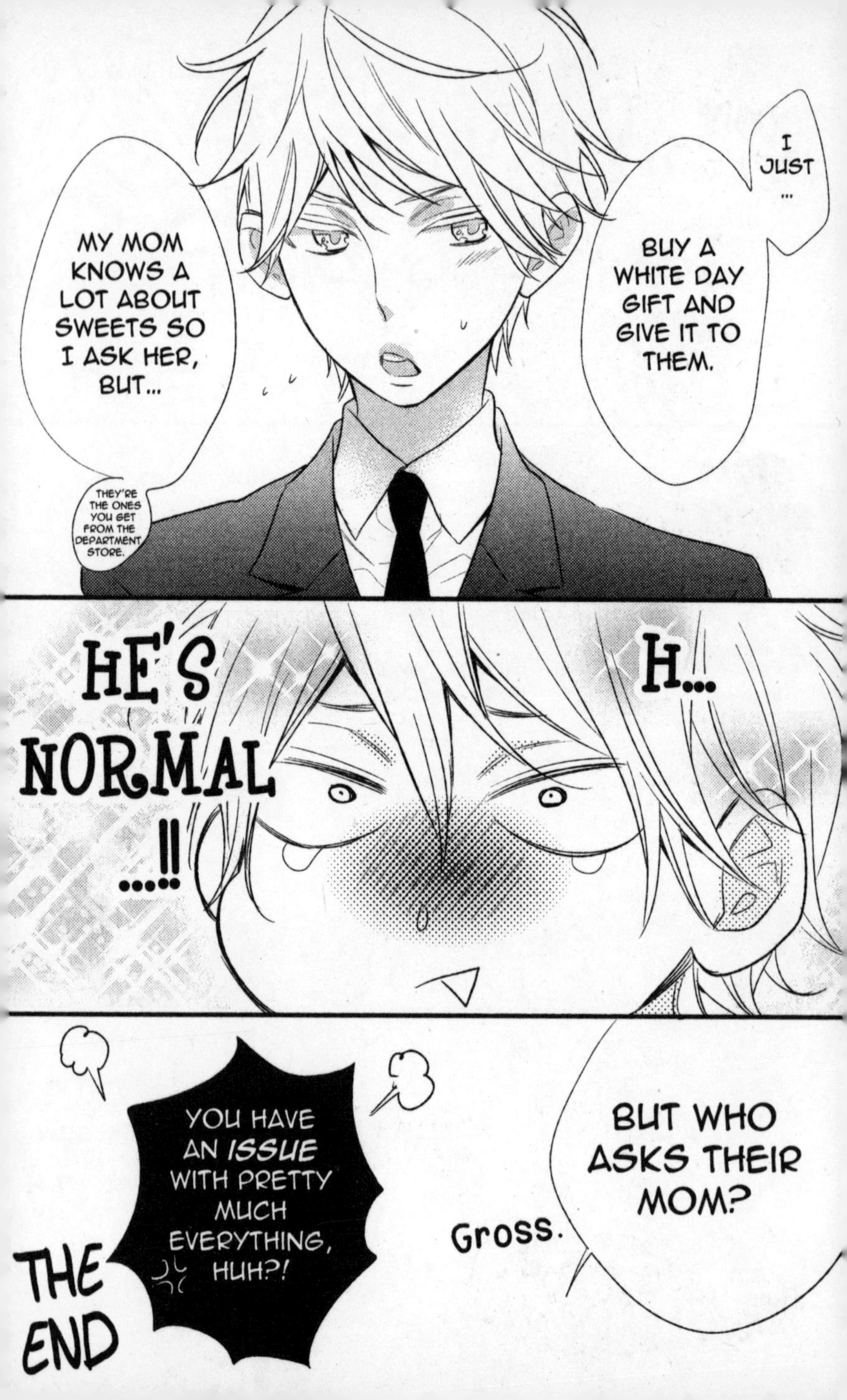
I JUST ...
BUY A WHITE DAY GIFT AND GIVE IT TO THEM.
MY MOM KNOWS A LOT ABOUT SWEETS SO I ASK HER, BUT...
THEY'RE THE ONES YOU GET FROM THE DEPARTMENT STORE.
H...
HE'S NORMAL ...!!
BUT WHO ASKS THEIR MOM?
Gross.
YOU HAVE AN *ISSUE* WITH PRETTY MUCH EVERYTHING, HUH?!
THE END

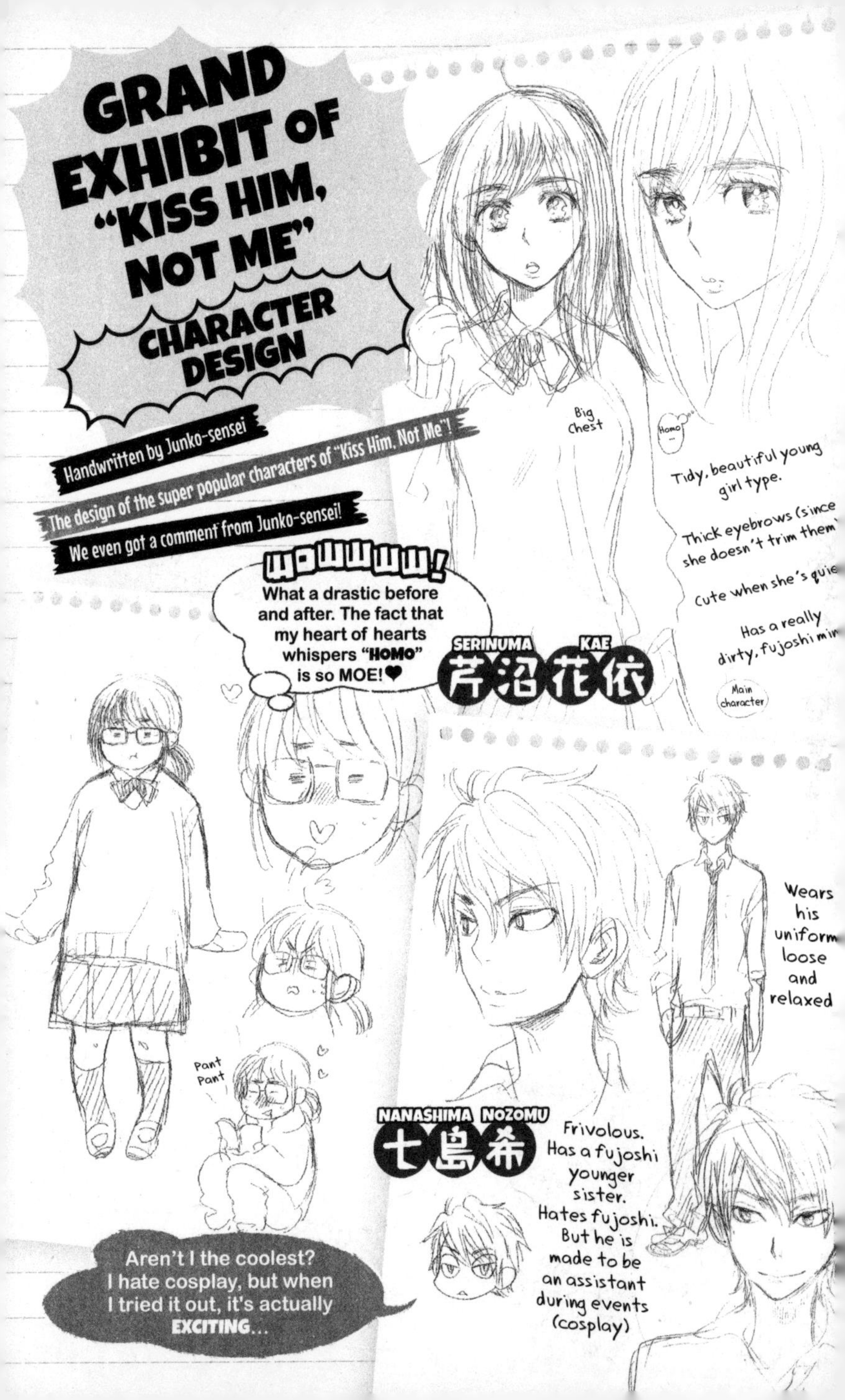
GRAND EXHIBIT OF "KISS HIM, NOT ME" CHARACTER DESIGN
Handwritten by Junko-sensei
The design of the super popular characters of "Kiss Him, Not Me"!
We even got a comment from Junko-sensei!
Big Chest
Homo...
Tidy, beautiful young girl type.
Thick eyebrows (since she doesn't trim them
Cute when she's quie
Has a really dirty, fujoshi min
Main character
WOWWWW! What a drastic before and after. The fact that my heart of hearts whispers "HOMO" is so MOE!❤
SERINUMA KAE 芹沼花依
Pant Pant
Aren't I the coolest? I hate cosplay, but when I tried it out, it's actually EXCITING...
Wears his uniform loose and relaxed
NANASHIMA NOZOMU 七島希
Frivolous. Has a fujoshi younger sister. Hates fujoshi. But he is made to be an assistant during events (cosplay)

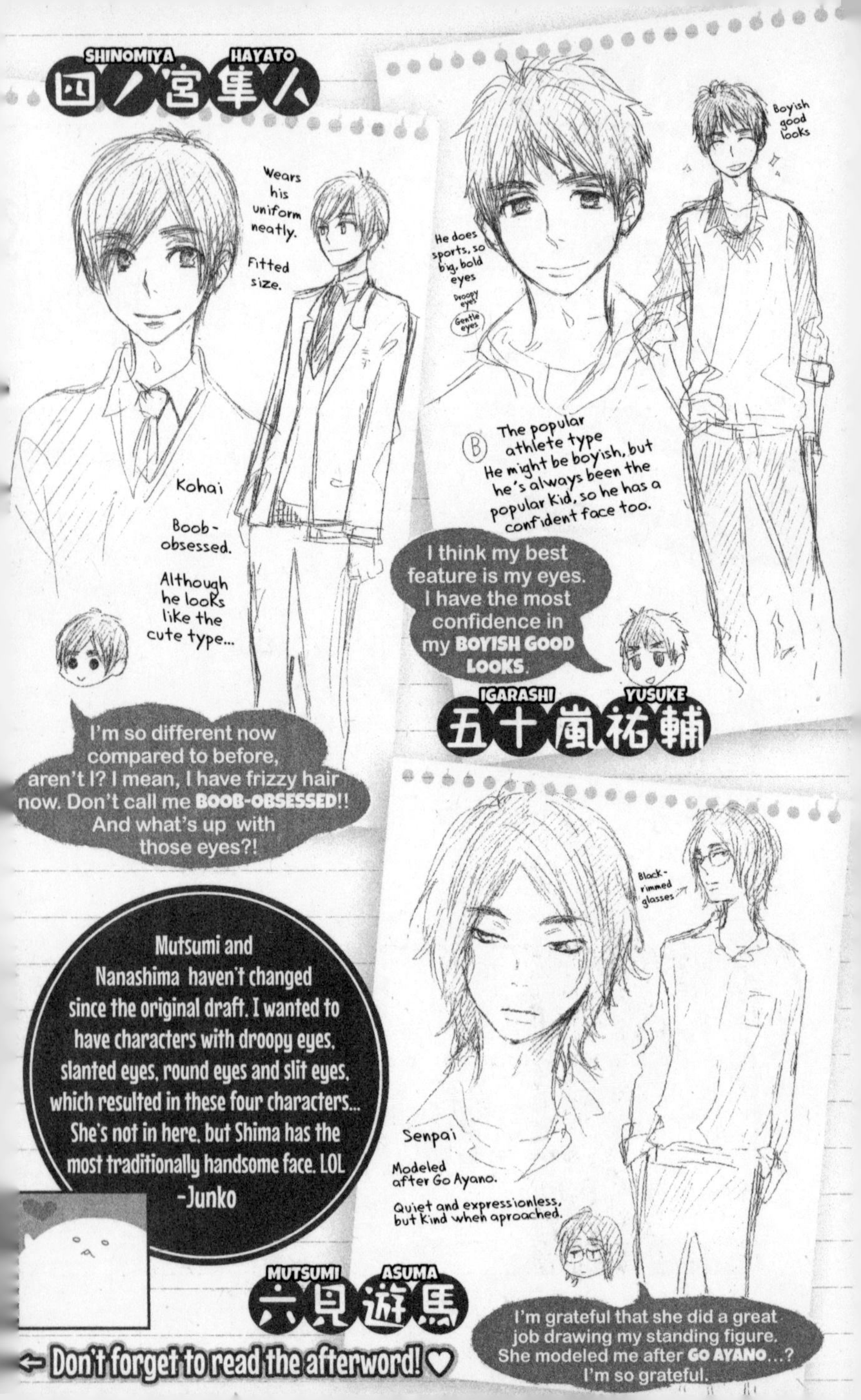
Boyish good looks
He does sports, so big, bold eyes
Droopy eyes
Gentle eyes
B The popular athlete type
He might be boyish, but he's always been the popular kid, so he has a confident face too.
I think my best feature is my eyes. I have the most confidence in my BOYISH GOOD LOOKS.
IGARASHI YUSUKE
五十嵐祐輔
SHINOMIYA HAYATO
四ノ宮隼人
Wears his uniform neatly.
Fitted size.
Kohai
Boob-obsessed.
Although he looks like the cute type...
I'm so different now compared to before, aren't I? I mean, I have frizzy hair now. Don't call me BOOB-OBSESSED!! And what's up with those eyes?!
Black-rimmed glasses
Senpai
Modeled after Go Ayano.
Quiet and expressionless, but kind when aproached.
I'm grateful that she did a great job drawing my standing figure. She modeled me after GO AYANO...? I'm so grateful.
MUTSUMI ASUMA
六見遊馬
Mutsumi and Nanashima haven't changed since the original draft. I wanted to have characters with droopy eyes, slanted eyes, round eyes and slit eyes, which resulted in these four characters... She's not in here, but Shima has the most traditionally handsome face. LOL
-Junko
← Don't forget to read the afterword! ♥

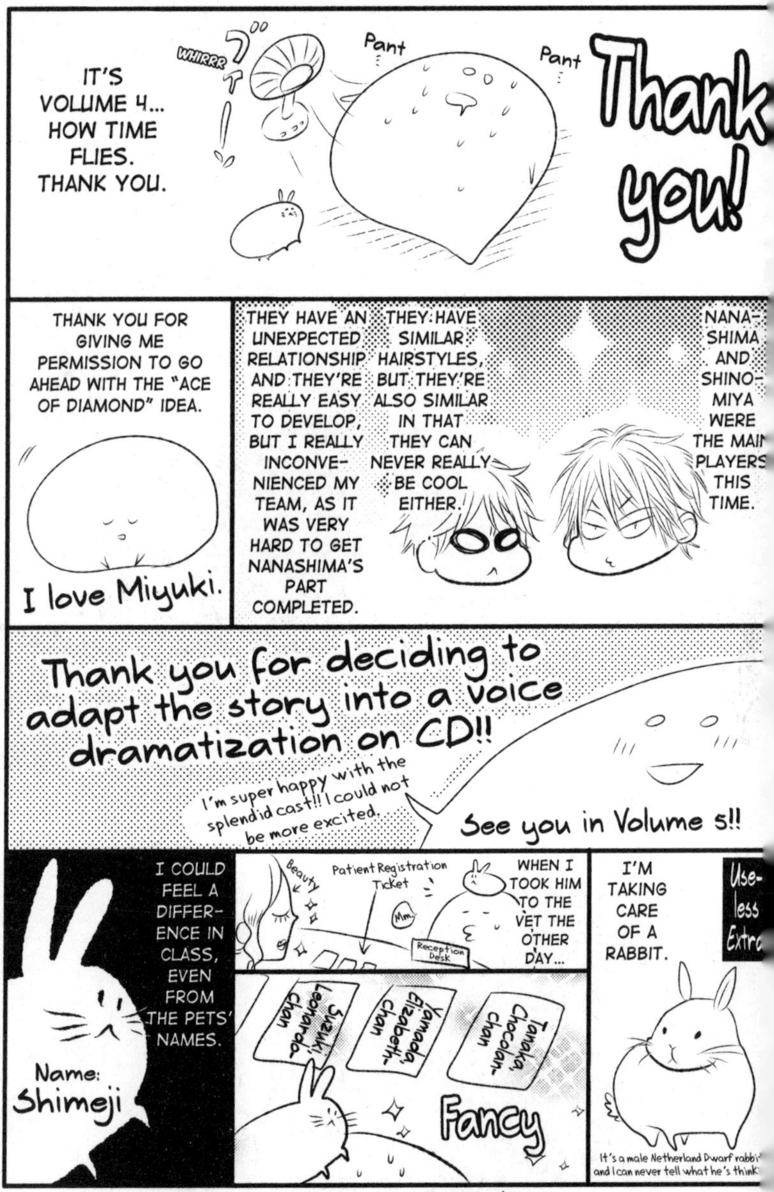
Thank you!
Pant
Pant
WHIRRR
IT'S VOLUME 4... HOW TIME FLIES. THANK YOU.
NANA-SHIMA AND SHINO-MIYA WERE THE MAI PLAYERS THIS TIME.
THEY HAVE SIMILAR HAIRSTYLES, BUT THEY'RE ALSO SIMILAR IN THAT THEY CAN NEVER REALLY BE COOL EITHER.
THEY HAVE AN UNEXPECTED RELATIONSHIP AND THEY'RE REALLY EASY TO DEVELOP, BUT I REALLY INCONVE-NIENCED MY TEAM, AS IT WAS VERY HARD TO GET NANASHIMA'S PART COMPLETED.
THANK YOU FOR GIVING ME PERMISSION TO GO AHEAD WITH THE "ACE OF DIAMOND" IDEA.
I love Miyuki.
Thank you for deciding to adapt the story into a voice dramatization on CD!!
I'm super happy with the splendid cast!! I could not be more excited.
See you in Volume 5!!
Use-less Extr
I'M TAKING CARE OF A RABBIT.
It's a male Netherland Dwarf rabbi and I can never tell what he's think
WHEN I TOOK HIM TO THE VET THE OTHER DAY...
Patient Registration Ticket
Beauty
Mm.
Reception Desk
Tanaka, Chocolan-Chan
Yamada, Elizabeth-Chan
Suzuki, Leonardo-Chan
Fancy
I COULD FEEL A DIFFER-ENCE IN CLASS, EVEN FROM THE PETS' NAMES.
Name: Shimeji

'Cause it was in a certain high-class area...

AUTHOR'S NOTE

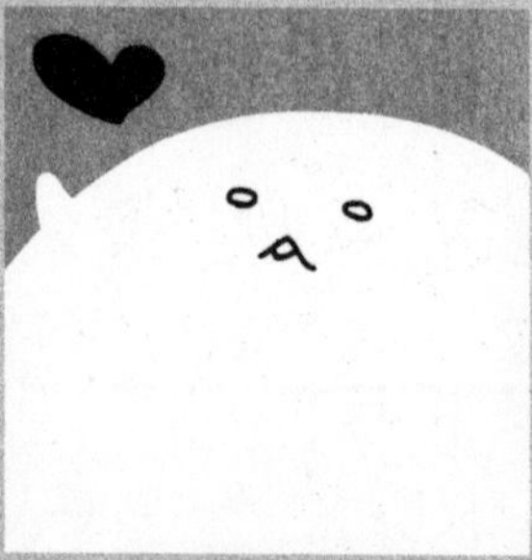

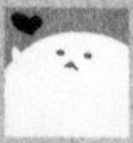

I'M NOT REALLY IN TOUCH WITH MY OLDER SISTER, BUT I CAN CONFIRM THAT SHE'S STILL ALIVE WHEN WE SEND EACH OTHER ITEMS IN MOBILE GAMES (LOL).

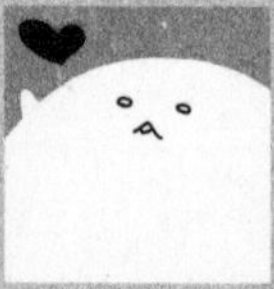

-JUNKO

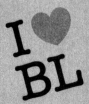

I ♥ BL

Translation Notes

Miyuki-senpai/Ace of Diamond, page 13

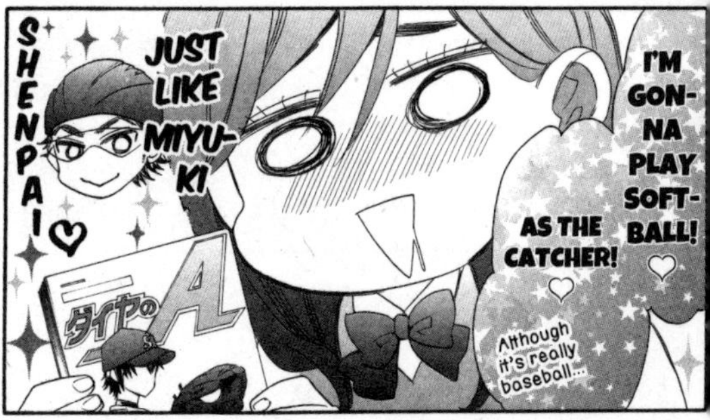
SHENPAI!
JUST LIKE MIYUKI
I'M GONNA PLAY SOFTBALL!
AS THE CATCHER!
Although it's really baseball...

Ace of Diamond, written and illustrated by Yuji Terajima, is an award-winning baseball-themed manga published by Kodansha. The series follows the adventures of Eijun Sawamura and his teammates on an elite high school baseball team. The catcher of this high school baseball team is Kazuya Mizuki, whose appearance matches the image shown in this volume.

Mamachari, page 54

Mamachari, which literally translates to "mama-bikes," are a common style of bicycle found in Japan. They can be often seen with a front basket as well as a rear rack for loading goods/groceries and are associated with housewives who use them as transportation during their daily errands. They are cheap—usually between $100-$200—and because of this, are considered to be disposable objects. Most people would rather buy a new bike than repair them and it's not a big loss if one is stolen or confiscated.

Clara stood up!, page 97

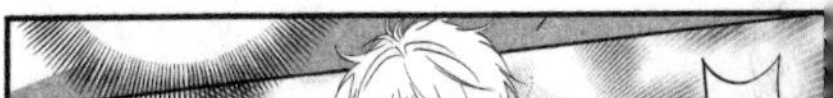
AHH!!
S...SHE STOOD UP!! CLARA STOOD UP!!
BOOM

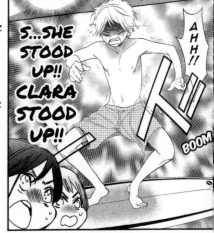

This particular line references *Heidi*, the novel by Swiss author Johanna Spyri. The novel follows the the titular character, Heidi, as she lives her life in the Swiss Alps with her grandfather. The series has been made into multiple live-action and animated films/series, but most Japanese people are familiar with the 1974 anime version, *Heidi, Girl of the Alps* (JP: *Arupusu no Shôjo Haiji*). Perhaps one of the most famous scenes from the anime is the one where Clara, the paralyzed daugther of a wealthy merchant, miraculously stands up and begins to walk without assitance. In this particular scene, Shinomiya tries to stand on his surfboard and his slow, nervous rise is reminiscent of Clara's scene of triumph in *Heidi*.

Nanmaidaa, page 139

Nanmaidaa is a shortened version of *Namuamidabutsu*, a common Buddhist prayer/chant. The phrase translates to something to the effect of "I entrust myself to Amida Buddha" and can be interpreted as "may Buddha have mercy." In a near-death situation, it can function in the same way as someone doing the Lord's Prayer or any other religious chant in preparation for one's possible demise.

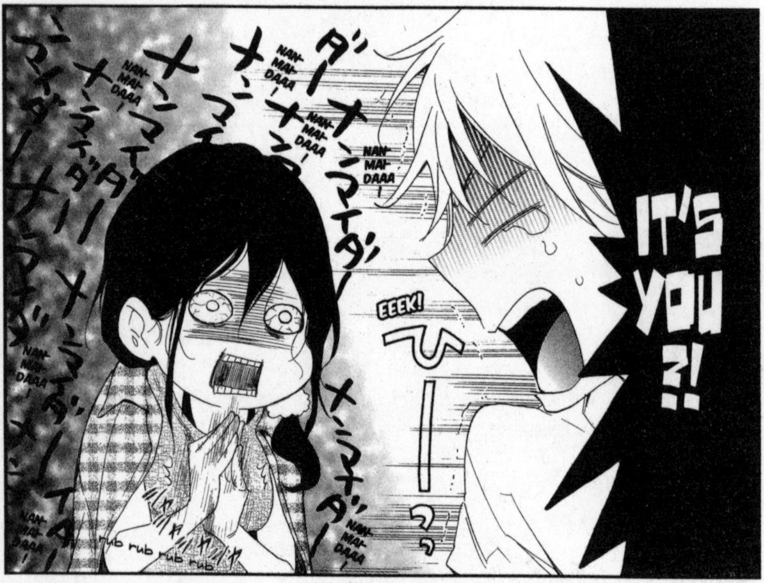
IT'S YOU?!
EEEK!
NAN-MAI-DAAA!
NAN-MAI-DAAA!
NAN-MAI-DAAA!
NAN-MAI-DAAA!
NAN-MAI-DAAA!
NAN-MAI-DAAA!
NAN-MAI-DAAA!
rub rub rub rub

Sleep and wait for good things, page 152

In Japanese, the idiom used here was "*kahô wa nete mate.*" This literally translates to "for good fortune, sleep and wait" but it is often translated as "everything comes to those who wait." The sense behind the original Japanese is that good fortune is not something that anyone can really do anything about since it is determined by luck or chance, so it is best to not fret–good things will come when it is time. The difference in nuance between this meaning and the usual English translation are slight, but the English translation doesn't work so well with the joke that Igarashi used the idiom incorrectly, so a literal translation was used to make the joke come through a little better.

Bean-throwing ritual, page 156

The bean-throwing ritual (*mamemaki*) is a custom held on the Japanese holiday of *Setsubun*, a holiday to celebrate the start of spring. Usually, *mamemaki* is done by throwing roasted soybeans from inside one's house outside at someone in an ogre mask while saying "Orges out! Luck in!" However, the same custom is often held at shrines where the beans are thrown at a crowd of people under a tall stand or stage. As you can guess from the phrase that's said when throwing the beans, this custom is a type of purification ritual to rid one of bad luck and evil spirits. In *Kiss Him, Not Me*, Igarashi is so popular that he has to give out White Day candy like it's the bean-throwing ritual.

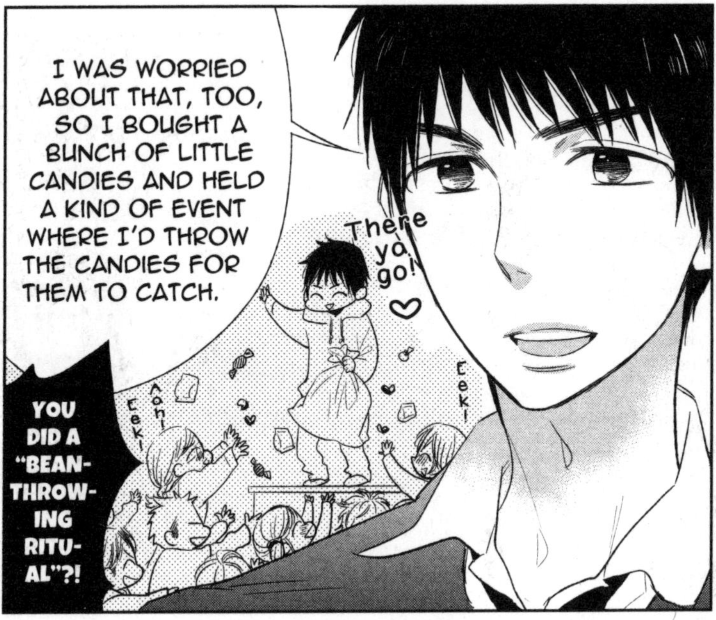
I WAS WORRIED ABOUT THAT, TOO, SO I BOUGHT A BUNCH OF LITTLE CANDIES AND HELD A KIND OF EVENT WHERE I'D THROW THE CANDIES FOR THEM TO CATCH.
There ya go!
Eek!
Aah!
Eek!
YOU DID A "BEAN-THROWING RITUAL"?!

Go Ayano, page 162

A Japanese actor who has starred in many big Japanese films in recent years. A good number of these films are adaptations of manga/anime, such as *Sakigake! Otoku Juku, Crows, Gantz, Usagi Drop, Ruroni Kenshin, Gatchaman,* and more recently *Lupin III* in which he played Goemon Ishikawa.

A Kodansha Comics Trade Paperback Original.

Kiss Him, Not Me volume 4 copyright © 2014 Junko
English translation copyright © 2016 Junko

Published in the United States by Kodansha Comics,
an imprint of Kodansha USA Publishing, LLC, New York.

Publication rights for this English edition arranged through Kodansha Ltd.,
Tokyo.

First published in Japan in 2014 by Kodansha Ltd., Tokyo, as *Watashi Ga Motete Dousunda* volume 4.

ISBN 978-1-63236-207-0

Printed in the United States of America.

www.kodanshacomics.com

9 8 7 6 5 4 3 2 1

Translation: David Rhie
Lettering: Hiroko Mizuno
Editing: Ajani Oloye
Kodansha Comics Edition Cover Design: Phil Balsman